ISRAEL IN EGYPT

ISRAEL IN EGYPT

*The Evidence
for the
Authenticity
of the
Exodus
Tradition*

JAMES K. HOFFMEIER

New York   Oxford • Oxford University Press

Oxford University Press

Oxford   New York
Athens   Auckland   Bangkok   Bogotá   Buenos Aires   Calcutta
Cape Town   Chennai   Dar es Salaam   Delhi   Florence   Hong Kong   Istanbul
Karachi   Kuala Lumpur   Madrid   Melbourne   Mexico City   Mumbai
Nairobi   Paris   São Paulo   Singapore   Taipei   Tokyo   Toronto   Warsaw

and associated companies in
Berlin   Ibadan

Published by Oxford University Press, Inc.
198 Madison Avenue, New York, New York 10016

First issued as an Oxford University Press paperback, 1999

Oxford is a registered trademark of Oxford University Press, Inc.

Library of Congress Cataloging-in-Publication Data
Hoffmeier, James Karl, 1951 –
Israel in Egypt : the evidence for the authenticity of
the Exodus tradition / James K. Hoffmeier
p. cm.
Includes bibliographical references and index.
ISBN 0-19-509715-7
ISBN 0-19-513088-X (Pbk.)
1. Exodus, The.   2. Egyptian literature — Relation to the Old Testament.
3. Bible. O.T. Exodus I-XV — Extra-canonical parallels.
I. Title.
BS680.E9H637 1997
222'.12095—dc20   96-31595

5 7 9 8 6 4

Printed in the United States of America
on acid-free paper

To Professor Kenneth A. Kitchen
on the occasion of his retirement
from the University of Liverpool in appreciation for
his many years of friendship,
support,
and encouragement

PREFACE

The biblical stories about Israel's origins in Egypt are so well known to people of Europe and the English-speaking world that one hardly has to rehearse the details. Whether people know them from reading the Bible, children's books, or from viewing epic film classics such as Cecil B. DeMille's *The Ten Commandments*, the Hebrew heroes Abraham and Sarah, Joseph, Moses, Miriam, and Joshua are celebrated as the founders of the nation of Israel. By and large, historians over the centuries have considered these individuals and the events in which they participated to be historical. The advent of archaeology and the deciphering of cuneiform inscriptions from Mesopotamian and Egyptian hieroglyphics brought the Western world into direct contact with the world of the Bible, making the fathers and mothers of Israel come alive. Sensational discoveries by Flinders Petrie and Edouard Naville in the Delta and Wadi Tumilat at the end of the nineteenth and the beginning of twentieth centuries were initially thought to provide firsthand evidence for the presence of the Hebrews in Egypt. Meanwhile, John Garstang's finds at Jericho seemed to support claims that the city was burned and its defense walls flattened, as related in Joshua 6. But subsequent investigations of these sites reversed earlier interpretations, and the evidence that originally appeared to confirm the stories concerning Israel's origin was met instead by embarrassing silence; for some this implied the repudiation of the Hebrew tradition.

Since the pioneering days of Petrie, Naville, and Garstang considerably more archaeological data has been uncovered in Egypt, and yet, even as the discipline of archaeology is about to enter a new millennium, direct evidence for the events and figures of Genesis and Exodus remains elusive. Prior to the nineteenth century only a few scholars questioned the historicity of the patriarchal narratives of Genesis and stories of the sojourn-exodus and Joshua's conquest of the land of Canaan. Beginning in middle of the nineteenth century and continuing into the twentieth, however, many western scholars considered these tales to be sagas, legends, and etiologies, but not historical records. In response to this critical climate, the biblical archaeologist William Foxwell Albright and his followers set a positive tone from the 1940s through early 1970s. Within these circles, the veracity of the biblical stories of Israel's Patriarchs in Genesis to the conquest of the "Promised Land" as described in Joshua and Judges seemed assured. However, a new generation of skeptics, or historical minimalists, have come to the fore over the past twenty years and challenged such a positive assessment.

In the first two chapters, I survey these developments and critique the new approaches and conclusions. The position of the minimalist school is that there was no Joseph serving Pharaoh, no Israelite bondage in Egypt, no Moses and the exodus, and certainly no military invasion of Canaan under the leadership of Joshua. In place of the biblical accounts of Israel's origin, new, provocative hypotheses have been advanced. While different methodologies have been employed, a new consensus seems to be emerging within a small but influential circle that maintain that Israel was a purely Levantine, indigenous development. So important has been this development that the cover story in the December 18, 1995, issue of *Time* magazine was entitled, "Is the Bible Fact or Fiction?" The subtitle read "Archaeologists in the Holy Land are shedding new light on what did—and didn't—occur in the greatest story ever told." This subtitle reflects the mood and thinking of some involved in the origins of Israel debate. In this book, I will challenge the premise that the absence of archaeological evidence can prove what did or did not happen in Bible history.

The "origins of Israel" debate of the past two decades has, by and large, been an intramural exercise with biblical historians and biblical/Syro-Palestinian archaeologists leading the way; however, little if any, attention has been given to materials from Egypt, except the Merneptah (Israel) stela, that might shed light on Israel's origin. While historians of ancient Israel have not seriously considered Egyptian sources, neither have Egyptologists over the past fifty years shown much interest in the Hebraic connection to the Nile Valley. This is a strange attitude for Egyptologists considering that the Bible has been a partner in historical inquiry from the beginnings of Egyptology. In recent decades, though, Egyptology has developed into a discipline in its own right, independent of Old Testament studies, and consequently there has been little interest in studying the Hebrew Bible and even a reluctance to enter biblical debates. This reticence is evident in an article by Manfred Bietak, the director of the Austrian excavations at Tell el-Dabᶜa. In response to a paper presented by Donald Redford at a symposium on Egypt and the Bible, Bietak confessed, "Being an Egyptologist I feel somehow embarrassed to comment on problems surrounding the theme of 'the Exodus,'"[1] but he later demurred, "I do not necessarily share Professor Redford's pessimism." Bietak went on to offer helpful insights into the various biblical sources bearing on the geography of the exodus and how the terms should be understood in the second millennium and in the first. Thus Bietak, a brilliant Egyptologist, presents a credible argument for the authenticity of geographical descriptions in Exodus, while remaining dispassionate about the Old Testament material. He seems to have no agenda for or against the historicity of the Hebrew narratives.

Thus, when Egyptologists do write about connections between Egypt and the Old Testament, they have generally accepted the Bible's claims. In Nicolas Grimal's *A History of Ancient Egypt*, the French Egyptologist seems totally unaware of the controversy brewing among biblical scholars and comfortably observes, "It is considered possible that the Jewish Exodus may have taken place during the reign of Ramesses II."[2] He finds the lack of surviving evidence for this event "not in itself surprising, given that the Egyptians had no reason to attach any importance to the Hebrews."[3] Grimal's approach seems to be fairly representative of most Egyptologists over the past twenty years.

While as a rule Egyptologists have not occupied themselves with scholarly integration of Egyptian and Hebrew sources, there have, of course, been a number of outstanding exceptions over the past thirty years. Two of my graduate-school mentors from the University of Toronto, Donald Redford and Ronald Williams, along with Kenneth Kitchen from Liverpool University, are examples of Egyptologists who were also trained in Old Testament studies and other cognate Near Eastern languages. All three have published widely on matters of contact between Israelite and Egyptian history and culture. Over twenty years ago, Williams identified why biblical scholars tend to ignore Egyptian sources when studying the Hebrew Bible:

> By the very nature of their training, Old Testament scholars are more likely to have acquired a first-hand knowledge of the Canaanite and cuneiform sources than they are to have mastered the hieroglyphic and hieratic materials of Egypt. For this reason they have had to depend to a greater degree on secondary sources for the latter. It is not surprising, then, that Israel's heritage from Western Asian in such areas as mythology, psalmody, theodicy, proverb collections, legal "codes" and practices, suzerainty treaties and royal annals has been more thoroughly investigated. Yet Egypt's legacy is by no means negligible.[4]

He, of course, believed that Israel had its birth as a nation in Egypt and, by virtue of being a neighbor in the following centuries, had ongoing contact with it. Hence, Williams maintained that Egyptian influence could be found within the pages of the Old Testament. He concluded his seminal essay by saying, "Due caution must always be observed in assessing the claims of direct influence, but the evidence is overwhelming that Israel drank deeply at the wells of Egypt. In a very real sense the Hebrews were 'a people come out of Egypt (Num. xxii 5, 11).'"[5] While this book was in the early stage of preparation, the scholarly world lost Professor Williams after a lengthy illness. His sagely approach, command of a wide range of sources and positive contributions to Egyptian–Old Testament studies will be sorely missed, but I hope that something of his legacy will be borne out by this volume.

On the other hand, Redford's important contributions to biblical studies have leaned in the minimalist direction, although he did reject the prevailing status quo in biblical studies regarding the story of Joseph (see chap. 4). In many places in this book, I have disagreed with my esteemed professor with whom I read Late and Old Egyptian texts, and from whom I had the pleasure of learning extensively while working for two seasons on the Akhenaten Temple Project's excavations at East Karnak that he directed. It is most uncomfortable to differ publicly with one's mentor, but I do so with the utmost respect for his brilliance and substantial scholarly contributions.

I concur with Ronald Williams that "the evidence is overwhelming" for Egypt's influence on the Hebrews because of their lengthy sojourn in the Nile Valley and subsequent association during the monarchy period in Israel. One of the glaring weaknesses of much of the recent literature that has questioned the historicity of the biblical records is that it has lacked serious investigation of Egyptian historical and archaeological materials. I intend to introduce (or, in some cases, reintroduce) Egyptian material that does shed light on the pertinent questions raised by the historical minimalists. Our differences illustrate how scholars can look at the same body of material and arrive at different interpretations.

It goes without saying, as Grimal has reminded us, that there is presently no known direct evidence for Israel's presence in the Nile Delta during the second millennium. This silence has resulted in the historical minimalists, for the most part, ignoring the available indirect evidence. It is my contention, and the purpose of this book, that in the absence of direct archaeological or historical evidence, one can make a case for the plausibility of the biblical reports based on the supporting evidence.

The reader will soon realize, as I did early on, that each chapter could have been expanded into a book of its own. Certainly, each of the main subjects warrants such thorough research, but time would not allow it. Because decades of scholarly discussion about the Israelite sojourn in Egypt and the exodus and entry into Canaan are behind us, it is not feasible to introduce every article and book that has dealt with these issues. Even the scholarly contributions of the past fifteen years cannot be covered thoroughly. Consequently, I have had to be selective in the sources treated, but have attempted to consider those studies that have been most influential in the recent debate. Rather than reviewing all the secondary literature on the subject, I will address the bigger picture of the narratives from Genesis 39 through Exodus 15 and to answer the following questions. Is the picture portrayed within these chapters compatible with what we know of Egyptian history? Did the peoples of Canaan go to Egypt for relief during times of drought and famine? Could a Semite like Joseph be elevated to such a position of prominence as reported in Genesis 45? Did the Egyptians press foreigners into hard labor projects as portrayed in Exodus? Could a non-Egyptian like Moses have been raised in the court? Do the plagues of Exodus 7–13 make ecological sense in an Egyptian setting? If so, what social, political, and religious implications are there for Egypt? Finally, do the geographical features and place-names in the Hebrew record accord in any way with Egyptian toponymy and geography?

In the following chapters, in order to answer these questions, a wide range of Egyptian sources—archaeological, geographical, textual, and pictorial—will be introduced and discussed. Some of the materials will not be new, but need to be placed on the table again because they have been ignored or trivialized in the past twenty years. At the same time, I shall provide fresh information from ongoing excavations in the Delta and Sinai, some not yet published in even preliminary form. For this new information, I made two visits to Egypt's Delta and Sinai in the spring of 1994 and 1995 and initiated the Eastern Frontier Canal Research Project during those visits. This work is ongoing, although some preliminary information is reported in chapters 7 and 8. Both trips to Egypt were made possible by funds from Wheaton College. Dr. Ward Kriegbaum, vice president for academic affairs, and Dr. James Stamoolis, graduate dean, made these grants available, and I thank them for their tangible support. A travel grant was also made possible from Wheaton for me to attend the Seventh International Congress of Egyptologists at Cambridge University (September 1995), where I presented a preliminary report on my investigations in north Sinai. I am grateful to Professor John Ray of Cambridge, chairman of the organizing committee of the congress, and his committee for naming my paper as the first runner-up to the best interdisciplinary presentation of the congress. Some of the material presented in the paper appears in chapters 7 and 8.

There are a host of others whose assistance, encouragement, and support throughout this nearly three-year effort must be acknowledged. Professor Kitchen, to whom this book is gratefully dedicated, helped me greatly by reading each chapter and offering his criticism, encouragement, and vast bibliographic knowledge so generously. Likewise, Professor Alan Millard of Liverpool University also read the entire manuscript. His insights into Old Testament scholarship and Hebrew and Semitic linguistics were most helpful. Dr. Mohamed Abd el-Maksoud of the Supreme Council of Antiquities of Egypt and director of all the North Sinai archaeological projects and his associate, Chief Inspector Abdul Rahman el-Ayedi provided the much needed logistical support for my work in Sinai. Dr. Manfred Bietak was kind enough to host me during my visit to Tell el-Dabᶜa in 1994. Also during my time in the Delta and Sinai in March 1994, Mr. Ted Brock, then director of the Canadian Institute in Egypt, worked very closely with me. While the results of the Shuttle Imaging Radar from the 1994 missions of the space shuttle *Endeavour* were not available to me, Dr. Jonathan Van Lepp of the Jet Propulsion Laboratory was my liaison. I have been assured by the project director, Neil Herman, that a future Imaging Radar mission, perhaps as early as 1998, will complete its mapping of Egypt and Sinai. I am hopeful that the data provided will be of great value for studying the topography of the region, learning more about the Eastern Frontier canal, and will enable us to settle questions about the course of Pelusiac branch of the Nile in Sinai. In connection with this canal (see chap. 7), I am grateful to Drs. Amihai Sneh and Tuvia Weissbrod for hosting me in Jerusalem in June 1993 when I visited the offices of the Geological Survey of Israel. Dr. Weissbrod and I have continued to have many conversations about the canal and the course of the Pelusiac via E-mail. He has been a tremendous resource.

A number of colleagues offered insights and criticism with specific chapters or problems with which I was wrestling. These include Dr. K. Lawson Younger (LeTourneau College), Dr. Richard Hess (Roehampton Institute), Dr. Mark Chavalas (University of Wisconsin, LaCrosse), Dr. Gary Rendsburg (Cornell University), Dr. Randall Younker (Andrews University), Dr. David Lorton (The Johns Hopkins University), Dr. Donald Spanel (Brooklyn Museum), Dr. John Foster (Roosevelt University), and Dr. James Hoch (Akhenaten Temple Project, Toronto). All of my Wheaton Colleagues in the Old Testament and archaeology department (Alfred Hoerth, Hassell Bullock, Herbert Wolf, Andrew Hill, and Richard Schultz) were always ready to entertain and critique my ideas. Professor Hoerth's knowledge of the excavations at Tell el-Retabeh was a boon, thanks to his work there in the late 1970s. Richard Schultz particularly helped me with German authors, and Andrew Hill readily shared his time, knowledge, and library with me. Dr. Charles Weber of the history department at Wheaton College introduced me to David Hackett Fischer's book, *Historian's Fallacies,* which proved to be a wonderful resource. Drs. Jeffrey Greenberg and Steven Moshier of the geology department provided me with equipment for my work on Sinai and have graciously allowed me to use their laboratory to study soil samples from north Sinai. They continue to be key players in the ongoing project. The resident marine biologist, Dr. Nadine Folino, has provided me with information about the shell samples taken from north Sinai (cf. chap. 8). Two graduate assistants who helped me in different ways must be mentioned: Darlene Brooks-Hedstrom (now a doctoral student at Miami University, Ohio) and Nathanael Heller (currently completing his master's degree). A personal friend and engineer who was a part of the work in north Sinai during the 1995 season, Mr. Ronald Bull, directed the mapping and auguring work around the site of Hebua. Much of what was accomplished could not have taken place without him. Because of the travel required in the preparation of this book, my wife, Cathy, and children, Jessica and Benjamin, have been without me for weeks at a time. Their patience, love, and support throughout the past three years were greatly appreciated.

It is clear that while many colleagues and friends have contributed in some way to this book, I alone must assume the responsibility for the contents of this work. On the publication side, I must thank Cynthia Read at Oxford University Press for her patience and professionalism at every stage of this project. She has been a delight to work with.

Throughout the following pages, the reader will encounter many translations of Egyptian texts and biblical passages. Unless otherwise stated, the Egyptian translations are my own, while the biblical translations are from the Revised Standard Version, unless another translation is specified.

J. K. H.

Notes

1 "Comments on the 'Exodus,'" in *Egypt, Israel, Sinai: Archaeological and Historical Relationships in the Biblical Period,* ed. A. F. Rainey (Tel Aviv: Tel Aviv University Press, 1987) 163. Redford's article "An Egyptological Perspective on the Exodus Narrative," is published in the same volume, 137–161. Both of these articles will be discussed below, especially in chapters 8 and 9.

2 *A History of Ancient Egypt* (Oxford: Blackwell, 1992) 258.

3 Ibid.

4 "'A People Come Out of Egypt': An Egyptologist Looks at the Old Testament," *VTS* 28 (1975) 231–232.

5 Ibid., 252.

CONTENTS

ABBREVIATIONS

AASOR   *Annual of the American Schools of Oriental Research*

ÄAT   *Ägypten und Altes Testament* (Wiesbaden: Otto Harrassowitz)

ABD   *Anchor Bible Dictionary*, 5 vols., ed. D. N. Freedman (New York: Doubleday, 1992)

ABL   Harry Frank and Roger Boraas, *Atlas of the Bible Lands*, rev. ed. (Maplewood, NJ: Hammond, 1990)

AEO   *Ancient Egyptian Onomastica*, 2 vols. (London: Oxford University Press, 1947)

AJA   *American Journal of Archaeology*

AJSL   *American Journal of Semitic Languages*

ÄL   *Ägypten und Levant / Egypt and the Levant* (Vienna)

ANET   James B. Pritchard, *Ancient Near Eastern Texts Relating to the Old Testament*, 3d ed. (Princeton: Princeton University Press, 1969)

AOAT   *Alter Orient und Altes Testament*

AOS   American Oriental Society

ARAB   D. D. Luckenbill, *Ancient Records of Assyria and Babylon,* 2 vols. (Chicago: University of Chicago Press, 1926 – 1927)

ARCE   *American Research Center in Egypt*

ASAE   *Annales du service des antiquites de l'Egypte* (Cairo)

ASOR   *American Schools of Oriental Research*

BA   *Biblical Archaeologist*

BAR   *Biblical Archaeology Review*

BASOR   *Bulletin of the American Schools of Oriental Research*

BES	Bulletin of the Egyptian Seminar
BIFAO	Bulletin de l'Institut Français d'Archéologie Orientale (Cairo)
BN	Biblische Notizen (Bamberg)
BZAW	Beiheften zur Zeitschrift für die alttestamentlichen Wissenschaft (Berlin)
CAD	The Assyrian Dictionary of the Oriental Institute of the University of Chicago, ed. I. J. Gelb, et. al. (Chicago: University of Chicago Press, 1956–)
CAH	Cambridge Ancient History, vol. 2 (Cambridge: Cambridge University Press, 1973, 1975)
CBQ	Catholic Biblical Quarterly
Cd'É	Chronique d'Égypte
CDME	R. O. Faulkner, Concise Dictionary of Middle Egyptian (Oxford: Oxford University Press, 1962)
CRIPEL	Cahiers de recherches de l'institut de Papyrologie et d'Egyptologie de Lille
DE	Discussions in Egyptology (Oxford)
DLE	Leonard H. Lesko, A Dictionary of Late Egyptian, 5 vols. (Berkeley: BC Scribe, 1982–1990)
DtrH	Deuteronomistic History or Historian
EA	El-Amarna = Amarna Letters
EAEHL	Encyclopedia of Archaeological Excavations in the Holy Lands, ed. M. Avi Yonah (Englewoods, N.J., Prentice-Hall, 1975)
EEF	Egypt Exploration Fund
EES	Egypt Exploration Society
ERB	Adriaan de Buck, Egyptian Readingbook, 3d ed. (Leiden: Nederlands Instituut voor het Nabije Oosten, 1970)
FT	Faith and Thought (Transactions of the Victoria Institute, England)
GM	Göttinger Miszellen
HAB	The Harper Atlas of the Bible, ed. J. B. Pritchard (New York, Harper and Row, 1987)
HTR	Harvard Theological Review
IDB	Interpreter's Dictionary of the Bible, 4 vols. and suppl., ed. G. A. Buttrick (Nashville: Abingdon Press, 1962, 1976)
IEJ	Israel Exploration Journal
IFAO	Institut français d'archéologie orientale
ISBE	International Standard Bible Encyclopedia, 4 vols., ed. G. W. Bromiley (Grand Rapids, Mich.: Eerdmans, 1979–1988)
JANES	Journal of the Ancient Near Eastern Society
JAOS	Journal of the American Oriental Society
JARCE	Journal of the American Research Center in Egypt
JEA	Journal of Egyptian Archaeology
JETS	Journal of the Evangelical Theological Society
JB	Jerusalem Bible
JBL	Journal of Biblical Literature
JCS	Journal of Cuneiform Studies
JEOL	Jaarbericht ex Oriente Lux
JNES	Journal of Near Eastern Studies
JSOT	Journal for the Study of the Old Testament
JSS	Journal of Semitic Studies
JSSEA	Journal of the Society for the Study of Egyptian Antiquities
JTC	Journal for Theology and the Church

JTS	*Journal of Theological Studies*
KB	Ludwig Koehler and Walter Baumgartner, *Lexicon in Veteris Testamenti Libros* (Leiden: Brill, 1903).
KJV	King James Version
KRI	Kenneth Kitchen, *Ramesside Inscriptions, Historical and Biographical*, 7 vols. (Oxford: Blackwell, 1968 –)
LEM	Alan H. Gardiner, *Late Egyptian Miscellanies* (Bibliotheca Aegyptiaca; Brussels: Édition de la Fondation Égyptologique Reine Élizabeth, 1937)
Les.	Kurt Sethe, *Aegyptische Lesestüche zum Gebrauch in akademischen Unterricht* (Leipzig: J. C. Hinrichs, 1928)
LXX	Septuagint (Greek translation of the Hebrew Bible)
MBA	Yohanan Aharoni and Michael Avi-Yonah, *The Macmillan Bible Atlas*, rev. ed. (New York: Macmillan, 1977)
MIFAO	*Memoires de l'institut français d'archéologie Orientale*
MMJ	*Metropolitan Museum Journal*
MT	Masoretic Text
NAS	New American Standard Bible
NBA	*New Bible Atlas*, ed. J. J. Bimson, J. P. Kane, J. H. Patterson, D. J. Wiseman, and D. R. W. Wood (Downers Grove/Leister: IV Press, 1985)
NBD	*New Bible Dictionary*, rev. ed., ed. J. D. Douglas (Wheaton, Ill.: Tyndale House, 1982)
NEAEHL	*New Encyclopedia of Archaeological Excavations in the Holy Land*, 4 vols., ed. Ephriam Stern (New York: Simon and Schuster, 1993)
NEB	New English Bible
NIV	New International Version
NIVAB	Carl Rasmussen, *NIV Atlas of the Bible* (Grand Rapids, Mich.: Zondervan, 1989)
OBA	Herbert G. May, *Oxford Bible Atlas* (London/New York: Oxford University Press, 1974)
OBO	*Orbis Biblicus et Orientalis* (Freiberg)
OMRO	*Oudheidkundige Mededelingen uit he Rijksmuseum van Oudheden te Leiden*
PM	B. Porter and R. Moss, *Topographical Bibliography of Hieroglyphic Texts, Reliefs and Paintings*, 7 vols. (Oxford: Griffith Institute 1927 – 51, 1960 – 72)
PEQ	*Palestine Exploration Quarterly*
PSBA	*Proceedings of the Society of Biblical Archaeology*
RB	*Revue Biblique*
Rd'É	*Revue d'Égyptologie*
RITA	K. A. Kitchen, *Ramesside Inscriptions Translated and Annotated: Notes and Comments*, 7 vols. (Oxford: Blackwell, 1993 –)
RSV	Revised Standard Version
RV	Revised Version
SAK	*Studien zur Altägyptischen Kultur*
SBL	Society of Biblical Literature
SJOT	*Scandanavian Journal of Old Testament*
TB	*Tyndale Bulletin* (Cambridge)
TDOT	*Theological Dictionary of the Old Testament*, 6 vols., ed. G. J. Botterweck and Helmer Ringgren (Grand Rapids, Mich.: Eerdmans, 1974 –)
TLZ	*Theologische Zeitschrift*

CHRONOLOGICAL CHARTS

Syro-Palestinian Chronology

Middle Bronze II	1800–1650 B.C.
Middle Bronze IIc or III	1650–1550 B.C.
Late Bronze I	1550–1400 B.C.
Late Bronze IIA	1400–1300 B.C.
Late Bronze IIB	1300–1200 B.C.
Iron Age IA	1200–1150 B.C.
Iron Age IB	1150–1000 B.C
Iron Age IIA	1000–925 B.C.
Iron Age IIB	925–720 B.C.
Iron Age IIC	720–586 B.C.

Dates based on Amihai Mazar's *Archaeology of the Land of the Bible* (New York: Doubleday, 1990)

Egyptian Chronology

Old Kingdom (Dynasties 3–6)	2700–2190 B.C.
First Intermediate Period (Dynasties 7–11)	2190–2106 B.C.
Middle Kingdom (Dynasties 11–12)	2106–1786 B.C.
Second Intermediate Period (Dynasties 13–17)	1786–1550 or 1539 B.C.
The Hyksos Period (Dynasties 15–16)	1648–1550 or 1540 B.C.
The New Kingdom (Dynasties 18–20)	1550 or 1539–1069 B.C.
The Eighteenth Dynasty	1550 or 1539–1295 B.C
The Nineteenth Dynasty	1295–1186 B.C.
The Twentieth Dynasty	1186–1069 B.C.

Dates based on the Chronologies of R. Krauss and K. A. Kitchen in *High, Middle or Low? Acts of an International Colloquiium on Absolute Chronology Held as the University of Gothenburg 20th–22nd August 1987*, parts 1–3, ed. Paul Åström (Gothenburg: Åströms Förlag, 1987–1989) and laid out in convenient chart form in *ABD* 2, 328–329.

ISRAEL IN EGYPT

1

ISRAEL'S EARLY HISTORY
IN RECENT SCHOLARSHIP

How are the mighty fallen . . . ?

1 Sam. 1:27a

I. The Demise of Israel's Early History

David lamented the news of the death of King Saul and Prince Jonathan with the famous words, "How are the mighty fallen . . . ?" The same question might be asked of the central figures of Israel's early history—Abraham, Moses, and Joshua—in the scholarly literature of the past two decades. The 1970s witnessed a number of unrelenting critiques of the comparative method of studying the Hebrew Bible, which sought to show that parallels between the social and legal practices described in the Patriarchal narratives of Genesis are attested to in ancient Near Eastern literature of the mid to early second millennium B.C. Such parallels were adduced as evidence that the biblical events were historical and characters real. Scholars such as John Van Seters and Thomas Thompson argued, however, that many of the so-called parallels were not compelling and could also be documented for the first millennium.[1] The result has been an abandonment by many Old Testament scholars of the conclusions of historical maximalists such as William F. Albright, John Bright, and Ephraim A. Speiser.[2] Thus the pendulum began to swing towards a more minimalist reading of the Hebrew Bible, especially the material found in Genesis through Joshua concerning the origin of Israel, namely, the Patriarchal, the sojourn-exodus, Sinai, and "conquest" traditions.

For centuries the Israelite exodus from Egypt has been considered to be a historical event central to the formation of ancient Israel as a nation and its faith. The historicity of this event was affirmed by John Bright as recently as 1981 in the third edition of *A History of Israel*: "There can really be little doubt that ancestors

3

of Israel had been slaves in Egypt and had escaped in some marvelous way. Almost no one today would question it."[3] Since that positive assessment was penned, however, the tide has shifted toward historical minimalism and led to the questioning or denial of the historicity of the events of Exodus. In 1986 the late Gösta Ahlström's *Who Were the Israelites?* sought to answer the pressing question of Israel's origin without referring to the commonly dismissed Pentateuch and book of Joshua. Ahlström's reductionist thesis will be treated in the next chapter. More recently, Robert Coote made the bold assertion: "The writers of ancient Israel knew little or nothing about the origin of Israel, although the Scriptures can provide much information relevant to the investigation of early Israel. The period under discussion, therefore, does not include the period of the patriarchs, exodus, conquest, or judges as devised by the writers of the Scriptures. These periods never existed."[4] When Bright's claim is read beside those of more recent biblical historians, like Ahlström and Coote, with only a decade separating them, we are forced to ask why the central event in Israel's history has so quickly lost its credibility in the eyes of many leading scholars? No single reason can be offered. In fact, a number of factors have been responsible for this decline and the present crisis.[5]

1. The collapse of the Albright-Wright synthesis of the "conquest" of Canaan by Joshua and the Israelites.
2. The demise of the Wellhausenian, or traditional-source critical certainties regarding the composition of the Pentateuch and the traditional dating of those sources. New literary and sociological approaches now rival older Continental methods.
3. The redefining of historiography or history writing in the Bible, resulting in the spurning of biblical writings for reconstructing Israel's early history.
4. The emergence of a new skepticism towards the historical reliability of the biblical text, what might be called a "hermeneutic of suspicion."

Let us now briefly sketch how these developments took place and how they set the stage for the present investigation.

The Collapse of the Albright-Wright Synthesis

William F. Albright, followed by his student G. Ernest Wright, significantly shaped and defined biblical archaeology from the 1940s through the 1970s.[6] The so-called archaeological (thirteenth-century) date for Israel's militaristic entry into Canaan was a direct result of Albright's discoveries at Tell Beit Mirsim (which he thought was biblical Debir) and Wright's work at Beitîn, possibly biblical Bethel.[7] Writing in the mid-1950s, Wright reflected on his work at the site:

> Sometime during the 13th century the city was destroyed by a tremendous conflagration. It was the privilege of the writer to participate in this excavation, and even for a beginner in the field of archaeology there was absolutely no mistaking the evidences of by far the worst destruction which the city experienced in all its history. In some places the debris of fallen walls and charred, ash-filled earth was almost five feet thick. The Canaanite city destroyed was a fine one with excellent

houses, paved or plastered floors and drains. Compared with them the poor straggly houses of the next town were poverty itself. The break between the two is so complete that there can be no doubt but that this was the Israelite destruction.[8]

This type of correlation between the archaeological data and Joshua narratives was the dominant view during the 1960s and 1970s, especially in North America, and has more recently been dubbed the "conquest model or theory."[9] To be sure, there were those who early on rejected the Albright school's conquest model. In his seminal essay of 1925, "Die Landnahme der Israeliten in Palästina," Albrecht Alt, who carefully utilized Egyptian historical sources, argued for a gradual migration of Israelite tribes into Canaan, rather than a wholesale conquest by a unified Israel under the leadership of Joshua.[10] This view was subsequently championed by Martin Noth, who asserted:

> It is clear that, to begin with, the occupation of the land by the tribes took place fairly quietly and peacefully on the whole and without seriously disturbing the great mass of the previous inhabitants. We may think of it as having proceeded rather in the way in which even today semi-nomadic breeders of small cattle from the adjoining steppes and deserts pass over into a settled way of life in the cultivated countryside, the only difference being that at that time there was more uninhabited space available than there is today.[11]

Alt (understandably in 1925) and Noth reached these conclusions based on their reconstructions of the Hexateuch and by largely ignoring or trivializing the archaeologically based approach of the Albright-Wright school. While Noth did not reject the evidence of widespread thirteenth-century destruction of Canaanite cities that Albright attributed to the Israelites, he believed that the archaeological evidence for assigning the destructions to the Israelites was lacking. True, there is nothing about these Late Bronze Age destructions that points toward Israel or any other culprit for that matter.[12] I have argued similarly in the case of the widely held view that Egyptian armies at the beginning of eighteenth Dynasty (sixteenth–fifteenth centuries B.C.) were responsible for the rampage that terminated the Middle Bronze Age.[13] In both cases, ascribing a destruction level at the sites to a particular perpetrator comes from inferences derived from texts, biblical in the former, and Egyptian in the latter. Noth rejected Albright's thesis on the basis of his conclusion that the text of Joshua was etiological in nature.[14] One result of the disintegration of the conquest model is a return to the Alt-Noth hypothesis, and variations of it, as in the works of Manfred Weippert and Adam Zertal.[15] One problem with the "infiltration" or "migrations" model that has not been thoroughly addressed by its advocates is its failure to explain the demise of the Late Bronze Canaanite city-states.[16]

Another development that grew out of the tension between the German and American positions on the nature of Israel's arrival in Canaan was George Mendenhall's "peasant revolt" theory, presented first in *Biblical Archaeologist* in 1962[17] and developed more fully in his subsequent monograph.[18] Dever recently hailed Mendenhall's contribution as "one of the most original contributions to twentieth-century American biblical scholarship."[19] While not eliciting widespread support in the 1960s, this model has gained in popularity more recently

among adherents to more sociological approaches, like that of Norman Gottwald,[20] who expanded upon Mendenhall's thesis, giving it a Marxist bent. However, Mendenhall has bristled at the way Gottwald has skewed his original thesis,
saying,

> I was quite aware at the time (1962) that the thesis could be subjected to exploita-
> tion by political propagandists interested only in "socio-political processes," and
> now we have a large work that systematically attempts to force the ancient histori-
> cal data into the Procrustes' Bed of nineteenth century Marxist sociology. My at-
> tempts to warn against such reductionistic interpretations of the history of society
> radically different from that of the nineteenth century after the industrial revolution,
> are derided by Gottwald in his *magnum opus, The Tribes of Yahweh*.[21]

Nevertheless, Gottwald's work, in turn, has influenced the conclusions of more recent studies such as those by Marvin Chaney and Robert Coote.[22] The peasant-
revolt model's support has come largely from scholars sympathetic to sociological
methods of biblical studies. Anson Rainey, a sharp critic of this approach, demurs
in his review of Gottwald's work: "This book could safely and profitably be ignored. Unfortunately, it represents the most recent fad in Old Testament studies.
. . . This 'Revolting Peasant Theology' has become popular among students and
scholars of Old Testament; it may even be the new panacea of late twentieth century Old Testament Studies."[23] Regardless of the present acceptability or the future of the Mendenhall-Gottwald theory, it has posed problems for both earlier
American and German models.

Perhaps the most severe blow to the conquest theory has been the archaeological problems posed at Jericho and et-Tell, thought to be Ai. Since these are
among the most thoroughly documented and celebrated sites of Israelite victories
in Joshua (2, 6–8:29), and since the text is explicit about the cities being burned
(Josh. 6:24; 8:28), these sites should both serve as test cases for the conquest model
and the historicity of the Joshua narratives.

Liverpool University archaeologist John Garstang excavated Tell es-Sultan
(Jericho) from 1930–1936. City IV had undergone a massive destruction and
conflagration. Based on the ceramic and scarab evidence, along with the absence
of Mycenaean ware, Garstang dated this destruction to ca. 1400 B.C., associating
it with the Israelite conquest as described in Joshua 6.[24] This discovery and its dating correlated nicely with the now marginalized "early" exodus and conquest
dates (ca. 1447 and 1407 respectively) based on the Masoretic Text (MT) of 1
Kings 6:1.[25] The "conquest model" and the book of Joshua basked in the light for
less than two decades before the walls came tumbling down. The highly respected
archaeologist Dame Kathleen Kenyon, utilizing more exacting methods of excavation and ceramic analysis, reworked the site from 1952 to 1958. Because of her
stature and reputation, Kenyon's conclusions were accepted immediately by biblical scholars and archaeologists alike: Garstang's dating of City IV from the Late
Bronze Age was in fact the termination of the Middle Bronze Age (ca. 1550 B.C.)
and the destruction could be tied to Egyptian military activity in connection with
the expulsion of Hyksos from Egypt and the beginnings of the Egyptian empire
in the Levant.[26] Kenyon also discovered that during the Late Bronze period, when

the Israelites were thought to have "conquered" Jericho, it was scarcely occupied and the levels were badly eroded.[27]

Thus, Jericho became a liability to the conquest theory. Recently, however, Bryant G. Wood has reassessed the Jericho material by comparing Garstang's publications, the material in *Excavations at Jericho* volumes three through five, and unpublished Jericho ceramics.[28] He argues for returning to Garstang's original dating and suggests attributing the destruction to the Israelites. Wood's suggestions have not been received warmly by Syro-Palestinian archaeologists.[29] However, his arguments for redating the ceramics that Kenyon assigned to the Middle Bronze Age to the Late Bronze Age must be considered carefully, and the presence of mid-fifteenth through mid-fourteenth-century Egyptian scarabs from the Jericho tombs cannot be ignored. Thus the problem of Jericho has been reopened for discussion and firm conclusions concerning the Israelites must be withheld until the recent publications on Jericho have been studied thoroughly, or there are new excavations.

The second critical site is et-Tell, thought to be biblical Ai by its excavators. Like Jericho, Ai was dug first by Garstang in 1928, then in the 1930s by Judith Marquet-Krause of France, and finally by Joseph Callaway from 1964 to 1976.[30] A hiatus from the end of the Early Bronze III (ca. 2400) down to Iron I (ca. 1200 B.C.) posed problems for the 1400 date of Garstang and the mid to late thirteenth-century date of Albright and Wright. These discoveries caused Albright and Wright to posit a contorted hypothesis, namely, that Beitîn (which they had excavated earlier) was really the site destroyed by the Israelites, but the tradition was transferred to the site of et-Tell because of the impressive destruction there.[31] Thus, Ai joined Jericho as a major embarrassment for proponents of the conquest model, and consequently Noth's etiological explanation for the Joshua narratives has enjoyed a resurgence of popularity.[32] Even the normally conservative Yigael Yadin, who in the main defended the conquest theory, had to acquiesce the point on Ai; "we must interpret the Biblical account as etiological."[33]

Interestingly, the identification of et-Tell with Ai is based on the geographical description in Joshua 7–8, so, while many biblical scholars are prepared to trust Joshua's information about the location of the site, they reject what it reports to have occurred there. Methodologically, selective use of the biblical materials in this manner should be viewed with suspicion. Ziony Zevit is a good example of a scholar who is willing to accept the location of Ai at et-Tell based on the information in Joshua but rejects the factuality of the account, even though he admits it is "an untendentious, realistic story that does not tax credulity."[34] It should be noted that the equation of et-Tell with Ai of the Joshua narratives has been questioned.[35]

The Demise of the Wellhausenian, or
Traditional-Source-Critical Certainties

With his *Die Composition Des Hexateuch* (1877), Julius Wellhausen left an enduring mark on critical Old Testament scholarship.[36] If ever there was an assured conclusion of biblical scholarship, it was that the Hexateuch was a composite document that could be tied to four primary, separate, datable documents: the Jahwist (J)

from the ninth century, the Elohist (E) from the eighth century, the Deuteronomist (D) from the seventh century (the Josianic reforms), and the Priestly source
(P) from the fifth century. For nearly a century, Wellhausen's views (with some
minor variations), also known as the Documentary Hypothesis, dominated Old
Testament Studies, and, except for some "conservative" Jewish and Christian
scholars, these conclusions were uncritically embraced by succeeding generations
of scholars. With the emergence of Near Eastern and cognate studies, however,
which investigate comparable biblical and Near Eastern literature, a number of
scholars began to question the prevailing consensus,[37] although they have generally been viewed with suspicion by members of the guild. But in recent years a
number of serious biblical scholars have begun to distance themselves from the
nineteenth-century synthesis. While some are revising the conclusions of the last
century, others are rejecting them altogether. For instance, John Van Seters has argued for downdating J to the sixth century and the elimination of E as an independent source.[38] For him, D is the earliest source of true history, dating to the late
seventh century.[39] The traditional fifth-century dating for the P materials has also
been questioned on linguistic grounds. Avi Hurwitz argues for a late pre-exilic
date,[40] as does Zevit, who suggests a *terminus ad quem* of 586 for P on socioreligious
grounds.[41] Building on the works of Hurwitz and Zevit, Gary Rendsburg has also
argued for pushing the P materials back to the united monarchy (tenth century).[42]

Starting in the mid 1980s, the period around the centennial of Wellhausen's
influential work, a number of studies appeared that dared not only to question
Wellhausen's long accepted dates for JEDP but also to challenge his methodology,
assumptions, and conclusions. A critical essay by Moshe Weinfeld well illustrated
the changing mood.[43] Isaac M. Kikawada and Arthur Quinn's book bears the
telling subtitle on its cover: "A Provocative Challenge to the Documentary Hypothesis."[44] This work compares the structure of early Genesis with that of the
Atrahasis myth as the basis for the view that Genesis follows and adapts the structural and thematic features of its Babylonian counterpart. They observe: "The five-
part Atrahasis structure is a crucial inheritance of the Hebrew tradition from the
ancient Near Eastern civilizations. In a more general sense we have shown that at
least one Hebrew author—and a most important one at that—has assumed on the
part of the audience a knowledge of this convention."[45] Regarding traditional-
source criticism they conclude: "One thing, if anything, we are certain of: the
documentary hypothesis at present is woefully overextended."[46]

In 1987 R. N. Whybray offered perhaps the most comprehensive critique of
the Documentary Hypothesis. He poses many tough questions that undermine
the theological and stylistic reasons for identifying a certain pericope with a particular source or date.[47] For him the Pentateuch is a collection of fragments assembled into its present form in the post-exilic period by a single author. Whybray's proposal represents a return to the old, long-rejected, fragmentary theory of
the late eighteenth-century scholar Geddes. (Vater further developed this hypothesis in his 1805 commentary on the Pentateuch.)[48] While Whybray's critique of
orthodox source criticism is well reasoned and compelling, his theory concerning
the composition of the Pentateuch does not advance Pentateuchal studies but
takes it back two centuries.[49]

As the Documentary Hypothesis has lost some of its luster over the past fifteen years, the tradition-history approach has gained in popularity. Built on the foundation of Hermann Gunkel's form criticism, tradition criticism is interested in investigating the prehistory of the text, both oral and written,[50] as advocated in recent years by Rolf Rendtorff.[51] Indeed, tradition criticism has had a role in the demise of source criticism's dominance in Old Testament studies, but Whybray questions its validity in Pentateuchal studies.[52] While investigating the tradition history of biblical texts has some merit, the degree of subjectivity in this method remains a problem, and, like Wellhausen's source-critical method, certain historical, social, and religious assumptions are made that just cannot be substantiated convincingly.

Although source criticism and tradition criticism remain pillars in Old Testament studies, their monopoly seems to have given way to new literary approaches that have diverted scholars from a microscopic study of the Hebrew Bible to a macro or panoramic view of the text. Building on the findings of an earlier generation of scholars, such as Umberto Cassuto, the "new literary approach" is interested in the broader literary characteristics of a story or passage. The fact that chiasmus operates both on the micro and macro levels has, for instance, resulted in recognizing the literary unity of the flood story. For over a century the flood story, along with the creation narratives, was the locus classicus of the Documentary Hypothesis.[53]

Robert Alter has perhaps been most influential in defining the new literary readings,[54] and a host of biblical scholars now employ this more comprehensive approach.[55] Such analyses have enabled the reader to see the tapestry of the text, shedding new light on the rhetorical and thematic dimensions of narratives that have long been overlooked while scholarly investigation of the past century has been preoccupied with identifying the literary threads or strands (i.e., sources), thus missing the design of the fabric. One of the problems raised by Alter's preoccupation with the literary dimension of biblical texts is the lack of interest in the historical, social, and legal aspects of the narratives that are the concern of most biblical scholars and historians. For Alter, biblical literature is largely "prose fiction."[56] However, using a literary framework that includes such features as doublets need not militate against the historicity of the events. I have argued for this, for example, in the case of celebrated and oft studied patriarchal wife-sister stories in Genesis 12, 20, and 26.[57]

The use of new literary approaches by biblical scholars has significantly contributed to the decline of the old source-critical consensus. The old historical moorings of the Documentary Hypothesis are in serious trouble, and the result has been a scramble to determine the dates and reliability of the sources or traditions. As Whybray explains, "With regard to written sources, the rejection of the Documentary Hypothesis simply increases the range of possibilities."[58] The tendency has been to push these sources even later than Wellhausen ever would have imagined.[59] The trend towards late dating (viz. lowering the composition date to the fifth century or later) and abandoning traditional dates for the sources has been resisted by some. The title of E. W. Nicholson's 1991 essay, "The Pentateuch in Recent Research: A Time for Caution" rightly expresses the concern of not a few traditional Old Testament scholars. Also, "new literary approaches" to Old

Testament studies have had their detractors.[60] Some, like Nicholson and John Emerton,[61] continue to follow the Documentary Hypothesis and adhere to nineteenth-century conclusions.[62] Nevertheless, it is abundantly clear that "the assured results" of nineteenth-century source criticism no longer have ascendancy in the study of the Hebrew Bible; rather, sociological and literary methods are enjoying widespread use.[63]

The Redefining of Historiography or History Writing in the Bible

Over the past twenty years a number of scholarly works have appeared on the historiography of the ancient Near East.[64] It is no exaggeration to say that "historiography" has been one of the most discussed topics in Near Eastern and Old Testament studies during this period, but it has not yet become as controversial an issue in Egyptology or Assyriology as it has in biblical studies. A number of the recent publications on Near Eastern historiography grew out of a symposium held at the University of Toronto in 1974.[65] These include essays by Harry A. Hoffner on the Hittites,[66] A. Kirk Grayson on Assyria and Babylon,[67] John Van Seters on Israel (which laid the foundation for his *In Search of History*),[68] and Donald B. Redford on Egypt.[69]

In response to a more maximalist reading of texts that characterized the 1950s to the mid 1970s,[70] the pendulum has definitely swung in the minimalist direction, and skepticism is presently widespread, especially towards the Old Testament. Many historians and biblical scholars now maintain that a text's claims must be corroborated before they can be considered historical. This expectation is the opposite of the Western legal tradition of "innocent until proven guilty."[71] In 1976 Maxwell Miller drew the following distinction between the approach of earlier and more recent historians: "1) he generally takes a more critical stance toward his sources. 2) he is inclined to disregard the supernatural or miraculous in his treatment of past events."[72] Egyptologist Gun Björkman in 1964 put it this way: "It may be said that the burden of proof does not rest on the sceptical scholar but on the scholar who accepts the statements of his source as credible evidence. He has to realise that the narrative cannot be taken at its face value: it does not give the fact itself but only the reproduction of it, or it might even be, more or less, a product of his imagination."[73]

In fairness to Björkman, she was primarily concerned with extracting history from wisdom literature, particularly with the "Wisdom for Merikare," a Middle Egyptian wisdom treatise. However, since she refers to "narrative" it appears that her comments extend beyond instructional literature. Unfortunately, her assertion that the burden of proof does not rest on the critical (minimalist) historian has become the prevailing attitude in biblical scholarship for the past several decades. In shifting the burden of proof to the ancient document and demanding that the maximalist historian "prove" the historicity of a text's claim, the minimalist historian commits a methodological fallacy. Historian David Hackett Fischer labels this practice the "fallacy of presumptive proof," which "consists in advancing a proposition and shifting the burden of proof or disproof to others."[74] Additionally, the minimalist approaches an ancient text as "guilty until proven innocent," whereas the maximalist accepts what appears to be a historical statement unless there is evidence to prove the contrary.

Historical minimalism has dominated the "origins of Israel" debate over the past fifteen years. Nevertheless, the maximalists have not been silent and I will examine their critique of minimalist tendencies. But first, let us examine how historiography has been redefined.

Van Seters, in his influential *In Search of History*, has done a commendable job of surveying the different cultures of the Near East, including Greece, Mesopotamia, Anatolia, Egypt, Syria-Palestine, and Israel. Van Seters's analysis of ancient texts follows Johan Huizinga's definition of history: "History is the intellectual form in which a civilization renders account to itself of its past."[75] With this definition as the starting point, Van Seters offers five criteria by which the reader can be certain he is dealing with "history writing":

    1) History writing is a specific form of tradition in its own right. Any explanation of the genre as merely the accidental accumulation of traditional material is inadequate.

    2) History writing is not primarily the accurate reporting of past events. It also considers the reason for recalling the past and the significance given to past events.

    3) History writing examines the causes of present conditions and circumstances. In antiquity these causes are primarily moral—who is responsible for a certain state of affairs? (It goes without saying, of course, that modern scientific theories about causation or laws of evidence cannot be applied to the ancient writer).

    4) History writing is national or corporate in character. Therefore, merely reporting the deeds of the king may be only biographical unless these are viewed as part of the national history.

    5) History writing is part of the literary tradition and plays a significant role in the corporate tradition of the people.[76]

It is clear that by these criteria there is little, if any, historiography in the ancient Near East and Egypt. Van Seters maintains that a specific genre of "historiography" is essential (cf. point one). But this raises the obvious question: By what criteria are modern historians able to determine whether a genuine historiographic genre existed in Egypt or Babylon in the second millennium B.C.? Since Van Seters embraces the conclusions of earlier German historians, such as Ernst Troeltsch[77] and Hugo Gressmann, who rejected the historical trustworthiness of a text when it reports divine intervention in human affairs (a point already noted in Miller's study), there is a built-in bias against ancient writers for whom there was no church-state, religion-history separation or dichotomy between secular and sacred worlds.[78]

Point four appears to be a no-win situation for the modern historian who examines the writings of his ancient counterpart. How does one know what motivated the ancient writer to record history? Was it an individual effort or was the writer commissioned? What tools are at our disposal to determine if a given work is "national or corporate in character"? A closer look at Huizinga's essay and how Van Seters has interpreted this fourth point reveals a number of problems. Baruch Halpern, in his review of *In Search of History*, critiqued Van Seters's use of Huizinga, noting that "strangely, Van Seters does not remark that in appropriating this

definition he restricts it to comprehensive histories, excluding what Huizinga explicitly hoped to include, not least Huizinga's own work."[79] K. Lawson Younger
likewise identified the same problem: "It appears that Van Seters has misunder-
stood Huizinga's definition and invested it with a meaning quite different from
the Dutch historian's."[80] Younger made the same point in his subsequent monograph on historiography.[81] The scholar who takes Van Seters's five points to their
logical conclusion and tries to write a history of any ancient, literate culture becomes bogged down in an exercise in futility.

Giovanni Garbini's monograph is one of the most radical works to appear on
Hebrew historiography.[82] He, like many biblical historians in the 1980s, tends to
read biblical texts skeptically and dates the books late, concluding:

> we may say that the book of Joshua reflects a historical situation markedly later than
> the exile and an ideology which it is difficult to date before the third century B.C.
> To rely on it and on the book of Judges as a basis for a unitary framework of He-
> brew history prior to the monarchy leads to accepting such a historical absurdity as
> a fairly large social body completely without a head. . . . The lack of a head, a king,
> while improbable for social groups in Palestine at the beginning of the Iron Age, is,
> however, conceivable for a small group with a hierocratic government like that of
> Jerusalem after the exile—a "Hebrew people" without a "king" in Palestine existed
> only before the Hasmonaeans.[83] [i.e. 165–37 B.C.]

In other words, the ideology of the books of Joshua and Judges reflects the ideology and *Sitz im Leben* of the final centuries of the Intertestamental Period when
these works were written. It defies logic to believe that Joshua and Judges originated in the very period when the Qumran scribes were already copying the
same documents because they were deemed to be canonical. And it must be recalled that the Septuagint was already translated a century before the beginning of
the Hasmonaean period. It seems, rather, that Garbini's observations reflect his
own ideology, not an accurate portrayal of Hebrew historiographic ideology.

Writing on royal inscriptions from the Near East, Garbini states, "Everything
that we know about the culture of pre-exilic Israel confirms that there were no
structural or ideological differences between the Israelites and the neighboring
peoples; and all the rulers of these peoples produced inscriptions."[84] Consequently, he is perplexed that no royal Israelite inscriptions have survived. However, as Alan Millard points out, "The accidents of survival and discovery are
partly responsible for that. Jerusalem has been so long occupied, destroyed and rebuilt that the lack of monuments of her Hebrew kings, early or late, is no sur-
prise."[85] Concerning the absence of archival materials for the Davidic-Solomonic
period, Millard adds: "Archives from the tenth century B.C. will probably never be
unearthed in Palestine because the normal writing material at that time was papyrus, which only lasts when buried in unusually dry places."[86] Historians must
recognize the limitations of archaeology. It cannot at every point substantiate historical records, be they from the Bible or the archives of the ancient Near East.

For Garbini, in order for a king's claim in a text to be considered historically
reliable, it must be corroborated by an external source,[87] by which he means a text

from a neighboring state. For example, Garbini questions the accuracy of the reports in 1 Kings and 2 Chronicles about the construction of Solomon's temple because the annals of Tyre make no mention of the temple.[88] He notes that "the virtually complete silence of epigraphy of Hebrew history seems all the more disconcerting when we compare it with the epigraphic evidence from neighboring peoples: Phoenicians, Aramaeans, Moabites, Philistines and now even Ammonites have left more or less numerous inscriptions, if only just one, but in them we find a record of the name and actions of rulers, of relations with neighboring peoples, of wars and works of peace."[89] With the exception of the Phoenicians and Aramaeans, there is a dearth of texts among the neighbors cited. One has to wonder to which Philistine texts Garbini is referring. I am unaware that any have survived, nor is it even known what script the Philistines employed. As for the most celebrated Moabite text, the Mesha Stela, it refers directly to the Israelite kings Omri and Ahab and events described in 1 and 2 Kings, and, if André Lemaire is correct in restoring a line in the stela, the expression "House of David" is attested therein.[90]

During the summer of 1993, Avraham Biran discovered a fragment of a basalt stela at Tell Dan that mentions the "king of Israel" and the "House of David," thought to be the first ancient, extrabiblical attestation of King David.[91] Two more fragments of the stela came to light in the summer of 1994.[92] The new pieces contain what appears to be the names (partially preserved) of Jehoram, king of Israel, and Ahaziah, king of Judah, the former of whom fought against Hazael of Damascus and was injured at Ramoth-Gilead (2 Chron. 22:5).[93] Hazael, or one of his generals, then, is the likely erector of the stela, commemorating his victory. With the name of the Judaean monarch being probable, *bytdwd* indeed appears to be an epithet, "House of David."[94]

Although not an "Israelite" inscription, this Aramaic stela was erected in Israel and describes events that took place in the Northern Kingdom and are reported in the Bible. Despite this important discovery, there are still very few extant documents from Israel's immediate neighbors. When those sources mention Israel, however, they describe events or figures found in the Bible.[95]

When we move to Mesopotamia, we find Assyrian and Neo-Babylonian texts concurring with the political history preserved in the Old Testament. While there may be differences in perspective and theology between the Assyrian annals and 1–2 Kings, there are no fundamental disagreements. A good example of this concurrence is the events of 701 B.C., where Sennacherib's annals and 2 Kings 18–20 and Isaiah 36–38 can be favorably compared.[96]

A Renewed Skepticism Toward the Historical Value of the Old Testament

The redefinition of which biblical texts are historiographic, the downdating of the sources, and the final redacting of the Old Testament documents has understandably resulted in a high degree of skepticism regarding Israel's origins in Canaan as well as that segment of their national history that places them in Egypt. Thomas Thompson well illustrates this climate of skepticism when he says, "a valid history of Israel's origins must be written within a historical geography of Palestine, based primarily on Palestinian archaeology and ancient Near Eastern studies . . . Israel's own origin tradition is radically irrelevant to writing such a history."[97] It is precisely this type of condescension toward the biblical literature that has given rise to revisionist histories of Israel over the past two decades, chief among them being the denial of the Hebrew presence in Egypt and the subsequent departure for Canaan. By minimizing or dismissing the Bible as a source for Israel's early history, revisionist histories can be written without the constraint of any controls.

The skeptical mood of many in Western scholarship, it appears, reflects the type of questioning that has directed at the media, politicians, and authority in general since the 1960s. Iain Provan has recently described this situation in similar terms: "We live in a culture that is slowly but steadfastly losing faith in the technological age and its high priests, as the confidence, even arrogance, of earlier times has given way to the disillusionment and cynicism of the nineties."[98] Hence there is a tendency to revise history to reflect the author's concerns and agenda. John Dewey has rightly observed the way in which the modern historian's ideology shapes the reading of earlier sources and writing history: "all history is necessarily written from the standpoint of the present, and is, in an inescapable sense, the history not only of the present but of that which is contemporaneously judged to be important in the present."[99] This cogent analysis captures what has been transpiring in the origins of Israel debate. Simply put, the widespread skepticism of the eighties and nineties reflects the ideology of the modern historian.

II. Response to the Current Climate of Skepticism

In response to the rising tide of skepticism among biblical scholars, Yale University Assyriologist and Hebrew Bible specialist William Hallo penned a brilliant essay entitled "The Limits of Skepticism."[100] Hallo offers a helpful guide to analyzing an ancient text: "treat the ancient sources critically but without condescension."[101] Likewise, Harvard's Jon Levenson has added his voice to the growing number of distinguished scholars who are openly questioning the current skeptical trends in scholarship. Levenson believes the time has come to suspect "the hermeneuts of suspicion."[102] Provan's critique of some of the works of key minimalist historians of Israel's origins has also called attention to excessive skepticism.[103] In response to the speculation that the biblical writers were writing ideological works and not history, Provan charges that these minimalist scholars too have ideologies and agendas: "The reality is, of course, that the approach to historiography that [Philip] Davies advocates with such passion is no less representative of a confessional stance or ideology, is indeed no more free of unverifiable presuppositions, than those other approaches he so vehemently attacks."[104] There has been the tendency for minimalist scholars to think of themselves as strictly objective investigators, the implication being that the historical maximalist is biased, credulous and naive.[105] But Provan is right: Everyone has assumptions when approaching a text or archaeological data that influence how one reads a text.[106] Anyone who thinks that he or she is totally objective and free from presuppositions commits the Baconian fallacy, the idea that a historian has no prejudices and assumptions.[107]

Let us return now to Van Seters's use of Huizinga's definition of history. He accepts the Dutch historian's definition that history is the "intellectual form in which a civilization renders account to itself of its past." It seems, however, that the word "intellectual" takes on a decidedly "Western" orientation while ignoring the conventions of the Near Eastern historian, a point also noted by Hallo some years ago.[108] It has been customary to celebrate Herodotus as "the father of history," owing to his Greek (Western) philosophic and "scientific" orientation, and because he apparently investigated information and was somewhat critical in his use of sources.[109] However, it has been noted that Herodotus could also be quite credulous,[110] and some recent commentators on Herodotus have doubted his reliability.[111]

Van Seters rightly observes that the true historian is "objective"[112] [if that is really absolutely possible], but ancient writers never reach this ideal, according to him, until well into the first millennium. Halpern characterizes Van Seters's assessment of the ancient biblical writers by saying he "imagines him (the Deuteronomic historian) a rogue and a fraud, a distributor of taffy."[113] On the other hand, historians like Hallo and Kitchen, who might be called maximalists, have greater faith in the ancient writer's integrity. One reason for the disparity between historical maximalists and minimalists is that the former tend to be trained in Near Eastern languages, history, and archaeology with the Hebrew Bible as a cognate discipline, whereas the latter are largely trained in Old Testament studies in the nineteenth-century European mold and treat cognate languages and sources as ancillary rather than central to their discipline.

Another of Huizinga's guiding principles, which serves to balance his definition of history cited above, is "every civilization creates its own form of history."[114] Van Seters, it appears, failed to consider this important proviso in Huizinga's essay, which allows for a variety of ways of writing history, not only one that conforms to certain Western codes or interpretations based on recently developed anthropological or sociological models. Halpern also makes this point when referring to the "variety of biblical historiographic forms and practices."[115] Van Seters's definition of history writing is thus overly restrictive and not as broad as that of Huizinga, whose definition he claims to follow.

The tendency to credit the Greeks as the first "true" historians is not the product of nineteenth- and twentieth-century historians. Nineteen hundred years ago, the Jewish historian Flavius Josephus protested the same attitude, prevalent in his own day:

> My first thought is one of intense astonishment at the current opinion that, in the study of primeval history, the Greeks alone deserve serious attention, that the truth should be sought from them, and that neither we nor any others in the world are to be trusted. In my view the very reverse of this is the case, if, that is to say, we are not to take idle prejudices as our guide, but to extract truth from the facts themselves. For in the Greek world everything will be found to be modern, and dating so to speak, from yesterday or the day before: I refer to the foundation of their cities, the invention of the arts, and the compilation of a code of laws; but the most recent, or

nearly the most recent, of all their attainments is care in historical composition. On
the contrary, as is admitted even by themselves, the Egyptians, the Chaldaeans, and
the Phoenicians . . . possess a very ancient and permanent record of the past.[116]

The ability of the ancient scribes to record history must not be diminished by
modern notions of historiography or by the current proclivity to give late dates to
the Hebrew narratives based on the groundless assumption that the Israelites were
unable to write history until the middle third of the first millennium, a position
held by Van Seters. On the contrary, Hallo maintains "that history begins where
writing begins and I see no reason to exempt Israel from this working hypothesis."[117] There is no reason to deny the ability to write and record information
prior to the Iron Age, as an ostracon discovered at ᶜIzbet Sartah from the twelfth-
century demonstrates.[118]

In view of Huizinga's position that "every civilization creates its own form of
history," the modern historian must exercise caution in employing modern, Western investigative methods on ancient Near Eastern documents. If the historian
thinks there is a problem with the text's trustworthiness, the burden of proof lies
with the modern investigator, not the ancient writer who cannot explain himself
to the modern investigator. Writing on this point nearly thirty years ago, Kitchen
stated, "It is normal practice to assume the general reliability of statements in our
sources, unless there is good, explicit evidence to the contrary. Unreliability, secondary origins, dishonesty of a writer, or tendentious traits—all these must be
clearly proved by adduction of tangible evidence, and not merely inferred to support a theory."[119]

I will follow this principle and use the "scripture in context," or "contextual
approach" of Hallo as the narratives of Israel in Egypt and Exodus are investigated.[120] Three decades ago, Roland de Vaux similarly described this methodology
regarding the early Hebrew history of Israel:

> Israel is one of the peoples of the ancient Near East whose place and role [the his-
> torian] puts in general history. He reconstructs its political and economic history,
> studies its social, political, and religious institutions and its culture, as he does or
> would do for any other people. The Bible is for him a document of history which
> he criticizes, and controls, and supplements by the information which he can obtain
> outside of the Bible. The result is a history of Israel.[121]

This method of investigating biblical texts, then, insists we examine the linguistic,
historical, and social setting of the Hebrew writings in the light of cognate literature of Israel's neighbors.

Unfortunately, over the past decades, comparative work with Old Testament
literature has not always been undertaken carefully and critically. Van Seters's and
Thompson's works on the Patriarchal narratives successfully exposed some of the
shortcomings of the social or legal parallels that Albright, Speiser, and others drew
between second-millennium cuneiform sources and Genesis.[122] Concerning this
aspect of their critique, Kitchen offers praise to these scholars: "Thus, their works
do perform the useful function of ruthlessly exposing sloppy argumentation of
others, false or inadequate parallels, refuting the wilder excrescences of speculation, and emphasising the need to look at all periods (not only the second mil-

lennium) in reviewing possible background to the patriarchal narratives."[123] On the other hand, Kitchen chides them for other methodological inconsistencies in their approach: "However, these same advocates themselves then fail to match up to this selfsame standard of reviewing the patriarchal data against *all* periods. Instead, they neglect the 3rd millennium BC. entirely, along with whole sections of relevant evidence from the early second millennium, and give exaggerated attention to the 1st-millennium materials."[124] By virtue of using parallels (albeit exclusively late ones) to date biblical texts, Thompson and Van Seters show that they find the comparative method a valid one in biblical research. But what they have done is to swing to the opposite extreme of Albright and Speiser.

The failures of earlier practitioners of the comparative method do not invalidate the approach. "Rather," as Hallo explains, "it invites a reconsideration of the terms of the comparison."[125] As a matter of academic integrity, the use of comparative material in the study of parallels *must* employ sources from *all* periods, as Kitchen avers, and texts where there is a spatial association with the Hebrew scribes.[126] Since the dating of the narratives of the first six books of the Bible remains an open question, one should not exclude Near Eastern documents because they are early or late when trying to determine the setting and origin of the Hebrew narratives.

I concur with Hallo, Levenson, and Provan that there has been too much condescension and suspicion of biblical documents by historians and biblical scholars during the past couple of decades. In this study, I shall seek to go where the biblical, historical, and archaeological evidence leads rather than being guided by anthropological or sociological models or subjective theories about the dating and origin of the biblical documents. Furthermore, I shall strive to treat both biblical and Near Eastern texts as witnesses to history and avoid the double standard of treating the Bible more critically than cognate literature from Israel's neighbors.

Notes

1 See two of the most important works: John Van Seters, *Abraham in History and Tradition* (New Haven: Yale University Press, 1975) and Thomas Thompson, *The Historicity of the Patriarchal Narratives*, *BZAW*, vol. 133 (Berlin, 1974). While these books were influential, most of the concerns they raised were adequately answered, see K. A. Kitchen, *The Bible in Its World* (Exeter: Paternoster, 1977) chap. 4; *Essays on the Patriarchal Narratives*, ed. A. R. Millard and D. J. Wiseman (London/Winona Lake: IV Press/Eisenbrauns, 1979/1980).

2 W. F. Albright, *From Stone Age to Christianity* (Baltimore: The Johns Hopkins University Press, 1946); John Bright, *A History of Israel*, 3d. ed. (Philadelphia: Westminster Press, 1981); and E. A. Speiser, *Genesis* (Anchor Bible: Garden City, N.Y., 1964). These represent only some of the works of these authors who advocated a second millennium setting for the Genesis narratives and considered the stories historical.

3 *History of Israel*, 120.

4 Robert B. Coote, *Early Israel: A New Horizon* (Minneapolis: Fortress, 1990). Interestingly, R. S. Hess began a recent article ("Early Israel in Canaan: A Survey of Recent Evidence and Interpretations," *PEQ* 125 [1993] 125-142) by comparing quotes from Bright and Coote, but different ones. My thanks to Dr. Hess for giving me an offprint of this study. The comparison drawn between the two here was made before seeing his study. It

is intriguing that, independently of each other, we both saw the contrast between Bright and Coote as exemplifying the radical change that has occurred among Old Testament scholars in a short period of time.

5 The following points are listed randomly and not in the order of their development or importance to the unraveling of the consensus of the 1950s to the 1970s.

6 Concerning the impact of the Albright-Wright school, see William G. Dever, *Recent Archaeological Discoveries and Biblical Research* (Seattle: University of Washington Press, 1990) 3–36. See also Dever's "Archaeology and the Israelite 'Conquest,'" in *ABD*, vol. 3, 546–547.

7 G. Ernest Wright, *Biblical Archaeology* (Philadelphia: Westminster Press, 1957) 80–81. Here Wright followed the views of Albright and Kelso, who were directing this excavation; see William F. Albright and James L. Kelso, *The Excavations of Bethel (1934–1960)*, *AASOR*, vol. 39 (Cambridge, Mass.: ASOR, 1968) 30–31.

8 Wright, *Biblical Archaeology*, 80–81.

9 Dever, *Recent Archaeological Discoveries*, 45; Dever offers a good overview of the consensus from 1930 to 1960 on pp. 40–49.

10 Albrecht Alt, *Essays on Old Testament History and Religion* (Garden City, N.Y.: Doubleday, 1967; orig. 1925).

11 Martin Noth, *The History of Israel* (London: Adam and Charles Black, 1960) 69.

12 This point has been made by John Bimson (*Redating the Exodus and Conquest* [Sheffield: Almond Press, 1981] 30–103), but this section of his work has been ignored largely because of the position he champions in the second part of the book, namely an early (fifteenth-century) exodus and conquest, which requires the lowering of the date for the end of the Middle Bronze IIC. Thus, for Bimson, the widespread destructions of Middle Bronze sites should be attributed to the Israelites around or before 1400 B.C.

13 James K. Hoffmeier, "Reconsidering Egypt's Part in the Termination of the Middle Bronze Age in Palestine," *Levant* 21 (1989) 181–193.

14 Noth, *History of Israel*, 82, n. 2. His position regarding the Joshua narratives was formulated earlier in his *Das Buch Josua* (Tübingen: J. C. B. Mohr, 1953).

15 Manfred Weippert, *The Settlement of the Israelite Tribes in Palestine*, Studies in Biblical Theology, vol. 21 (London: SCM Press, 1971) and "The Israelite 'Conquest' and the Evidence from Transjordan," in *Symposia Celebrating the Seventy-Fifth Anniversary of the Founding of the American Schools of Oriental Research (1900–1975)*, ed. Frank Moore Cross (Cambridge, Mass.: ASOR, 1979) 15–34 and Adam Zertal, "Israel Enters Canaan—Following the Pottery Trail," *BAR* 17 no. 5 (1991) 28–47.

16 A point also made by Volkmar Fritz. See his "Conquest or Settlement? The Early Iron Age in Palestine," *BA* 50 no. 2 (1987) 84.

17 George E. Mendenhall, "The Hebrew Conquest of Palestine," *BA* 25 no. 3 (1962) 66–87.

18 *The Tenth Generation* (Baltimore: The Johns Hopkins University Press, 1973).

19 Dever, *Recent Archaeological Discoveries*, 50.

20 *The Tribes of Yahweh: A Sociology of the Religion of Liberated Israel, 1250–1050 B.C.E.* (Maryknoll, N.Y.: Orbis, 1979).

21 George E. Mendenhall, "Ancient Israel's Hyphenated History," in *Palestine in Transition: The Emergence of Ancient Israel*, ed. D. N. Freedman and D. F. Graf (Sheffield, England: Almond Press, 1983) 91.

22 Marvin L. Chaney, "Ancient Palestine Peasant Movements and Formation of Premonarchic Israel," in *Palestine in Transition*; Coote, *Early Israel*.

23 Anson F. Rainey, Review of N. K. Gottwald's *The Tribes of Yahweh: A Sociology of the Religion of Liberated Israel, 1250–1050 B.C.E.*, *JAOS* 107 (1987) 541–543.

24 Field reports of Garstang's work can be found in *Liverpool Annals of Archaeology and Anthropology*, vols. 19, 20, 21, 22, and 23 (1932–1936), and in *Palestine Exploration Fund Quarterly Statement* 1930, 1931, 1932, and 1936.

25 The question of dating will be further discussed in chapter 5 §V.

26 Kathleen M. Kenyon, *Digging Up Jericho* (London: Ernest Benn, 1957); "Jericho," *EAHL*, vol. 2, 674–681. Her final reports of the tell material were published posthumously with T. A. Holland, vol. 3 of *Excavations at Jericho* (London: BSA, 1981); *The Pottery Type Series and Other Finds*, vol. 4 of *Excavations at Jericho* (London: BSA, 1982); and *The Pottery Phases of the Tell and Other Finds*, vol. 5 of *Excavations at Jericho* (London: BSA, 1983). For a recent, condensed review of the archaeology of Jericho, see T. A. Holland, "Jericho" in *ABD*, vol. 3 (1992) 723–737.

27 For a detailed study of the Late Bronze Age in Jericho, see Piotr Bienkowski, *Jericho in the Late Bronze Age* (Warminster, England: Aris and Phillips, 1986).

28 Bryant Wood, "Did the Israelites Conquer Jericho: A New Look at the Archaeological Evidence," *BAR* 16 no. 2 (1990) 44–59.

29 Wood's thesis has been challenged by Piotr Bienkowski, "Jericho Was Destroyed in the Middle Bronze Age, Not the Late Bronze Age," *BAR* 16 no. 5 (1990) 45, 46, and 69, to which Wood has offered a careful response ("Dating Jericho's Destruction: Bienkowski Is Wrong on All Counts," *BAR* 16 no. 5 (1990) 45, 47–49, 68–69.

30 For Callaway's survey of the archaeological history of the site and his own synthesis of the archaeological and biblical data, see "Ai" in *ABD* vol. 1, 125–130, and "Ai" in *EAEHL*, vol. 1, 39–45.

31 Wright, *Biblical Archaeology*, 80–81; "The Literary and Historical Problem of Joshua 10 and Judges 1," *JNES* 5 (1946) 107–108, and W. F. Albright, "The Kyle Memorial Excavation at Bethel," *BASOR* 62 (1934) 11.

32 Ziony Zevit, "Archaeological and Literary Stratigraphy in Joshua 7–8," *BASOR* 251 (1983) 23–35 and "The Problem of Ai," *BAR* 11 no. 2 (1985) 58–69.

33 Yigael Yadin, "Is the Biblical Account of the Israelite Conquest of Canaan Historically Reliable?" *BAR* 8 no. 2 (1982) 16–23.

34 *BASOR* 251 (1983) 23 and see *BAR* 11 no. 2 (1985) 58–69.

35 J. M. Grintz, "'Ai Which Is Beside Beth-Aven," *Biblica* 42 (1961) 201–216; Kenneth Kitchen, *Ancient Orient and Old Testament* (Downers Grove, Ill.: IV Press, 1966) 63–64.

36 Baruch Halpern's important work, *The First Historians: The Hebrew Bible and History* (San Francisco: Harper and Row, 1988), provides a helpful discussion of the philosophical and religious setting in which nineteenth-century biblical scholars wrote.

37 E.g., Umberto Cassuto, *The Documentary Hypothesis* (Jerusalem: Central Press, 1941; English trans. 1961); Cyrus H. Gordon, *The Ancient Near East*, 3d ed., rev. (New York: W. W. Norton; 1965); Kitchen, *Ancient Orient and Old Testament*, chaps. 1 and 6.

38 *Abraham in History and Tradition*.

39 John Van Seters, *In Search of History: Historiography in the Ancient World and the Origins of Biblical History* (New Haven: Yale University, 1983), and further developed in his more recent monographs, *Prologue to History: The Yahwist as Historian in Genesis* (Louisville: Westminster/John Knox Press, 1992) and *The Life of Moses: The Yahwist as Historian in Exodus-Numbers* (Knoxville: Westminster/John Knox Press, 1994).

40 Avi Hurwitz, "The Evidence of Language in Dating the Priestly Code—A Linguistic Study in Technical Idioms and Terminology," *RB* 81 (1974) 24–36 and *A Linguistic Study of the Relationship Between the Priestly Source and the Book of Exodus* (Paris: Cahier de la Rèvue Biblique 20, 1982). It should be noted that Philip Davies has recently challenged Hurwitz's approach as based on the unfounded assumption that Ezekiel is dated to

the sixth century (cf. Philip R. Davies, *In Search of Ancient Israel*, *JSOT* Supp. Series, vol. 148 (Sheffield: *JSOT* Press, 1992) 102. That Davies should question the sixth-century dating of Ezekiel reflects his own metachronistic tendencies. It was pointed out over twenty-five years ago that the chronological data interspersed throughout the book of Ezekiel makes it one of the most securely dated books in the Hebrew canon; see K. S. Freedy and D. B. Redford, "The Dates in Ezekiel in Relation to Biblical, Babylonian and Egyptian Sources," *JAOS* 90 (1970) 462–485.

41 Ziony Zevit, "Converging Lines of Evidence Bearing on the Date of 'P,' " *ZAW* 94 (1982) 481–511.

42 Gary Rendsburg, "Late Biblical Hebrew and the Date of 'P,' " *JANES* 12 (1980) 65–80; "A New Look at Pentateuchal *HW*," *Biblica* 63 (1982) 351–369 and *The Redaction of Genesis* (Winona Lake, Ind.: Eisenbrauns, 1986) chap. 7.

43 *Getting at the Roots of Wellhausen's Understanding of the Law of Israel on the 100th Anniversary of the Prolegomena*, Institute for Advanced Studies Report no. 14/79 (Jerusalem: The Hebrew University of Jerusalem,1979).

44 *Before Abraham Was: The Unity of Genesis 1–11* (Nashville: Abingdon, 1985). Kitchen had argued along similar lines nearly a decade earlier in *The Bible in Its World* (Exeter: Paternoster, 1977) 31–34, but Kikawada and Quinn's study makes no mention of Kitchen's comparing the thematic structure of Atrahasis and Genesis.

45 Kikawada and Quinn, *Before Abraham Was*, 124.

46 Ibid., 125.

47 *The Making of the Pentateuch: A Methodological Study*, *JSOT* Supplement Series vol. 53 (Sheffield: *JSOT*, 1987).

48 For a discussion of these works, see R. K. Harrison, *Introduction to the Old Testament* (Grand Rapids, Mich.: Eerdmans, 1969) 14–15.

49 E. W. Nicholson, "The Pentateuch in Recent Research: A Time for Caution," *VTS*, vol. 43 (1991) 10–21, offers a number of criticisms of Whybray's work.

50 See Douglas Knight, "Tradition History," *ABD* vol. 6, 633–634.

51 E.g., *Das überlieferungsgeschichtliche Problem des Pentateuch BZAW* vol. 147 (Berlin: 1977).

52 Whybray, *The Making of the Pentateuch*, 133–219.

53 Gordon J. Wenham, "The Coherence of the Flood Narrative," *VT* 28 (1978) 336–348, and repeated in his *Genesis 1–15* (Waco: Word, 1987) 155-169. Wenham's chiastic analysis was subsequently accepted by Kikawada and Quinn (*Before Abraham Was*, 103–104).

54 Robert Alter, "A Literary Approach to the Bible," *Commentary* 60 no. 6 (1975) 70–77 and *The Art of Biblical Narrative* (New York: Basic Books, 1981).

55 The following works represent a range of literary approaches: Michael Fishbane, *Text and Texture: Close Readings of Selected Biblical Texts* (New York: Schocken, 1979) and "I Samuel 3: Historical Narrative and Narrative Poetics," in *Literary Interpretations of Biblical Narratives*, vol. 2 ed. Kenneth R. R. Gros Louis (Nashville: Abingdon, 1982) 191–203; Jack Sasson, "The 'Tower of Babel' as a Clue to the Redactional Structuring of the Primeval History (Gen. 1–11:19)" in *The Bible World: Essays in Honor of Cyrus H. Gordon*, ed. Gary Rendsburg, et al. (New York: Ktav, 1980) 211–219; Kenneth R. R. Gros Louis, ed., *Literary Interpretations of Biblical Narratives*, vol. 2; David W. Baker, "Diversity and Unity in the Literary Structure of Genesis," in *Essays on the Patriarchal Narratives*, ed. A. R. Millard and D. J. Wiseman (Winona Lake, Ind., 1983) 197–215; Kikawada and Quinn, *Before Abraham Was*; Joel Rosenberg, *King and Kin: Political Allegory in the Hebrew Bible* (Bloomington, Ind.: Indiana University Press, 1986); Rendsburg, *The Redaction of Genesis*; David Damrosch, *The Narrative Covenant: Transformations of Genre in the Growth of Biblical Litera-*

ture (San Francisco: Harper and Row, 1987); Regina Schwartz, ed., *The Book and the Text: The Bible and Literary Theory* (Oxford: Blackwell, 1990); Leland Ryken and Tremper Longman III, eds., *A Complete Literary Guide to the Bible* (Grand Rapids, Mich.: Zondervan, 1993); and D. F. Watson and A. J. Hauser, *Rhetorical Criticism of the Bible: A Comprehensive Bibliography with Notes on History and Method* (Leiden: Brill, 1994). I am using the expression "literary approaches" in a rather broad sense.

56 *Art of Biblical Narrative*, 23–46.

57 James K. Hoffmeier, "The Wives' Tales of Genesis 12, 20 & 26 and the Covenants at Beer-Sheba," *TB* 43 no. 1 (1992) 81–99.

58 Whybray, *The Making of the Pentateuch*, 236.

59 See for instance Garbini's quote in §3 below. Philip Davies's recent monograph argues that the biblical works dealing with early Israel date to the sixth through third centuries, with his inclination being toward the latter end of that horizon (*In Search of 'Ancient Israel,'* see chap. 6–9).

60 E.g., J. Emerton, "An Examination of Some Attempts to Defend the Unity of the Flood Narrative in Genesis, Part I," *VT* 37 (1987) 401–420 and "An Examination of Some Attempts to Defend the Unity of the Flood Narrative in Genesis, Part II," *VT* 38 (1988) 1–21.

61 Ibid.

62 E.g., R. E. Friedman, *Who Wrote the Bible?* (San Francisco: Harper, 1988).

63 Sociological approaches have not seriously impacted source criticism the way literary readings of biblical texts have. By their nature, sociological investigations are not particularly interested in literary and compositional questions. Hence, the contribution sociological investigations of the Old Testament has not been considered here. However, some representative works include: Robert R. Wilson, *Sociological Approaches to the Old Testament* (Philadelphia: Fortress, 1984); Norman Gottwald, *The Hebrew Bible: A Socio-Literary Introduction* (Philadelphia: Fortress, 1985); a forthcoming book containing a number of important essays is Charles Carter and Carol Meyers, eds., *Community, Identity, and Ideology: Social Scientific Approaches to the Hebrew Bible*, Sources for Biblical and Theological Study vol. 6 (Winona Lake, Ind.: Eisenbrauns, 1997).

64 Some of these studies include: Mario Liverani, "Memorandum on the Approach to Historiographic Texts," *Orientalia* 42 (1973) 178–194; J. Maxwell Miller, *The Old Testament and the Historian* (Philadelphia: Fortress, 1976); Van Seters, *In Search of History*; H. Tadmor and M. Weinfeld, eds., *History, Historiography and Interpretation: Studies in Biblical and Cuneiform Literatures* (Jerusalem/Leiden: Magnes/Brill, 1983); Piotr Michalowski, "History as Charter: Some Observations on the Sumerian King List," in *Studies in Literature from the Ancient Near East Dedicated to Samuel Noah Kramer*, AOS vol. 65 (1984) 237–248; Giovanni Garbini, *History & Ideology in Ancient Israel* (New York : Crossroad, 1988); Baruch Halpern, *The First Historians*; Robert B. Coote and David R. Ord, *The Bible's First History* (Philadelphia: Fortress, 1989); K. Lawson Younger, *Ancient Conquest Accounts: A Study in Ancient Near Eastern and Biblical History Writing*, JSOT Supp. Series, vol. 98 (Sheffield: JSOT Press, 1990); and *Faith, Tradition, History: Essays on Old Testament Historiography in its Near Eastern Context*, ed. A. R. Millard, J. K. Hoffmeier, D. W. Baker (Winona Lake, Ind.: Eisenbrauns, 1994). Some of the ideas presented in this section were presented in a different form in my essay "The Problem of 'History' in Egyptian Royal Inscriptions," in *VI Congresso Internazionale De Egittologia Atti*, ed. Silvio Curto (Turin: 1992) 291–299.

65 I had the privilege of attending this symposium during graduate studies at the University of Toronto.

66 "Histories and Historians of the Ancient Near East: The Hittites," *Orientalia* 49 (1980) 283–332.

67 "Histories and Historians of the Ancient Near East: Assyrian and Babylonia," *Orientalia* 49 (1980) 140–194.

68 "Histories and Historians of the Ancient Near East: The Israelites," *Orientalia* 50 (1981) 137–185.

69 *Pharaonic King-Lists, Annals and Day-Books: A Contribution to the Study of the Egyptian Sense of History* (Mississauga, Ont.: Benben, 1986).

70 Good examples of the earlier, more positive, and less skeptical approach are found in Robert C. Dentan, ed., *The Idea of History in the Ancient Near East* (New Haven: AOS, 1954, repr. 1983) and Bright, *History of Israel*.

71 I have maintained just the opposite in an exchange with Syro-Palestinian archaeologist W. G. Dever. Cf. "Some Thoughts on William G. Dever's 'Hyksos, Egyptian Destructions, and the End of the Palestinian Middle Bronze Age,'" *Levant* 22 (1990) 83–89.

72 Miller, *The Old Testament and the Historian*, 12–13.

73 "Egyptology and Historical Method," *Orientalia Suecana* 13 (1964) 11.

74 A number of methodological fallacies of historical minimalists will be exposed here that are identified in David Hackett Fischer, *Historians' Fallacies: Toward a Logic of Historical Thought* (New York: Harper and Row, 1970) 48.

75 Johan Huizinga, "A Definition of the Concept of History," in *Philosophy and History: Essays Presented to Ernst Cassirer*, ed. R. Kiblansky and H. J. Paton (New York: Harper Torchbooks, 1963) 1–10 (Orig. Oxford: Clarendon Press, 1936).

76 Van Seters, *In Search of History*, 4–5. His definition is applied to Israel, but I expect that he would apply these criteria to any body of literature in the Near East.

77 Troeltsch lived from 1865 to 1923, and although he is not specifically cited by Van Seters, his works influenced those, such as Gressmann and Gunkel, to whom Van Seters is indebted. Troeltsch's works were primarily concerned with biblical studies, cf. *Gesammelte Schriften*, vols. 1 and 2 (Tübingen: J.C.B. Mohr, 1913). His methodology, however, influenced virtually all fields of history in Europe. It may be said that he is also responsible for the skepticism that has dominated German biblical scholarship since.

78 For a critique of this approach, see Bertil Albrektson, *History and the Gods* (Lund: Gleerup, 1967) and Hoffmeier, in *VI Congresso Internazionale De Egittologia Atti*, 296–297.

79 Baruch Halpern, Review of *In Search of History, JBL* 104 (1985) 507.

80 *JSOT* 40 (1988) 111.

81 Younger, *Ancient Conquest Accounts*, 27.

82 *History and Ideology*.

83 Ibid., 132.

84 Ibid., 18.

85 "Texts and Archaeology: Weighing the Evidence, The Case for King Solomon," *PEQ* 123 (1991) 25. Even from the first century A.D., few inscriptions have been found in excavations of the area around the south and western (south end) of the Temple Mount in Jerusalem; cf. Alan Millard, *Discoveries from the Time of Jesus* (Oxford: Lion Books, 1990) 78–97.

86 Millard, *PEQ* 123 (1991) 25.

87 Garbini, *History & Ideology*, 23.

88 Ibid.

89 Ibid., 17.

90 "'House of David' Restored Moabite Inscription," *BAR* 20 no. 3 (1994) 30–37.

91 "An Aramaic Stele Fragment from Tel Dan," *IEJ* 43 nos. 2–3 (1993) 1–18. Biran and Naveh's identification of the reading *bytdwd* with "The House of David" has, not surprisingly, been challenged by Philip Davies ("'House of David' Built on Sand: The Sins

of the Biblical Maximizers," *BAR* 20 no. 4 [1994] 54 – 55). One of Davies's major objections to reading *bytdwd* as "House of David" is the absence of a word divider between *byt*
and *dwd*. But see a rejoinder by Anson Rainey, "The 'House of David' and House of the
Deconstructionists," *BAR* 20 no. 6 (1994) 47, Baruch Halpern, "The Stela from Dan:
Epigraphic and Historical Considerations," *BASOR* 296 (1994) 63 – 80, and Gary Rendsburg "On the Writing ביתדוד in the Aramaic Inscription from Tel Dan," *IEJ* 45 (1995)
22 – 25. Subsequently, additional studies have come out against Biran and Naveh's reading
of the text: F. H. Cryer, "A 'BETDAWD' Miscellany: DWD, DWD' or DWDH," *SJOT* 9
(1995) 52 – 58; and Thomas Thompson, "House of David": An Eponymic Referent to
Yahweh as Godfather," *SJOT* 9 (1995) 59 – 74. The discovery of additional fragments of
the stela (see n. 92) supports Biran and Naveh's reading of the first portion and undermines the arguments of Davies, Cryer, and Thompson. See also my discussion of the
methodological assumptions of the minimalists in the current debate, "Of Minimalists
and Maximalists," *BAR* 21 no. 2 (1995) 20 – 22 and "The Recently Discovered Tell Dan
Inscription: Controversy & Confirmation," *Archaeology in the Biblical World* 3 no. 1 (1995)
12 – 15.

   92 Avraham Biran and Joseph Naveh, "The Tel Dan Inscription: A New Fragment,"
IEJ 45 (1995) 1 – 15.

   93 Ibid., 9 – 11.

   94 Rendsburg, *IEJ* 45 (1995) documents the high frequency of toponyms in Aramaic
texts that follow the formula *byt*-X (22 – 25). In fact, Rendsburg observes that Aramaic
inscriptions have the greatest concentration of this name formula among Semitic languages. He concludes, "The totality of the evidence demonstrates that X-בית was a strong
characteristic of Aramaic phraseology. This fact explains why an Aramaic scribe would
use the expression ביתדוד for Judah, writing it as one lexeme not requiring a word
divider" (25).

   95 A notable exception would be Shalmaneser III's annals that mentions Ahab's
involvement in the battle of Qarqar in 853 B.C. on which the Bible is silent.

   96 On the correlation between the biblical and Assyrian sources, see A. R. Millard,
"Sennacherib's Attack on Hezekiah," *TB* 36 (1985) 61 – 77; K. A. Kitchen, "Egypt, the
Levant and Assyria in 701 B.C.," *Fontes Atque Pontes: Eine Festgabe für Helmut Brunner*, ÄAT
vol. 5 (1983) 243 – 253. Kitchen's study also incorporates Egyptian sources.

   97 Thomas L. Thompson, *The Origin Tradition of Ancient Israel*: vol. 1 *The Literary For-
mulation of Genesis and Exodus 1–23* (Sheffield: *JSOT* Press, 1987) 41.

   98 "Ideologies, Literary and Critical: Reflections on Recent Writing on the History
of Israel," *JBL* 114 (1995) 585 – 606.

   99 John Dewey, "Historical Judgments," in *The Philosophy of History in Our Time*, ed.
Hans Meyerhoff (Garden City, N.Y.: Doubleday, 1959) 168.

   100 *JAOS* 110 no. 2 (1990) 187 – 199.

   101 Ibid., 189.

   102 Jon D. Levenson, *The Hebrew Bible, the Old Testament and Historical Criticism*
(Louisville: Westminster/John Knox Press, 1993) 116.

   103 *JBL* 114 (1995) 585 – 606.

   104 Ibid., 600.

   105 This issue comes up in bristling rejoinders to Provan by Davies and Thompson
in *JBL* 114 (1995) 683 – 698 and 699 – 705 respectively, and Davies, *BAR* 20 no. 4 (1994)
55 – 56.

   106 See the interesting essay by Stephan Fowl on this point, "Texts Don't Have Ideologies," *Biblical Interpretation* 3 (1995) 15 – 33.

   107 Fischer, *Historians' Fallacies*, 4.

108 Hallo, "Biblical History in its Near Eastern Setting: The Contextual Approach," in *Scripture in Context: Essays on the Comparative Method*, ed. Carl D. Evans, William W. Hallo, and John B. White (Pittsburgh: Pickwick Press, 1980) 1-26.

109 In fairness to Van Seters, he argues that the Deuteronomistic historian of the Old Testament was the first historian; he wants to date him to the sixth century, a century before Herodotus. See *In Search of History*, 322-362.

110 A. R. Millard has recently cited examples of lapses in Herodotus in "Story, History, and Theology," *Faith, Tradition, and History*, 39-40. See also John Wilson, *Herodotus in Egypt* (Leiden: Brill, 1970).

111 For example, Alan B. Lloyd continually berates Herodotus's credibility as an historian, cf. *Herodotus Book I and II* (Leiden: Brill, 1988).

112 Van Seters, *In Search of History*, 212.

113 Halpern, *The First Historians*, 31.

114 Huizinga, in *Philosophy and History*; 7-8.

115 *Emergence of Israel*, in *Canaan*, Society of Biblical Literature Monograph Series No. 29 (Chico, Calif.: Scholars Press, 1983) 19.

116 I call Josephus a historian over the objections of Garbini who boldly states, "Josephus was not a historian"(*History & Ideology*, 23). The above quotation is from *Contra Apion* 1.6-8. trans. H. St. J. Thackeray (Cambridge, Mass.: Loeb Classical Library, 1926) 165-167.

117 Hallo, *Scripture in Context*, 10.

118 Moshe Kochavi, "An Ostracon from the Period of the Judges from ᶜIzbet Sartah," *Tel Aviv* 4 (1977) 1-13; A. Demsky, "A Proto-Canaanite Abecedary Dating from the Period of the Judges and Its Implications for the History of the Alphabet," *Tel Aviv* 4 (1977) 14-27; Frank M. Cross, "Newly Found Inscriptions in Old Canaanite and Early Phoenician Scripts," *BASOR* 238 (1980) 1-20; Benjamin Sass, *The Genesis of the Alphabet in the Second Millennium B.C.*, ÄAT, vol. 13 (1988). For a general study on the subject of literacy, see A. R. Millard, "Literacy (Ancient Israel)" *ABD* vol. 4 (1992) 337-340 and "The Knowledge of Writing in Iron Age Palestine," *TB* 46 (1995) 207-217.

119 Kitchen, *Ancient Orient and Old Testament*, 29.

120 Hallo, in *Scripture in Context*, 1-26.

121 "Method in the Study of Early Hebrew History," in *The 100th Meeting of the Society of Biblical Literature, December 1964*, ed. J. P. Hyatt (Nashville: Abingdon, 1965) 15.

122 See n. 1, above.

123 Kitchen, *Bible in Its World*, 58.

124 Ibid. The selective use of Near Eastern texts by Van Seters in his investigation of the nomadic lifestyle portrayed in Genesis was noted by me in "Tents in Egypt and the Ancient Near East," *Society for the Study of Egyptian Antiquities Newsletter* 7 no. 3 (1977) 13-28. More recently, I have shown again that Van Seters is selective in citing only Neo-Assyrian texts to try to date the Joshua "conquest" narratives to the seventh century because it "was an invention of DtrH." He has ignored earlier cuneiform records, cf. "The Structure of Joshua 1-11 and the Annals of Thutmose III," in *Faith, Tradition and History*, 165-179.

125 Hallo, in *Scripture in Context*, 12.

126 I agree completely with Hallo's call for a chronological proximity between biblical and Near Eastern sources (ibid., 12-15). Henri Frankfort argued along similar lines many years ago concerning religious similarities between two ethnic groups. If a parallel between two cultures is to be established, a chronological and geographical association is essential. *The Problem of Similarity in Ancient Near Eastern Religions: The Frazer Lecture 1950* (Oxford: Clarendon Press, 1951).

2

THE ORIGINS OF ISRAEL

The Current Debate

> So Joshua defeated the whole land, the hill
> country and the Negeb and the lowland and
> the slopes, and all their kings; he left none
> remaining, but utterly destroyed all that
> breathed, as the LORD God of Israel com-
> manded.
>
> Josh. 10:40

I. The Recent Developments

"Of making many books there is no end, and much study is a weariness of the
flesh" (Eccles. 12:12). Hebrew wisdom writer Qoheleth uttered these words of
exasperation sometime during the first millennium B.C. over the multitude of
writings available in his day. I share this frustration in the mid-1990s as I try to follow the unfolding debate on the origins of Israel over the past twenty years. The
old consensus (if there ever was one) regarding Israel's entry into Canaan, as the
book of Joshua claims, has been largely abandoned because the archaeological
record has not corroborated a literal interpretation and because, in the view of
historical minimalists, the nature of the biblical sources is not historiographic but
ideological and etiological. The purpose of this book is not to concentrate on the
problem of when and under what conditions Israel entered Canaan but rather to
investigate seriously the sojourn narratives from the vantage point of Egypt.
However, because of the link the Bible makes between these events (i.e., Egyptian sojourn → Sinai period → entry into Canaan), the Exodus and Joshua materials are inseparable. Consequently, the events described in both books rise or fall
together. Baruch Halpern sees the connection between the two when he comments on the implications of Alt's "peaceful infiltration" thesis (discussed in chap.
1): "Once Alt had knocked the props out from under the conquest account, he
had destroyed the moorings of the exodus."[1] While Halpern is right that this link-

age has led some scholars to question or even reject the sojourn in Egypt, I do not think it follows logically that if the Israelites migrated peacefully into Canaan that they could not have come from Egypt. Since we cannot ignore the archaeological problems and the textual issues related to the nature of Israel's appearance in Canaan, I shall examine some of the key developments from the 1980s to the present and evaluate them before looking at the biblical data on the Egyptian sojourn-exodus tradition.

In a 1993 essay, Richard Hess offered a helpful survey of the range of models found in scholarly literature regarding Israel's origins in Canaan. He outlines four main positions; namely, the conquest, peaceful infiltration, peasant revolt, and pastoral Canaanites.[2] The second and third of these were cursorily, but sufficiently for this study, treated in chapter 1, but the fourth model, that the Israelites were pastoral Canaanites is a new development that must be examined here. We shall then revisit the "conquest" theory in the light of what the biblical texts actually say and claim and then examine literary factors that impact how these narratives are interpreted. Finally, the Joshua narratives will be examined comparatively with other ancient Near Eastern military writings in order to determine whether or not this Hebrew literature can be considered historical.

Lemche's Evolutionary Hypothesis

The lack of archaeological evidence to support the theory of an invasion of outsiders, coupled with the absence of direct historical information from Egypt concerning the departing Hebrews, have naturally led to the questions of where they came from and what circumstances led to the formation of Israel. Niels Peter Lemche has written a lengthy, thorough critique of George Mendenhall's "peasant revolt" theory and Norman Gottwald's expansion of that model.[3] Lemche argued that Gottwald's use of anthropological data was inadequate, dated, and too limited. He likewise condemned the "immigration" hypothesis pioneered by Alt.[4] Like many other recent reconstructers of Israel's early history, Lemche's disdain for the historical value of the Old Testament materials is unabashed, declaring the material regarding early Israel to be "a fiction written around the middle of the first millennium."[5] Furthermore, he boldly asserts, without offering any evidence, "We know that the OT [Old Testament] scarcely contains *historical* sources about Israel's past."[6] Here the condescension that William Hallo decried is evident.[7]

The immigration theory and the peasant-revolt model are both dismissed because they require the Israelites to have come from outside of Canaan. Since there is an absence of archaeological evidence to demonstrate the presence of a new people in Canaan in the Late Bronze Age and Iron I, except for the Sea Peoples, the idea of the Israelites being foreigners rests solely on the biblical traditions that Lemche has called "fiction." Hence, an intrusion from outside Canaan is rejected. The only alternative, then, is to have "Israel" originate within Canaan. Lemche postulates that the Israelites derived from the *ḥabiru* (here he agrees with the old Mendenhall hypothesis) whom he takes to be refugees from another part of Canaan.[8] During the turbulent days of the end ·of the Late Bronze Age when Egypt's hegemony over the Levant was coming to an end, Lemche speculates, bands or tribes of *ḥabiru* evolved into a people that ethnically became identifiable as "Israel" by the time of Merneptah's campaign in Canaan.[9]

One of the valuable contributions of recent scholarship has been to examine the beginnings of Israel in the social, archaeological, historical, and anthropological setting of the Late Bronze and Iron I periods. However, one reviewer of Lemche's thesis, Alan J. Hauser, has cautioned: "L. assumes that the social, economic, cultural and political analysis he presents concerning Palestine after 1500 BCE relates directly to the origin of Israel, but that certainly is not a given, and constitutes no less a leap of faith than the assumption that certain core elements in the biblical traditions, such as Israel's coming to the land from the outside, may be true."[10] The strength of Lemche's work lies in his careful investigation of the process of tribalization, which may shed light on how Israel became a tribal entity on its way to nationhood.

Similar to Lemche's evolutionary hypothesis is Volkmar Fritz's "symbiosis hypothesis."[11] Although he makes no mention of Lemche's work (both works were in press at the same time), Fritz believes that the Iron Age remains have close affinities with the previous Late Bronze Age, suggesting that a symbiotic relationship existed between the Israelites and the Canaanites. Fritz calls the early Israelites "culture-land nomads."[12] He does not, however, identify these nomads with the *ḥabiru* as Lemche does. Nevertheless, their ideas are remarkably close and equally reductionistic. Fritz asserts, "The book of Joshua is of no historical value as far as the process of settlement is concerned. The stories of Joshua 1–11 are aetiological sagas."[13]

Ahlström's Canaanite > Israelites theory

The late Gösta Ahlström argued in the mid-1980s for an Israel indigenous to Canaan.[14] Like Lemche, he was highly critical of the revolutionary model, but did not associate the Israelites with the *ḥabiru*. He allows, however, that the *ḥabiru* mentioned in connection with Labaya of Shechem in the Amarna letters might be connected with the Israelites because of the biblical association of Jacob's family with Hamor of Shechem (Gen. 34).[15] The central tenet of Ahlström's provocative thesis revolves around his idea that "Israel" in the Merneptah stela (fig. 1) referred originally to a geographical region and was subsequently appropriated by or applied to the mixed population of the central hill country, which was largely Canaanite.[16] His analysis of the chiastic structure of the closing pericope of the stela, which mentions Israel, is interesting but not beyond criticism.[17] Based upon the suggested structural correspondence between Canaan and Israel in the poem, he posits a parallel geopolitical relationship between the two.[18] Many years ago, however, Ronald Williams considered the word "Israel" to be parallel to Harru, not Canaan, in the text.[19] Lawrence Stager and John Bimson concur with Williams's observation and reject Ahlström's analysis.[20] On the other hand, Frank Yurco has lately argued that Canaan and Harru are in a chiastic relationship.[21]

Michael Hasel has offered a masterful review and critique of the discussions about the structure of the closing hymn of the stela and the many historical interpretations of "Israel."[22] He then proposes another structural analysis in which

Harru (C) and Canaan (C') "correspond to each other metaphorically as husband
and wife as two corresponding geographical regions," and that the city-states
Ashkelon, Gezer, and Yenoam, along with an ethnic group "Israel," together represent a region within Canaan.[23] In the chiastic structure advanced by Hasel, this
section is D, the apex of the chiasm.

This analysis has some merit but also some shortcomings. First, I fail to see
how Canaan and Harru are metaphorically presented as husband and wife. To be
sure, Harru is described as a widow (*ḫȝrt, a nice play on ḫȝrw*) because of Merneptah's devastating blow against it, but there is no corresponding male or husband
terminology for Canaan. Rather, if there is to be a husband-wife correlation, it
would seem to be between Israel and Harru, which occur side by side and share
the same grammatical relationship. Thus, "his seed" (*prt.f*) would apply to Israel's
children, making him childless and Harru the widow.[24] Stager has also seen a connection between Israel (husband) and Harru (wife/widow)[25] that further militates
against the meaning "grain" for *prt*.[26] Further, if Canaan and Harru correspond to
each other as Hasel believes, why are toponyms in Canaan introduced while none
are detailed for Harru? Another problem for Hasel's structure is that coupling
Ashkelon, Gezer, Yenoam, and Israel as a single unit entails mixing different grammatical patterns, which I believe reveals a lack of appreciation for the Egyptian
poetic flow of this section.

These differing interpretations of the same text illustrate why, until there is
greater certainty about the poetic structure of this paean, it is imprudent to draw
firm conclusions about the geopolitical divisions of the Levant. Paying more careful attention to the grammatical features of the poem may yield some fruitful
results.

One of the problems for non-Egyptologists who have tried to understand the
structure of the "Israel" stanza is that in an English translation, it is difficult to distinguish between the passive *sḏm.f* and the old perfective forms. Both are usually
rendered by English passive verbs, whereas in Egyptian there is a complete reverse
in word order between the two forms. A grammatical analysis of the poem concerning Merneptah's enemies follows, and the translation is intended to show the
word order and reflect the grammatical patterns.

Passive *sḏm.f*	Old Perfective
1. (a) *captured is* Libya,[27]	(b) Hatti *is pacified*
2. *plundered is* Canaan with every evil	3. Yenoam *is made* into nonexistence
carried off is Ashkelon	Israel *is wasted*, its seed is not
captured is Gezer	Harru *is become* a widow

Three grammatically based, distinguishable units are evident. The first bicolon
follows a pattern of passive *sḏm.f* + subject (a) and subject + old perfective (b).
The pattern of the bicolon is verb-subject, subject-verb. This pericope sets the
grammatical sequence that is followed in sections 2 and 3. 1a uses the passive
sḏm.f, as do phrases in 2, while in 1b the old perfective is employed, which is likewise used in the colons in 3. In the tricolon of section 2, each line begins with the
verb, the passive *sḏm.f* (as does 1a), and 3 follows the pattern subject + verb, in this

case, the old perfective is written (as does 1b). Here is not the place for a full discussion of the geopolitical implications of this poem based on my grammatical
analysis, but a few brief observations are in order.

Section 1, made up of Libya and Hatti (Anatolia-North Syria) probably represented the western and northern extremities of Merneptah's realm. He had fought
Libyans as reported earlier in this stela, and the treaty with the Hittites established
by his father, Ramesses II, was still being observed.[28] Within these two distant
lands fit the toponyms of the following two sections. The names in section 2 are
geographically closer to 1a (Libya), and section 3 is closer to 1b, Hatti.

Section 2 is made up of Canaan, Ashkelon, and Gezer. The toponym Canaan,
p3 k3n^cn^c in New Kingdom texts can be another term for Gaza, and not the land
of Canaan.[29] In fact, Donald Redford's recent translation of line 27 of the stela begins "Pakana^can (Gaza) is plundered."[30] With this possibility in mind, the cities of
Gaza, Ashkelon, and Gezer represent a nice geographical unit within a limited
area of what would later be known as Philistia.[31] The third grammatical unit consists of Yenoam, Israel, and Harru.[32] Yenoam is usually identified with Tell el-
Ubeidiya, located south of the Sea of Galilee.[33] Harru is understood to be a territorial term for at least part of Syria.[34] And third Israel is named. The tribes of Israel
appear to have been located primarily in the central Hill Country and Upper
Galilee.[35] The geographical range of this third section, then, constitutes an area that
includes the Canaanite Hill Country, Galilee, and north and east into Syria.

These three grammatical units in the poem, it might be suggested, conform to
geopolitical regions. If this grammatically based analysis has merit, then a number
of the earlier attempts to associate various geopolitical entities based on literary
parallels are called into question. Whatever chiastic arrangements the poem may
have (and thereby possible geographical or political relationships), they must be
scrutinized in view of the grammatical structures of the poem. Certainly, my
analysis raises serious questions about Ahlström's linking Canaan and Israel.

Another major problem with Ahlström's treatment of the Merneptah stela is his
cavalier attitude toward the text. Since its discovery by Petrie in 1896,[36] the name
"Israel" alone of the eight toponyms in the pericope is known to be written with
the 𓏤𓏤 determinative, thus suggesting it refers to a people and not a land (fig. 1).[37]
Naturally, this paleographic detail should derail Ahlström's suggestion. He is un-
daunted, however, claiming that "biblical scholars have generally blown the determinative issue out of proportion. Egyptologists attach little significance to the
choice of determinative here, recognizing that determinatives were generally used
rather loosely by scribes, especially when a people was called by the name of the
territory they inhabited."[38] It may be true that some Egyptologists have "attach[ed]
little significance" to the determinatives in this text, but the majority take them
seriously. Indeed in certain cases Egyptian scribes were not always consistent in
their use of determinatives. In fact, different determinatives could be written with
the same word in the very same document. But an examination of the text of the
Merneptah stela is instructive. In the coda containing "Israel," there are a total of
eight toponyms, and with the other seven the same combination of 𓈙 + 𓈉 is
used.[39] The 𓈉 sign is associated with a territory, while the sign 𓈙 applies to a foreign people.[40] Israel is written with 𓈙 + 𓏤𓏤 . None of the other toponyms use the

people determinative. The consistent writing of the determinatives in the seven toponyms and the variation in the writing of "Israel" suggests that there was something different about this entity.[41] In this regard, John Wilson declared: "Much has been made of the fact that word Israel is the only one of the names in this context which is written with the determinative of people rather than land. Thus we should seem to have the Children of Israel in or near Palestine, but not yet as a settled people. This is a valid argument."[42] However, he does allow that there could have been a scribal error involved in the writing of Israel.

Williams, who was both a competent Egyptologist and Old Testament scholar concluded, "the fact that the hieroglyphic determinative for the people rather than land is used with the name suggests that Israel was not yet permanently settled. This would fit the OT context, for Joshua's campaigns were most probably conducted during the third quarter of the thirteenth century."[43] In the final analysis, Ahlström wants to emend the text to fit his theory about the origin of Israel, a practice that must be viewed with suspicion.

Before Ahlström, Martin Noth and Otto Eissfeldt also tried to distinguish the Israel of the Merneptah stela from Israel of the Bible. For Noth, the former refers to an "older entity which bore the name 'Israel' and then for some now obscure historical reason passed it on to the 'Israel' that we know."[44] Of course, there is no evidence for the existence of a people named "Israel" in Canaan other than the Israel of the Bible. Eissfeldt took a different tack, proposing that the name on the stela could be read as "Jezreel" rather than "Israel."[45] Despite the many problems with this interpretation, it has been renewed again by Othniel Margalith.[46] Linguistically, a correlation between the Egyptian writing *ysri3r* and Hebrew *yizr^{e}e'l* is impossible.[47] The hieroglyphic signs ⟶ and ⎮ in Old Egyptian (ca. 2700–2300 B.C.) represented the sounds *z* and *s* respectively. This distinction is important for Eissfeldt and Margalith's interpretation. However, from the Middle Kingdom onwards (after 2106 B.C.) the two signs are used interchangeably for *s*.[48] Thus, the use of ⟶ in the late New Kingdom Merneptah stela cannot represent *z* as required for the reading "Jezreel." Nearly thirty years ago, Kenneth Kitchen, an authority on Ramesside inscriptions and Semitic languages, responded to this same attempt. His comment is equally cogent in the case of Margalith's and Ahlström's treatments: "Why these evasions? Simply that the tribal Israel as an entity in W. Palestine in 1220 B.C., pictured by the Old Testament and tacitly by the Merenptah-stela (by determinative of 'people'), does not suit their particular theories about Israelite origins, and they prefer these theories to the first-hand evidence of the stela."[49] Anson Rainey's response to Ahlström's handling of this text is even stronger, maintaining that he has "simply demonstrated that Biblical scholars untrained in Egyptian epigraphy should not make amateurish attempts at interpretation."[50] Emending the writing of Israel to include the land determinative is superficially plausible, but to build a theory about the origin of Israel based on such a reconstructed text is methodologically ill-advised. In the final analysis, Ahlström commits "the fallacy of the lonely fact"[51] by building a historical reconstruction that relies so much on one phrase in a single historical document, and even then it requires emending the critical word.

The use of archaeological data, epigraphic and anepigraphic, by Ahlström,

Lemche, Thompson, and Philip Davies[52] in their works on Israel's origin has been criticized by both epigraphers (e.g., Rainey) and archaeologists. Reacting to their use of archaeological sources, William Dever, the dean of North American Syro-Palestinian archaeologists declared: "There is no longer any need for the biblical scholar to resort to histories of Israel like those of Thompson and Ahlström, which presume to make competent use of archaeological data, but in fact only misled the nonspecialist because they cannot control the data. There is even less excuse for taking seriously the *obiter dicta* of 'new nihilists' like P. R. Davies, whose use of archaeology in *The Search for Ancient Israel* (1992) is a travesty."[53] Fortunately, competent archaeologists have entered the discussion of the origins of Israel in Canaan, and Israel Finkelstein's study has attempted to address the problem of Israel's arrival from a purely archaeological perspective.

Finkelstein's Resedentarizing-Nomads Model

Israel Finkelstein's 1988 monograph is the most thoroughly archaeologically based of the recent investigations of the origins of Israel.[54] While his conclusions are not substantially different than those of Robert Coote and Keith Whitelam,[55] Finkelstein's work incorporates all available archaeological data provided by excavations as well as comprehensive surveys of Ephraim and Manasseh. Hence, Finkelstein's work has been received by many as authoritative and representing the state of the art on the origins of Israel. In fact, Dever has gone so far in his praise of Finkelstein as to claim that his conclusions are "rapidly becoming a consensus."[56]

Finkelstein maintains that Israel's origins can be determined by the archaeological record alone. He builds on the earlier ideas of Yohanan Aharoni that the Iron I villages in the Upper Galilee and Hill Country represented the beginnings of the Israelite settlement of Canaan.[57] His general thesis is that as the Middle Bronze culture of Canaan declined during the sixteenth century B.C., large segments of the population became nomadic; later, toward the end of the Late Bronze period, the process of resedentarization began.[58] For him, one of the pieces of evidence supporting the idea of a nomadic population is the presence of religious shrines, such as Shiloh, because of the significant size of the cultic facility relative to the size of the population.[59] But Finkelstein is unable to offer any archaeological evidence for identifying Shiloh as an Israelite site during the settlement period, other than the prominence given to Shiloh in the text of Joshua and Judges. Thus, he is forced to rely on the very biblical text that he eschews on methodological grounds.

While there is general agreement that the settlements in question are Israelite, the evidence for assigning them to Israel is far from convincing. Finkelstein arranges his evidence into five categories: (1) geographical location, (2) size of sites, (3) settlement pattern, (4) architecture and site layout, and (5) pottery.[60] These features, however, do not necessarily occur all together in these Iron I villages. The late Douglas Esse critiqued this aspect of Finkelstein's work, observing, "A number of sites are thus accepted as Israelite even though they do not possess all the traits mentioned above. At the same time, he occasionally rejects sites as Israelite even though they do possess some of the defining traits."[61] Concerning the first of his five points, he violates his own purely archaeological approach; namely, minimizing the biblical text in archaeological investigation, for he is forced to consult Joshua and Judges to learn where the Israelites are said to be situated. Thomas Thompson attacked Finkelstein for this slip: "Finkelstein asserts *a priori*, on the apparent basis of unexamined later biblical traditions, that Israel's origins are to be found uniquely in specific clusters of new settlements of the central hills and Galilee. Certainly the patterns of settlement which he does examine are of paramount importance, but we have no reason to claim that either the hill country population, or the new settlers of that region, are uniquely to be identified with emerging Israel."[62]

As for the architecture, Finkelstein points to the pillared buildings or "four-room house" as being typically Israelite, tracing the origins of this type of architecture (i.e. tents with surrounding stone walls and various chambers to nomadic precursors).[63] Except for possibly one such house from Tell Batash in a Late Bronze context, the "four-room house" is found exclusively in Iron I levels, thus leading Finkelstein to conclude that it is an Iron I Israelite innovation.[64] Yet he offers no evidence that the four-room house was developed by the Israelites. An additional problem for Finkelstein's thesis is that a four-room house from western Thebes, dated to the reign of Ramesses IV (1153–1147 B.C.), has been identified by Manfred Bietak.[65] Bietak believes that the builders of the house were prisoners of war, likely taken by Ramesses III (1184–1153 B.C.) during his campaigns in Palestine, who were pressed into labor projects. This dating fits nicely into the beginning of the Iron I period and the appearance of the four-room house in Canaan. Since the chances are remote that the Theban house is of Israelite construction, Finkelstein's belief that this type of house is an Israelite innovation is questionable. Thus, caution must be used when assigning an ethnic origin to the four-room house until more conclusive evidence appears.

Finkelstein's ethnographic study of Bedouin encampments from earlier in the present century is an intriguing explanation for the origin of the type of architecture and site layout, but this explanation has not been universally accepted by Syro-Palestinian archaeologists.[66] Furthermore, he can offer no evidence for why they should be ascribed to the Israelites. What prevents this architectural tradition from belonging to sedentarizing *ḫabiru*, Amalekites, Shasu, or any other nomadic group known from Late Bronze texts?

This is not to say that I reject Finkelstein's identification—they may well be Israelite villages. The reason for raising these questions is to show that the archaeological evidence alone at this point in time cannot demonstrate that the sites in question are Israelite without drawing inferences from the biblical text. Furthermore, the villages do not tell us how long the settlers had been pastoralists in the area before settling, or whether they had moved about inside or outside of Canaan, or both, before becoming sedentary. Finkelstein's very thorough investigation in no way precludes the possibility that the Israelites entered Canaan, as the biblical record claims, after a period of seminomadic life in Sinai and the Transjordan that was preceded by a sedentary existence in Egypt for a greater period of time.

Another issue that Finkelstein and others who have studied the Iron I settlements have failed to resolve is the dating for the beginning of Iron I.[67] The round figure of 1200 B.C. is still widely used and is associated with the coming of the Sea Peoples (and Philistines), even though their battle with Ramesses III in Egypt dates to ca. 1177 B.C.[68] If the Sea Peoples are a significant factor in the beginning of the Iron Age, then their impact on the transition from the Late Bronze to Iron I would, it appears, postdate 1177.[69] While there has been considerable discussion over the dating of the Middle-Late Bronze transition, a similar debate has not yet taken place for the Late Bronze–Iron I.[70] Among Syro-Palestinian archaeologists a range of a century still exists for the end of the Middle Bronze Age—from ca. 1550 B.C. to 1450 B.C.[71] The mention of Israel in the Merneptah stela (ca. 1208 B.C.) suggests that tribal Israel was already a significant presence in the Levant prior to the sedentarization described in Finkelstein's masterful study.[72] If Lemche's anthropologically based conclusion that the Israel of the Merneptah stela is "a fully developed tribal organization" is correct[73]—and this would predate the beginning of the Iron I settlements—then Israel was known to Egyptian scribes prior to the beginning of their settlement in Canaan. Hence, the Iron I villages tell us nothing about Israel's origin, only its sedentarization.[74]

II. The "Conquest" Theory and the Book of Joshua

The Albright-Wright synthesis has been rightly challenged by virtually every recent scholarly investigation concerned with the origins of Israel debate. Because the Baltimore School took a moderately conservative maximalist position relative to the biblical narratives, its critics have widely assumed that the "conquest" theory of Albright-Wright and their followers is one and the same as the "biblical" description. Therefore, the repudiation of the former has resulted in the abrogation of the latter. Before the connection between the two is accepted uncritically, an examination of the biblical text vis-à-vis the Albright-Wright synthesis is in order.

A quote from Wright well illustrates that he often overstated or went beyond what the biblical text actually claimed: "The books of Joshua, Judges, and Samuel carry the story from triumph to triumph, until even the greatest of Canaanite walled fortresses were destroyed (Lachish about 1220 B.C., Megiddo, Beth-Shan, Jerusalem and finally Gezer shortly after 1000)."[75] Wright goes on to assign a destruction around 1220 B.C. to nearly every site mentioned in connection with Israel's campaigns in Joshua 6–11 and ascribes the Late Bronze II destruction of Beitîn (Bethel ?) to Israel even though the Bible makes no such claim.[76] Wright includes Megiddo in his list of cities conquered by Israel, and yet nowhere in Joshua or Judges is Megiddo reported to be conquered. The killing of its king (which could have occurred in a battle elsewhere) is recorded in Joshua 12:21, but a coexistence between the Israelites and residents of Megiddo is described in Joshua 17:21 and Judges 1:27.

William Dever has recently compiled archaeological and biblical data into helpful charts to show the lack of corroboration between the two.[77] According to Dever, sixteen cities are said to be destroyed in the biblical narratives, but only three have yielded evidence for destruction around 1200 B.C. He also notes that no destruction level for that period was found at the five excavated cities out of the twelve cities that the Bible states were not destroyed.[78] For Dever, like many other critics of the Albright-Wright school from the 1970s to the present, the lack of destruction levels at sites reportedly attacked by the Israelites means that the Joshua narratives are not historical.

This conclusion rests on some fallacies and unfounded assumptions. First, it has long been assumed that if there was a conquest it took place around 1220 B.C. (for a discussion of chronological issues, see chap. 5). This conclusion, of course, is based on the theory (which though possibly correct has never been proven) that the exodus from Egypt took place early in the reign of Ramesses II (ca. 1270–1260), allowing forty years in the Sinai wilderness prior to the Israelites' entry into Canaan. However, if this chronological scenario is wrong, then archaeologists should not expect to find cities destroyed in Canaan as the biblical materials report. The result of this assumption, if wrong, is "the fallacy of anachronism."[79]

A second problem for recent reconstructions that reject the idea of conquest is the fallacy of "negative proof"—that is, "an attempt to sustain a factual proposition merely by negative evidence."[80] Concerning this type of fallacy, David Hackette Fischer has cogently observed, "evidence must always be affirmative. Negative evidence is a contradiction in terms—it is no evidence at all."[81] By pointing out these two fallacies, we are not attempting to revive or give credibility to the conquest model but merely to point out that the rationale for dismissing the Israelite conquest of Canaan rest upon fallacies and unverifiable assumptions.

Critics of the conquest model have also been contemptuous in their treatment of the text of Joshua relative to the archaeological record. J. Maxwell Miller well illustrates this attitude in summing up his reading of the pertinent Old Testament books: "The overriding impression one receives from Numbers—Joshua is that, after an initial delay of forty years, *the whole of the promised land was conquered systematically and in a relatively short period* of time by a unified Israel under the leadership of Moses and Joshua."[82] In his critique of the "invasion hypothesis," Fritz points out that it rests on a "naive adoption of the traditional interpretation of the book of Joshua."[83] However, a close look at the terms dealing with warfare in Joshua 10 reveals that they do not support the interpretation that the land of Canaan and its principal cities were demolished and devastated by the Israelites.

For instance, *lkd* (לכד) means "rush upon" or "capture," *lhm* (לחם) means "to fight," *nkh* (נכה) means "to wound" or "smite," and *hnh* (חנה) means "to besiege."[84] These terms alone do not indicate that a city was deliberately set ablaze and destroyed. To "besiege," "assault," or "take" a city does not mean it was destroyed, as Dever claims. Abraham Malamat, after investigating the so-called "conquest" narratives, labels early Israel's military tactics as indirect.[85] He observes that Israel quickly learned that direct attacks on fortified cities had disastrous results (e.g., the first assault on Ai in Josh. 7:4–5). Hence, the indirect stratagem was adopted and proved successful. Malamat summarizes early Israel's tactics: "Among the early wars of the Israelites, we find no actual description of an outright, successful assault upon an enemy city. The adoption of an indirect military approach finds ex-

pression in two principal tactics employed by the Israelites: covert infiltration—
neutralizing the city defenses; and enticement—drawing the defenders out into
the open."[86]

Given the indirect strategy of military conquest, we should expect only limited, if any, discernible destruction in the archaeological record. On the other
hand, one would expect that if a city was destroyed it was the result of a calculated
act of burning or dismantling.[87] Donald Redford has argued that when the Egyptians destroyed a city, it was deliberately demolished and a specific word, ḥb3 (or
b3), was used to describe such action.[88] Referring to the demolition of Middle
Bronze IIC Canaanite cities, he comments, "It must be maintained, however, that
the destructions could never have been effected in the heat of battle but must
have been in the nature of intentional demolition demanded of the conquered by
the king himself."[89] Given the description in Joshua 10, that a city is "taken" and
then Israelites quickly move on, it is hard to conceive of such intentional demo-
litions taking place. Consequently, the cities enumerated in Joshua 10 probably
were not destroyed or leveled, thus leaving no detectable evidence in the archaeological record. This does not mean, however, that fighting did not occur at these
ancient cities. Consequently, when destructions from the end of the Late Bronze
Age are absent from cities where the Israelites fought (according to Joshua), the
archaeologist should not be surprised. The Joshua narratives, on the other hand,
are very clear when the Israelites' did in fact burn a city, which *would* leave its
mark in the archaeological record. The book of Joshua reports only three cities
destroyed by fire, śārap bā'ēš (שָׂרַף בָּאֵשׁ) or śārap (שָׂרַף); that is, Jericho (Josh. 6:24), Ai
(Josh. 8:19–20, 28), and Hazor (Josh. 11:11). (See chap. 1 § 1 for a discussion of
some of the archaeological problems with these sites.)

Presently, of the three, only Hazor is currently being dug. In 1996 Amnon Ben
Tor's team uncovered the sensational, charred remains of the Late Bronze Age
palace.[90] The deliberate decapitation and mutilation of statues of deities, in keeping with the charge of Moses to the Israelites in Deuteronomy 7:5, is one factor
that has led Ben Tor to provisionally suggest that this destruction is the work of
the Israelites. Until additional evidence is available, the excavator is not prepared
to pinpoint an absolute date in the Late Bronze Age for this conflagration. Since
the study of these remains are at a preliminary stage, and the exacavations ongoing, firm conclusions should not be made. The emerging picture, however, is consistent with the description of the sack of Hazor in Joshua 11.

The problem of correlating text with tell also exists for the transition from the
Middle to Late Bronze Age in Canaan. There has been a tendency to attribute the
widespread destruction of no less than twenty Middle Bronze cities to the Egyptians, based upon their royal and private inscriptions.[91] A careful reading of the
relevant Egyptian texts and an examination of the terms used to describe the outcome of the battles, though, reveal that these interpretations lack the support of
the very texts summoned to explain the cause of the destruction.[92]

Like Dever, Redford recently has caricatured the Joshua narratives by saying,
"Cities with massive fortifications fall easily to rustic nomads from off the desert,"
and he describes the conquest as "a whirlwind annihilation."[93] In reviewing Redford's work, Kitchen responds by saying that he is "superficial in dealing with the

Biblical data" and goes on to point out that Joshua does not describe a widespread destruction of the land.[94] Rather, as Joshua admits (13:1), there was still much land not in Israelite hands, and it proceeds to outline those areas (Josh. 13:2–8). There is a continual reminder of this situation in the "territorial allotment" chapters that follow (14–19). This picture is completely consistent with Judges 1, making the oft-cited contradiction between Joshua and Judges 1 illusory.[95] Kitchen also reminds us that only three cities are explicitly said to be burned between Joshua 6 and 11. Following the campaign in the Galilee region, Joshua 11:12 reports: "But none of the cities that stood on mounds [tells] did Israel burn, except Hazor only; that Joshua burned." Contrary to a blitzkrieg and "whirlwind annihilation" conquest of Galilee region as understood by some critical readers of Joshua, quite the opposite is reported. In a retrospective of that campaign, Joshua 11:18 records: "Joshua made war a long time against those kings" in northern Canaan and south Lebanon.

A careful reading of the text of Joshua suggests a far more modest military outcome than those advanced by twentieth-century biblical scholars either supporting or critiquing the conquest model. So it appears that the real contradiction was between the model and the archaeological record, not the record and the narratives of Joshua and Judges. The conquest model has become something of a straw man that ostensibly represented the biblical record, the latter being guilty by association with the former.

Furthermore, if we consider that Jericho's city IV destruction may have resulted from an earthquake that facilitated the taking of the city,[96] and that Ai was seized by a ruse that drew the defenders out of the city (Josh 10:23), the conquest of two of the three cities Joshua claims to have destroyed becomes less sensational and quite believable.[97]

In this section, we have sought to draw attention to lexical issues that have not been seriously considered as new models for explaining Israel's origins have begun to replace older ones. Minimalist readers of Joshua have also overlooked the literary nature of the conquest narratives.

III. Literary Consideration of the Joshua Narratives

Most of the literary analysis of the Hebrew Bible during the first half of this century has marched in lockstep with German source-critical conclusions of the nineteenth century. Joshua has traditionally been assigned to D, which dates to the seventh-century B.C.[98] Martin Noth, however, departed from Wellhausen's synthesis,[99] placing parts of Joshua (chaps. 1 and 12) within the Deuteronomistic History (DtrH; i.e., Deuteronomy through 2 Kings) and thus detaching it from the primary Pentateuchal sources. For Noth, the majority of the military narratives, chapters 2 through 11, derived from earlier etiological legends that were added to the DtrH during the period of compilation in the mid-sixth century B.C.[100] Noth's analysis has had widespread support over the past thirty years, but John Van Seters has recently challenged Noth's idea, concluding, "The invasion of the land of Canaan by Israel under Joshua was an invention of the DtrH."[101] Van Seters's claim derives from his peculiar use of the comparative approach, which will be examined below.

Literary approaches to Joshua have shown that, far from being a patchwork of carelessly thrown together and often contradictory tales, the book appears to have been creatively and skillfully crafted. H. J. Koorevaar studied the structure of the book of Joshua and identified four thematic units that are arranged chiastically: 1) Cross over (עבר - ᶜbr) 1:1–5:12; 2) Take (לקח - lqh) 5:13–12:24; 3) Divide (חלק - hlq) 13–21; and 4) Serve (עבד - ᶜbd) 22–24.[102] Koorevaar concludes that this pattern was established for didactic purposes and that the work was redacted before the destruction of the Shiloh sanctuary in the eleventh century B.C. Based upon archaeological evidence, this sanctuary, so central to early Israelite worship, is believed to have been destroyed by the Philistines in the days of Eli and Samuel.[103]

Around fifteen years ago Robert Boling and Ernest Wright recognized chiastic structures within sections of Joshua. They demonstrated that the southern campaign (Josh. 10:16–39) is palestrophic in nature, with the subthemes of ban and oracle dominating the chiasm.[104] Lawson Younger expanded upon the "iterative scheme" of this unit, identifying eight episodes that use eleven syntagms.[105] Independently of Younger, I came to virtually the same conclusions some years earlier.[106] Younger's careful analysis showed the intricate and complex interplay between expressions in Joshua 10:28–42. It might be further observed that when the terminology used to describe what happened to each city is read carefully, a further chiasmus emerges.[107]

A (28)	(took -lkd) לכד
B (29)	(fought -wyllhm) וילחם
C (30)	(smote -wykh) (ויכה נכה)
D (31)	(siege and assault -wyhn – wyllhm) ויחן וילחם
E (33)	(smote him - wykhw) ויכהו
	[The king of Gezer, not Gezer]
D' (34)	(siege and assault -wyhn – wyllhm) ויחן וילחם
B' (36)	(fought -wyllhm) וילחם[108]
B' (38)	(fought -wyllhm) וילחם
C' (40)	(smote -wykh) (ויכה נכה)
C' (41)	(smote -wykh) (ויכם נכה)
A' (42)	(took -lkd) לכד

Throughout this unit, four different roots are used repeatedly to describe the attacks on cities. These terms (lkd = לכד, lhm = לחם, nkh = נכה, hnh = חנה) share both phonemic (especially the first two pairs and the second pair) and semantic relationships.[109] That there is a repetition of these terms in a calculated manner is critical to understanding the literary fabric of the text.

The important question that demands an answer is: What is the relationship between such complex literary compositions and history? For Alter and many proponents of new literary readings of Hebrew texts, the narratives are "prose fiction."[110] Kenneth Gros Louis, another champion of the "new literary approach," has analyzed Joshua and Judges and addresses the relationship between literary narratives and historical records.[111] In response to recent tendencies to label the Joshua and Judges narratives "fiction," Gros Louis and Willard Van Antwerpen protest, charging that "the terms *history* and *fiction*, however, are elusive, and the distinction between the literary and nonliterary often seems arbitrary."[112] Moreover, they maintain that "new literary" critics, by virtue of their discipline, are not interested in historical questions, but rather, proceeding from the assumption of literary unity (which may be valid), their primary goal is to "probe themes and threads that hold a given work together."[113]

Michael Fishbane also addresses the relationship between complex literary narratives and history.

> Surely these phonemic/semantic meanings add to the historical "fact" of the composition and bring out more forcefully that in the Hebrew Bible historical narrative is always narrative history, and so is necessarily mediated by language and its effects. It is thus language in its artistic deployment that produces the received biblical history—a point that must serve to deflect all historistic reductions of these texts to "pure" facts. And if this requires a reconception of the truth-claims of the biblical historical narrative, then it is to this point that reflection has long been due.[114]

While Fishbane's comments arose out of his study of 1 Samuel 3, they are applicable to the conquest narratives of Joshua that share the same literary characteristics he identified in the Samuel narratives. Consequently, the literary nature of the military narratives does not preclude the essential historicity of this body of literature. In the final analysis, Fishbane says that the literary structure of a text needs to be apprehended before interpretation can take place. Having sought to do this here, we need to compare the military narratives of Joshua with other Near Eastern military writings.

IV. The Military Narratives of Joshua in the Near Eastern Setting

Owing to the supposed etiological nature, theological affirmations, and ideological framework of the conquest narratives in Joshua, coupled with hyperbolic claims of wiping out the population of certain parts of Canaan (particularly in chap. 10), many studies of the Joshua narratives, especially those since the 1970s, have marginalized the biblical account of Israel's arrival in Canaan to the point of oblivion. Even if one could demonstrate that a story is etiological, that does not mean the story is imaginary.[115] With the Hebrew scripture confined to the sidelines, Egyptian texts, particularly the Merneptah or Israel stela, become the primary written source upon which Israel's origins are reconstructed. Suddenly, historical minimalists such as Ahlström and Lemche become maximalists, accepting at face value an Egyptian document, despite the fact that it too is religious and ideological, replete with hyperbole and propaganda. Yet when similar literary devices and rhetoric are found in Joshua, the historical value of those narratives is summarily dismissed. The methodological inconsistency is self-evident.

Not until recently has there been any serious comparative analysis of the Joshua materials alongside cognate Near Eastern military writings. Moshe Weinfeld in his study of the Deuteronomistic School offered parallels between Neo-Assyrian texts and Joshua to show the seventh-century date of the latter.[116] Weinfeld completely failed, however, to consider earlier texts of the second millennium. Jeffrey Niehaus has examined features that Joshua and Neo-Assyrian texts share in common (e.g., war oracles, the command-fulfillment chain, divine involvement in warfare) and agrees that "it is only fair to recognize that the literary phenomena in Joshua have first-millennium extra-Biblical analogues."[117] However, Niehaus goes on to show that these very same features are well attested in Ugaritic and Middle Assyrian texts of the second millennium, thus severely weakening the rationale for an exclusive connection between DtrH and Neo-Assyrian texts. Weinfeld also averred that within the Joshua narratives there were two traditions, the Deuteronomistic one portraying Joshua as a national military hero and another in which he appears as a national religious leader à la Moses.[118] Here, too, Niehaus shows, the military writings of Tiglath-Pileser I (1115–1077 B.C.) and Tukulti-Ninurta I (1244–1208 B.C.) portray these conquering kings in both ways. He quotes the following statement by the latter monarch: "When Ashur my lord faithfully chose me for his worshiper, gave me the scepter for my office of shepherd, presented me in addition the staff for my office of herdsman, granted me authority so that I might slay my enemies (and) subdue those who do not fear me, (and) placed upon me the lordly crown—(at that time) I set my foot upon the neck of the lands (and) shepherded the extensive black-headed people like animals."[119] These Middle-Assyrian references demonstrate that 1) portraying Joshua in these two different manners is not contradictory; 2) the different images are not necessarily indicative of divergent traditions; and 3) these motifs are also at home in the latter third of the second millennium.[120]

Lawson Younger's investigation offers the first comprehensive investigation of military records of the Egyptians, Assyrians, and Hittites and compares them with the rhetorical devices used in Joshua.[121] He discovered that Near Eastern scribes used similar, if not identical, theological perspectives and literary conventions and devices in their military writing. Hyperbole, he notes, was widely used in describing the magnitude of enemy defeats. Younger notes that this type of hyperbole is in view in Joshua 10 when the entire population of city after city is said to be wiped out.[122] Younger does not restrict his investigation to the first millennium nor to one geographical area. Instead, he considers second-millennium materials from Anatolia, Mesopotamia, and Egypt, and draws the following conclusion:

> This study has shown that one encounters very similar things in both ancient Near Eastern and biblical history writing. While there are differences (e.g., the characteristics of the deities in the individual cultures), the Hebrew conquest account of Canaan in Joshua 9–12 is, by and large, typical of any ancient Near Eastern account. In other words, there is a common denominator, a certain commonality between them, so that it is possible for us to speak, for purposes of generalization, of a common transmission code that is an intermingling of the texts' figurative and ideological aspects.[123]

In contrast to Younger's comprehensive study, an essay published by Van Seters in the same year drew parallels solely between the Joshua narratives and Neo-Assyrian royal inscriptions.[124] I have written a critique of this essay, which I will briefly summarize here.[125] Like Weinfeld, Van Seters was trying to demonstrate that the conquest narratives of the DtrH originated at the time suggested by Neo-Assyrian parallels. All ten parallel motifs Van Seters draws between Joshua and Neo-Assyrian royal inscriptions are treated by Younger, who has identified comparable second-millennium analogues.

Van Seters, for instance, believes that the motif of the Israelites crossing the Jordan during the flood stage is borrowed from reports of Sargon II and Ashurbanipal's crossing the Tigris and Euphrates during "high water of the spring of the year."[126] Based on just these two texts, he asserts, "The special emphasis on the crossing can only be explained as a topos taken from the Assyrian military accounts."[127] Van Seters's treatment of this matter fails on two points. First, the spring of the year was the traditional time for kings to go to war in Israel (cf. 2 Sam. 11:2) as well as in Mesopotamia. As Robert Gordon has observed, "Spring was the time for launching military campaigns, when the winter rains had stopped and the male population was not yet involved in harvesting."[128] Spring is also when the rivers, the Jordan as well as the Tigris and Euphrates, are at their highest levels because of melting snow from the mountains to the north. Secondly, the seemingly miraculous crossing of raging rivers by a king is well attested in earlier Near Eastern sources. Hattusili I (ca. 1650 B.C.) boasts of his accomplishments in this respect, likening them to those of Sargon the Great (ca. 2371–2316 B.C.).[129] On one occasion, Tiglath-Pileser I records that a particular crossing of the Euphrates was his twenty-eighth, and it was "the second time in one year."[130] It is clear that when Sargon II (721–705 B.C.) broadcasts his achievement, he is emulating his warrior predecessors rather than inventing a new motif. Consequently, there is no basis for Van Seters's assertion. The river crossing in Joshua 3 by Israel's forces accurately reflects the seasonal realities of military life in the Near East throughout the three millennia B.C.

Another literary practice the DtrH borrowed from Assyria, according to Van Seters, is the pattern of describing a few major battles in a report and giving only cursory accounts of others. This characteristic is well known in New Kingdom Egyptian military writings, especially in the Annals of Thutmose III. There, lengthy reports (e.g., the Battle of Megiddo) can be compared with those in Joshua (e.g., Jericho), and terse reports such as Thutmose III's sixth campaign are similar to Joshua 10:28–42. It has been suggested that these differences can be attributed to different scribal practices used concurrently in Egypt, even in the same document, with the short reports being traced to the Egyptian Day Book Style.[131]

Van Seters also saw an Assyrian prototype behind Joshua's use of the fame and terror of Israel's army causing the enemies to submit. However, I showed many years ago that such motifs are well known in second-millennium Egyptian royal inscriptions.[132] A few examples will suffice to illustrate this point. Concerning Thutmose III it is said, "He (Amun-Re) caused that all foreign lands (come) bowing because of the power of my majesty, my dread being in the midst of the Nine Bows, all lands being under my sandals."[133] The poetical stela of Thutmose III records the speech of Amun-Re who recalls that he placed his "bravery" (*nḥt*), "power" (*bȝw*), "fear," (*snd̲*) and "dread" (*ḥryt*) in the king so that all lands would submit to him.[134] This type of language abounds during the New Kingdom. In Mesopotamia, similar expressions are used, as Alan Millard has demonstrated from Middle Assyrian texts from the end of the second millennium.[135]

The summary statement—a device used in Joshua 10:4–43, 11:16–20, and 12—is another feature Van Seters considers borrowed from the Neo-Assyrian scribal tradition. Here, too, earlier analogies from Middle Assyrian and Eighteenth-Dynasty Egypt are readily available.[136] The *shwy* (review or summary) of Egyptian texts is found in Thutmose III's annals as well as in the Armant stela of the same pharaoh.[137]

Egyptian New Kingdom royal inscriptions are replete with examples of exaggerated claims of military success. Consider the following Egyptian examples: The Poetical Stela of Thutmose III has Amun-Re speak of the victories of the king through divine agency: "The great ones from every foreign land are united in your grasp . . . I fettered Nubian Bowmen for you by ten thousand thousands and northerners as a hundred thousand prisoners of war . . . you trod on *all* foreign lands."[138] The grandiose claims continue, "The heads of Asiatics are severed, none escape (death)."[139] The stela claims that there were no survivors because of the swashbuckling king, but later in the same text thousands of prisoners of war are reported to have been taken.[140]

That the Poetical Stela is describing real events, albeit with rhetorical flourishes and propaganda, is undeniable. In fact, the Euphrates campaign, which is the subject of the grandiose lines in the poem, is one of the best documented expeditions from the Egyptian New Kingdom.[141] This same type of language, which at face value appears contradictory, is found in Joshua where all the enemy forces are said to be wiped out in a battle, followed by reference to survivors, i.e. "the remnant". Joshua 10:20 reads: "When Joshua and the men of Israel had finished slaying them with *a very great slaughter, until they were wiped out*, and *when the remnant which remained* of them had entered into the fortified cities, all the people returned safe to Joshua at the camp of Makkedah."[142]

In the Sphinx stela of Amenhotep II, it is said concerning the king, "He (Amun-Re) commanded him (Amenhotep) to capture *all* lands without fail. . . . *all* foreign lands were bound under his soles."[143] Comparing the statements of Amenhotep with those of his father Thutmose, we must ask that if Thutmose's campaigns were so thorough, why did his son have to conquer the Levant too? A similar situation exists between Joshua 6–11 and Judges 1.

Exaggerated numbers are also found in Ramesses II's Battle of Kadesh report, which boasts of "prevailing over a hundred thousand men."[144] The much quoted Merneptah stela also contains far-fetched claims of decimating entire regions within the same section that makes reference to conquest of particular cities such as Gezer and Ashkelon. It begins with the boast that none of the Nine Bows (Egypt's traditional enemies) could so much as lift a head after Pharaoh's onslaught, and then concludes by saying that "*all* lands are united" (under Merneptah) and "*all* who roamed have been subdued."[145] Thus, we have in the same literary unit, lofty assertions of universal conquest side by side with sober statements about taking individual cities. This precise combination is found in the Joshua narratives.

Concerning "Israel" in Merneptah's stela, if his boast that Israel's seed is no more is taken literally, then the annihilation of Israel (or possibly its grain) is in view.[146] Whatever happened between the Egyptian forces and Israelites tribes toward the end of the thirteenth century B.C., it is clear that the Egyptian scribe was not writing for the benefit of twentieth-century biblical scholars and historians seeking answers for the origins of Israel problem. If the Egyptian claim is taken literally, the text can only tell us about Israel's demise, not its origin.

One of the troubling features of the summary statements and other descriptions of vanquished cities in Joshua are the sweeping claims about conquering an area and decimating its population (e.g., "So Joshua defeated the whole land, the hill country and the Negeb and the lowland and the slopes, all their kings; he left no one remaining, but utterly destroyed all that breathed, as the LORD had commanded," Josh. 10:40). But since hyperbole, as Younger has shown, was a regular feature of Near Eastern military reporting,[147] the failure of Miller, Dever, Redford, and others to recognize the hyperbolic nature of such statements in Joshua is ironic because the charge usually leveled at maximalist historians is that they take the text too literally. As a consequence of this failure, these historical minimalists have committed "the fallacy of misplaced literalism" that Fischer defines as "the misconstruction of a statement-in-evidence so that it carries a literal meaning when a symbolic or hyperbolic or figurative meaning was intended."[148]

The above-quoted Egyptian statements must be understood as hyperbole that perpetuates Egyptian royal ideology.[149] This does not mean that the Levantine campaigns of Thutmose III and Amenhotep II, Ramesses' Battle of Kadesh, and Merneptah's invasion of Canaan did not take place. Egyptologists, while recognizing the propagandistic nature of the material, nevertheless ascribe some historical worth to the bombastic claims.[150] The critical reader of the texts needs to understand the rhetoric and the propagandist nature of the material but should not throw out the proverbial baby with the bathwater by dismissing the more sober reports in the body of the same text. Yet when similar hyperbole is found in the Bible, the account is often summarily dismissed as unhistorical, especially if there is a hint of divine intervention. And yet divine involvement or intervention in military affairs is a regular feature of Near Eastern military writing.[151] The Merneptah stela provides an excellent illustration. In line 14, the capture of the Libyan chieftain is described as "a great wonder (or miracle) happened" (*bi3t c3t ḥprt*).[152] Despite the claim of a miracle and the use of hyperbole in this inscription, no Egyptologist rejects the historicity of the Libyan war of Merneptah.[153]

To conclude, I maintain that comparative study of the Joshua material must include documents from the second millennium, not just the first. Van Seters is absolutely right when he concludes, "His (DtrH) historiographic method is to write past history in the form and style of contemporary historical texts."[154] The question is what contemporary historical texts influenced the Hebrew scribal tradition. By restricting his parallels to Neo-Assyrian texts of the first millennium and ignoring those of the Late Bronze Age (as Weinfeld did earlier), Van Seters is able to manipulate the results to his desired conclusion. As Niehaus, Younger, and I have shown, though, sources from the previous millennium cannot be ignored simply because the material invalidates one's presuppositions about the dating of the Joshua narratives and DtrH. The earlier parallels are just as valid, if not more compelling, and thus allow for a date centuries before the reforms of Josiah at the end of the seventh century B.C.

V. Conclusion

The recent discussions on the origins of Israel have grown out of the demise of the conquest model and the rise of more archaeological, sociological, and anthropological approaches toward reconstructing Israel's early history. While there seems to be something of a school developing that believes the Israelites were indigenous to Canaan, there is little evidence to support this assertion. Despite the current movement towards minimalist and reductionist readings of the biblical text and the elevation of the newer approaches, Siegfried Herrmann has argued for more traditional, text-based methods to answer the problems of Israel's origins. He maintains, "we need theories with a closer connection to the biblical and extrabiblical texts, together with careful consideration of the archaeological results. The question is which source provides some certainty regarding the real Israelite Settlement in the premonarchial period? This is a very old question, but should be raised afresh in order to limit new theories and speculations."[155] I agree with Herrmann's assessment. The biblical texts have been set aside in favor of "new theories and speculations." This development is why so much disagreement persists about Israel's emergence in Canaan. With the traditional view of a forceful invasion by the Israelites now increasingly discarded as a viable option, the emergence of new schools of thought have resulted in internecine disputes. For instance, we have seen Lemche, with his anthropological approach, disagreeing with Gottwald's sociological reconstruction, and Thompson, a biblical historian, critiques Finkelstein's archaeological analysis. The current climate among scholars of the Bible and the archaeology of Syria and Palestine who are historical minimalists is one of discord. Edwin Yamauchi's characterization of this situation is insightful: "Though scholars are united in their lack of confidence in Scripture and supremely confident in their own theories, they are highly critical of each other's views."[156] In his survey of the four primary positions held in the 1990s, Richard Hess offers a generous compromise to these apparently conflicting views by saying, "Aspects of each of the models may be attested in the biblical accounts of early Israel. Aspects of each of them may well have been true in some measure."[157]

When Joshua is viewed as a piece of Near Eastern military writing, and its literary character is properly understood, the idea of a group of tribes coming to Canaan, using some military force, partially taking a number of cities and areas over a period of some years, destroying (burning) just three cities, and coexisting alongside the Canaanites and other ethnic groups for a period of time before the beginnings of monarchy, does not require blind faith. Finally, the idea that the Israelites would have destroyed and leveled cities indiscriminately, makes little sense for they intended to live in this land. A scorched-earth policy is only logical for a conqueror who has no thought of occupying the devastated land. After the battles had been fought and the land divided up among the tribes, Israel is said to have occupied "a land on which you have not labored, and cities which you had not built, and you dwell therein; you eat the fruit of vineyards and oliveyards which you did not plant" (Josh. 24:13). This suggests that the arrival of the Israelites did not significantly affect the cultural continuity of the Late Bronze Age and may explain why there is no evidence of an intrusion into the land from outsiders, for they became heirs of the material culture of the Canaanites.

Notes

1 *The Emergence of Israel in Canaan* (Chico, Calif.: Scholars Press, 1983) 249.

2 Richard S. Hess, "Early Israel in Canaan: A Survey of Recent Evidence and Interpretations," *PEQ* 125 (1993) 125–142.

3 Niels Peter Lemche, *Early Israel: Anthropological and Historical Studies on the Israelite Society before the Monarchy* (Leiden: Brill, 1985). Lemche's critique of Gottwald's *Tribes of Yahweh* (Maryknoll, N.Y.: Orbis, 1979) is found throughout the first 300 pages.

4 Ibid., 35–48.

5 Lemche, *Early Israel,* 412.

6 Ibid., 414.

7 W. W. Hallo, "The Limits of Skepticism," *JAOS* 110 (1990) 187–199.

8 Lemche, *Early Israel*, 421–429.

9 Ibid., 430–431.

10 Alan J. Hauser, Review of Niels Peter Lemche, *Early Israel: Anthropological and Historical Studies on the Israelite Society Before the Monarchy, CBQ* 51 (1989) 526.

11 "Conquest or Settlement," *BA* 50 no. 2 (1987) 84–100.

12 Ibid., 97–98.

13 Ibid., 98.

14 *Who Were the Israelites?* (Winona Lake, Ind.: Eisenbrauns, 1986).

15 Ibid., 16.

16 Ibid., 37–43. Because of the criticism received, Ahlström offered some modifications of the interrelationships between the toponyms ("The Origin of Israel in Palestine," *SJOT* 2 [1991] 19–34). Ahlström's posthumously published work, *The History of Ancient Palestine* (Minneapolis: Fortress, 1993) 282–288, reasserts his thesis.

17 The distinguished German Egyptologist and specialist in Egyptian literature Gerhard Fecht understood Canaan and Israel to be arranged in parallelism ("Die Israelstele, Gestalt und Aussage," in *Fontes Atque Pontes: Eine Festgabe für Hellmut Brunner*, ed. M. Görg, ÄAT vol. 5 [1983] 106–138.

18 *Who Were the Israelites?* 39. This idea was presented in an earlier work, "Merneptah's Israel," *JNES* 44 (1985) 59–61.

19 In D. Winton Thomas, ed., *Documents from Old Testament Times* (New York: Harper and Row, 1958) 140.

20 Lawrence E. Stager, "Merenptah, Israel and the Sea Peoples: New Light on an Old Relief," *Eretz Israel* 18 (1985) 61* and John J. Bimson, "Merneptah's Israel and Recent Theories of Israelite Origins," *JSOT* 49 (1991) 20–23.

21 Frank Yurco, "Merneptah's Canaanite Campaign," *JARCE* 23 (1986) 190.

22 "Israel in the Merneptah Stela," *BASOR* 296 (1994) 45–61.

23   Ibid., 51.

24   It is noteworthy that the Egyptian scribes referred to Israel in the masculine gender since normally foreign nations are treated as feminine. This anomaly might indicate that the Egyptian scribes understood "Israel" to be the name of a man.

25   Stager, *Eretz Israel* 18 (1985) 61*.

26   *Prt* can mean grain or (human) seed (*Wb*, vol. 1, 530), just like its Hebrew counterpart *pᵉrî* (KB, 778). When it means grain, the determinatives ⸗ or ⸗ over ⸗⸗⸗, signify grain or seed in the plural form (A. H. Gardiner, *Egyptian Grammar*, 3d ed. [Oxford: Clarendon Press, 1975] 490). For the meaning human seed, the phallus sign is written, likewise, over the ⸗⸗⸗. The writing in the Merneptah stela has a single grain over plural strokes, thus making the reading ambiguous.

27   This line is a thorny one grammatically. It reads *ḥfᶜ n thnw*. The problem lies with the *n*, which is either a preposition or the *n* of a *sḏm.n.f* form. I appreciate Professor Kitchen's lengthy discussion of this grammatical problem with me. Professor Allan Millard kindly gave me a photocopy of a personal note on this problem by Professor H. W. Fairman. I am inclined to agree with Fairman that a *sḏm.n.f* form makes no sense in this context, where all the verbs are passive. (The *sḏm.n.f* is active.) Furthermore, if the *sḏm.n.f* was intended, the subject of the verb is missing. If the *n* is preposition, *ḥfᶜ* would have to be a noun, but a nominal form for this verb is not otherwise attested. The anomolous *n* could be a type of dittography with the *n* below it in the writing of *thnw*. Kitchen informs me that in a forthcoming article in the Ronald J. Williams *Gedenkschrift*, he suggests that Williams's translation "Destruction for Tehenu" (*Document from Old Testament Times*, 139) is a viable option. In this case, the *n* is a dative (cf. Gardiner, *Egyptian Grammar*, §114), but would be contrary to the obvious verbal pattern of the poem. If the *n* be taken as a scribal error, *ḥfᶜ* would become a passive *sḏm.f*, which fits the grammatical pattern noted here admirably. While I usually resist emending any text, I think one may be justified in this case given the consistent use of either old perfectives or passive *sḏm.f* forms throughout this poetic unit.

28   Kenneth Kitchen, *Pharaoh Triumphant: The Life and Times of Ramesses II* (Warminster: Aris and Phillips, 1982) 215.

29   H. Jacob Katzenstein, "Gaza in Egyptian Texts of the New Kingdom," *JAOS* 102 (1982) 111–113.

30   Donald Redford, "The Ashkelon Relief at Karnak and the Israel Stela," *IEJ* 36 (1986) 197. Yurco points out that since the Egyptians in the nineteenth Dynasty wrote *Gdt* for Gaza, *p3 k3nᶜn* probably refers to the region of Canaan and not the city-state of Gaza. Yurco, "Merneptah's Canaanite Campaign," 190. For an opposing view see *JAOS* 102 (1982) 112.

31   Yurco believes this since Gaza (*Gdt*) occurs in other texts from Merneptah's time.

32   Placing these three together in no way diminishes the obvious linking of the destruction of Israel's seed with Harru's widowhood, a brilliant point made by Stager (*Eretz-Israel* 18 [1985] 61*).

33   The identification of Yenoam remains a problem, see Shmuel Aḥituv, *Canaanite Toponyms in Ancient Egyptian Documents* (Leiden/Jerusalem: Brill/Magnes, 1984) 206–208; K. A. Kitchen, *RITA*, vol. 1, 18.

34   *Wb*, vol. 2, 232. The term may have a more limited scope, as Stager observes (*Eretz-Israel* 18 [1985] 61*).

35   See chap. 2, §I above for discussion of the archaeological evidence for Israel's presence in these areas.

36   W. M. F. Petrie, *Six Temples in Thebes in 1896* (London: Egyptain Research Acount, 1897).

37   The use of the land determinative rather than the city sign in Ashkelon, Gezer, and Yenoam indicates that the Egyptians understood these to be city-states. This practice is seen in the eighteenth Dynasty toponym lists where Megiddo, Kadesh, and other cities are so written, cf. *Urk.* IV, 781 – 786.

38   *Who Were the Israelites?* 40.

39   For the most authoritative collation of the text, see KRI vol. 4, 19.

40   Gardiner, *Grammar,* sign list N 25 = 488 and T 14 = 513.

41   I agree with Frank Yurco that the Karnak reliefs and inscriptions belong to Merneptah and that they represent a pictorial counterpart to the stela, cf. Yurco, *JARCE* 23 (1986) 189 – 215. However, the section where Israel would have been written has not survived. Thus, no textual support for Ahlström's proposed emendation can be found on the relief.

42   *ANET* 378 n. 18.

43   *Documents from Old Testament Times,* 141.

44   *History of Israel* (London: Adams and Charles Black, 1960) 3.

45   "Palestine in the Time of the Nineteenth Dynasty," *CAH,* vol. 2, pt. 2 (1965) 26a, 14. Interestingly, by the time the 1975 printing of *CAH,* this proposal was omitted.

46   "On the Origin and Antiquity of the Name 'Israel,'" *ZAW* 102 (1990) 225 – 237.

47   Kenneth Kitchen, "Historical Method and Early Hebrew Tradition," *TB* 17 (1966) 63-97 and *Ancient Orient and Old Testament* (Downers Grove, Ill.: IV Press, 1966) 59 n.12.

48   Gardiner, *Grammar,* 27.

49   Kitchen, *Ancient Orient,* 60 n.12.

50   Anson F. Rainey, "Rainey's Challenge," *BAR* 16 no. 6 (1991) 93.

51   David Hackett Fischer, *Historians' Fallacies: Toward a Logic of Historical Thought* (New York: Harper and Row, 1970) 109.

52   Davies study was briefly discussed in chap. 1, nn. 40, 59.

53   Review of *The Archaeology of Ancient Israel* (Ed. Amnon Ben-Tor: New Haven: Yale University Press, 1992) in *JBL* 114 (1995) 122.

54   *The Archaeology of the Israelite Settlement* (Jerusalem: Israel Exploration Society, 1988).

55   Robert G. Coote and Keith Whitelam, *The Emergence of Early Israel in Historical Perspective* (Sheffield: *JSOT* Press, 1987).

56   William G. Dever, "'Hyksos,' Egyptian Destructions, and the End of the Palestinian Middle Bronze Age," *Levant* 22 (1990) 79 n.3.

57   Finkelstein, *Archaeology,* chaps. 1 – 2.

58   Ibid., 339 – 348.

59   Ibid., 228 – 234.

60   Ibid., 29 – 31.

61   Douglas Esse, Review of Israel Finkelstein's *Archaeology of the Israelite Settlement, BAR* 14 no. 5 (1988) 8.

62   Thomas Thompson, Review of *The Archaeology of the Israelite Settlement, JBL* 109 (1990) 323.

63   Finkelstein, *Archaeology,* 236 – 259.

64   Ibid., 257.

65   Manfred Bietak, "An Iron Age Four-Room House in Ramesside Egypt," *Eretz Israel,* Avraham Biran Vol. (Jerusalem: IES, 1992) 10*– 12*.

66   E.g., Esse, *BAR* 14 no. 5 (1988) 11.

67   This point has been cogently made recently by Bimson, *JSOT* 49 (1991) 5 – 13.

68   The Medinet Habu relief depicting the invasion of the Sea Peoples is dated to year

8. Following Kitchen's chronology (*ABD*, vol. 2, 329), Ramesses III reigns from 1184 to 1153 B.C., making the eighth year ca. 1177 B.C.

69 We do not know how long the Sea Peoples were in Canaan before their attempted invasion of Egypt. Was there some initial settlement of those tribes prior to the invasion? Did they move quickly down the coast of the Levant and directly into Egypt? To date, the historical and archaeological data have not provided convincing answers to these important questions that impinge on the date of the beginning of the Iron Age.

70 Bryant Wood's dissertation *Palestinian Pottery of the Late Bronze Age: An Investigation of the Terminal LB IIB Phase* (University of Toronto: University Microfilms, 1985) brings together ceramic, epigraphic, and historic data to help refine the chronology. Since it remains unpublished, it has not been adequately reviewed by Syro-Palestinian archaeologists, but there is some discussion of LBA ceramics in his *The Sociology of Pottery in Ancient Palestine* (Sheffield: JSOT Press, 1990).

71 For a discussion of this problem see my exchange with W. G. Dever, see "Reconsidering Egypt's Part in the Termination of the Middle Bronze Age in Palelestine," *Levant* 21 (1989) 185-186, "Some Thoughts on William G. Dever's '"Hyksos," Egyptian Destructions, and the End of the Palestinian Middle Bronze Age,'" *Levant* 22 (1990): 83-89. See *Levant* 22 (1990) 75-81, where Dever critiques my article in *Levant* 21 (1989).

72 Bimson has argued along similar lines in *JSOT* 49 (1991) 18-24.

73 Lemche, *Early Israel*, 430-431. Halpern agrees that the Israel of the stela is an ethnic group and not a region (*ABD*, vol. 5, 1132).

74 This observation has also been made by a number of scholars, e.g. Hess, *PEQ* 125 (1993) 138; Bimson, *JSOT* 49 (1991) 19.

75 G. Ernest Wright, *Biblical Archaeology* (Philadelphia: Westminster Press, 1957) 69.

76 Ibid., 80-83.

77 William G. Dever, *Recent Archaeological Discoveries and Biblical Research* (Seattle: University of Washington Press, 1990) 57-59.

78 Ibid., 61.

79 Fischer, *Historians' Fallacies*, 132-133.

80 Ibid., 47.

81 Ibid., 62.

82 J. Maxwell Miller, "The Israelite Occupation of Canaan," in *Israelite and Judaean History*, ed. John H. Hayes and J. Maxwell Miller (Philadelphia: Westminster Press, 1977) 215. Emphasis added.

83 Fritz, *BA* 50 no. 2 (1987) 84.

84 KB 481, 478, 615, 314.

85 "The Israelite Conduct of War in the Conquest of Canaan," in *Symposia Celebrating the Seventy-Fifth Anniversary of the Founding of the American Schools of Oriental Research (1900–1975)*, ed. F. M. Cross (Cambridge, Mass.: ASOR, 1979) 44-54 and "How Inferior Israelite Forces Conquered Fortified Canaanite Cities," *BAR* 8 no. 2 (1982) 24-35.

86 Malamat, in *Symposia*, 46-47.

87 It is true that accidental burning of houses or sections of an ancient site can result from fighting or an earthquake.

88 Donald B. Redford, "Contact Between Egypt and Jordan in the New Kingdom," *Studies in the History and Archaeology of Jordan*, vol. 1, ed. A. Hadidi (Amman: Department of Antiquties, 1982) 117 n. 23a. See my discussion of the terminology used for destroying a city in *Levant* 21 (1989) 183-184.

89 Donald B. Redford, *Egypt, Canaan, and Israel in Ancient Times* (Princeton: Princeton University Press, 1992) 139 n. 49.

90 This information is based upon Professor Ben Tor's slide lecture presented at the annual meeting of the Society of Biblical Literature and the American Schools of Oriental Research in New Orleans, November 25, 1996. Presently, published material on the new finds at Hazor is not available.

91 The most recent champion of this view is James Weinstein, cf. "The Egyptian Empire in Palestine: A Reassessment," *BASOR* 241 (1981) 1–28.

92 Hoffmeier, *Levant* 21 (1989) 181–193; *Levant* 22 (1990): 83-89; and Hoffmeier, "James Weinstein's 'Egypt and the Middle Bronze IIC/Late Bronze IA Transition': A Rejoinder," *Levant* 23 (1991) 117–124.

93 Redford, *Egypt, Canaan, and Israel*, 264.

94 Kenneth A. Kitchen, "Review of Donald B. Redford's *Egypt, Canaan, and Israel in Ancient Times*," *BAR* 19 no. 1 (1993) 6–8.

95 Wright was very much aware of this problem, see "The Literary and Historical Problem of Joshua 10 and Judges 1," *JNES* 5 (1946): 105–114 and *Biblical Archaeology*, 69-70. Miller considers the differences between Joshua and Judges to be a major problem in *Israelite and Judaean History*, 215. Dever has commented on this problem recently in *Recent Archaeological Discoveries*, 40–42. The tendency has been to give weight to the Judges material on the grounds that it was believed to be older and, perhaps, because it seemed to portray a picture more closely resembling the view of Alt—i.e., an infiltration of individual tribes rather than a pan-Israelite invasion as in Joshua.

96 J. R. Bartlett, *Jericho* (Grand Rapids, Mich.: Eerdmans, 1982) 94. Geologist Amos Nur of Stanford University believes that city IV's demise was the result of seismic activity. This information comes from his video, "The Walls Came Tumbling Down: Earthquakes in the Holy Land," (Stanford University).

97 The problem that et-Tell represents for the historicity of Joshua 7–8 has been raised in chap. 1. While Callaway was convinced that the site he excavated was biblical Ai, no evidence from the site has actually proven the identification, and indeed J. M. Grintz was convinced that et-Tell was Beth-Aven, not Ai, and that biblical Ai might be identified with Khirbet Haiyân (see J. Grintz, "Ai which is beside Beth-aven," *Biblica* 42 [1961] 201–216). See also Bimson's helpful review of the problem of et-Tell and the documentation of those who doubt that it is Ai (*Redating the Exodus and Conquest* [Sheffield: Almond Press, 1981] 201–214). Concerning Grintz's suggestion that Khirbet Haiyân might be identified with Ai, subsequent, albeit limited, excavations there have turned up no Late Bronze or Iron I materials. J. A. Callaway and M. B. Nicol, "A Sounding at Khirbet Haiyân," *BASOR* 183 (1966) 12–19 and J. A. Callaway, "The 1968–1969 ᶜAi (Et-Tell) Excavations," *BASOR* 198 (1970) 10.

98 R. G. Boling and G. E. Wright accept the seventh-century dating of Joshua, but allow for pre-Deuteronomic material, see *Joshua* (Garden City, N.Y.: Doubleday, 1982) 41–72. Likewise, Alberto Soggin also makes such allowances, see *Joshua* (Philadelphia: Westminster Press, 1972) 7–14.

99 Martin Noth, *Überlieferungsgeschichtliche Studien*, 2d ed. (Tübingen: Niemeyer, 1957) = *The Deuteronomistic History* (trans. Jane Doull, et al., Sheffield: *JSOT* Press, 1981) and *Das Buch Joshua*, 3d ed. (Tübingen: J. C. B. Mohr, 1971).

100 *Das Buch Joshua*, 9–13.

101 John Van Seters, "Joshua's Campaign and Near Eastern Historiography," *SJOT* 2 (1990) 12.

102 H. J. Koorevaar, *De opbouw van het Boek Jozua* [*The Structure of the Book of Joshua*] (Brussels: Centrum voor Bijbelse Vorming België [Protestant Faculty of Theology], 1990).

An abstract appeared in *Old Testament Abstracts* 13 (1990), no. 1047. A longer English abstract of this dissertation is appended to the end of the work, 291–294.

103 The most recent excavations at Shiloh have confirmed the conclusions of the Danish expedition of 1926–1932. See Finkelstein, *Archaeology*, 228–232 and Excavations at Shiloh 1981–1984, Preliminary Report," *Tel Aviv* 12 (1985) 123–180.

104 Boling and Wright, *Joshua*, 293–294.

105 K. Lawson Younger, *Ancient Conquest Accounts: A Study in Ancient Near Eastern and Biblical History Writing* (Sheffield: *JSOT* Press, 1990) 226.

106 James K. Hoffmeier, "The Structure of Joshua 1–11 and the Annals of Thutmose III," in *Faith, Tradition and History: Old Testament Historiography in its Near Eastern Context*, ed. A. R. Millard, J. K. Hoffmeier, and D. W. Baker (Winona Lake, Ind.: Eisenbrauns, 1994) 167–169. This analysis of the structure of this section of Joshua was made in 1975 but not published until 1994. In November 1990 the ideas were presented at a symposium at Wheaton College, the proceedings of which were published in *Faith, Tradition and History*. An earlier version of the paper was presented at the SBL annual meeting in November 1991.

107 Younger has sent me a copy of his paper, "The 'Conquest' of the South (Joshua 10:28–39)" in which he demonstrated, independently of me and using different criteria, that this passage is chiastic in structure. It appears in *Biblische Zeitschrift* 199 (1995) 255–264 . He too considers the Gezer episode to be the turning point of the palestrophe (259–260). Once again, my analysis was reached independently of Dr. Younger's. The fact that we both arrived at similar conclusions on this pericope suggests that we are on the right track.

108 I have no explanation for why B' and C' have been reversed from the sequence in the first half of the chiasmus.

109 See the previous section where the meanings were discussed.

110 See above, in chap. 1 §2 for discussion.

111 Kenneth R. R. Gros Louis and Willard Van Antwerpen, Jr., "Joshua and Judges," in *A Complete Literary Guide to the Bible*, ed. Leland Ryken and Tremper Longman III (Grand Rapids, Mich: Zondervan, 1993) 137–150.

112 Ibid., 137.

113 Ibid., 138.

114 Michael Fishbane, "I Samuel 3: Historical Narrative and Narrative Poetics," in *Literary Interpretations of Biblical Narratives*, vol. 2, ed. Kenneth R. R. Gros Louis (Nashville: Abingdon, 1982) 203.

115 Alan Millard ("Story, History and Theology," in *Faith, Tradition and History*, 41) has recently argued that while some etiologies are folklorist in nature, it is "illogical" to assume that all etiologies are by their nature "imaginary stories."

116 Moshe Weinfeld, *Deuteronomy and the Deuteronomic School* (Oxford: Clarendon, 1972) 50.

117 Jeffrey J. Niehaus, "Joshua and Ancient Near Eastern Warfare," *JETS* 31 (1988) 45–50.

118 Weinfeld, *Deuteronomy*, 50.

119 Niehaus, *JETS* 31 (1988) 46

120 Ibid., 37–50.

121 *Ancient Conquest Accounts*, chaps. 2–4.

122 Ibid., 190–192, 227–228, and 241–247.

123 Ibid., 265.

124 Van Seters, *SJOT* 2 (1990) 1–12.

125 Hoffmeier, in *Faith, Tradition and History*, 165–179. In addition, some of the com-

ments in this section were presented in a paper ("Recent Developments in Historiography: Implication for the Study of Egyptian 'Historical' and Old Testament Texts") at the SBL annual meeting in November 1993 in Washington, D.C.

126   *SJOT* 2 (1990) 6-7.

127   Ibid., 7.

128   *1 & 2 Samuel: A Commentary* (Grand Rapids, Mich.: Zondervan, 1986) 252.

129   See Hoffmeier, in *Faith, Tradition and History*, 178 for references.

130   *ARAB*, vol. 1, § 330.

131   Hoffmeier, in *Faith, Tradition and History,* 168-178.

132   James K. Hoffmeier, "Some Egyptian Motifs Related to Enemies and Warfare and Their Old Testament Counterparts," In *Egyptological Miscellanies: A Tribute to Professor Ronald J. Williams*, vol. 6 of *Ancient World*, ed. James K. Hoffmeier and Edmund S. Meltzer (Chicago: Ares, 1983) 53 - 70. Van Seters apparently did not see this study.

133   Translation, ibid., 66. Orig. text in *Urk.* IV, 161.14 - 16.

134   *Urk.* IV, 612.7 - 9.

135   "The Old Testament and History: Some Considerations," *FT* 110 (1983) 46.

136   Younger, *Ancient Conquest Accounts*, 231 - 232, 251 - 253.

137   See Hoffmeier, in *Faith, Tradition and History* 175 - 176, for references and discussion.

138   *Urk.* IV, 612.12 - 613.4.

139   Ibid., 614.1 - 2.

140   Ibid., 612.14 - 16.

141   Hoffmeier, *Levant* 22 (1990) 85.

142   The italics show the contrasting statements.

143   *Urk.* IV, 1278.4, 1283.9.

144   Miriam Lichtheim, *Ancient Egyptian Literature*, vol. 2 (Berkeley and Los Angeles: University of California Press, 1976) 66.

145   KRI, vol. 4, 19.3, 8.

146   The translation *prt* as human "seed" or "grain" is problematic. Egyptologists have tended to go with the former. While Michael Hasel (*BASOR* 296 [1994] 45 - 61) makes a good case for *prt* having a floral meaning, I still favor the traditional interpretation of *prt* as argued above in §I.

147   Younger, *Ancient Conquest Accounts*, 190 - 192, 227 - 228, 241 - 247.

148   Fischer, *Historians' Fallacies*, 58.

149   John Wilson, "The Royal Myth in Ancient Egypt," *Proceedings of the American Philosophical Society* 100, no 5 (October 1956) 439-442, and A.R. Schulman, "The Great Historical Inscription of Merneptah at Karnak: A Partial Reappraisal," *JARCE* 24 (1987) 22.

150   For examples, see Georges Posener, *Littérature et politique dans l'Égypte de la XII dynastie* (Paris: Bibliothèque de l'École des Hautes Études, 1956) 14 - 15 and Ronald J. Williams, "Literature as a Medium of Political Propaganda in Ancient Egypt," *Seed of Wisdom: Essays in Honour of T. J. Meek*, ed. W. S. McCullough (Toronto: University of Toronto Press, 1964) 14 - 30.

151   See A. R. Millard, *FT* 110 (1983) 34 - 53; Niehaus, *JETS* 31 (1988) 37 - 50; and Younger, *Ancient Conquest Accounts* for numerous examples. I have also dealt with this issue in Egyptian "historical" texts, see James K. Hoffmeier, "The Problem of 'History' in Egyptian Royal Inscriptions," in *VI Congresso Internazionale De Egittologia Atti*, ed. Silvio Curto (Turin: 1992) 296 - 97.

152   KRI, vol. 4, 19.4 - 5.

153   See, for example, R. O. Faulkner in *CAH*, vol. 2, pt. 2, 232 - 235 and A. R. Schul-

man, *JARCE* 24 (1987) 21 – 22. Even though Redford is somewhat reductionist about the historic worth of the Asian campaign, he nevertheless believes that there was a smaller-scale campaign during Merneptah's tenure. He does not appear to question the Libyan invasion in which "the great miracle" took place. See Redford, "The Ashkelon Relief at Karnak and the Israel Stela," *IEJ* 36 (1986) 188 – 200. Robert Coote takes Redford's scaled-down campaign and offers a further reduction, saying, "While Merneptah might have sent soldiers to Palestine during the first year or two to display imperial muscle, the campaign implied by the stela inscription may never have occurred." *Early Israel: A New Horizon* (Minneapolis: Fortress, 1990) 74.

154 Van Seters, *SJOT* 2 (1990) 11 – 12.

155 Siegfried Herrmann, "Basic Factors of Israelite Settlement in Canaan," in *Biblical Archaeology Today: Proceedings of the International Congress on Biblical Archaeology, Jerusalem, April 1984*, ed. Janet Amitai (Jerusalem: Israel Exploration Society 1985) 47.

156 Yamauchi, in *Faith, Tradition and History*, 31.

157 Hess, *PEQ* 125 (1993) 132.

3

SEMITES IN EGYPT

The First and Second Intermediate Periods

A wandering Aramean was my father, he
went down into Egypt and sojourned there

Deut. 26:5

These words make up the opening line of an ancient Israelite creed.[1] If Israel had
its origins within Canaan as an indigenous people who either evolved from the
Habiru or were formerly urban dwellers of the great Middle Bronze cities of the
Levant that for several centuries were nomadic before resedentarizing at the beginning of the Iron Age to become "Israel," then this creed and an overwhelming body of biblical evidence is patently wrong.

Here is a simple outline of the biblical events from Genesis 37 to Exodus 14:
owing to a famine in Palestine, the extended family of Jacob/Israel emigrated to
Egypt and settled peacefully there for some time until their fortunes changed.
Under a new king or dynasty, they were pressed into hard labor for a period of
some decades or longer before being released by a recalcitrant pharaoh with the
help of a Hebrew named Moses to return to Canaan from whence they had
come. Is such a scenario implausible? Should the overwhelming weight of biblical evidence for this sojourn–exodus tradition be denied in the light of new, revisionist histories of the origins of Israel? I maintain that there is nothing in the
main points of this story that defies credulity to justify the recent reductionist tendencies among biblical scholars. While the biblical materials have been spurned
because they are believed to be ideologically and theologically shaped and so late
in composition as to be useless for historical investigation, the ultimate reasons for
the rejection are also ideological and reflect the predisposition to skepticism of the
late twentieth century.[2]

For many, the underlying reason for rejecting the history of the Israelite sojourn in Egypt and the exodus tradition is the absence of corroborating historical or archaeological evidence in Egypt. Recently, Niels Peter Lemche has noted that "the silence in the Egyptian sources as to the presence of Israel in the country" is "an obstacle to the notion of Israel's 400 year sojourn."[3] Thus, scholars are faced with a dilemma not unlike that encountered in Canaan with the absence of evidence for an invasion by Israel and have arrived at a similar conclusion: the lack of evidence means the events described in Genesis and Exodus are retrojections of a later period and do not reflect historical reality. Indeed, no one has been able to identify any unimpeachable evidence in Egypt, either historical or archaeological, to support the biblical accounts of the sojourn and exodus events. To draw any conclusions from the current state of knowledge (or ignorance), would be to succumb to the fallacy of negative proof.[4]

The biblical evidence, apart from the Pentateuch, consistently supports the testimony of the book of Exodus, and yet proof from Egypt is lacking. How do we deal with this dilemma? Here I will examine the main points of the story line described in Genesis and Exodus to see if they are plausible within the limits of our present knowledge of ancient Egypt.

The book of Genesis contains several reports of the Hebrew patriarchs going to or anticipating a trip to Egypt to avoid drought and famine in Canaan. The first report, ascribed to Abraham, is in Genesis 12:10, which reads, "Now there was a famine in the land. So Abram went down to Egypt to sojourn there for the famine was severe in the land." On another occasion, Isaac, son of Abraham, considered going to Egypt because of famine conditions in Canaan: "Now there was a famine in the land, besides the former famine that was in the days of Abraham" (Gen. 26:1).[5] Like his father before him, Isaac anticipated going to Egypt, but in a theophany he is told "Do not go down to Egypt" (Gen. 26:2). Finally, Genesis 46:26–29 reports that the family of Israel moved to Egypt in order to escape the grips of a prolonged drought in Canaan (Gen. 41:50–46:7) and were settled in the northeast Delta (Gen. 47:11). The historian naturally will ask if there is evidence for such migrations. Do these references reflect a documented pattern of migration from Canaan to Egypt during times of drought? Does the biblical story fit into any period of Egyptian history when such migrations were taking place? Should there be no evidence for such movements of people from the Levant into the Nile Valley during the second millennium B.C., one might be inclined to question the historical worth of the Genesis narratives. It has been well known for decades, however, that there were Semites in the Delta starting after the collapse of the Old Kingdom (ca. 2190) and reaching a zenith during the Hyksos or Second Intermediate Period (ca. 1700–1550 B.C.) and on into the New Kingdom (1550–1069 B.C.).

I. Semites in Egypt: Epigraphic Evidence

Throughout the millennia, Egypt's lush Delta was like a magnet to the pastoral nomads of the Sinai and Canaan. "On the borders of the Delta, from time immemorial," writes Jean Bottero, "small groups of these bedawin came to pasture their flocks, tempted by the proximity of better grazing-grounds and possible loot."[6] As early as Dynasty 1 the pharaoh had to defend Egypt's borders and commercial interests in Sinai from troublesome Bedouin. An ivory label of King Den reads, "the first occasion of smiting Easterners."[7] From throughout the Old Kingdom reliefs have survived depicting pharaoh smiting Egypt's enemies, and not a few of these have come from the Sinai.[8]

The biography of Weni, a Sixth Dynasty official, reports on his five raids against "sand-dwellers" (ḥryw šꜥ), probably from the Sinai-Negev region, and a sortie against "the Gazelle's Nose,"[9] perhaps the Mount Carmel ridge in northern Canaan.[10] The evidence furnished by Weni's biography suggests these were preemptive actions against the pastoral-nomadic population east of Egypt. Defensive strategies were also needed to prevent infiltration by these peoples. Evidence for such activities, Hermann Kees observed, is found in the Fifth Dynasty title "Overseer of the barriers, the deserts and the royal fortresses in the Nome of Heliopolis."[11]

With Memphis no longer the seat of a united Egypt as it had been during the glory days of the Old Kingdom (ca. 2700–2190 B.C.), the First Intermediate Period saw the rise of the power of local governors or nomarchs, resulting in two rival claimants to the kingship during Dynasties 9 and 10 and into 11 (ca. 2160–2050 B.C.), Thebes in the south and Hnes (Herakleopolis) near the base of the Delta.[12] Hostilities between the north and the south only exacerbated the problem, with Herakleopolis exercising only minimal control over the Delta, thus allowing for a significant incursion of people from western Asia. William C. Hayes described the Delta of this period as having a "mixed Egyptian and Asiatic population."[13] Who were these Asiatics? Where did they come from? And why did they settle in Egypt? Fortunately, answers to these questions are furnished by both epigraphic and anepigraphic sources. Let us consider the written material first.

The Instruction for Merikare

The literature of the First Intermediate Period and the following Middle Kingdom describe a foreign presence in the north. In "Merikare," a Tenth Dynasty Herakleopolitan king provides his son with detailed information about the Delta.[14] The speaker, apparently King Khety Nebkaure, in lines 81 to 105 advises his son to take note of his policies toward foreigners in the Delta and follow his lead:[15]

81. Then I arose as lord of (my) city
     and was upset because of (the condition of) the Northland (or Delta),
     from Ḥwt Šnw to Smb3k3,
82. its southern border goes to the 2 Fish Canal.[16]
     I pacified the entirety of the West, even as far as the Delta coast.[17]
83. They pay revenue from it, it gives mnw wood.[18]
     One sees juniper, they give it to us.
84. The east (Delta) abounds with foreigners, their revenue [comes in].

The central Delta[19] is turned back, and every one within it.

The administrative districts say,

85. "you (the king) are greater then I."

See, [the land] which they destroyed has been transformed into nomes.

Every great town [/////]. What was ruled by one

86. is now in the charge of ten men.

Official(s) should be appointed who will provide you

with revenue lists for taxation.[20] Freeman are provided with fields.

Like a single gang (they) work for you.

87. Rebellion does not exist there (in the Delta).

Because the inundation will not fail for you so that it does not flood,

the revenue of the Delta will be under your control.

88. Look, the mooring post is pounded [in the region][21]

which I have made in the east,

from the border of *Hbnw* [22] to the Way of Horus[23]

89. which is settled with citizens, filled with Egyptians,

90. the finest of the entire land, in order to repulse barbarians[24] among them.

91. Now speaking about these foreigners,

as for the miserable Asiatic, wretched is the place where he is;

92. Lacking in water, hidden because of trees.

Many and difficult are the paths therein because of mountains.

He has not settled in one place.

93. Food causes his feet to roam about.

He fights since the time of Horus.

He does not conquer nor is he conquered.

94. He does not declare war,

(but) is like a thief darting about in a group.

95. But as I live and will be what I am, these foreigners were indeed a sealed wall, its

gates were opened when I besieged it.[25]

96. I caused the Delta to attack it. I plundered their inhabitants,

having captured their cattle.

97. I slaughtered [the people] among them so that the Asiatics abhorred Egypt. So

don't be anxious about him,

98. for the Asiatic is a crocodile on his bank.

He robs on an isolated road,

he does not steal in the vicinity of a populated city.

99. Dig a canal to its [///][26] Flood its half to the Bitter Lakes.

Look, it is a navel cord for the foreigners.

100. Its walls are warlike, its army numerous.

The farmers in it know how to take up arms,

101. besides the freemen within.

The region of *ddw swt* totals ten thousand citizens who are free and not taxed.

102. Officials have been in it since the time the Capital was established.

The borders are established, the garrisons strong.

103. Many northerners flood it near the Delta

who pay taxes in barley alongside the freeman.

104. [corrupt line]

Look, it is the door [/ / / /] the delta,

105. they having made a canal to Herakleopolis.

Ward's thematic arrangement of this section enables us to understand the king's approach to the Delta, especially his dealings with the Asiatic presence: lines 81–85, "Summary of conditions in the north"; 85–88, "Instructions for reorganizing the Middle (?) Delta"; 88–90, "(the king's) outpost in the Eastern Delta"; 91–98, "Digression: the nature of and (the king's) initial skirmishes with them"; and 99–105, "Instructions for fortifying the Eastern Delta."[27]

Throughout this passage and others discussed below, the term "Bowman" (pḏtyw, ll. 84, 91, 95) means "foreigner,"[28] and is a synonym for ꜥꜣm(w) (ll. 91, 97, 98) here as the parallelism suggests. The term ꜥꜣm(w) has traditionally been translated "Asiatic" or "Semite,"[29] and refers to "speakers of a West Semitic tongue."[30] These Asiatics, it appears, were driven to Egypt by their need for food (l. 93). Khety does not claim to have expelled the Asiatics from Egypt; rather, he launched an attack on them and captured cattle (ll. 96–97). The result of this action against the Delta aliens seems to have resulted in scattering them, making them less of a threat (ll. 97–98). In order to prevent further upheaval in the north and to discourage further infiltration of the Nile valley by peoples from western Asia, the king took further measures. Military defenses were established, garrisons of troops deployed, and Egyptian farmers in the northeast Delta were armed (ll. 99–100).

A part of the defensive network described (or envisioned) by Khety was a canal that line 99 appears to describe. Ward renders this as, "Dig a canal until it is un[hindered]. Flood its half as far as Lake Timsah."[31] John Wilson understood it similarly; "Dig a dyke . . . flood it as far as the Bitter Lakes."[32] R. O. Faulkner's translation of this line is virtually the same: "Dig a moat against [. . .] and flood the half of it at the Bitter Lakes."[33] In a note Faulkner explains the defensive nature of this feature, saying, "it is the key to the frontier against the desert dwellers."[34] Kees has also recognized the defensive nature of this feature, translating the critical line as follows: "A wall is set at his side, its (other) side is covered with water up to the Bitter Lakes. Its walls are strong against attack."[35] In fact, he also thought that this defense structure was the "Walls of the Ruler" from the tale of Sinuhe (discussed below).[36] Other translators, however, have come to different conclusions. Miriam Lichtheim renders this critical line as "Medenyt has been restored to its Nome, Its one side is irrigated as far as Kem-Wer."[37] Wolfgang Helck has interpreted this passage similarly,[38] as has Joachim Quack in his recent investigation, although he considers Ward's emendation (i.e., dropping the ⊗ determinative) a possibility.[39]

The reason for the different translations lies in the textual reading preferred by the translator: šd mdnit, or šd m(y) dnit. The reading mdnit would be Aphroditopolis or Atfih, in the Twenty-second Nome just south of Memphis.[40] Of the three manuscript witnesses of "Merikare" in Helck's critical edition, only Papyrus Petersburg has the city determinative written after m dnit, suggesting that the New Kingdom scribe who made this copy thought the city of Atfih was meant. This line, however, is completely lost in Papyrus Moscow, while only šd m is preserved in Papyrus Carlsberg. Consequently, caution must be exercised reading this line, and firm conclusions must be avoided.

Ward considers the m following šd to be the particle m(y) that is occasionally written after imperatives.[41] *Dnit* would mean canal, dike, or ditch.[42] Since Khety continues by indicating that this structure was meant for defensive purposes (cf. ll. 100–101) and included walls (*inbw*), Helck's and Lichtheim's interpretation does not seem to fit the context as well. Also, in support of Ward, the presence of troublesome foreigners or desert dwellers (*ḥ3styw*, Pap. Petersburg) or bowman (*pḏtyw*, Pap. Carlsberg)[43] at Atfih, south of Memphis, seems unlikely in view of Khety's apparently successful measures taken against them further north in the Delta. It is hard to believe that Khety would have been able to deal with the Asiatics in the Delta up to the eastern frontier and not control them in his own neighborhood.

In lines 104–105, *dnit* occurs again, this time in association with Khety's capital, Hnes (Herakleopolis), and there is no preceding *m* nor is the city sign used as a determinative. Interestingly, here Lichtheim renders it "dyke," suggesting that it has a metaphorical nuance for "protection."[44] We suggest that the idea of a defensive feature near Hnes called a *dnit* that Lichtheim understood in lines 104–105 is also in view in lines 100–101 in the Bitter Lakes–Wadi Tumilat area.

One might be inclined to favor Ward, Wilson, Faulkner, and Kees's interpretation of this line and locate the activity recommended by Khety in the Bitter Lakes region (*km wr*). However, Lichtheim observes that *km wr* could also be located in the Fayum, following J. Yoyotte's investigation of the geography of that area.[45] It should be noted, however, that Yoyotte's sources for this identification are largely from the Greco-Roman period and may be of little value for identifying place-names of the First Intermediate Period. At this point, one must be careful not to draw firm conclusions about the line *šd m dnit* because of the lacunae in key points in the various manuscripts. However, the possibility that a canal was excavated in this area as a part of a defensive system cannot be ruled out and in fact seems to be supported by line 100, which states "Its (the *dnit*)[46] walls are warlike, its army numerous." An effective defense network in the area between the Bitter Lakes and the Mediterranean in the eastern Delta Sinai region would be essential to deny further access to people infiltrating from the east. For this reason Ward interpreted lines 99–101 as follows:

> Merikare is to build a canal, presumably from the fortress at Ways-of-Horus southward to Lake Timsah (lines 99ff.). This line of defense, once completed, would be the logical one since it would guard the whole area from the southeastern shore of Lake Manzeleh to Lake Timsah. Its northern terminus would be at the land-route which entered Egypt through Ways-of-Horus and its southern terminus at the entrance to the Wadi Tumilat at Ismailiyah. Precisely this region was the main point of entry for nomads wishing to move out of the desert into the Delta. A fortified canal, half-filled with water, would be an ideal defensive position, easily manned by troops and mobile units of rafts or small boats patrolling the length of the canal.[47]

Soon after Ward's book was published in 1971, a canal was discovered by members of the Israel Geological Survey in the north Sinai.[48] Aerial photographs and examination of this feature on the ground led to the discovery of a seventy-meter-wide waterway that might be the feature Khety had in mind, even if he or Merikare did not begin or complete the project. (For a discussion of archaeological and historical evidence for the canal, see chap. 7) Whatever the Herakleopolitan kings achieved in terms of militarizing the northeast Delta and Sinai, it is clear that their policy was continued by their Twelfth Dynasty successors, as the following sections illustrate. (For archaeological evidence of Herakleopolitan activity in this area, see § II below.)

The Prophecy of Neferti

The "Prophecy of Neferti" most likely originated in the Twelfth Dynasty court of Amenemhet I[49] or Senusert I,[50] otherwise the propagandistic value attached to the work would have been meaningless.[51] Set in the Fourth Dynasty court of Sneferu (l. 1), this prophecy anticipates the coming of Ameny (short for Amenemhet), who would bring order out of chaos (l. 58ff.) and reestablish *m3ᶜt*, political and cosmic order. Although half a century had passed since Egypt had been reunited under Montuhotep II Nebhepetre, ending Egypt's first dark age and ushering in the Middle Kingdom, conditions of the First Intermediate Period are described.[52] Recently, Donald Redford has observed that it "preserves a vivid picture of the state of affairs in Egypt and adjacent parts of Asia during the last decades of the third millennium B.C."[53] Before Neferti, a lector priest and "native of On" (Heliopolis), utters his prophecy, we hear his thoughts:[54]

> He (Neferti) was concerned for what would happen in the land.
> He thinks about the condition of the east.
> Asiatics (ᶜ3mw) travel with their swords,[55]
> terrorizing those who are harvesting,
> seizing the oxen from the plow.
>
> A strange bird[56] will reproduce in the marsh of the Delta,
> having made its nest by the people, the people
> have caused it (the bird) to approach because of want.
>
> All happiness has gone away, the land is cast down in trouble
> because of those feeders,[57] Asiatics (sṭṭyw) who are throughout the land.
> Enemies have arisen in the east, Asiatics have come down to Egypt.
> A fortress is deprived of another beside it,
> the guards do not pay attention to it.[58]

The scenario in "Neferti" is like that of "Merikare." The eastern Delta has become home to unruly Asiatics who came to Egypt for food and in the process terrorized the Egyptian population. The metaphor, likening the Asiatics to a "strange bird" that reproduces in the Delta and builds its nest, suggests that the foreign population was growing and intended to stay permanently. The closing line translated here suggests that Egypt's defenses along its eastern border were unable to stop the infiltration.[59] While it is recognized that "Neferti" has a propagandist bent, the references to the presence of Asiatics are consistent with the picture portrayed in

"Merikare."[60] Hence, they should be taken as a realistic allusion to conditions in Egypt during the First Intermediate Period and into the Middle Kingdom.

According to Neferti's prophecy concerning the messianic Ameny, he is to deal with the problem of the Asiatic infiltration by building up Egypt's border defenses.

One will build the "Walls of the Ruler," life prosperity and health,
to prevent Asiatics (ʿȝmw) from going down into Egypt.
They beg for water in the customary manner
in order to let their flocks drink.[61]

The "Walls of the Ruler" (inbw ḥkȝ) is believed to have been a fortification or network of forts at the end of the Wadi Tumilat. (More will be said about this in the following section.) This section indicates that water for flocks has been and still is the primary reason that Levantine pastoral nomads come into the Nile valley. Drought, it must be recalled, is the reason the biblical Patriarchs gave for coming to Egypt.

Miscellaneous Middle Kingdom References

The Admonitions of Ipuwer continues in the complaint genre like that of "Neferti," bemoaning the conditions in Egypt.[62] Although its dating is debated, the work seems to reflect the kind of disruption of political and social life that characterized parts of the First Intermediate Period.[63] Ipuwer, while not devoting the same space to the problem of foreigners in the Delta as "Merikare," briefly describes the nature of the problem. Delta residents maintain defensive postures, carrying shields (1, 4); the same is said of farmers plowing their fields (2, 1). "The nomes are destroyed" complains Ipuwer, "Foreign bowmen (pḏtyw) have come to Egypt" (3,1). In the lacunae-filled final section of the work, several references are made to "Bowmen" and "Asiatics" (ʿȝmw). Thus, while this work does not describe the foreign presence in the Delta in great detail, their contribution to the upheaval is unmistakable.

With the establishment of the Twelfth Dynasty, significant efforts were made to secure Egypt's borders and guard her frontiers. The well-known fortresses of Nubia were built to defend Egypt's southern flank and to serve as a springboard for economic ventures in that area.[64] Many of these forts were investigated during the Nubian campaign in connection with the Aswan Dam salvage project in the 1960s. Given the problems of west Asian migrants entering Egypt from the northeast during the First Intermediate Period, the border between Egypt and Sinai likely became a similar militarized zone. Certainly, that is what the "Instruction for Merikare" anticipates, though, we know very little about this area during the Middle Kingdom. Neferti's reference to the coming Amenemhet I and building the "'Walls of the Rulers' to prevent Asiatics (ʿȝmw) from going down into Egypt" finds a parallel in the Tale of Sinuhe.

Sinuhe fled Egypt upon learning of the assassination of Amenemhet I. He reports:

I reached the "Walls of the Ruler"
which were made to repulse the Asiatics (*sttyw*),
to trample the Bedouin (*nmiw šc*).
It was in fear that I took to crouching in a bush
lest the sentry on the wall on duty see (me).[65]

The precise location of this feature and its nature remains problematic. Since *km wr* ("the Great Black") or the Lake Timsah–Bitter Lakes region is mentioned in the following lines, a location on the Egyptian border with Sinai seems assured.[66] The fact that both Neferti and Sinuhe mention the "Walls of the Ruler" (*inbw ḥḳ3*) in connection with keeping Asiatics at bay, and since Neferti associates it with Amenemhet (and in Sinhue it is functioning at that monarch's death), strongly suggests that early in the Twelfth Dynasty, measures were taken to secure Egypt's frontier with western Asia. Some additional textual evidence further supports this suggestion. A stela, found in two parts in 1913 and 1914 in Kerma (Sudan), dating to the 33d regnal year of Amenemhet III (ca. 1810 B.C.), appears to allude to this defense network.[67] The stela mentions a shipment of 35,300 bricks north to "*Snbt* which is in the Walls-of-Amenemhet, the Justified"—*snbt ntt m inbw imn-m-ḥ3t m3c ḥrw*.[68] Hans Goedicke has observed that since the royal name "Amenemhet" has the epithet "*m3c ḥrw*" appended to it, indicating that this king was dead, it must refer to either Amenemhet I or II.[69] He opts for the former, equating "the Walls of Amenemhet" (*inbw imn-m-ḥ3t*) of the Kerma stela with "the Walls of the Ruler" (*inbw ḥḳ3*) of Sinuhe and Neferti.[70] Consequently Amenemhet I is credited with either building or refurbishing the "Walls of the Ruler," a defense network in the Bitter Lakes region running north to the coast.[71] Goedicke further suggests that the project alluded to in the stela was to reinforce the area in view of a real threat from Canaan.[72]

Currently, there is no archaeological evidence for such a fort or network of forts dating to the Twelfth Dynasty in this area. But thanks to a concerted international effort, teams of archaeologists are now surveying and excavating north Sinai. To date, the most significant fort discovered is Tell Hebua (fig. 22), situated northeast of modern El-Qantara. Mohamed Abd el-Maksoud, the discoverer and excavator of this site, has provisionally identified Hebua with Tjaru, the well-known frontier town of the New Kingdom.[73] Portions of a massive fort with New Kingdom pottery have been uncovered, and an inscription of the Second Intermediate Period king Nehsy has been found, indicating that the this site goes back at least to the seventeenth century B.C.[74] As excavations continue, Middle Kingdom levels could come to light.[75] Other forts in the area are also being excavated (e.g., Tell Qedua = T 21 and Tell el-Herr), but they have not yet exposed even New Kingdom levels.[76] In the coming decade our knowledge of this important area should increase considerably, providing information about the end of the third and early second millenniums in this strategic region.

What became of the Semitic people who entered Egypt during the First Intermediate Period? The fate of these peoples during this period is not altogether clear. Certainly there is no evidence of any organized effort to rid Egypt of these people, like that at the end of the Hyksos period. Since many were pastoral nomads, some may have returned to the Levant, though it appears that a significant portion stayed on and assimilated into Egyptian culture.

There is ample documentation during the Middle Kingdom of a significant Semitic-speaking population in Egypt. An oft-cited document that provides information on Semites in Egypt during the late Middle Kingdom is Papyrus Brooklyn 35.1446 (fig. 3).[77] This document, probably of Theban origin and dating to the late Twelfth or early Thirteenth Dynasty, contains a ledger with the names of the servants of an Egyptian estate. Over forty are labeled ꜥ3m or ꜥ3mt (feminine) and bear names of Northwest Semitic type indicating their Syro-Palestinian ethnicity.[78] Since over forty Semites were attached to this single estate in the Thebaid, the number across Egypt, especially in the Delta, was likely considerable. To account for this presence, Hayes suggests that there was a large number of Syro-Palestinians throughout Egypt in the service of Egyptian nobility.[79] In the absence of any historical evidence for major military campaigns into the Levant by the Twelfth Dynasty monarchs, which would account for prisoners of war, Hayes suggests that there was "a brisk trade in Asiatic slaves carried on by the Asiatics themselves, with Egypt" not unlike that reported in Genesis 37:28, 36.[80]

Since virtually nothing is known of such a slave trade from Egyptian sources, Hayes's explanation alone can hardly account for the significant number of Semites in Egypt during the first half of the second millennium. Recently, a historical inscription of Amenemhet II (1901–1866 B.C.) has come to light which reports on campaigns into the Levant that resulted in the capture of 1,554 prisoners of war.[81] This demonstrates that some of the Asiatics in Egypt during the Middle Kingdom were transplanted to Egypt as a result of war. This same text also reports that Asiatic rulers and chieftains from Canaan sent individuals as tribute to the Egyptian court.[82] The same text also reinforces what has been known earlier: that Asiatics entered Egypt on commercial ventures.[83] There was commercial contact between Egypt and Canaan as far back as the close of the predynastic and Archaic period (Dynasties 1 and 2).[84] During the Old Kingdom (ca. 2700–2190 B.C.) commercial contacts between Egypt and the Levant flourished, with Egyptians desiring timber from Lebanon.[85]

The famous Beni Hasan scene and accompanying inscriptions report of 37 ꜥ3mw coming to Egypt with Abi-Sha has been known for over a century.[86] Since Newberry's original publication, it has been commonly thought that these ꜥ3mw were engaged in trade, probably transporting eye paint or kohl (e.g., msdwt) to Egypt, though Goedicke has argued that this group was brought to the area of Beni Hasan to prospect for galena.[87] He concludes, "This should be seen as a commercial enterprise for which foreigners were imported to Egypt."[88] On the other hand, Detlef Franke has recently argued along more traditional lines that the eye paint is a gift, although he places these Asiatics in Egypt's eastern desert, rather than Sinai or the Levant, because of the presence of galena there.[89] Barry Kemp, however, reports that according to Eleventh Dynasty texts galena was extracted in the Sinai.[90] Despite differences in the interpretation of this scene, there is agreement that this group of Semites was in Egypt for commercial reasons.

While "slave trade," as Hayes described it, might account for the presence of some Semites in Egypt during the Middle Kingdom, the evidence now shows that foreigners from western Asia entered Egypt as POWs, as tribute or diplomatic gifts, and as participants in commercial venturers. Furthermore, it is quite logical to believe that a portion of the Semitic peoples in Egypt during the Middle Kingdom and beyond were descendants of immigrants from the First Intermediate Period who had settled in the Delta.[91]

Other papyri—such as Papyrus London UC XL.1 and the Papyri Berol 10002, 10004, 10021, 10034, 10047, 10050, 10055, 10066, 10111, 10228, and 10323—point to a significant number of Asiatics ($^c3m[w]$). While these remain largely unpublished, Ulrich Luft has begun a thorough investigation of these sources.[92] Some of the professions associated with these Asiatics are singers, dancers, temple workers and doorkeepers, couriers, corvée laborers, and mining-expedition workers.[93] While most of them bore Semitic names, others had good Egyptian names like Senusert, but were prefixed by ^c3m, indicating their foreign origin despite the Egyptian name.[94]

II. Archaeological Evidence for Semites in Egypt

The literature of the First Intermediate Period and Middle Kingdom place the infiltrating ^c3mw primarily in the northeast Delta, and the emerging archaeological remains support the written record. After decades of neglect, the Delta is beginning to receive the scientific investigation it deserves. A number of factors have contributed to the neglect, not the least of which is that many sites have been badly denuded by farming activity. The sites of Tell El-Dab^{c}a/Avaris, and Qantir/Pi-Ramesses, for example, today are fields with surrounding villages (figs. 2, 13). Consequently, much has been lost, discouraging early generations of archaeologists from exploring such areas. In addition, since 1948, sites close to and in Sinai have been off-limits for military reasons, and many Delta sites did not have visible architectural remains, as sites in Middle and Upper Egypt did, prompting many Egyptologists to turn to greener pastures. The result of the neglect is that there is a dearth of information about Lower Egyptian cities and villages from the Pharaonic period. This situation is well reflected in Baines and Málek's *Atlas of Ancient Egypt* (1980), which devotes ninety-five pages to sites from Middle and Upper Egypt, but just ten pages on the Delta. Redford describes further problems for Delta archaeology: "Many Delta sites had been picked over before archaeology became the scientific endeavor it is today, while others have . . . permanently concealed their Middle Kingdom strata below a high water table."[95] As further industrialization, urbanization, and changing ecological forces threaten the archaeological record, the past two decades have witnessed a surge in interest and work on these endangered sites. Because of the recent exploration of this important region, information about the Semitic peoples who left their mark on northern Egypt is beginning to emerge from the fog.

Tell el-Dab^c a

Beginning in 1966, Manfred Bietak of University of Vienna has led the excavations at Tell el-Dab^c a, arguably the most important Delta site ever excavated (figs.
2, 13). That it was Avaris, the capital established by the Hyksos rulers of Dynasties
15 through 17 is widely accepted today by Egyptologists.[96] The earliest remains
uncovered go back to the First Intermediate Period. A Twelfth Dynasty stela
mentions a "Temple (or estate) of Khety," which led Bietak in 1979 to surmise
that the earliest settlement at Tell el-Dab^c a-Khata^c na "probably began as an outpost constructed by Herakleopolitan kings of the First Intermediate Period in
order to check the Asiatic infiltration of that time."[97] A few years later, archaeological evidence for this period came to light. As might be expected of a military
outpost, "it was protected by a strong wall" and "the settlement had an orthogo-
nal plan," says Bietak.[98] While our knowledge of the earliest history of what later
became Avaris is still quite limited, it furnishes us with what is likely the first
known settlement built in the northeast Delta in response to the Asiatic threat.
Also, it confirms that in the "Instruction for Merikare," Khety is describing a real
strategy utilized by the Egyptians to defend against unwanted emigration from
the Levant. It appears, however, that this particular site, probably *Hwt-r3 w3ty-ḫty*
("the estate of Rowaty of (King) Khety") was abandoned in the Twelfth Dynasty,
while other areas of Tell el Dab^c a enjoyed a long period of buildup by immigrants
from the Levant.[99]

A number of inscribed blocks have been uncovered from the early Twelfth
Dynasty, bearing the names of Amenemhet I and Senusert I.[100] Eric Uphill considers Amenemhet I to have been a key figure in the history of the site because of
the strategic location of Avaris and the need to secure his northeastern border,
much as he had initiated the building of defensive structures in Nubia.[101] Tell
el-Dab^c a has well-stratified remains from the end of the Twlefth Dynasty (after
Amenemhet III), through the Hyksos period (ca. 1648–1540 B.C.), after which it
was thought that Avaris was abandoned before some rebuilding in the Seth temple precinct during the reign of Horemheb (1323–1295 B.C.).[102] These levels
correspond to the Middle Bronze IIA–C and Late Bronze I periods in Canaan.
The domestic and religious architecture, burial traditions, ceramics, and bronzes
all show strong connections to the Levant, although there was an increased Egyp-
tianization of the pottery as time went on. Concerning the earliest Asiatic settlement, stratum H and d/2 of the Middle Bronze IIA period, Bietak concludes,
"Donkey sacrifices in connection with tombs, and bronzes from the tombs reveal,
however, in combination with the house-types that the inhabitants of this settlement were Canaanites, however, highly Egyptianized."[103] Up until this point the
residents of this site were not the ruling Hyksos who dominated Lower Egypt
during the Second Intermediate period.

The arrival of the Hyksos has long been thought to have been a military invasion by a ruthless people. Josephus's citations from Manetho, the third century B.C.
Egyptian priest-historian, are largely responsible for this view. Josephus quotes
from book two of Manetho's *History of Egypt*:

Tutimaeus. In his reign, I know not why, a blast of God's displeasure broke upon us. A people of ignoble origin from the east, whose coming was unforeseen, had the audacity to invade the country, which they mastered by main force without difficulty or even a battle. Having overpowered the chiefs, they then savagely burnt the cities, razed the temples of the gods to the ground, and treated the whole native population with the utmost cruelty, massacring some, and carrying off the wives and children of others into slavery. Finally they made one of their number, named Salitis, king. He resided at Memphis, exacted tribute from Upper and Lower Egypt, and left garrisons in the places most suited for defense.... Having discovered in the Sethroite nome a city very favorably situated on the east of the Bubastis arm of the river, called after some ancient theological tradition Auaris, he rebuilt and strongly fortified it with walls, and established a garrison there numbering two hundred and forty thousand to protect his frontier.[104]

This statement by Manetho, coupled with the belief that advanced weaponry such as composite bows and horse-drawn chariots were introduced to Egypt by the Hyksos, has contributed to the view of many modern historians that the Hyksos easily conquered Egypt. Consider the following affirmations by scholars from the 1930s through 1960s.

In 1939, R. M. Engberg said, "Just as it is plausible to believe that much of the success of the Hyksos was due to their superior weapons and fortifications, so it may be presumed that horses and chariots played a large part in their fortunes."[105] John Wilson spoke of "invading hordes" and tied their success to the "speed and striking power of the horse and chariot" that "gave them the most obvious superiority."[106] H. E. Winlock and, more recently, Yigael Yadin attributed the success of the Hyksos invasion of Egypt to their superior weaponry, especially the chariot.[107] Despite the widespread support for a military invasion of Egypt, this view has been challenged in recent years by some scholars, including Torgny Säve-Söderberg[108] and John Van Seters.[109] They believe that the Hyksos Dynasty emerged from the Asiatics who infiltrated Egypt at the end of the Middle Kingdom when political and royal power were waning. The Manethonian tradition was subsequently defended by Helck[110] and Redford, first in 1970 and again in 1992.[111] Interestingly, Redford adopts a maximalist stance with Manetho whereas, as we shall see in the following chapters, he is a historical minimalist with Genesis and Exodus. Regarding the archaeological evidence at Tell el-Dabᶜa, Redford cogently observes that "what remains to be explained are the major sites such as Tel ed-Dabᶜa, Tel el-Yehudiyeh and Maskhuta, where an urban but thoroughly Middle Bronze Canaanite population had insinuated itself. And this population surely did not take shape through sporadic infiltration but through the migration en bloc of communities already urban in nature."[112]

Perhaps these two opposing positions (invasion versus infiltration) on the Hyksos' origin in Egypt are not mutually exclusive. The excavations at Tell el-Dabᶜa show a pre-Hyksos, Asiatic population of Middle Bronze IIA, Canaanite origin beginning to settle toward the end of the Twelfth Dynasty and into the Thirteenth, around 1800–1700 B.C. (viz. strata G - E/3 and c - b/2).[113] Dynasties 15 through 17 are represented by strata E/2 - D/2 and b/1 -a/2.[114] There appears to have been no major destruction to mark what Bietak called "the second major

Canaanite incursion": the arrival of the Hyksos (stratum E/3).[115] But that does not mean they were not invaders, since they may not have needed to conquer cities occupied by fellow Semitic-speaking people. Their targets would have been Memphis (as Manetho states) and other Egyptian cities of the Middle Kingdom. Furthermore, Manetho does not claim that Avaris was founded by the Hyksos king, Salitis; rather, he "rebuilt and strongly fortified it with walls." Thus, I do not believe the Manethonian tradition is invalidated by the absence of a Hyksos-era destruction at Avaris. Instead, Manetho's claim that Salitis rebuilt and fortified Avaris is consistent with the archaeological picture at Tell el-Dab^ca.

The excavations at Tell el-Dab^ca in recent years show that the so-called expulsion of the Hyksos by King Ahmose at the outset of the Eighteenth Dynasty did not result in the obliteration of the city, although tombs were plundered.[116] While the site for the most part seems to have been abandoned, the Seth Temple continued to be used through the Eighteenth Dynasty until major renovations were initiated under Horemheb (1323–1295 B.C.).[117] Since the Seth temple was permitted to function on some basis, it appears there must have been a sufficient number of possibly Asiatic devotees. Apparently, the entire Asiatic population of the Hyksos capital was not eliminated or forced to retreat to Canaan, even though the elite and certainly the military departed. If this scenario was true for Avaris, then other Delta sites where Semitic-speaking aliens resided may not have been entirely depopulated. Only further excavation of the suburban areas of Avaris will settle this issue. (For information about the recently discovered early Eighteenth Dynasty fortification at Tell el-Dab^ca, see pages 122–23.)

The Wadi Tumilat

The Wadi Tumilat is a narrow, fertile band that extends east from the Nile Delta and runs to modern Ismailiya on Lake Timsah. It was one of the primary highways in and out of Egypt from earliest antiquity until modern times (fig. 2).[118] Because of its proximity to Sinai and the availability of fresh water, it attracted Asiatics from the Negev and Sinai from earliest times. Extensive archaeological-survey work was undertaken by the Wadi Tumilat Project from the late 1970s to the mid-1980s. A part of this project entailed excavations at Tell el-Maskhuta (see next section). A University of Chicago dissertation by Carol Redmount has brought together the data from this comprehensive project.[119] Of the seventy-one sites identified, twenty-one yielded Middle Bronze II, Levantine materials that correspond to the Second Intermediate through Hyksos Periods.[120] Most sites are regarded as campsites or villages that were seasonally occupied by transhumants, while five of the sites were actually on tells, Maskhuta being the largest.[121] Redmount describes the foreign presence in the Wadi as "rural" and notes that the finest burial objects are poor when compared to the tombs of their counterparts at Tell el-Dab^ca.[122] The comparison of materials from these two areas suggest that during Egypt's Second Intermediate Period, Semitic-speaking peoples at opposite ends of the socioeconomic spectrum resided in Egypt.

Tell el-Maskhuta

Situated toward the eastern end of the Wadi Tumilat, Tell el-Maskhuta commanded an important position that guarded the entrance to this important route into Egypt from Sinai (fig. 2). Excavations at Maskhuta from the late 1970s and early 1980s uncovered Middle Bronze, Canaanite remains.[123] The earliest phase is described as a "marginal settlement" by John S. Holladay, who directed the University of Toronto project; he dates the site to the Middle Bronze IIA period based on the broken cooking pots, apparently from a campsite.[124] The second phase witnessed more signs of permanence, such as mud-brick tombs with donkey burials and ceramics suggestive of the late Middle Bronze IIA and into IIB.[125] A scarab bearing the name of the Thirteenth Dynasty monarch was discovered. It reads, "Sobekhotep (IV), born of the king's mother Kemi" and was found in one of the tombs of this period, offering a *terminus post quem* around 1740 or 1730 B.C., according to Holladay.[126] Recent chronological studies of the Second Intermediate Period by Kenneth Kitchen, however, have resulted in lowering the dates of Sobekhotep IV down to 1712 to 1705 or even later (1685 to 1678, according to Rolf Krauss).[127] The people of this second phase have been labeled "Egyptian based 'Asiatics.'"[128] Given the later appearance of these transhumant pastoralists from the Levant, they cannot be associated with Asiatics who came to Egypt during the First Intermediate Period. Nevertheless, this evidence illustrates the recurrence of the same type of emigration to Egypt that occurred after the collapse of the Old Kingdom. The Maskhuta material demonstrates that in the waning decades of the Twelfth Dynasty and early into the Thirteenth, Asiatics were once again penetrating Egypt as they had after the collapse of the Old Kingdom.

Tell el-Retabeh

This important site, second only in size to Maskhuta in the Wadi Tumilat (fig. 2), was excavated in the final years of the last century and early in the twentieth by Edouard Naville and Flinders Petrie.[129] In addition to the Ramesside remains, Petrie discovered Middle Kingdom and what he believed to be Old Kingdom materials.[130] The presence of Ramesside materials from Retabeh led Petrie to suggest provisionally that it was the site of Ramesses.[131] Petrie also uncovered an inscribed weight bearing the name of *Nb k3w ḥty*.[132] Mention of the Tenth Dynasty Herakleopolitan King Khety has led Redford to suggest that "Retabeh in the Wadi Tumilat was apparently fortified in the 10th Dynasty."[133] This intriguing hypothesis would be further evidence for the policy prescribed in "Merikare" to defend Egypt's frontier against further Asiatic infiltration in the First Intermediate Period.

As for Middle Bronze Canaanite remains, the picture is not clear. Nevertheless, Redmount believes that a child burial uncovered by Petrie "looks and sounds suspiciously like an Middle Bronze Age/Second Intermediate Period burial such as those found at Tell el-Maskhuta and Tell el-Dabᶜa."[134] In the mid-1970s small-scale excavations directed by Hans Goedicke were undertaken at Retabeh. While there appears to be evidence of Middle Bronze Age materials, it remains unpublished.[135] Thus, it is possible that, like Maskhuta, there is evidence of foreign presence in the Second Intermediate Period, though we shall have to await its publication. The question of Retabeh's association with the "store-cities" of Exodus 1:11 will be taken up in chapter 5 §IV.

Tell el-Yehudiyeh

The Arabic name, "mound of the Jew," tantalizingly suggests a memory of a foreign presence at this unique site located in the thirteenth Lower Egyptian nome of Heliopolis (fig. 2). It was here that the so-called "Tell el-Yehudiyeh" juglets were first found, hence the name. Petrie worked this tell in the early years of this century following upon the earliest probes of Naville and Griffiths in the 1880s.[136] His excavations led him to think that it was a Hyksos camp, measuring 515 × 490 yards externally and 390 × 390 internally.[137] This interpretation, however, was challenged in the 1930s by Hermann Ricke who proposed that this sandy mound was actually a temple foundation.[138]

The sloped glacis on the outer edge of the tell, a common feature of Middle Bronze II sites from Syria through Canaan,[139] led G. R. H. Wright in turn to question Ricke's conclusion, since there is no architectural evidence for a massive temple covering this mound.[140] He postulates that the plastered glacis, otherwise unattested in Egypt, was a technique employed to protect a tell against weathering and erosion. If Wright is correct, then the presence of the glacis at this Delta site further ties it to the Middle Bronze Canaanite culture.

About a kilometer east of the tell is the Second Intermediate Period cemetery.[141] The mud-brick vaulted tombs, Olga Tufnell has recently observed, are like those found at Tell el-Dabᶜa.[142] The ceramic remains are of Palestinian type and Tufnell suggests a horizon of 1700 to 1600 B.C., based on her reexamination of the contents of these tombs.[143] She also thought that the people buried in these tombs were "a poor community of shepherds."[144] Clearly, such people would not have been responsible for building up this large site. Tell el-Yehudiyeh should be excavated again, utilizing the more precise archaeological methods of the late twentieth century, but the site is being lost due to farming and building activities in the area. Nevertheless, it is certain that an Asiatic element resided at Tell el-Yehudiyeh during the Second Intermediate Period, though many questions remain unanswered about the early history of this important site.

Inshas

This site was excavated in a limited manner in the 1940s and the discoveries were commented upon only in a brief report (fig. 2).[145] Remains from the Hyksos Period were found, including vaulted tombs like those discovered at Tell el-Dabᶜa, Maskhuta, and Tell el-Yehudiyeh.[146]

Tell Farasha

Tell Farasha is located midway between Tell Basta to the southwest and Tell el-Dabᶜa to the northeast (fig. 2). Although it was excavated in the early 1970s, it was not until 1983 that a brief preliminary report appeared.[147] Once again, vaulted tombs of the type from Tell el-Dabᶜa were uncovered, complete with Tell el-Yehudiyeh juglets.[148] While full publication is required before firm conclusions are drawn, the preliminary reports show yet another Delta site with Middle Bronze Canaanite remains.

Tell el-Kebir

Late in 1993, members of the Egyptian Antiquities Organization discovered tombs at this eastern Delta site (fig. 2). The contents were from the 2nd Intermediate Period and the high quality of the remains has led to the speculation that these were perhaps royal tombs. To date, preliminary publication of this material has not appeared, nor has the historical range for these tombs been announced. But it is safe to say that another delta site has revealed Canaanite materials prior to the New Kingdom.

III. Conclusion

This review of epigraphic and archaeological data clearly demonstrates that Egypt was frequented by the peoples of the Levant, especially as a result of climatic problems that resulted in drought (as "Merikare" reports) from the end of the Old Kingdom (ca. 2190 B.C.) through the Second Intermediate Period (ca. 1786–1550 B.C.). Even during the Empire Period, there are records of hunger and thirst driving people from Canaan and Sinai to Egypt for relief.[149] Despite the problem of placing the Genesis Patriarchs in a precise historical context, and even a denial by some scholars that these figures ever existed,[150] they seem to fill in a period covering the nineteenth through mid-sixteenth centuries, a range followed by scholars who accept the essential historicity of Genesis.[151] This horizon coincides with the period from the end of the Middle Kingdom and into the Second Intermediate Period (ca. 1786–1550 B.C.) when Egypt was for a second time visited by emigrating Semitic-speaking peoples who occupied the eastern Delta. During the century of Hyksos domination of the Delta (ca. 1650–1540 B.C.), Egypt was apparently also accessible to the transhumant population of Canaan and the Sinai. Thus, for a period roughly from 1800 to 1540 B.C., Egypt was an attractive place for the Semitic-speaking people of western Asia to migrate, and during the final century, Lower Egypt was controlled politically by rulers of Syro-Palestinian origins in Avaris. This span of time coincides with the traditional "Patriarchal Period" and therefore fits the period and circumstances described in Genesis when Abraham, Isaac (almost), and Jacob went to Egypt in search of food, water, and green pastures.

Notes

1 Gerhard von Rad, *The Problem of the Hexateuch and Other Essays* (Edinburgh: Oliver and Boyd, 1966) 3–8 (German orig. 1938); A. D. H. Mayes, *Deuteronomy* (London: Marshall, Morgan, and Scott, 1979) 333–334; J. A. Thompson, *Deuteronomy* (Downers Grove, Ill.: IV Press, 1974) 254–255.

2 Concerning the skepticism of our times and the ideological nature of historical minimalists, see Iain Provan, "Ideologies, Literary and Critical: Reflections on Recent Writing on the History of Israel," *JBL* 114 (1995) 585–606.

3 *Ancient Israel: A New History of Israelite Society* (Sheffield: *JSOT* Press, 1988) 31.

4 David Hackett Fischer, *Historians' Fallacies: Toward a Logic of Historical Thought* (New York: Harper and Row, 1970) 47–48.

5 For a discussion of the source- and form-critical questions raised by this so-called "doublet" and the sociolegal issues, see James K. Hoffmeier, "The Wives' Tales of Genesis 12, 20 & 26 and the Covenants at Beer-Sheba," *TB* 43 no. 1 (1992) 81–99.

6 "Egyptians in Sinai and Palestine," *CAH,* vol. 1, pt. 2, 351.

7 The label is British Museum 55586 and pictures of it are available in many publications including Cyril Aldred, *Egypt to the End of the Old Kingdom* (New York: McGraw-Hill, 1965) 64; Emma Swan Hall, *The Pharaoh Smites His Enemies*, Münchner Ägyptologische Studien 44, (Munich: 1986) fig. 9.

8 Hall, *Pharaoh Smites His Enemies*, figs. 10–20.

9 *Urk.* I, 103–104. Translation in Miriam Lichtheim, *Ancient Egyptian Literature*, vol. 1 (Berkeley and Los Angeles: University of California Press, 1975) 20.

10 Bottero, *CAH,* vol. 1, pt. 2, 361; A. H. Gardiner, *Egypt of the Pharaohs* (New York: Oxford University Press, 1961) 96; and Donald B. Redford, *Egypt, Canaan, and Israel in Ancient Times* (Princeton: Princeton University Press, 1992) 55 n.78.

11 *Ancient Egypt: A Cultural Topography* (Chicago: University of Chicago Press, 1961) 191–192. Text in H. Junker, *Giza III*, Akademie des Wissenschaften in Wien (Vienna: Holder-Pichler-Tempsky, 1938) 172–173.

12 For a useful survey of this period, see William C. Hayes, "The Middle Kingdom in Egypt: Internal History from the Rise of the Heracleopolitans to the Death of Ammenemes III," *CAH*, vol. 1, pt. 2, 464–479.

13 Ibid., 464.

14 Most Egyptologists regard "Merikare" as a reliable source for constructing the history of the Tenth Dynasty, but there have been dissenters, e.g., Gun Bjorkman, "Egyptology and Historical Method," *Orientalia Suecana* 13 (1964) 9–33. Against Bjorkman's skepticism, see William A. Ward, *Egypt and the East Mediterranean World 2200–1900* (Beirut: American Univesity Press, 1970) for a more positive assessment of this text.

15 This translation is my own, based on the late Professor Wolfgang Helck's critical edition, *Die Lehre für König Merikare*, Kleine Ägyptische Texte (Wiesbaden: Otto Harrassowitz, 1977), and rests heavily on the work done with my late, lamented professor, Ronald Williams, in his seminar on reading Egyptian wisdom texts about twenty years ago. His insights and comments were always most helpful. The standard anthologies all contain translations of "Merikare," e.g., John Wilson in *ANET*, 414–418; R. O. Faulkner, *The Literature of Ancient Egypt*, ed. W. K. Simpson (New Haven: Yale University Press, 1973) 180–192; Lichtheim, *Ancient Egyptian Literature* vol. 1, 97–109. The passage about the Asiatics in Egypt has been throughly studied, translated, and commented upon by Ward, *Egypt and the East Mediterranean*, 23–35, and a fresh rendition of part of this lengthy unit has recently been made by Redford, *Egypt, Canaan, and Israel*, 67–68. A thorough study has been made by Joachim F. Quack, *Studien zur Lehre für Merikare* (Wiesbaden: Otto Harrassowitz, 1992).

16 The precise location of these Delta toponyms is uncertain, althought *Ḥwt šnw* has been located near Heliopolis (Ward, *Egypt and the East Mediterranean*, 25 n.95).

17 There is little certainty about the translation of *pdswt nt s.Wb*, vol. 1, 567 offers "delta coast" or "inland sea," while Helck suggests "lagunendinün" (*Lehre für König Merikare*, 51), and Faulkner (*Literature of Ancient Egypt*, 187) and Lichtheim (*Ancient Egyptian Literature*, vol. 1, 103) suggest "sand dunes" and "coast of the sea" respectively.

18 I.e., the people of the Delta he subjected are paying tribute to Khety.

19 Literally "the inner islands." For the meaning "central Delta," see N. C. Grimal, *La Stèle Triomphale de Pi(ᶜnkh)y au Musée du Caire* (Cairo: IFAO, 1981) 38, no. 88.

20 There are several textual problems with this line, and thus a certain translation is impossible.

21 Helck (*Lehre für König Merikare*, 53) restores this as 𓄿𓂝 𓆣, however in hieratic 𓆣 is easily confused with 𓋴, which is what we would expect. The likely reading is 𓄿𓂝𓋴. The point is that boats are able to dock (and sail) in this part of the Delta that had previously been dangerous for commercial ventures from Hnes, Khety's capital.

22 An eastern Delta location seems to fit the geographical context for this toponym despite a number of scholars who have identified *Ḥbnw* with a site in middle Egypt, however, the context is more suggestive of a eastern Delta site. (See Ward's lengthy note on this identification in *Egypt and the East Mediterranean* 28 n.113.) Ward postulates that *Ḥbnw* is a corrupt writing for *ḥwt-bnw*, a topopnym near *T̲3rw* that makes good sense.

23 Normally written *W3wt ḥr*, "Ways of Horus," but here for some unknown reason *w3t* (singular) is written. The "Ways of Horus" is the so-called "military road" across north Sinai to Palestine; cf. A. H. Gardiner, "The Ancient Military Road Between Egypt and Palestine," *JEA* 6 (1920) 99–116. For recent archaeological work along this route, see Eliezer Oren, "The 'Ways of Horus' in North Sinai," in *Egypt, Israel, Sinai: Archaeological and Historical Relationships in the Biblical Period*, ed. A. F. Rainey (Tel Aviv: Tel Aviv University Press, 1987) 69–119. However, in a recent article, Dominique Valbelle argues against the traditional interpretation that *w3t ḥr* is the name of the road or route ("La (Les) Route(s)-D'Horus," in *Hommages à Jean Leclant* vol. 4, Bibliothèque de l'École des Hautes Études 106, [Cairo: IFAO,1994] 379–386). Rather, she believes a geographical region is meant that includes north Sinai and the coastal highway. Clearly *W3t ḥr* is refering to the region that includes the northeast Delta and into Sinai. Along these same lines, Gardiner referred to "the Ways of Horus" in the Herakleopolitan period as "a garrison town" in *JEA* 6 (1920) 115.

24 Only one witness of this line survives: Pap. Petersburg. The word has one ⟞ upon another, suggesting the word *ᶜᶜi*, "jabber" (*CDME* 38) or "babbler (of a foreign language)" (see Faulkner, *Literature of Ancient Egypt*, 187 n.39). R. J. Williams thought that Faulkner was right. However, Ward (*Egypt and the East Mediterranean*, 29 n.116) thinks that the text is corrupt and suggests emending *ḥsf ᶜᶜ.wy* to read *ḥsf-ᶜ*, "oppose." Lichtheim (*Ancient Egyptian Literature*, vol. 1, 103) follows Ward's suggestion. Since the other two witnesses to "Merikare" have lacunae at this juncture, one cannot be certain how to read this word. Regardless of which reading is followed, it is clear that the king populated the eastern frontier with Egyptians whose presence would be a deterent to further Asiatic infiltration.

25 This line is difficult to translate. Lichtheim (*Ancient Egyptian Literature*, vol. 1, 104) offers "When the Bowmen (*pdtyw*, "foreigners') were a sealed wall, I breached [their strongholds]." "A sealed wall" would have been metaphorical for protection, Lichtheim suggests, meaning that the sheer numbers and strength of the Asiatics made them like a fortified stronghold (ibid., 109 n.20).

26 Opinions differ on the translation of *šd m dnit* and will be fully discussed below.

27 *Egypt and the East Mediterranean*, 25–30.

28 *CDME*, 97; *Wb*, vol. 1, 570 renders it "Barbarenstamm."

29 *CDME*, 38; *Wb*, vol. 1, 167–168.

30 Redford, *Egypt, Canaan, and Israel*, 100. It might be suggested that this term could apply to other speakers of foreign languages, not just Semites.

31 *Egypt and the East Mediterranean*, 31.

32 J. Wilson, *ANET*, 417.

33 Faulkner, *Literature of Ancient Egypt*, 188.

34 Ibid.

35 *Ancient Egypt*, 192.

36 Ibid.

37 *Ancient Egyptian Literature*, vol. 1, 104.

38 *Lehre für König Merikare*, 63.

39 *Studien zur Lehre für Merikare*, 59 n.d.

40 Ibid.

41 Ward, *Egypt and the East Mediterranean*, 30 n.125; Cf. A. H. Gardiner, *Egyptian Grammar*, 3d ed. (London: Oxford University Press, 1969) § 250.

42 *Wb*, vol. 5, 465.

43 Pap. Moscow contains a lacuna here. See Helck, *Lehre für König Merikare*, 61.

44 Lichtheim, *Ancient Egyptian Literature*, vol. 1, 104, and n.20.

45 Ibid., n.20; J. Yoyotte, "Processions Géographiques Mentionnant le Fayoum et ses Localités," *BIFAO* 61 (1962) 116–117.

46 "Its" in this line is the 3d feminine suffix and must refer back to *dnit*, which is feminine.

47 Ward, *Egypt and the East Mediterranean*, 34.

48 Amihai Sneh, Tuvia Weissbrod, and Itamar Perath, "Evidence for an Ancient Egyptian Frontier Canal," *American Scientist* 63 (1975) 542–548.

49 Hans Goedicke, *The Protocol of Neferyt* (Baltimore: Johns Hopkins University Press, 1977) is quite certain of assigning it to the founder of Dynasty 12, stating, "There can be no doubt that the text was written in the time of Amenemhet I."

50 Redford, *Egypt, Canaan, and Israel*, 68.

51 On the propagandist nature of this and other Twelfth Dynasty works, see A. de Buck, "La Litterérature et la politque sous la douzième dynastie égyptienne," in M. David, B. A. van Groningen, and E. M. Meijers, eds., *Symbolae ad jus et historian antiquitatis pertinentes Julio Christiano van Oven dedicatae* (Leiden: Brill 1946), 1–28; E. Otto, "Weltanschauliche und politische Tendenzschriften," in B. Spuler, ed., *Handbuch der Orientalistik*, Vol 1.: "Aegyptologie," "Literatur" (Leiden: Brill, 1952) 111–119; G. Posener, *Littérature et politique dans l'Egypte de l'Egypte de la XIIᵉ dynastie* (Paris, Bibliothèque de l'École des Hautes Études 1956); R. J. Williams, "Literature as a Medium of Political Propaganda in Ancient Egypt," in *Seed of Wisdom: Essays in Honour of T. J. Meek*, ed. W. S. McCullough (Toronto: University of Toronto Press, 1964) 14–30.

52 I concur with Lichtheim (*Ancient Egyptian Literature*, vol. 1, 139) that what is portrayed here is "artificial gloom" and the "national distress topos." However, I believe that the topos had its origin in the First Intermediate Period and reflects the problems of that era. This suggestion is supported by the similar language in "Merikare" that undoubtedly dated to the First Intermediate Period. Redford (*Egypt, Canaan, and Israel*, 68) also sees a similarity between the manner in which the Asiatic is portrayed in "Merikare" and "Neferti," saying, "In some respects that Asiatic in Neferty resembles the description vouchsafed by the Instruction for Merikare, about one hundred years earlier."

53 Redford, *Egypt, Canaan, and Israel*, 68.

54 The translation is my own, based on Wolfgang Helck's critical edition, *Die*

Prophezeiung des Nfr.tj, Kleine Ägyptische Texte (Wiesbaden: Otto Harrassowitz, 1970) 16–28.

55 I render *m ḫpš.sn* as "with their swords" because *ḫpš* has the determinative ⏧.

56 This is clearly a metaphor. That the bird refers to the Asian presence is clarified in the following paragraph.

57 I agree with Lichtheim's treatment of the word *ḏf3w* (*Ancient Egyptian Literature*, vol. 1, 144, n. 6). Goedicke's translation, "those aiming for food" (*Neferyt*, 87), also captures the essence.

58 The translation of this sentence is most difficult, Lichtheim offered only "If the fortress is [crowded]..............," and did not even suggest a translation of the end of line 34 and the beginning of 35.

59 Goedicke (*Neferyt*, 92) believes that these refer to fortifications that go back to the Old Kingdom, as well as to those mentioned in "Merikare" that were built by the Herakleopolitan monarchs.

60 See Redford's comment quoted above in n. 53.

61 The text is in Helck's *Nfr.tj* 56–57.

62 The publication of the text is in A. H. Gardiner, *Admonitions of an Egyptian Sage* (Leipzig: J. C. Hinrichs 1909). Translations are available in Lichtheim, *Ancient Egyptian Literature*, vol. 1, 149–163; Faulkner, *Literature of Ancient Egypt*, 210–229; and John Wilson, *ANET*, 441–444.

63 Gardiner (*Admonitions*, 111) maintains that it was written during the Twelfth Dynasty, but looked back to the preceding Intermediate Period. John Van Seters ("A Date for the 'Admonitions' in the Second Intermediate Period," *JEA* 50 [1964] 13–23) argued that the period of turmoil reflected in Ipuwer was the Second Intermediate Period. This view has been overwhelmingly rejected (see Redford, *Egypt, Canaan, and Israel*, 66 n. 47).

64 A. H. Gardiner, "An Ancient List of the Fortresses of Nubia," *JEA* 3 (1916) 184–192; Bruce Trigger, "The Reasons for the Construction of the Second Cataract Forts," *JSSEA* 12 no. 1 (1982) 1–6; and Stuart Tyson Smith, "Askut and the Role of the Second Cataract Forts," *JARCE* 28 (1991) 107–132.

65 A. M. Blackman, *Middle Egyptian Stories*, Bibliotheca Aegyptiaca, vol. 2 (Brussels: Édition de la Fondation Égyptologique Reine Élizabeth 1932) 11–12.

66 Pierre Montet, *Géographie de L'Égypte Ancienne*, vol. 1 (Paris: Imprimerie Nationale, 1957) 216.

67 For a reexamination of the text, see Ronald Leprohon, "A New Look at an Old Object: Stela M.F.A. 13.3967/20.1222," *JSSEA* 12 no. 2 (1982) 75–76.

68 The text of the inscription can be seen in a photograph ibid., pl. 6, and in Hans Goedicke's follow-up study, "Another Look at an Old Object," *BES* 4 (1982) 77.

69 *BES* 4 (1982) 72-75.

70 Ibid.

71 Gardiner, *Egypt of the Pharaohs*, 131–132; Nicholas Grimal, *A History of Ancient Egypt* (Oxford: Blackwell, 1992) 160.

72 *BES* 4 (1982) 75.

73 "Une nouvelle forteresse sur la route d'Horus: Tell Heboua 1986 (North Sinaï)," *CRIPEL* 9 (1987) 13–16. His suggestion that it is Tjaru was made verbally to me during my visit to the site in March 1994.

74 Dr. Mohamed Abd el-Maksoud was kind enough to show me a drawing of the inscription prior to its publication in *ASAE* 69 (1988) 1–3.

75 During my visit to Hebua in April 1995, Dr. Mohamed informed me that Hyksos-era materials had recently come to light, including a horse burial from what he called a

"late Hyksos" period locus. At present this material is not published. Dr. Mohammed believes that Twelfth Dynasty remains will be found.

76 Excavations at T 21 were undertaken initially by Eliezer Oren ("Migdol: A New Fortress on the Edge of the Eastern Nile Delta," *BASOR* 256 [1984] / 44) but now is being dug by Donald Redford and a team from the University of Toronto. Their work has only begun and publications are not yet prepared. In a report on the Toronto excavations at the annual meetings of the American Research Center in Egypt (April 1994), Dr. F. T. Miosi reported that only Persian levels had been reached. For an overview of the archaeological work underway in North Sinai, see Dominique Valbelle et al., "Reconnaissance archéologique à la pointe du Delta. Rapport préliminaire sure les saisons 1990 et 1991," *CRIPEL* 14 (1992) 11-31 and Maryvonne Chartier-Raymond et al., "Reconnaissance archéologique à la pointe orientale du Delta, Campagne 1992," *CRIPEL* 15 (1993) 45-71.

77 William C. Hayes, *A Papyrus of the Late Middle Kingdom in the Brooklyn Museum* [Papyrus Brooklyn 35.1446] (New York: The Brooklyn Museum, 1955).

78 Ibid., 92-99. For a thorough discussion of Semitic names in this document, see William F. Albright, "Northwest-Semitic Names in a List of Egyptian Slaves from the Eighteenth Century B.C.," *JAOS* 74 (1954) 222-233 and Georges Posener, "Les Asiatiques en Égypte sous les XIIᵉ et XIIIᵉ Dynasties," *Syria* 34 (1957) 145-163.

79 *A Papyrus of the Late Middle Kingdom*, 99.

80 Ibid.

81 Jaromír Málek and Stephen Quirke, "Memphis, 1991: Epigraphy," *JEA* 78 (1992) 14, l. 16.

82 Ibid. See a recent discussion of this text by Kenneth Kitchen, "Genesis 12-50 in the Near Eastern World," in *He Swore an Oath: Biblical Themes from Genesis 12-50*, ed. R. S. Hess et. al. (Cambridge: Tyndale House, 1993) 79. On this practice in the New Kingdom, see J. K. Hoffmeier, *TB* 43 no. 1 (1992) 87-91, and discussion below in chap. 6, §V.

83 Málek and Quirke, *JEA* 78 (1992) 14.

84 Michael Hoffman, *Egypt Before the Pharaohs* (London: ARK Paperbacks, 1980) 176, 189, 197, 201-204, 338-339; W. B. Emery, *Archaic Egypt* (Baltimore: Penguin Books, 1961) 204-205; S. Yeivin, "Early Contacts between Canaan and Egypt," *IEJ* 10 (1960) 193-205; R. Gophna, "Egyptian Immigration into Canaan during the First Dynasty?" *Tel Aviv* 3 (1976) 31-37; A. Ben-Tor, "New Light on the Relations Between Egypt and Southern Palestine During the Early Bronze Age," *BASOR* 281 (1991) 3-10; R. Amiran, "An Egyptian Jar Fragment with the Name of Narmer from Arad," *IEJ* 24 (1974) 4-12; R. Amiran, "The Narmer Jar Fragment from Arad: An Addendum," *IEJ* 26 (1976) 45-46; Amihai Mazar, *Archaeology of the Land of the Bible 10,000-586 B.C.E.* (New York: Doubleday, 1990) 106-107.

85 D. B. Redford, "The Acquistion of Foreign Goods and Services in the Old Kingdom," *Scripta Mediterranea* 2 (1981) 5-16; D. B. Redford, "Egypt and Western Asia in the Old Kingdom," *JARCE* 23 (1986) 125-143; Redford, *Egypt, Canaan, and Israel*, chap. 2; Barry Kemp, *Ancient Egypt: A Social History*, ed. B. G. Trigger et al. (Cambridge: Cambridge Univesity Press, 1983) 137-149.

86 Percy E. Newberry, *Beni Hasan I* (London: EEF, 1893) 63, pl. 30-31.

87 "Abi-Sha(i)'s Representation in Beni Hasan," *JARCE* 21 (1984) 206-207.

88 Ibid., 207.

89 "The Career of Khnumhotep III of Beni Hasan and the So-Called 'Decline of the Nomarchs,'" in *Middle Kingdom Studies*, ed. Stephen Quirke (New Malden, Surrey: SIA, 1991) 56.

90 *Ancient Egypt*, 142.

91   A view expressed earlier on by Posener, *Syria* 34 (1957) 158–160.

92   "Asiatics at Lahun: A Preliminary Report," in *Sesto Congresso Internazionale di Egittologia Atti*, vol. 2, ed. S. Curto et al. (Turin: 1992) 291–297.

93   Ibid.

94   Ibid., 296.

95   Redford, *Egypt, Canaan, and Israel*, 102–103.

96   E.g., Kemp, *Ancient Egypt*, 156–157; Redford and Weinstein, "Hyksos," *ABD*, vol. 3, 341, 344–345.

97   *Avaris and Piramesse: Archaeolgical Exploration in the Eastern Nile Delta*. Proceedings of the British Academy, vol. 65 (London: Oxford University Press, 1986) 228–229.

98   Bietak, "Canaanites in the Eastern Delta," in *Egypt, Israel, Sinai: Archaeological and Historical Relationships in the Biblical Period*, ed. A. F. Rainey (Jerusalem: Tel Aviv University Press, 1987) 41. The First Intermediate Period material is also discussed in *Avaris and Piramesse*, 293, and is labeled as stratum "e."

99   Ibid., 292.

100   Eric Uphill, *The Temples of Per Ramesses* (Warminster: Aris and Phillips, 1984) 199–200.

101   Ibid., 204–205.

102   Manfred Bietak, "The Middle Bronze Age of the Levant—A New Approach to Relative and Absolute Chronology," in *High, Middle or Low? Acts of an International Colloquium on Absolute Chronology Held at the University of Göthenburg 20th–22nd August 1987*, pt. 3, ed. Paul Åström (Gothenburg: Paul Åström, 1989) 93, 99; cf. Bietak, *Avaris and Piramesse*, which reviews the stratigraphic history.

103   Ibid., 89.

104   Josephus, *Against Apion I*, trans. H. St. J. Thackeray (Cambridge, Mass.: Harvard University Press, 1926) §§65–79.

105   *The Hyksos Reconsidered*, Studies in Ancient Oriental Civilization, vol. 18 (Chicago: University of Chicago Press, 1939) 23.

106   *The Culture of Ancient Egypt* (Chicago: University of Chicago Press, 1951),158, 163.

107   *The Rise and Fall of the Middle Kingdom of Thebes* (New York: Macmillan, 1947) and *Art of Warfare in Biblical Lands*, vol. 1 (New York: Macmillan, 1963) 75, 86.

108   "The Hyksos in Egypt," *JEA* 37 (1951) 53–71.

109   *The Hyksos: A New Investigation* (New Haven: Yale University Press, 1966) 121–126.

110   *Die Beziehungen Ägyptens zu Vorderasien im 3. und 2. Jahrtausend V. Chr*, Ägyptologische Abhandlungen, vol. 5 (Wiesbaden: Otto Harrassowitz, 1962) 92–97.

111   "The Hyksos in History and Tradition," *Orientalia* 39 (1970) 1–51; *Egypt, Canaan, and Israel*, 101–106; and "Hyksos" *ABD*, vol. 3 (1992) 341–344.

112   *Egypt, Canaan, and Israel*, 102.

113   Bietak, in *High, Middle or Low?* 82–88. The term "Hyksos" is applied to the rulers of Dynasties 15–17.

114   Ibid., 114, fig. 7, to see Bietak's helpful chart.

115   *Avaris and Piramesse*, 256.

116   Ibid., 268; Bietak, "Zur Herkunft des Seth von Avaris," *ÄL*, vol. 1 (1990) 9–16.

117   Ibid., 9–16. In a letter to me dated August 21, 1989, Professor Bietak wrote, "Our findings are that the town was not deliberately destroyed, but plundered and deserted. The only area where we found some evidence of continuity in settlement is the area of the temple of Sutekh [Seth], but even this does not exclude an interval of let us say 20 or 30 years. So, there is a possibility that in the temple area alone a continuation of the cult was permitted, while the rest of the town had been deserted throughout the 18th

Dynasty." This position has now changed with new discoveries of the past two years. They are introduced below in chap. 5, §V.

118 Kees, *Ancient Egypt,* 29, 35.

119 *On an Egyptian/Asiatic Frontier: An Archaeological History of the Wadi Tumilat* (University of Chicago: UMI Dissertations, 1989).

120 Ibid., 71–81.

121 Ibid., 177, 227–270; Carol Redmount, "Wadi Tumilat Survey," *The ARCE Newsletter* 133 (1986) 22–24.

122 *Egyptian/Asiatic Frontier,* 261.

123 John S. Holladay, Jr., *Tell el-Maskhuta: Preliminary Report on the Wadi Tumilat Project 1978–1979, Cities of the Delta, Part III, ARCE* Reports, vol. 6 (Malibu: Undena Publications, 1982) 44–47, 50.

124 Ibid., 247.

125 Ibid.

126 Ibid., 245, pl. 45.

127 These dates appear together in the charts in Kitchen's entry "Egypt, History of (Chronology)" in *ABD,* vol. 2, 329.

128 Holladay, *Tell el-Maskhuta,* 146.

129 E. Naville, *The Shrine of Saft El-Henneh and the Land of Goshen* (London: EEF, 1887) and *The Store-city of Pithom and the Route of the Exodus* (EEF Memoir, 1888); W. M. F. Petrie, *Hyksos and Israelite Cities* (London: British School of Archaeology, 1906) 28–34.

130 Ibid., 32–34.

131 Ibid., 28.

132 Ibid., pl. 33, 4.

133 *Egypt, Canaan, and Israel,* 80 n.50.

134 *Egyptian/Asiatic Frontier,* 128–129.

135 My colleague Alfred Hoerth was a member of this expedition in 1977–1978. He tells me he believes there were Middle Bronze Age materials, including a Syrian seal. While Goedicke has not published the material, he has offered some historical observations based on his finds. Cf. "Ramesses II and the Wadi Tumilat," *VA* 3 (1987) 13–24 and "Papyrus Anastasi VI 51–61," *SAK* 14 (1987) 83–98.

136 *Hyksos and Israelite Cities,* 1–16.

137 Ibid., 3–5, pl. 2.

138 "Der 'hohe Sand in Heliopolis,'" *ZÄS* 71 (1935) 107–111.

139 Mazar, *Archaeology of the Land of the Bible,* 198–204.

140 G. R. H. Wright, "Tell el-Yehudiah and the Glacis," *ZDPV* 84 (1968) 1–17.

141 Petrie, *Hyksos and Israelite Cities,* 10–16.

142 "Graves at Tell el-Yehudiyeh: Reviewed after a Life-time," in *Archaeology in the Levant: Essays for Kathleen Kenyon,* ed. R. Moorey and P. Parr (Warminster: Aris and Phillips, 1978) 76.

143 Ibid., 81.

144 Ibid., 87.

145 *Bulletin de la Société Française d'Egyptologie* 1 (1949) 12–13.

146 Ibid., 8, shows one such tomb.

147 Fouad Yacoub, "Excavations at Tel Farasha," *ASAE* 65 (1983) 175–176.

148 Ibid., pl. 4–5.

149 For the tomb of Horemheb at Sakkara (*ANET,* 251) and Pap. Anastasi VI (*LEM,* 76) and R. A. Caminos, *Late-Egyptian Miscellanies* (London: Oxford University Press, 1954) 293.

150 Van Seters and Thompson (for discussion and references see chap. 1, n.1) in the mid-1970s argued against the historicity of Abraham, Isaac, and Jacob and continue to maintain their view.

151 The historicity of the Hebrew Patriarchs and a date in first third of the second millennium is advanced by a number of British scholars, cf. K. A. Kitchen, *Ancient Orient and the Old Testament* (Downers Grove, Ill.: IV Press, 1966) 35 – 56 and *The Bible in Its World* (Exeter: Paternoster, 1977) 56 – 74; *Essays on the Patriarchal Narratives*, ed. A. R. Millard and D. J. Wiseman (Winona Lake, Ind.: Eisenbrauns, 1983) and A. R. Millard, "Abraham," *ABD*, vol. 1 (1992) 35 – 41. Cyrus Gordon opts for a lower chronology for the Patriarchal period, viz. the Amarna period or fourteenth century (cf. *The Ancient Near East* [New York: W. W. Norton, 1965] 115 – 125). While this scenario is plausible, I do not find the rationale very compelling. Those who have accepted this view, by and large, are Gordon's students.

Figure 1. The Merneptah Stela. Courtesy of the Petrie Museum, University College, London.

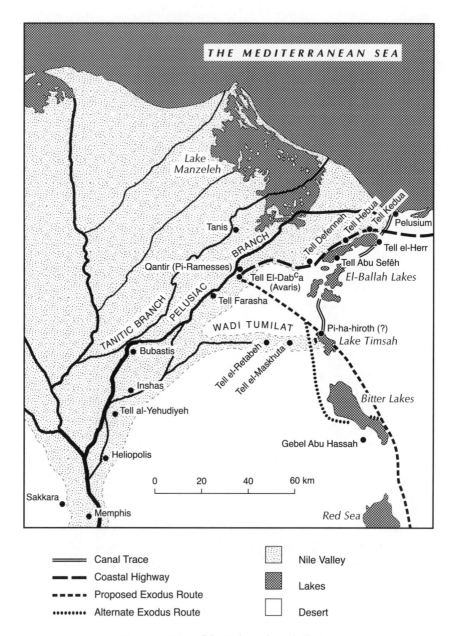

Figure 2. Map of the Delta and north Sinai.

THE MEDITERRANEAN SEA

Lake Manzeleh

Tanis

Qantir (Pi-Ramesses)

Tell El-Dab^ca (Avaris)

Tell Farasha

WADI TUMILAT

Bubastis

Tell el-Retabeh

Tell el-Maskhuta

Inshas

Tell al-Yehudiyeh

Heliopolis

Gebel Abu Hassah

Sakkara

Memphis

Tell Defenneh

Tell Hebua

Tell Kedua

Pelusium

Tell el-Herr

Tell Abu Sefêh

El-Ballah Lakes

Pi-ha-hiroth (?)

Lake Timsah

Bitter Lakes

Red Sea

TANITIC BRANCH

PELUSIAC

BRANCH

0   20   40   60 km

Canal Trace

Coastal Highway

Proposed Exodus Route

Alternate Exodus Route

Nile Valley

Lakes

Desert

Figure 3. Papyrus.
Brooklyn 35.1446, verso,
lines 1–16. Courtesy of
the Brooklyn Museum.

Figure 4. Papyrus. Chester Beatty, BM 10683: section of dream manual. Courtesy of the
British Museum.

Figure 5. Reward ceremony of General Horemheb (ca. 1350 B.C.) in his Sakkara tomb. Photo courtesy of the Rijksmuseum, Leiden.

Figure 6. Investiture of Vizier Paser. From tomb 106 in the Theban Necropolis. From drawing by Kristine Henriksen.

Figure 7. Figure of
Aper-el and his wife
from their Sakkara
tomb. Courtesy of
Alain Zivie.

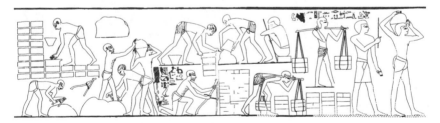

Figure 8. Semitic and Nubian POWs making bricks. From N. de Garis Davies, *The Tomb
of Rekhmire at Thebes* (New York: Metropolitan Museum of Art, 1943) 47. With permission
of the MMA.

Figure 9. Taskmaster with stick overseeing POWs in brickmaking work. Photo by James K. Hoffmeier.

Figure 10. Seti I returning from campaign against Shasu-bedouin. The canal is to the right of the POWs and Fortress Tjaru apparently straddles the canal. From The Epigraphic Survey, *The Battle Reliefs of King Sety I* (Chicago: The Oriental Institute, 1986), pl. 2. With permision of the OI.

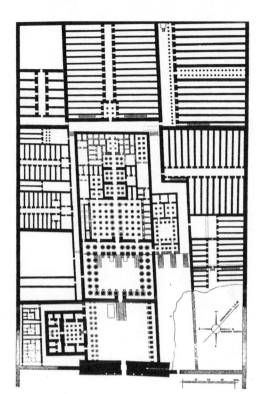

Figure 11. Plan of Ramesseum, Western Thebes, with brick storage facilities surrounding the temple. From J. E. Quibell, *The Ramesseum* (London: Egyptian Research account, 1896).

Figure 12. Brick storage facilities at rear of Ramesseum. Photo by James K. Hoffmeier.

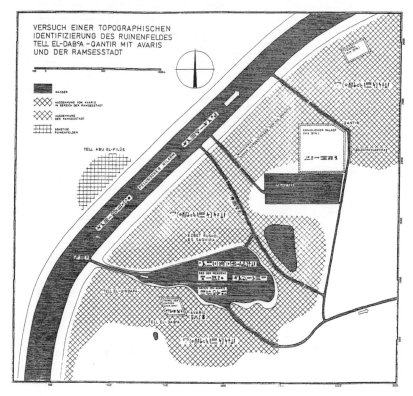

Figure 13. Map of Avaris-Qantir area. From Manfred Bietak, *Tell el-Dab^c a*, vol. 2 (Vienna: Österreichischen Akademie der Wissenschaft, 1975) fig. 44.

Figure 14. Ramesses II smiting the head of a foreigner before Atum, who is called "Lord of Tjeku." The block is from Tell el-Retabeh, perhaps from a Temple of Atum. From W. M. F. Petrie, *Hyksos and Israelite Cities* (London: British School of Archaeology, 1906), pl. 30.

Figure 15. Thutmose IV shown smiting the heads of his enemies. The text to the right of his arm reads *nb ḫpš*, "possessor of a powerful arm." From W. Wreszinksi, *Atlas zur altägyptischen Kulturgeschichte* (Leipzig: J. C. Hinrichs, 1923) 1.

Figure 16. Statue of Senusert I or II with the long shepherd's crook. Courtesy of Metropolitan Museum of Art, N.Y. (MMA 14.3.17).

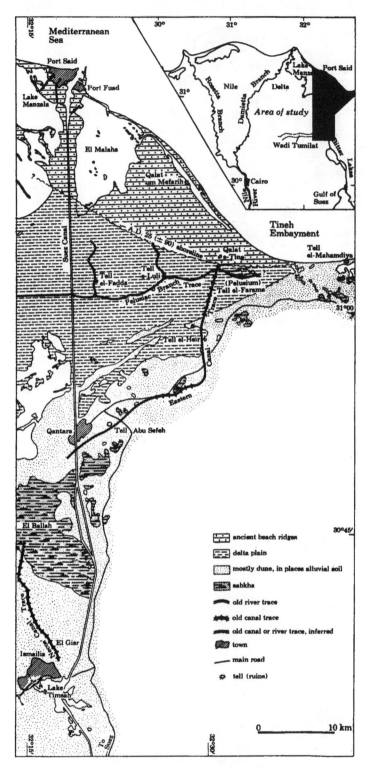

Figure 17. Israel
Geological Survey
map of the area
Eastern Frontier
Canal. Courtesy
of Tuvia Weissbrod.

Figure 18. Traces of the Eastern Frontier Canal from the air. This 2-kilometer stretch is located between Tell Abu Sefêh and Tell el-Herr. Courtesy of Tuvia Weissbrod, Israel Geological Survey.

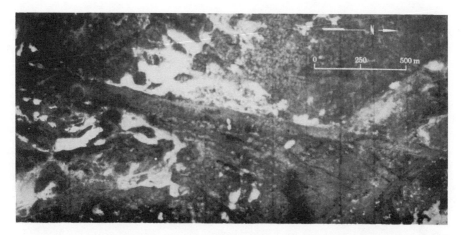

Figure 19. Traces of the Eastern Frontier Canal from the air. This 2.5-kilometer stretch is located north of Tell el-Herr. Courtesy of Tuvia Weissbrod, Israel Geological Survey.

Figure 20. Ismailiya Canal. The high embankments show the long history of this section, well back into pharaonic times.

Figure 21. Canal through the Wadi Tumilat by Tell el-Maskhuta.

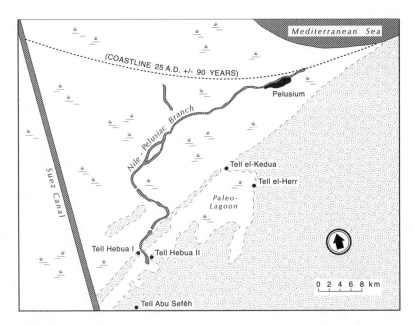

Figure 22. Based on Bruno Marcolongo's map of north Sinai showing his reconstruction of Pelusiac. From *CRIPEL* 14 (1992) fig. 1. Map by Patricia Neumann.

Figure 23. Sequence of forts and water sources along north Sinai in Seti I relief at Karnak. The Epigraphic Survey, *The Battle Reliefs of King Sety I* (Chicago: The Oriental Institute, 1986) pl. 5. With permission of the OI.

Figure 24. The defensive wall around the fortress at Tell Hebua.

Figure 25. The elevated strip of land on which Hebua sits is on the left. This area is sandy, whereas the low-lying area is darker and in the winter still has standing water (see left center). Photo by James K. Hoffmeier.

Figure 26. Ancient lake bed, looking west toward Hebua I. Photo by James K. Hoffmeier.

Figure 27. Lake Timsah with reeds surrounding it. Courtesy of Alfred J. Hoerth.

Figure 28. Reeds growing along the Suez Canal. Photo by James K. Hoffmeier.

Figure 29. Reed-filled swamps near Qantara in the area that was part of the El-Ballah lake system. Photo by James K. Hoffmeier.

4

JOSEPH IN EGYPT

> Now Joseph was taken down to Egypt, and
> Potiphar, an officer of Pharaoh . . . bought
> him from the Ishmaelites who had brought
> him down there
>
> Gen. 39:1

Because of the Egyptian setting of the Joseph narratives (Gen. 39–50), they have attracted the attention of several generations of Egyptologists and biblical scholars with interest in Egyptology. The Joseph story became a testing ground to determine if Egyptology had anything to contribute to Pentateuchal studies. Also, some thought that if sufficient Egyptian background could be detected, then the views of Gunkel, Gressmann, and Noth that treated the story as romance or novella could be challenged and the authenticity of the story demonstrated.[1] My intention is not to offer a complete history of the investigation of the Joseph story nor to present an exhaustive Egyptological analysis of the Egyptian backgrounds to the narrative. A major monograph would be required to accomplish this task. However, inasmuch as the Joseph story is central to the "Egypt in Israel" tradition, we are obliged to pay atention to this remarkable narrative. Consequently, this chapter will be limited to a brief sketch of some of the key works that have integrated Egyptological data with the Genesis material (I), a discussion of some recent form- and literary-critical developments (II), and a summary of the most compelling Egyptian data, including some new material (III), and then some conclusions will be drawn (IV).

I. Egyptological Investigations of the Joseph Story

A. S. Yahuda was one of the early pioneers of this approach.[2] His pan-Egyptianiz-ing tendencies did not win many supporters, although he made some valuable contributions. Many of his etymological shortcomings were pointed out by Joseph Vergote in the late 1950s.[3] Working within the confines of traditional source crit-icism, Vergote nevertheless viewed the narratives as historical, and he set the story within the New Kingdom. He has recently (1985) reaffirmed his early conclu-sions and defended his overall thesis against its critics, especially Redford and his tendency to date the origins of the Joseph story much later (see below).[4] Just prior to Vergote in the mid-1950s, the Dutch scholar J. M. A. Janssen also used his Egyptological training to discuss a number of aspects of the Joseph story, focusing attention on issues such as slavery, dreams, foreign officials in Egypt, Egyptian names and terms, famine, the life span of Joseph, and mummification.[5] Janssen concluded that the Egyptological materials do not answer all the questions one might hope, but they do demonstrate an authentic, although sometimes idealistic, presentation of Egypt.

In 1970 Donald Redford's influential monograph on the Joseph story was published,[6] it included sections dealing with the Egyptian backgrounds.[7] While acknowledging some Egyptianisms in the story, Redford argued that they pointed to the Saite-Persian period (i.e., late seventh to sixth centuries). In his lengthy re-view of Redford's study, Kenneth Kitchen thoroughly documented Redford's ten-dency to use late material selectively at the expense of earlier sources in his effort to date the Joseph narratives to the late period.[8] Some of Kitchen's differences with Redford will be discussed in the following sections. His general observation of Redford's appeal to Egyptian sources is that it was "at times over-hasty, less than accurate and (on presenting dating-evidence) occasionally misleading."[9] His pro-clivity towards selective in use of late sources prompts Kitchen to say, "Redford's treatment is reduced to the level of a Late-Period apologetic, not an impartial quest for the truth, 'early' or 'late.' "[10] Nevertheless, Redford's work has had a last-ing impact on Old Testament studies because it often departed from traditional source-critical analysis and thus broke new ground.[11]

Since Redford's monograph, there has been a dearth of scholarly investigation of the Joseph story from an Egyptological perspective. Though W. Lee Humphreys devoted a chapter of his 1988 literary monograph to Egyptian backgrounds, he of-fered nothing new from an Egyptological perspective.[12] Rather, he merely re-viewed the works of Vergote, Janssen, and Redford, occasionally citing parallels between Egyptian literature and the Joseph narratives, but his quotations come from dated translations, Breasted's *Ancient Records of Egypt* (1906) and Pritchard's *Ancient Near Eastern Texts* (1969). Furthermore, Humphreys naively accepts Re-ford's dating conclusions and is totally unaware of their shortcomings as pointed out by Kitchen. In fact, none of Kitchen's contributions to Joseph story studies are even cited.

In addition to his 1973 review, Kitchen has written a number of shorter stud-ies of this type over the past three decades and for some years now has been work-ing on a monograph that, when published, will be the first major study of Egyptological data related to the Joseph story since Redford's.[13] Given the continual appearance of new Egyptological data, especially because of the new emphasis on archaeological exploration in Egypt's Delta, Kitchen's work will be a welcome addition to the ongoing debate on the nature of the Joseph cycle.

While this is by no means an exhaustive treatment of those who have dealt with more specific details of the story, the results of the studies from Vergote (1959) to Kitchen's most recent observations (1993) agree that there are genuine Egyptian features present in the Genesis narrative, including terms, toponyms, and personal names. Redford stands alone among Egyptologists in thinking that these details point to the seventh through fifth centuries, but Janssen and Vergote believe the evidence points to the second half of the New Kingdom (ca. 1300–1100), while Kitchen maintains a late Middle Kingdom to Second Intermediate Period setting for Joseph, with the Ramesside period details indicating the compositional date of the narratives.[14]

II. Recent Literary Developments in Joseph Story Studies

Twentieth-century biblical scholars have invested considerable time in wrestling with source- and form-critical questions raised by the Joseph narratives. Naturally, the question of genre is imperative for guiding the reader to a proper interpretation of a piece of literature. So, too, with the Joseph narratives.

Source-Critical Developments

Since the end of the nineteenth century, it has become common to speak of the Joseph story being a blending of J and E sources. Gerhard von Rad followed his German forebears in this scenario even though he also argued that it was a novel and its *Sitz im Leben* was the wisdom school.[15] In recent years, confidence in a two-source analysis of this material has been waning.[16] R. N Whybray saw a dilemma in von Rad's position that it was a redaction of two separate sources and yet "a novel through and through."[17] He observes, "Composite authorship of a novel is not entirely unknown; but it is, to say the least, very difficult to believe that a novel of superlative merit could be the result of a *conflation* of two other novels. . . . If the Joseph Story as we now have it is a literary masterpiece in von Rad's sense, it must be a complete literary unity both in conception and execution; if it is a conflation of two sources, then von Rad's estimate of its high qualities as a novel must be largely illusory."[18] Simply put, von Rad (and his followers) cannot have it both ways. Consequently, Whybray rejects the two-source hypothesis and opts to call it a literary masterpiece in "Israel's wisdom tradition."[19]

Redford similarly dismissed the two-source reconstruction, but he also challenged the wisdom genre on the grounds that it was based on "a misinterpretation of the evidence."[20] This rejection of the didactic nature of the Joseph narrative was applauded by Kitchen.[21]

Despite the careful reasoning behind Whybray, Redford, and Kitchen's rejection of the two-source hypothesis, a number of Old Testament scholars continue to cling to nineteenth-century critical thinking. Robert B. Coote and David R. Ord, for instance, as recently as 1989 maintained that "the whole history of Joseph is actually an interweaving of the histories of Judah and Joseph."[22] Van Seters, on the other hand, denies the existence of E and asserts that the Joseph narratives are strictly the work of J.[23] What is clear is that there is a growing tendency to regard Genesis 39–50 as a literary unity and not a composite mélange. This development is due as much to the failures of source criticism to provide convincing answers regarding the nature of the material as it is the result of form-critical analysis and new literary approaches that undermine the documentary hypothesis (see chap. 1 § 2).

Structural and Genre Studies

The literary structure of the book of Genesis was the subject of several important investigations in the late 1980s. Gary Rendsburg showed that there are a series of chiastic cycles running from the primeval history through the Joseph narratives.[24] He demonstrates that the Joseph story is a chiastic unit with complementing themes and theme-words that link the episodes in the mirrored sections.[25] Rendsburg's work further succeeds in demonstrating the literary unity and the impossibility of discerning so-called secondary strands in the story, as well as underscoring the literary genius of the work. Approaching the Joseph story from a textlinguistic perspective that includes identifying macro- and microstructural chiasms led Robert Longacre to see the incredible complexity of the story and its literary unity.[26]

The past several decades have witnessed the appearance of a variety of genre studies of the Joseph story that differ widely on the nature of the Hebrew literature. Dorothy Irvin's 1977 study on the Joseph and Moses narratives unconventionally compared these Hebrew narratives with fictitious Egyptian folktales.[27] In so doing, she was able to produce a number of interesting parallels in plot motif. However, for valid comparative analysis of literature to take place, the works must be "commensurate," to borrow William Hallo's appropriate qualifier.[28] I maintain that it is inappropriate to compare two pieces of literature in order to identify the genre of the one from the other unless there is good evidence that the texts in question are indeed commensurate, although this is not to say that we cannot compare disparate pieces of Hebrew and Egyptian literature to provide general background information. My contention with Irvin is not how she compares motifs, but in how she moves from motif comparison to identifying the genre of the Hebrew material on the basis of noncomparable Egyptian sources. An example of what she does within Egyptian literature would be to take the "Taking of Joppa" (set in the reign of Thutmose III), which appears to be a legend, and compare it with the annalistic reports of the conquest of Megiddo. Based on this comparison, since both deal with the siege of a Canaanite city, should one identify the genre of the annals as legend? Obviously, such a conclusion would be absurd. But methodologically, this is what Irvin does.

By using "fiction" as her comparative category, Irvin ipso facto assumes that the Joseph and Moses stories are also fictitious. Kitchen has also questioned Irvin's approach, describing it as "the classic case of picking in advance one's comparative material to achieve a desired result (i.e., select only myths and tales to compare with the patriarchal narratives, so they are myths too).[29] It is not surprising then, that when she is joined by Thomas Thompson for the conclusion of the chapter, they speak of the "ahistorical nature of the tales which make up the Pentateuch."[30] J. B. Geyer has likewise pointed out some of Irvin's methodological shortcomings,[31] maintaining that the Genesis and Exodus narratives are minimally theological reflections on history that thus do tell us something about that history.[32]

An additional methodological problem with Irvin's work is that she holds the English Bible in one hand and Pritchard's *Ancient Near Eastern Texts*, or some other translation, in the other and draws comparative conclusions.[33] Irvin offers no comparison of the Hebrew or Egyptian terms in the literature she investigates. Consequently, the comparisons at times seem quite facile, paying attention to banal similarities while ignoring significant differences. For example, as in most treatments of the Joseph story, the "Tale of Two Brothers" is introduced.[34] As in the incident with Potiphar's wife, Bata is falsely accused by his sister-in-law of trying to seduce her when in fact she had made the advances to the upright lad (ll. 2.9 – 5.4).[35] This pericope occupies only about thirty lines out of around 330 in Gardiner's edition. The other 90 percent has nothing at all in common with the Joseph story.

The most recent, authoritative study of the "Tale of Two Brothers" with a comparison to the Joseph story was done by Egyptologist and folklorist Susan T. Hollis.[36] In a most exemplary manner, Hollis lists eleven features of the "spurned seductress" motif found in the Egyptian tale that are also found in Genesis 39.[37] Since "Tale of Two Brothers" dates to the late Nineteenth Dynasty, Hollis argues that the ideological and theological purposes of the two stories are significantly different. The Joseph story, she opines "tells of humans and human behavior and extols the actions of the one God who acts for his people in history, the former [Two Brothers] relates the actions of gods, albeit gods living on earth like humans."[38] Hollis also suggests that the Egyptian tale might "contain reflexes of an actual historical situation."[39] She goes on to postulate that the Egyptian story had its origins in the aftermath of the death of Merneptah (ca. 1203 B.C.) when there was a dispute about dynastic succession, and it may have served to help legitimate the successor. Her conclusion about the incident with Potiphar's wife is cogent: "Clearly, the Potiphar's wife motif encompasses more substance than is at first apparent and is not simply a folktale motif, at least in these early examples."[40] This observation is most damaging for the comparison Irvin and others try to make between these two pieces of literature.

Another problem with Irvin's comparative analysis is that often significant temporal differences exist between the Egyptian and Hebrew materials. For instance, she appeals to the "Tale of Three Wonders," where the motif of the treasure in the grain sacks (as in Genesis 42) and the parting water (as in Exodus 14) are found. The problem is that this tale has just one witness, Papyrus Westcar (P. Berlin 3033) and no schoolboy ostraca (inscribed potsherds) exist, as they did for classical works that were widely disseminated in Egypt.[41] Furthermore, the tale is written in classical Middle Egyptian and the manuscript dates to the Hyksos Period (seventeenth to mid-sixteenth century B.C.).[42] Given Thompson's propensity to date the pentateuchal narratives to the middle third of the first millennium, it is surprising that he defends Irvin's seeing an "analogy" between the Hebrew and Egyptian motifs.[43]

A more productive comparative approach is that of J. Robin King, who identifies the genre of literature in the Joseph story as "a special kind of hero tale," using ten narrative steps of the Egyptian "Tale of Sinuhe" as a model.[44] The ten steps include: 1) initial situation, 2) threat, 3) threat realized, 4) exile, 5) success in exile, 6) exilic agon, 7) exilic victory, 8) threat overcome, 9) return and reconciliation and 10) epilogue.[45] These narrative steps are found in other Near Eastern tales, including those of Idrimi of Alalakh, Hattusilis of Hattusas, Esarhaddon of Assyria, and Nabonidus of Babylon. Their stories are described by King as "much more historical and lack[ing] the rhetorical polish and romance of the Egyptian story [i.e., Sinuhe]. To be sure, they are all tendentious, but their tendentiousness is expected in the kind of history writing they are—dynastic apologetics."[46] It could well be that some aspects of this widely dispersed Near Eastern literary pattern were employed by the Hebrew author(s) to cast the story of Joseph. In view of the fact that Idrimi, Hattusilis, Esarhaddon, and Nabonidus were well attested historical rulers, there is no reason to deny Joseph the same status because of the use of this literary structure.[47] On the contrary, if the ten narrative steps of the hero tale are typically used for historical figures, then it is logical to assume that Joseph was a historical individual.

Von Rad's thesis that the Joseph story is a novella[48] has certainly garnered widespread support in the past thirty years.[49] In fact, George Coats recently claimed 'a consensus in that the Joseph story is a novella, a genre category that facilitates the original conceptions of an artist rather than the patterns of a traditional folk story handed down from one generation to the next."[50] The genre "novella" as understood by some biblical scholars is not just a short novel in the modern sense of "an invented prose narrative."[51] As Coats declares: "The [Joseph] story employs historical verisimilitude effectively. But effective description of a culture that did in fact exist does not establish the historicity of the events and personalities set out in the Joseph novella, nor does it deny it."[52] Humphreys's understanding of novella, at least as it relates to the question of historicity, is somewhat different. He places a novella between a novel and a short story, sharing the qualities of these two genres, and concludes, "it is an artfully crafted piece of prose fiction that entertains and seeks to give an accurate depiction of life."[53] He does allow for the possibility of historical "links" in a novella.[54]

One of the problems for advocates of novella regarding the Hebrew Bible is, as Humphreys himself concedes, that this genre "has developed in the West [only] since the 14th century [A.D.]."[55] Thus it must be asked if it is valid to take a relatively modern Western literary classification and impose it upon ancient texts. On this point, I heartily concur with Irvin who cautions that "modern application of [literary] terms is apt to be somewhat arbitrary, because it is not clear which ancient characteristics deserve which modern labels."[56]

To speak of a scholarly consensus regarding a Joseph novella, as Coats does, is a bit premature. (Given the present disarray in Old Testament scholarship, it is perhaps imprudent to speak of a consensus on any issue.) Indeed, Thompson differs from Coats, asserting that "we have evidence that the received text of the Joseph story does not reflect the individual composition of a 'novella.' Rather we have here a tradition of plot episode and motif development, akin to traditional narrative of the sort we have seen in both the Abraham and Jacob narratives."[57] Thompson considers the toledoth framework of Genesis (the "these are the generations of X" formulas that serve as dividers between different family histories) to be what unifies Genesis 1 through Exodus 23.[58] He describes the toledoth tradition as "a narrative unit, with its own theme, plot-line, and distinctive beginning and end"[59] that holds together the narrative blocks of Israel's origin tradition. The toledoth framework is the final redactive step that incorporated smaller units and tales, larger compound tales, and traditional, complex, chain narratives. I find Thompson's suggestions regarding the framework and subsections of Genesis and Exodus very plausible because he seriously considers the clues within Genesis to determine the structure and literary units rather than imposing modern, Western-oriented structural patterns on the narrative. Furthermore, Thompson's approach also puts an end to the futile, subjective quest for different sources that comprise the story.[60]

Despite more sophisticated literary and structural analyses of the Joseph narratives in the past decade, the questions of genre remains problematic. King's, "a special kind of hero tale" classification, however seems to be promising literary analysis.

III. Egyptian Dimensions of the Joseph Story

Scholars with Egyptological training have long recognized the Egyptian elements in the Joseph story. Alan R. Schulman claims the writer of this Hebrew narrative "had an exceedingly intimate knowledge of Egyptian life, literature, and culture, particularly in respect to the Egyptian court, and in fact, may even have lived in Egypt for a time."[61] Having surveyed the significant Egyptological investigations of the Joseph narratives, I now turn to discussing newer Egyptian material and more recent studies that have not been adequately considered by biblical scholars over the past twenty years as genre studies have advanced and questions of historicity have been raised.

Slavery in Egypt

Joseph, according to Genesis (37:28, 36; 39:1), was sold to traders who took him to Egypt were he was sold to an official. As noted, Hayes believed that slave trading accounts for the presence at least some of the Semites in Egypt during the Twelfth and Thirteenth Dynasties which he linked to the Joseph story.[62] Evidence for slave trade is limited, however, and further work in this area is needed.[63]

An interesting detail in the sale of Joseph is the price. Twenty shekels (Gen. 37:28) is the average price for slaves during the first half of the second millennium, whereas in the second half of that millennium, owing to inflation, the price was up to thirty shekels. By the first millennium, when many believe the Genesis stories originated, the price had risen to fifty or sixty shekels.[64] Is the twenty-shekel price of Joseph's sale and the average price during the first half of the second millennium just a trivial coincidence, or is it a little detail that points to the period of the original setting of the story? Certainly, this point alone will not settle the issue of the dating or the authenticity of the tradition, but when weighed along with other considerations, it cannot be brushed aside.

Once purchased by Potiphar, Joseph was made "overseer of his house" (Gen. 39:4), ^{c}al-bēytô, literally "over his house." Papyrus Brooklyn 35.1446 lists the Semitic names of dozens of male and female servants attached to a particular estate (fig. 3).[65] The third column from the right on the papyrus contains their trade or occupation. Interestingly, a number of these servants are identified as ḥry-pr,[66] literally, "he who is over the house," which is translated "domestic servant."[67] That the Hebrew ^{c}al bayit is a translation of the Egyptian expression ḥry-pr is likely and supported by the semantic correspondence between the two expressions. The fact that Joseph, a Hebrew, is portrayed in Genesis as serving in the house of an Egyptian official and that Asiatic men (^{c}ȝmw) work in the capacity of ḥry pr on Egyptian estates in the late Middle Kingdom and beyond, suggests that the Joseph story could be set within this period. It is also possible that as Joseph's skill and competence were recognized by his Egyptian master, he may have been promoted from ḥry-pr to imy-r pr (Gen. 39:4b) normally translated, "overseer of the house," or "steward."[68]

Egyptian Personal Names

The etymologies of the personal names in the Joseph story have been of considerable interest to scholars because names can provide a chronological horizon when a name was in vogue. If the data from the corpus of names converge on a specific time period, theoretically, they could provide parameters for the date of authorship or the setting of the story. The names in the Joseph narratives are Potiphar, Joseph's master (Gen. 39:1); Asenath, Joseph's wife (Gen. 41:45); Potipherah, Joseph's father-in-law (Gen. 41:45); and Zaphenath-paneah, Joseph's Egyptian name conferred upon him by Pharaoh (Gen. 41:45).

Potiphar (פוֹטִיפַר >pôtîp̱ar - Gen. 37:36; 39:1) and Potipherah (פּוֹטִי פֶרַע >pôtî p̱era^c - Gen. 41: 45, 50) have been widely understood to be the Hebrew writing of p3 di p3 r^c, "he whom Re has given."[69] It is generally thought that Potiphar is a shorter version of the name Potipherah, less the final ^{c}ayin. Indeed, the two names may share the same etymology. However, I am not convinced that the Septuagint writings, Πετεφρῆ/petephre and Πετεφρῆς/petephres, respectively, help settle the issue.[70] It is noteworthy that the final element of the priest's name is r^c or Re, the patron of On[71] or Heliopolis, where the Sun-god's most important cult center was situated from the Old Kingdom through the Third Intermediate Period. It is at this precise religious center that Potipherah is said to have been a priest in Genesis 41:45.

Assuming that the proper etymology for both names is p3 di p3 r^c, it is of a type that appears to have been most popular during the first millennium B.C. Redford has recently reaffirmed this long-held view, noting that this precise name is attested in several texts of the seventh through third centuries B.C.[72] Kitchen, however, has shown that this particular name (not the name formula) is found on a Twenty-first Dynasty stela (ca. 1070–945 B.C.) the text of which was published in 1939.[73] Schulman's investigation of the frequency of this name in Egyptian sources led him to place the name a bit earlier than Redford, in the Twenty-first or Twenty-second Dynasty, or during the period of David and Solomon.[74] Kitchen parts company with his Egyptologist colleagues because similar name formulas are documented as early as the New Kingdom. For example, *p₃ di R^c* (with the definite article *p₃*) and *p₃ di ḥnsw,* and *p₃ di sw r nḥḥ* date to the reign of Seti I.[75] These occurrences lead him to conclude that "the Egyptian original of Potiphera (and possibly of Potiphar) would not date before the 19th Dynasty (13 century B.C.) and would be current long after."[76] Kitchen goes on to argue that the late Egyptian name forms are modernized versions of ones that go back to the Middle Kingdom—that is, *dd(w)* or *ddt* +deity—and that the transition to the later form began at the start of the Eighteenth Dynasty with the feminine form *t₃ didi(t).s* ("the one that she [=goddess] has given"), and the masculine form beginning later on.[77] These factors lead Kitchen to aver that "given the clear existence of the sequence of types of name with the same meaning: *Ddi-X*, then *Pa-didi-X*, *Ta didi(t)-X*, then *Pa-di-X*, it is possible to suggest that in fact Joseph's father-in-law was originally called *Didi-Re,* a name which became later (if not *Pa-didi-(P)Re*) the present *Pa-di-Pre*."[78]

Asenath (אָסְנַת > '*āsnaṯ* - Gen. 41:45, 50) has long been thought to be derived from the Egyptian name *ns-nt,* "she who belongs to [the goddess] Neith."[79] According to Schulman, this name type (*n(i) + sw* or *si* + deity) is "most frequently attested from the beginning of the first millennium on."[80] Despite the broad support for this proposed interpretation, no example of the name *ns-nt* is known in ancient Egyptian onomastics.[81] Also, W. Spiegelberg noted nearly a century ago that the initial Hebrew א (*aleph*) in Asenath does not correspond with the expected vocalization of the *ns-* names.[82] Thus, he proffered the name formula *iw.s n nt* (As-en-Neit). However, this name likewise is not attested, and just one example of the type (with the goddess Mut) is catalogued by Ranke.[83] Because of the absence of *ns-nt* among the names of women from Pharaonic Egypt, the linguistic problems of equating *ns-nt* with Hebrew אָסְנַת, and the rare use of a theophoric name with the goddess Neith (not what would be expected of the daughter of the priest of On), Kitchen offers a different etymology.[84] The pattern *iw.s-n.i* ("she belongs to me") is found in Middle Kingdom inscriptions that could also appear as *iw.s n it.s* or *iw.s n mwt.s:* "she belongs to her father" or "she belongs to her mother."[85] He posits that this pattern lies behind the name Asenath, particularly *iw.s n.t* ("she who belongs to you" (2d per. fem. suffix), and concludes: "This explanation for Asenath eliminates the unrealistic link with Neith, fits the vocalic pattern in Hebrew and Egyptian, and derives from an attested name (even if in the masculine only at present).[86]

Zaphenath-paneah (צָפְנַת פַּעְנֵחַ > *ṣāpnaṯ pa^cnēaḥ* - Gen. 41:45) in the story is uttered by the Pharaoh, thus the reader would naturally expect that this name is of Egyptian derivation, and it indisputably is. However, the precise name pattern remains a subject of debate. Over a century ago, the Egyptologist Georg Steindorff proposed the etymology *ḏd p3 nṯr iw.f ꜥnḫ*, meaning, "the God has said: 'he will live,'"[87] and this interpretation has been widely accepted.[88] Yahuda offered a different interpretation of the name: *ḏf3 n t3 p3 ꜥnḫ*, meaning "food, sustenance of the land is living."[89] While he can point to the name type *ḏf3* + deity (e.g., *ḏf3 ḥꜥpy*, Hapi-djefa), the lack of a parallel for this name and grammatical problems have resulted in little enthusiasm for this proposal. In fact, Vergote criticized Yahuda and questioned Steindorff's time-honored view.[90] In Vergote's opinion, both the Masoretic and Septuagint spellings are corrupt. Consequently, he created a harmonized name by taking elements from Hebrew and Greek that he thought were correct, resulting in *p3 s nty ꜥm.f n3 iḫt)*, which appears to be a good Late Egyptian sentence meaning, "the man who knows things."[91] As ingenious as Vergote's suggestion is, it fails because the name lacks a counterpart in Egyptian onomastics, and his method of combining Greek and Hebrew elements is suspect.[92]

Because Yahuda's and Vergote's reconstructions have not garnered much support, Steindorff's *Ḏd p3 nṮr iw.f ꜥnḫ* continues to be the favored interpretation of the Egyptian name behind the Hebrew Zaphenath-Paneah.[93] While Redford admits that the Egyptian reading of the name "is not quite so certain," he nevertheless follows Steindorff's *ḏd p3 nṯr iw.f ꜥnḫ* and notes that this formula is found most frequently between 664 and 331 B.C., the Saite through Persian eras.[94] Schulman likewise agrees with Steindorff's proposed name formula for Zaphenath-Paneah, though he prefers to date the name some three centuries before Redford's earliest suggested date.[95]

For many years, Kitchen has resisted the Egyptian reading *ḏd p3 nṯr iw.f ꜥnḫ* for the Hebrew *ṣāpnat paꜥnēaḥ*. Around twenty-five years ago he protested that "Steindorff's explanation has become standard in many commentaries almost to the point of unjustifiable dogmatism."[96] Alternatively, he postulates the Egyptian name as "(Joseph) *ḏd (w) n.f 'Ip-ꜥnḫ*," which means "(Joseph) who is called 'Ip-Ankh,'" ["who recognizes life"][97] This pattern, according to Kitchen, runs from the Middle Kingdom through the Eighteenth Dynasty (ca. 2000–1300 B.C.). For this Egyptian formula to be at the root of the initial Hebrew word requires a metathesis of the *p* and *t* when going from Egyptian to Hebrew. Kitchen explains that such metatheses were common, with loan words going between languages. In this case, he notes that "the consonantal succession was totally foreign to a Semitic speaker and writer, so it was switched to a sequence that was familiar, z-p-n-(t). Hence, there is no problem in accepting Zaphnat from Egyptian Djad(u)-naf."[98]

In the early attestations of this formula, it is commonly used to refer to Semitic slaves attached to Egyptian estates. Once again, the Brooklyn Papyrus is instructive.[99] A tripartite pattern occurs: X who is called Y. The *ḏdw n.f* (masc.) or *ḏdt n.s* (fem.) is the passive participle in Middle Egyptian.[100] This form is used both for recording the Semitic birth name and the given Egyptian name, as well as birth and nicknames of Egyptians named in this document.[101] An example of the latter is, "Renes Seneb's son Ankhu who is called [*ḏdw n.f*] Hedjeri."[102] In the case of Semites, the first name is prefixed with the label *ꜥ3m*, "the Asiatic"—for example, "The Asiatic (fem.) Dodi-huat(u) who is called Ankhw em Hesut,"[103] "The Asiatic Qui/// who is called Res-Seneb,"[104] and "the Asiatic Aamu///, who is called Werni."[105] Of special interest is one "Ankhu who is called Pa-Aam [the Asiatic]"[106] because the use of the article *p3* is usually thought to be characteristic of Late Egyptian (from the fourteenth cenutry B.C. onward), and the chief reason why many Egyptologists have considered the element phenath / נתפ derive from *p3 ntr* ("God") thus suggestive of lateness.[107] The occurrence of definite article *p3* in this late Middle Kingdom document (ca. 1700 B.C.)—and other cases can be cited for the same period[108]—demonstrates that the use of *p3* or *t3* (fem.) is not limited to the late period, as is often claimed.

Kitchen's reading of the first part of the name, if correct, is a form well attested from the later Twelfth Dynasty on. The same is true of the name *(I)pi-ᶜnh* or *(I)pu-ᶜnh* since this name is well documented during the Middle Kingdom, "but not any later."[109] Thus, his alternative proposal is particularly worthy of consideration because it follows the formula used for foreigners in Egypt who had been given Egyptian names and because linguistically his proposed reading meets the rules for going from Egyptian to Hebrew.[110] The practice of giving Egyptian names to foreigners was not restricted to "slaves" or servants. For instance, the Hittite princess who married Ramesses II around 1246 was renamed "Maat-Hor-Nefer-ure, may she live, daughter of the Great Ruler of Hatti, and daughter of the Great Queen of Hatti."[111]

Despite the disagreement among Egypto-Semitic specialists concerning the precise etymology of the four personal names discussed here and their dating (an issue that will be taken up again in the conclusion to this chapter), all agree that they are undeniably Egyptian. All except Yahuda believed the first Hebrew element *s* to be *dd* ("to say"), and all agree that the final element *ᶜnh* is a perfect writing for Egyptian *ᶜnh*, "life." The differences on the middle elements are owing to the number of weak consonants (which approximate vowels) that to the Hebrew ear would have sounded like vowels and would not have been written, since in classical Hebrew vowels were not recorded. Consequently, there can be legitimate variations in reading the Hebrew: Does Hebrew p stand for vowel + *p* or *p* + vowel (*ip* or *p3*)? Regardless of these linguistic problems, the names in question are incontrovertibly Egyptian.

Historians have long lamented that the writer of the Joseph narratives (and those of Exodus, too) did not furnish the reader with the name of the Egyptian king. Throughout Genesis and Exodus, the well-known title "Pharaoh," derived from *pr ᶜ3*, literally "great house," is used. As a reference to the palace, this expression goes back into the Old Kingdom, but as an epithet for the monarch, it does not occur until the Eighteenth Dynasty,[112] sometime before the reign of Thutmose III (1479–1425 B.C.).[113] By the Ramesside period (1300–1100 B.C.), "Pharaoh" is widely used and continued to be popular in the late period.[114] From its inception until the tenth century, the term "Pharaoh" stood alone, without juxtaposed personal name. In subsqent periods, the name of the monarch was generally added on. This precise practice is found in the Old Testament; in the period covered from Genesis and Exodus to Solomon and Rehoboam, the term "pharaoh" occurs alone, while after Shishak (ca. 925 B.C.), the title and name appear together (e.g., Pharaoh Neco, Pharaoh Hophra).[115]

Thus, the usage of "pharaoh" in Genesis and Exodus does accord well with the

Egyptian practice from the fifteenth through the tenth centuries. The appearance of "pharaoh" in the Joseph story could reflect the New Kingdom setting of the story, or, if its provenance is earlier (i.e., the late Middle Kingdom through Second Intermediate Period), its occurrence in Genesis is suggestive of the period of composition.

The Magicians

In the Joseph story, magicians are referred to as interpreters of dreams (Gen. 41:8; 24), whereas in the Exodus narratives (Exod. 7:11; 8:3, 14, 15; 9:11) they take on the role of charmers. In both episodes, the word commonly rendered "magician" is *ḥarṭummîm* (חַרְטֻמִּים) for which an Egyptian origin has long been recognized. Early on it was posited that the priestly title *ḥry-ḥb* was behind the Hebrew word.[116] Subsequently, a more linguistically acceptable expression *ḥry-tp* was thought to be the root of the Hebrew term,[117] and now it is thought to be an abbreviation of *ḥry-tp ḥry-ḥb*, chief lector priest.[118] In a recent study of *ḥarṭummîm*, the late Jan Quaegebeur observed: "Due to the fact that these lector-priests, and especially those holding a higher rank, were also engaged in magic, *ḥry-tp* 'Chief' could come to mean 'Magician.'"[119]

Redford, on the other hand, argued that the word came into Hebrew via the Demotic *ḥry-tm* and thus was evidence for a first-millennium origin in Hebrew.[120] His claim has influenced quite a few, especially German scholars.[121] But Quaegebeur has shown that the reading of Demotic *ḥry-tm* thought to be the late-period vocalization of *ḥry tp* was mistaken. He goes on to show from Greek transcriptions of Egyptian texts of the Ptolemaic and Roman periods that the vocalization of *tp* had become *tb*, not *tm*, and, furthermore, that the same vocalization is found in Assyrian texts of the seventh century.[122] He then shows that at least from 1300 B.C. on the vocalization of *tp* was actually *tb*, and this accounts for the *ṭum* in the Hebrew writing *ḥarṭummîm*.[123] Therefore, Quaegebeur departs from Redford's late dating by observing, "the term may just as well have been borrowed in earlier times."[124]

What is known about the activities of the (chief) lector priests in Pharaonic Egypt? This priest may have been summoned to different temples or the palace, but the "House of Life" (*pr ꜥnḥ*) was the place where he studied and transmitted "ritual and magical texts."[125] The connection between the *ḥry-tp* and the "House of Life" is further established in the Coptic (Bohairic) translation of Genesis 41:8 and 11 where the translators depart from the Septuagint's translation of *ḥarṭummîm* with the term ⲥⲫⲣⲁⲛϣ (*sphransh*). Long ago, Battiscombe Gunn suggested that behind this Coptic term was the expression *sẖ pr ꜥnḥ*, "scribe of the house of life."[126] Subsequently, Jaroslav Černý, a specialist in Coptic etymologies, while agreeing with Gunn on his analysis of ⲫⲣⲁⲛϣ, observed that the Coptic ⲥ does not derive from *sẖ*, but from *sb(3)*.[127] This reading would mean, "teacher of the House of Life." The Coptic (B) translators of Genesis 41 clearly understood that behind interpreters of dreams was an official of the "House of Life" where dream-interpretation manuals, like Papyrus Chester Beatty (fig. 4)[128] were stored and studied.[129] Although this papyrus is of Ramesside date, Gardiner believed that the contents could date back to the Twelfth Dynasty, based on the grammar.[130] Concluding a recent grammatical study of this text, Sarah Israelit-Groll states: "It should also be noted that the biblical concepts expressed in the story of Joseph, that nightmares possess oracular power, but also that the effects of oracular nightmares can be avoided by reason, wisdom and justice, suit very well the concept of dream interpretation in the Dream Book."[131]

The story of the dreams of the butler and baker in Genesis 40 may be further illuminated by the preceding information. In prison they had dreams and were distraught (Gen. 40:5–6). The reason for this response may be that in prison they did not have access to the *ḥarṭummîm* and their dream-interpretation manuals. In Genesis 40:8 the two officials respond dejectedly to Joseph, "We have had dreams, and there is no one to interpret them." Joseph served as their "dream interpreter," as he did for Pharaoh a few years later (41:15–36).

Pharaoh's Birthday

During his incarceration, Joseph was joined by two of the king's officials, the chief baker and butler, who had fallen out of favor with the monarch. Genesis 40:20 mentions "Pharaoh's birthday," at which a feast for his officials served as the occasion for pardoning the butler. Redford acknowledges that Pharaoh's birthday, like that of a god, may have involved celebrations throughout Egyptian history, but no evidence exists for the practice prior to the first millennium.[132] Since the birthday of the emperor was a gala event during the Persian era, Redford believes that this practice was introduced into Egypt during the Persian or preceding Saite Period. Consequently, for Redford, this consideration further points to the period when the Joseph story was authored, the seventh through sixth centuries.[133]

Liesbeth Boddens-Hosang has recently drawn attention to a Second Dynasty year name on the Palermo Stone that contains the word *mswt*, "birth," beside the name of King Khasekhemui.[134] Over eighty years ago Kurt Sethe wrestled with the reading of this year name and argued that the word *mswt* had nothing to do with birth because the following sign or determinative (θ) is associated with metals.[135] Hence, he believed that the year name had to do with the year in which a copper statue of the king was fashioned. Having examined this rather minuscule text with a magnifying glass, I am inclined to agree with Sethe. While Boddens-Hosang was aware of Sethe's objections to the reading "birth," she nevertheless preferred the earlier interpretation. In the absence of a celebration of a king's birthday elsewhere in the Old Testament, she postulates: "the Genesis reference is obviously not a scribal interpretation or error. The passage may, then, record a genuine Egyptian festival."[136] It appears that she has too quickly applied a questionable reading of an Egyptian text to try to illuminate a biblical problem.

However, another interpretation of the expression יוֹם הֻלֶּדֶת אֶת־פַּרְעֹה - *yôm hulledet ʾet-parꜥōh*, "birthday of Pharaoh," needs to be considered. The second Psalm, thought by many commentators to be a royal psalm used at the coronation of the Judaean king and the annual celebration of that day,[137] states: "I will tell of the decrees of the LORD: He said to me, 'You are my son, today I have begotten you'" (Ps. 2:7). The final line of this verse is אֲנִי הַיּוֹם יְלִדְתִּיךָ - *ʾni hayôm ylidtîkā*.

The same root, ילד, (*yld*) is used in both Psalm 2:7 and Genesis 40:20. Although the same root is found in another royal, coronation Psalm (110:3) and appears to share the same idea as Psalm 2:7, the vowel pointing is different.[138] The use of *yld* in Psalms 2 and 110 suggests a technical meaning for this word that shows a connection between the Hebrew king's coronation and divine-birth theology is intended.[139] Concerning this matter, Peter Craigie declares, "'I have begotten you' is metaphorical language; it means more than simply adoption, which has legal overtones, and implies that a 'new birth' of a divine nature took place during the coronation."[140] The iconography of the Near East, especially Egypt, richly illustrates the divine conception, birth, and enthronement of its kings.[141] At a coronation in Egypt, the monarch is transformed into the divine king and the "immortal *ka*" of kingship.[142] In Egyptian royal theology, a close bond existed between the divine conception, birth, accession, and coronation.[143] For this reason the five-part royal titulary applied at coronation from the Fifth Dynasty onwards included the *s3 rᶜ* or Son of Re name.[144]

Thus, we see that in Egypt and in Israel the idea of kingship was closely associated with the divine birth of the king at coronation.[145] It is thought that the king's accession/coronation anniversary was annually celebrated in Israel,[146] although what was involved in these festivities is not reported in the Bible. Similarly, in Egypt the accession date, when the king's divine birth as the living Horus took place, was observed.

Redford has thoroughly studied texts related to the "appearance" (*hᶜy*) of the king.[147] It had been long held that the accession of Pharaoh occurred immediately upon the death of his predecessor, and a more elaborate coronation ceremony took place some time later.[148] Redford's dissertation corrected this notion. After examining over one hundred texts where the term *hᶜy* and its derivatives are used, he demonstrated that the accession and coronation occurred at the same time.[149] In his view, this finding does not preclude the possibility that at a later date a public and more elaborate ceremony was observed, but this occasion was not the coronation.[150]

It has long been known that there was a "festival of the king's appearance," *hb nsw hᶜw*,[151] or simply *hb n hᶜw* ("festival of appearance").[152] Based on Redford's conclusion that the *hᶜw/y* is the accession and the coronation, the celebration (*hb nsw hᶜw*) must be the anniversary of the accession, not a later coronation date.[153] As early as the Sixth Dynasty this festival is known from an inscription where an official boasted of his presence in the palace at *hbw nb(w) n hᶜw* - "every festival of appearance."[154] There is also textual evidence of the accession feast during the Eighteenth Dynasty for the reigns of Thutmose I and III and Amenhotep II.[155] In the following Ramesside period, the expression *irt hᶜy nsw* ("celebrating the king's appearance,") occurs.[156] Apparently, this expression replaced the earlier *hb nsw hᶜw*.

Since during the New Kingdom and earlier, the accession of the king—his birthday as Son of Re—was annually observed as a festive occasion, the celebration of his birth may not have been mythologically important enough to celebrate as well, thus possibly accounting for the absence of textual evidence for it. Because of the ideological similarity between the Egyptian and Israelite concept of divine birth (or rebirth) at accession/coronation, the so-called "birthday" of Pharaoh mentioned in Genesis 40:20 might be not a celebration of his physical birth, but of his divine birth, at "the festival of accession." This suggestion is further supported by the fact that the accession year of a new king was an occasion in the Near East for pardoning individuals, including political enemies. This happened to the Judaean king, Jehoiachin, in Babylon. 2 Kings 25:27b declares: "Evil-merodach king of Babylon, in the year that he began to reign graciously freed Jehoiachin king of Judah from prison." Perhaps the anniversary of the king's coronation also served as an occasion for pardoning as suggested by Pharaoh's pardoning of his butler in the Joseph story.[157]

Joseph's Investiture

> Then pharaoh took his signet ring from his
> hand and put it on Joseph's hand, and ar-
> rayed him in garments of fine linen, and put
> a gold chain about his neck. . . . Thus he set
> him over all the land of Egypt
>
> Gen. 41:42–43

With these words Joseph was ceremonially elevated to a prestigious position. The Egyptian background to this episode has been studied in detail because Egyptian officials frequently portrayed their promotion ceremonies in their tomb paintings or reliefs (fig. 5 and 6). Vergote discussed this detail in the Joseph story in light of the Egyptian evidence.[158] Subsequently, Redford expanded on the earlier works by gathering and analyzing over forty scenes spanning from the reign of Thutmose III to the Twenty-first Dynasty (ca. 1479–950 B.C.).[159] These scenes typically show the king sitting on a throne, often under a canopy, while the recipient stands before the monarch wearing a gold necklace and adorned in white linen. Redford carefully examined the scenes and determined that there are actually two types: those depicting an induction to a new office and others illustrating rewards for faithful service. He produced a list of thirty-two scenes (from Thutmose IV to the Twenty-first Dynasty, ca. 1400–950 B.C.) he thinks are of the reward genre and a second corpus of nine he identifies as investitures.[160] An important diagnostic feature of investiture scenes is the presence of some sort of insignia of the new office (standard, staff, or seal). He also observes that the reward scenes portray the decorated individual (gold collars on neck) with hands upraised in a joyful pose, whereas the induction ceremony is more somber.[161]

Kitchen disagrees with this latter distinction, however, noting that the celebrative feature of what Redford labels "reward" scenes are "*integral* to the scene of appointment of Tutu at Amarna."[162] In this case, the accompanying text makes it clear an appointment was taking place. The sequence shows 1) Tutu standing with arms upraised, decked with gold collars; 2) an additional collar being presented; 3) gifts on nearby stands; and 4) Tutu riding away in his chariot.[163] Parenthetically, the Joseph story records that after receiving the seal and gold chain, the king made

Joseph ride in his chariot (Gen. 41:43). Kitchen also cites the case of Huya at Amarna, who is depicted in the joyous pose, yet the text indicates that a promotion (*dhn*) was occurring, with a signet ring and staff being presented to the official.[164]

The case of Huy, Viceroy of Cush under Tutankhamun, is also introduced by Kitchen.[165] The painting shows Huy receiving a rolled-up linen object along with a gold signet ring. Here we recall Joseph's gift of linen (Gen. 41:42). Of particular interest here is that the word "linen," שֵׁשׁ (*šēš*), is of recognized Egyptian etymology, deriving from the term *ssr(w)*.[166] In view of the fact that there are four other Hebrew words for linen,[167] *šēš* in the Hebrew Bible probably refers to Egyptian linen, which was celebrated for its fine quality. In addition to use of *šēš* in Genesis 41:42, there are twenty-eight occurrences of this term in the Old Testament. Twenty-six are found in the book of Exodus, all having to do with priestly garments and features from the tabernacle. Since the Bible reports Israel's portable shrine being built shortly after the departure from Egypt, the use of the Egyptian term is not surprising, and it suggests that the tabernacle traditions have a much earlier history than acknowledged by source critics who assign the Exodus narratives to P in the fifth century.[168] In support of this observation, Avi Hurwitz has shown that the word *šēš* is replaced in late biblical Hebrew by *bûṣ*.[169]

Concerning the differences between Redford's two categories of scenes, reward and investiture, Kitchen concludes that one cannot assign certain motifs to one type and other features to the second. Rather, he believes that there were similarities between the two, and that artists occasionally had to be selective in what they showed.[170] In such cases, the accompanying texts clarify which scene is in view. The Joseph story may well reflect this combining of the reward and induction ceremony. He would have been rewarded for his successful dream interpretation and inducted into the office designated by Pharaoh to prepare Egypt for the coming years of famine.

Of Redford's thirty-two examples of his reward scenes, only one (no. 32) dates after the New Kingdom (and that one is from the Twenty-first Dynasty, ca. 930), while all nine of his investiture types range from Thutmose III to Ramesses II. To these Kitchen has added several more, all from the New Kingdom.[171] Despite the overwhelming evidence that the reward-investiture motif is at home in the artistic repertoire of the New Kingdom, Redford, alas, assigned the Joseph induction ceremony to the late period because it was a "popular *Märchen* in vogue in the middle of the First Millennium." His evidence is limited to a few neo-Assyrian examples, a Demotic text, the biblical book of Daniel, and Ahikar.[172] Given the dearth of Egyptian evidence for the late period and the abundance of material for the New Kingdom, Redford's conclusions seem to have been reached not on the merits of the evidence, but because of his penchant to late-date the story.

The evidence reviewed here strongly suggests that these ceremonies were most popular during the New Kingdom, at least as artistic representations of what was a regular part of the funerary repertoire of the fifteenth through twelfth centuries. Redford suggests the reward scene of General (later King) Horemheb was the result of a successful military campaign because of the Syrian POWs in the relief.[173] However, inscriptional evidence for military heroes being decorated can be traced back to the wars of liberation against the Hyksos (ca. 1560–1550 B.C.). Ahmose si Abena's tomb inscriptions record his acts of bravery and the subsequent decoration by the king: *wn.in tw ḥr rdit n.i nbw n ḳnt* [174]—"Then one (the king) gave to me the gold of valor." The fact that textual evidence for such rewards goes back to the transition between the Second Intermediate Period and the New Kingdom suggests that the practice actually predates the empire.

Joseph's Status

There has been considerable discussion as to the office and titles of Potiphar and Joseph, after Joseph's promotion by Pharaoh. Since the titles are apparently Hebrew equivalents of Egyptian ones and not of Egyptian etymology, there has been a range of opinion about the various offices. But all who have examined them in the light of actual Egyptian titulary concur that genuine Egyptian ranks are behind the Hebrew expressions. They certainly do not compare with known titles from Israel's monarchy in the first millennium. There have been differences of opinion on the Egyptian titles behind the Hebrew, which is understandable since over fifteen hundred titles have been isolated for the Middle Kingdom alone.[175] I do not believe that the present evidence allows us to come to any firm conclusions about the Egyptian equivalents of Joseph's titles, but the general impression is that the offices or rank mentioned in Genesis do reflect genuine Egyptian institutions.

In Genesis 41:40c Pharaoh declares "only as regards the throne will I be greater than you." This statement has led some to believe that Joseph was the vizier (*ṯзty*), the highest-ranking official in the realm.[176] But William Ward rejected this idea because, in his opinion, Joseph's titles as presented in Genesis and the responsibilities described therein do not match those of the vizier.[177] A new and thorough study on the duties of the vizier by Guido van den Boorn tends to support Ward's earlier claim.[178] However, van den Boorn's primary source for his investigation comes from the fifteenth-century tomb of Rekhmire, and his concern was the vizier in the early New Kingdom. Because our knowledge of the responsibilities of the vizier in the previous centuries remains obscured by the lack of evidence, this office cannot be ruled out.

After examining the biblical passages describing Joseph's responsibilities, Ward offered six titles that could be ascribed to Joseph: Overseer of the Granaries of Upper and Lower Egypt, Royal Seal-Bearer, God's Father, Great Steward of the Lord of the Two Lands, Foremost of Courtiers, and Chief of the Entire Land.[179] Ward may be right in his assessment that Joseph's titles and responsibilities do not accord with those of the vizier, but the office of vizier cannot be dismissed on the grounds that a foreigner in Egypt could not assume such a lofty position. Labeling the Joseph story a *Märchen*, a fairy tale employing the rags-to-riches or prison-to-palace motif, ignores the fact that such elevations did occur in the Near East in ancient times.[180]

It has long been known that during the dynastic turmoil that followed the death of Seti II in 1194 B.C. an official named Bay was instrumental in placing Siptah on the throne and bore the title "Great Chancellor of the entire land."[181]

Gardiner points out that this Syrian-born official was "possibly one of those court officials who in this age frequently rose to power by the royal favour."[182] Interestingly, as with the case of Joseph, Bay bore an Egyptian name, "Ramesse-Khamenteru." Černý observed that during the Ramesside era it "became quite usual for men of foreign origin to serve in high office at Court."[183] Under Hatshepsut (1479–1457 B.C.), a man with the Semitic name ꜥ-m-mi-ṯ-w, served as vizier.[184] But these cases have been known for many years. Now we can add the name of another Semite to the list of high-ranking officials of the New Kingdom, thanks to the discovery of a new tomb at Saqqara by the French Egyptologist Alain Zivie in the 1980s (fig. 7).[185]

Situated near the entrance to the famous necropolis, this tomb is still being studied and has been only partially published in a preliminary, semipopular report, complete with colored photographs of some of the reliefs and objects found, including the remains of the tomb owner, his wife, and their son (fig. 7). The name of man is ꜥpr-el. This name type is well known as Aper + deity (e.g., Resheph, Dagan) in the late Middle Kingdom,[186] and Aper-el was attested to in the New Kingdom prior to this discovery.[187] A partially damaged text on an offering table of the late Hyksos Period read imy-r sḏꜣt ꜥpr ///—"overseer of the Seal Aper ///), with a lacuna occupying the place where the divinity's name would have been written.[188] Thus, Aper-el, the formular Aper + deity is now attested in the Middle Kingdom, Second Intermediate Period, and the New Kingdom. In the name Aper-el, the second element, 'el, could be the generic term in Semitic languages for "god," or it could point to El, the head of the Canaanite pantheon.[189]

Aper-el's wife's name is titi or didi, a name documented in the late Middle Kingdom Brooklyn Papyrus,[190] and she has several Egyptian names, including twy, wriꜣi and tꜣ wrt.[191] Other attestations of this name are documented in the New Kingdom.[192] The son is named "knnꜣ who is called ḥwy," and he has a good Egyptian name: imn-m-ḥꜣt, Amenemhet.

Aper-el's titles include ṯꜣty, vizier, "mayor of the city," judge, it nṯr, "father of the god," as well as ḫrd n kꜣp, "child of the nursery."[193] He oversaw the king's affairs in Lower Egypt during the final years of Amenhotep III and well into the reign of Akhenaten, apparently dying in his tenth regnal year, to judge from the date on a wine docket.

Only when full publication of the tomb and its contents are made can firm comparative analysis with Joseph be advanced. But for the present, it is safe to say that in Aper-el, who was a vizier and a Semite, we have a striking parallel to Joseph in Genesis, and some provisional comments can be made.

First, this discovery is the first time this high-ranking official's name appeared on a monument after over a century of exploration at Sakkara. If such a high-ranking official as Vizier Aper-el was completely unknown to modern scholarship until the late 1980s, despite the fact that he lived in one of the better documented periods of Egyptian history, and was buried in arguably the most excavated site in Egypt, it is wrong to demand, as some have, that direct archaeological evidence for Joseph should be available if he were in fact a historical figure. This point is especially true for Joseph since his provenance in Genesis is the Delta, still an underexcavated area, and if he did live in the late Middle Kingdom through Second Intermediate Period for which there is even less documentation than the New Kingdom.

Second, Aper-el is a Semitic name, as those of his wife and son are, which strongly suggests he was a Semite. The fact that anthropoid coffins with their mummified remains were discovered in the same chamber might also point to their Levantine heritage. Group burial is not the expected practice for the New Kingdom elite like the family of the vizier. Thus, the Aper-el family not only bore Semitic names, but also followed the Late Bronze Age Canaanite tradition of family burials,[194] while adopting many Egyptian funerary practices.

Genesis 50:2 – 3 reports that Jacob was mummified according to Egyptian prescription, and Joseph himself was placed in a coffin (Gen. 50:26). Neither mummification nor the use of coffins was known in Canaan during the Bronze Age.[195] These clearly are Egyptian practices used by the Hebrew Patriarchs Jacob and Joseph, precisely like those employed for Aper-el and his family. Just as Aper-el chose to be buried with his family, so Jacob wished to return to the ancestral burial cave near Hebron (Gen. 49:29 – 32; 50:12 – 14).

Joseph's Age at Death

Genesis 50:22 reports Joseph's age as 110 when he expired. As long ago as 1864 it was recognized that this figure represents the ideal lifetime in Egypt that influenced the author of the biblical Joseph story.[196] Clearly, the life span 110 was not an Israelite ideal.[197] Rather, seventy is held up as a normative life span and eighty years as the ideal (cf. Ps. 90:10; 2 Sam. 19:32, 35).[198] The figure 110 was, in some cases, applied to sages like Djedy in Papyrus Westcar.[199]

J. M. A. Janssen, in a 1950 article, assembled about thirty occurrences of applications of this age to individuals in Egyptian texts, spanning from the late Old Kingdom down to the Ptolemaic period (ca. two thousand years).[200] Interestingly, the Ramesside period has the greatest number of usages (twenty), leading Janssen to state: "If we don't want to see Joseph's lifetime as accidentally agreeing with the ideal Egyptian lifetime but as an Egyptian peculiarity of the story I think it more probable that the 110 years should belong to the original text rather than to be a later addition. If we want to urge that this formula frequently occurs during the XIXth and XXth Dynasties we should first be sure of the time at which the Joseph episode got its final form."[201]

IV. Conclusions

Throughout this chapter, two issues remain in tension: the authenticity or historicity of the Joseph narratives and the date of their composition. Two factors influence the first of these problems: 1) the nature of the literature and historiographical assumptions, and 2) the problem of dating the narratives.

Genre and History

My survey of the genre studies of the Joseph story since von Rad in the 1950s and 1960s illustrates that while there is a significant number of scholars accepting the label "novella" for this literature, differences remain on the question of historicity. Humphreys and others generally believe that if it is a novella, it can't be historical, while Coats does not rule that out, and Schulman offers an even more positive assessment of the historicity of the "Joseph novella," but concedes that it is "an historical novel containing a core of historical memory."[202] He also maintains that the writer had an intimate knowledge of Egypt.[203] With this affirmation, he parts company with his fellow Egyptologist, Redford, who declared, "the Hebrew writer was not so well acquainted with Egypt as has often been imagined."[204]

Schulman presents an ingenious idea to rationalize the Joseph story.[205] He believes that the story was written during the Solomonic era as an apologetic for that monarch's cordial relations with Egypt that climaxed with the marriage treaty between the Israelite king and the daughter of Pharaoh (cf. I Kings 3:1; 9:16). In other words, Solomon needed to portray a time when Israel and Egypt peacefully coexisted to justify the current political harmony because of the bitter memories preserved in the oppression and exodus tradition where Israel was in bondage. Schulman also suggests that the Joseph story is essential to Genesis and Exodus because it explains how the Israelites came to live in Egypt.[206] Schulman's proposal certainly has merit, but a logical problem presents itself. If an eisodus story was required to bridge the sojourn and exodus tradition, it presupposes that the Israelites must have also known of their ancestors' emigration to Egypt prior to Solomon's day.

For Irvin, literary investigation led her to reject the classification of novella (and here I believe she is right), but her assertion that the Joseph narratives compare favorably with fictitious Egyptian folktales leads her (and Thompson) to the conclusion that they are not historical. I believe I have sufficiently exposed her methodological shortcomings so as to invalidate the comparison and the resulting conclusions regarding nature of the biblical literature and the historicity question.

In view of this observation, I find Thompson's more recent treatment on the relationship between the Joseph and Exodus narratives to be worthy of careful consideration. He argues that Genesis 12 through Exodus 23 is a "traditional complex-chain narrative," comprised of "five of the six major blocks of continuous narration from which the origin tradition of the Pentateuch (Genesis 1 – Exodus 23) has been formed (the sixth block being Genesis 1–11)."[207] If he is correct in understanding this section of the Pentateuch as a "continuous narration," then the origin and dating of the various "blocks" become a subjective exercise.

What is puzzling about Thompson's thesis is his conflicting historiographical conclusions. While he speaks of "early Israelite folk tradition" (38), "the biblical history is not a history at all" (39), "they are not history" (41), he appears to say just the opposite with claims such as, "an historiographically oriented parallel structure" (64), "the origin tradition, under the *Toledoth* structure, is aetiological and historiographical in form" (64–65), and "the historiographically oriented redaction of the Pentateuch" (172–173). He then concludes: "To reiterate: the plot of the Exodus chain narrative is historiographical" (178).

There apparently contradictory statements suggest that Thompson recognizes in the final form of the text genuine historiographical features that indicate the redactor considered his sources and the final product to be history—a description of events that really happened. Amazingly, around three millennia later, Thompson is able to discern what the ancient compiler could not: namely, that the components of the narrative chain are made up of etiologies, folktales, and ahistorical traditions. It seems to me, however, that if the narratives look like history, are structured historiographically, and the events described (especially in the Joseph story) are not incredible and compare favorably with the Egyptian backgrounds (as I have shown they do), then the narratives ought to be considered historical until there is evidence to the contrary. It seems that Thompson's conclusions about the historicity of the Joseph story are reached not by what the narratives appear to be, but because of his ideological assumptions.

Van Seters's recent monograph on Genesis also deals with the questions of genre and historiography. Because of the presence of what he calls myth, legend, and etiology in Genesis, he opines, "this material . . . has been judged as incompatible with historiography."[208] His conclusions regarding the historical worth of the Genesis narratives (Gen. 12–50) have not substantially changed since his 1977 work on Abraham and his 1983 volume on historiography.[209] He considers the Joseph cycle to "have an independence from the rest of the Pentateuch."[210] He believes the story is a " 'wisdom' novella," and thus "was not concerned to reflect tribal or national history."[211]

In the end, how a biblical scholar or historian reads the Genesis Joseph story, or the Exodus narratives for that matter, has more to do with the reader's assumptions about the texts than anything else. How else can Thompson, for example, say it looks like history, but it isn't? Why speak of "historical novel" since the modern critic has no tools available to penetrate the mind and determine the intentions of the author? Indeed, there are genuine problems with assigning genre to ancient texts, whether Hebrew or Egyptian. But in the end, interpretation becomes a philosophical question. The minimalist, despite the admitted historiographical characteristics, will call the Joseph story a saga, legend, folktale, or novella, and not a historical narrative, whereas the maximalist will accept the story as genuine until there is evidence to the contrary. To date, there is no direct evidence for the Hebrew Joseph being an official in the Egyptian court. However, the indirect evidence presented here tends to demonstrate the authenticity of the story. There is really nothing unbelievable or incredible about the narrative. The absence of direct evidence for Joseph, of course, does not disprove his existence because negative evidence proves nothing,[212] while the indirect evidence supports the historicity of the story and its protagonist.

The Question of Dating

The date of composition of the Joseph story also remains in dispute. Redford's study has convinced a number of Old Testament scholars of the lateness of the composition in the seventh or sixth century B.C. George Coats opines: "With his contribution in view, it is now impossible to consider seriously any suggestions about a direct historical line from the story to the Egyptian court of the Ramesside period."[213] This enthusiastic endorsement is not shared by Kitchen, Rendsburg, Quaegebeur, Herrmann,[214] and myself, who believe a New Kingdom date is preferable. Joining Redford's dating scheme is Van Seters, who attributes the Genesis narratives to the exilic (Babylonian-Persian) period,[215] partially because he is compelled by Redford's Saite-Persian period dating of the Egyptianisms. Van Seters's late date for J, with which he identifies the Joseph story, of course, stands apart from the traditional dating of J to the tenth or ninth century.

Kitchen, as detailed above, roundly criticized Redford for minimizing earlier evidence while overly emphasizing the late sources. Kitchen maintains that the setting of Joseph was the late Middle Kingdom to Second Intermediate Period, while recognizing Ramesside elements that point to the authorship of the work. Quaegebeur has come out in support of Kitchen's arguments and chides biblical scholars for ignoring them.[216]

In reviewing scholarly literature of the past several decades on the dating of the Joseph story, an interesting spread is evident: Vergote, Janssen and Kitchen, all Egyptologists, assign a Ramesside date. Schulman, also an Egyptologist, holds to a Twenty-first or Twenty-second Dynasty date that parallels the Solomonic era (a date that many source critics traditionally ascribed to J). Thompson prefers a late seventh-century date.[217] Redford dates the material to the sixth or fifth centuries, as does Van Seters. Then there are some, like Giovanni Garbini, who are prepared to push the origin of the Pentateuchal materials to the second or first centuries B.C.[218]

Thus 1200 years separate those at the early end of the spectrum from others on the late end. Curiously, Egyptologists (save Redford) tend to date the story early (New Kingdom) while recent biblical scholars, by and large, opt for dates in the middle third of the first millennium. This range strongly suggests that the methodologies used are inadequate to provide an incontrovertible date for the composition of the story. However, the story's details, such as the sale price of Joseph, his domestic service and titles, the reward and investiture ceremony, his titles and offices, and his age at death all point directly toward the second millennium B.C. If Kitchen's analysis of the personal names is correct, they, too, point to the same period. Consequently, I concur with Kitchen that the weight of the Egyptological data, when thoroughly examined, lends both credibility to the essential historicity of the narratives and points to a Late Bronze Age date (i.e., thirteenth century) for the composition of the Hebrew narratives, with possible editorial work being done in the period of Israel's united monarchy.

Notes

1 For a good, recent synthesis of early twentieth-century thinking about Genesis, and the Joseph story in particular, see John Van Seters, *Prologue to History: The Yahwist as Historian in Genesis* (Louisville: Westminster/John Knox Press, 1992) 20–42.

2 *The Language of the Pentateuch in Its Relation to Egyptian* (London: Oxford University Press, 1933).

3 *Joseph en Égypte: Genèsa chap 3r-5υ à la lumière des études égyptologiques récentes* (Louvain: Publications Universitaires, 1959).

4 "'Joseph En Egypte': 25 Ans Après," in *Pharaonic Egypt: The Bible and Christianity*, ed. Sarah Israellit-Groll (Jerusalem: Magnes Press, 1985) 289–306.

5 "Egyptological Remarks on the Story of Joseph in Genesis," *JEOL* 14 (1955–1956) 63–72.

6 *A Study of the Biblical Story of Joseph*, VTS, vol. 20 (Leiden: Brill, 1970).

7 Ibid., chaps. 5, 7.

8 *Oriens Antiquus* 12 (1973) 223–242. This work is not merely a book review but is in its own right a critical essay on Redford's metachronistic slant and where Kitchen makes a case for a Second Intermediate Period setting for Joseph.

9 Ibid., 238.

10 Ibid., 240.

11 Even Kitchen said that Redford's work "must be considered by future workers on this topic" (Ibid., 242).

12 *Joseph and His Family: A Literary Study* (Columbia, S.C.: University of South Carolina Press, 1988) chap. 8.

13 See "Joseph" in *NBD* 617–620; "Joseph," in *International Standard Encyclopedia*, vol. 2, ed. G. W. Bromiley (Grand Rapids, Mich.: Eerdmans, 1982) 1125–1130; "Genesis 12–50 in the Near Eastern World," in *He Swore an Oath: Biblical Themes from Genesis 12–50*, ed. R. S. Hess et al. (Cambridge: Tyndale House, 1993) 77–92; and a number of other articles in which he deals with different Egyptian backgrounds to other parts of the Pentateuch.

14 See especially *He Swore an Oath*, 90–92.

15 "Josephgeschichte und ältere Chokma," VTS, vol. 1 (1953) 120, trans. as "The Joseph Narrative and Ancient Wisdom," in *The Problem of the Hexateuch and Other Essays* (Edinburgh: Oliver and Boyd, 1966) 292–300; *Die Josephsgeschichte* (Neukerchen: Kreis Moers, 1956); *Genesis*, Old Testament Library (Philadelphia: Westminster Press, 1972).

16 Concerning the demise of the Wellhausian consensus, see chap. 1, §2.

17 "The Joseph Story and Pentateuchal Criticism," *VT* 18 (1968) 522–525.

18 Ibid., 525.

19 Ibid., 528. Whybray also suggests that his conclusion regarding the J and E makeup of the narrative is further evidence for rethinking the documentary hypothesis, which he did in *The Making of the Pentateuch*, JSOT Supp. Series, vol. 53 (Sheffield: JSOT Press, 1987). For a discussion of this book, see chap. 1, §2.

20 *The Biblical Story of Joseph*, 251–253.

21 *Oriens Antiquus* 12 (1973) 235–236.

22 *The Bible's First History* (Philadelphia: Fortress, 1989) 8–12, 172.

23 *Prologue to History*, 1–77, 311–324.

24 *The Redaction of Genesis* (Winona Lake, Ind.: Eisenbrauns, 1986).

25 Ibid., 79–97.

26 *Joseph: A Story of Divine Providence* (Winona Lake, Ind.: Eisenbrauns, 1989).

27 "The Joseph and Moses Narratives," in *Israelite and Judaean History*, ed. John Hayes and J. Maxwell Miller (Philadelphia: Westminster Press, 1977) §3. See also her subsequent, larger study, *Mytharion: The Comparison of Tales from the Old Testament and the Ancient Near East*, AOAT, vol. 32 (Neukirchen: Neukirchener Verlag-Vluyn, 1978). I am more concerned with her earlier study because of the historiographical conclusions drawn from her comparative work by her and Thompson.

28 William W. Hallo, "Biblical History in its Near Eastern Setting: The Contextual

Approach," in *Scripture in Context: Essays on the Comparative Method*, ed. C. D. Evans, W. W. Hallo, and J. B. White (Pittsburgh: Pickwick Press, 1980) 11–12.

29 "Israel Seen From Egypt: Understanding the Biblical Text from Visuals and Methodology," *TB* 42 no. 1 (1991) 117.

30 In *Israelite and Judaean History*, 210.

31 "The Joseph and Moses Narratives: Folk-Tale and History," *JSOT* 15 (1980) 51–56.

32 Ibid., 53–56.

33 Humphrey, *Joseph and His Family*, makes the same mistake when comparing this Hebrew narrative and Egyptian literature.

34 Irvin, in *Israelite and Judaean History*, 185–188.

35 For the text, see Alan H. Gardiner, *Late-Egyptian Stories, Bibliotheca Aegyptiaca*, vol. 1 (Brussels: La Fondation Égyptologique Reine Élizabeth, 1932) 9–30.

36 *The Ancient Egyptian "Tale of Two Brothers": The Oldest Fairy Tale in the World* (Norman, Okla.: University of Oklahoma Press, 1990).

37 Ibid., 97–99.

38 Ibid., 101.

39 Ibid., 102.

40 Ibid.

41 Adolph Erman, *Die Märchen des Papyrus Westcar*, Mitteilungen aus den orientalischen Sammlungen, vols. 5–6, (Berlin: 1890). For a more accessible version of the text, see *RB*, 79–88.

42 It should be noted that there are "Late Egyptianisms" in this text, but that does not mean the text dates from the late New Kingdom and beyond.

43 "History and Tradition: A Response to J. B. Geyer," *JSOT* 15 (1980) 57–61.

44 "The Joseph Story and Divine Politics: A Comparative Study of a Biographic Formula from the Ancient Near East," *JBL* 106 (1987) 577–584.

45 Ibid., 584.

46 Ibid., 581.

47 The matter of the historicity of Sinuhe remains a debated point among Egyptologists. He could have been the invention of the writer for purely propagandist ends. On the other hand, Sinuhe might have been an historical figure around which the story was embellished. Unfortunately, the preserved story cannot prove or disprove his existence.

48 The genre "novella" seems to have been applied to biblical studies after Alfred Hermann's study, *Die ägyptische Königsnovelle*, Leipziger Ägyptologische Studien, vol. 10 (Glückstadt-Hamburg: 1938). Siegfried Herrmann appears to have made the connection with Israel, cf. "Die Königsnovelle in Ägypten und Israel," *Wissenschaftliche Zeitschrift der Universität Leipzig* (1953–1954) 51–62 and "Joseph in Ägypten," *TLZ* (1960) 827–830.

49 Redford offers a slight variation, classifying the story as a "Märchen-Novelle" in that it shares the timelessness of the former and the "real-world" of the latter (*The Biblical Story of Joseph*, 66–67).

50 "Joseph, Son of Jacob," *ABD*, vol. 3 (1992) 980. See also Coats's earlier treatments of Joseph in *Genesis: With an Introduction to Narrative*, Forms of the Old Testament Literature series, vol. 1 (Grand Rapids, Mich.: Eerdmans, 1984) chaps. 9–10.

51 *Webster's Seventh New Collegiate Dictionary* (Springfield, Mass.: 1969) 577.

52 *ABD* 3 (1992) 980–981.

53 Humphreys, *Joseph and His Family*, 16–17. See also his "Novella," in *Saga, Legend, Tale, Novella, Fable: Narrative Forms in Old Testament Literature*, ed. G. W. Coats, *JSOT* Supp. Series, vol. 35 (Sheffield: *JSOT* Press, 1985) 82–96.

54 Ibid., 19.

55 Humphreys, *Joseph and His Family*, 15.

56 In *Israelite and Judaean History*, 184.

57 *The Origin Tradition of Ancient Israel, JSOT* Supp. Series, vol. 55 (Sheffield: *JSOT* Press, 1987) 122.

58 Ibid., 64.

59 Ibid.

60 I do, however, disagree with Thompson's date for the composition. The late seventh century (the reign of Josiah) is quite arbitrary, and he offers no real evidence to support his conclusion. The toledoth framework was articulated decades ago by P. J. Wiseman in *Creation Revealed in Six Days* (London: Marshall, Morgan, and Scott, 1948). However, Wiseman thought that the formulas were colophons in the cuneiform tradition rather than headings that joined family histories. In a somewhat modified manner, the late R. K. Harrison further expanded Wiseman's idea (*Introduction to the Old Testament* [Grand Rapids, Mich: Eerdmans, 1969] 547–551). Earlier on, S. R. Driver considered the framework of Genesis to be determined by the toledoth formulas (*The Book of Genesis* [London: Methuen, 1909] ii).

61 "On the Egyptian Name of Joseph: A New Approach," *SAK* 2 (1975) 236.

62 William C. Hayes, *A Papyrus of the Late Middle Kingdom in the Brooklyn Museum [Papyrus Brooklyn 35.1446]* (New York: The Brooklyn Museum, 1955) 99.

63 See A. M. Bakir's, *Slavery in Pharaonic Egypt*, Supplément aux *ASAE*, vol. 18 (Cairo: 1952).

64 Kenneth Kitchen, "Joseph," *ISBE*, vol. 2, 1127; Kitchen, *He Swore an Oath*, 79–80.

65 Discussed above, chap. 3, §I.

66 See Hayes, *Papyrus of the Late Middle Kingdom*, pl. 8, 1, 9, pp. 18, 19, 20, 68 for occurrences.

67 Janssen, *JEOL* 14 (1955-56) 64; *CDME*, 174.

68 *CDME*, 18.

69 See the entries "Potiphar" in *IDB*, vol. 3 (1962) 845 and *ABD*, vol. 5 (1992); Janssen, *JEOL* 14 (1955-56) 67–68.

70 Janssen (ibid., 67; see also *ABD*, vol. 5 [1992] 427) is among those who cite the LXX evidence here because both have the η that would correspond to the missing ᶜayin in Gen. 39:1. Kitchen declares himself to be "very sceptical" concerning the association of the two names given the absence of the final ᶜayin in Gen. 39:1 (*He Swore an Oath*, 85).

71 The Hebrew writing for On is the proper vocalization for the Egyptian *iwnw* (*Wb*, vol. 1, 54).

72 *ABD*, vol. 5 (1992) 426.

73 *He Swore an Oath*, 85.

74 Schulman, *SAK* 2 (1975) 241–243.

75 *He Swore an Oath*, 85. *T3* is the feminine definite article, while masculine is *p3*.

76 Ibid., 86.

77 Ibid.

78 Ibid.

79 *IDB*, vol. 1 (1962) 247–248; Janssen, *JEOL* 14 (1955-56) 68; Schulman, *SAK* 2 (1975) 238–239.

80 Ibid., 239.

81 Cf. Hermann Ranke, *Ägyptische Personennamen*, vols. 1, 2 (Hamburg: Augustin, 1935).

82 *Aegyptischen Randglossen zum Alten Testament* (Strasburg: Schlesier and Schweikhardt, 1904) 18–19.

83 *Personennamen*, vol. 1, 15.3.

84 *He Swore an Oath*, 84.

85 Ibid., 84–85; cf. Ranke, *Personnenamen*, vol. 1, 14.7, 15.4 for the former and 15.1, 7 for the latter.

86 *He Swore an Oath*, 85.

87 *ZÄS* 27 (1889) 41–42 and *ZÄS* 30 (1892) 50–52.

88 Janssen, *JEOL* 14 (1955-56) 67; Schulman, *SAK* 2 (1975), 239–240.

89 *Language of the Pentateuch*, 33.

90 *Joseph en Égypte*, 142–150.

91 Ibid., 144–145.

92 Kitchen has made this point in his review of *Joseph en Égypte*, *JEA* 47 (1961) 161.

93 See "Zaphenath-Paneah," *IBD*, vol. 4 (1962) 934.

94 Redford, *The Biblical Story of Joseph*, 230–231.

95 *SAK* 2 (1975) 239–243.

96 *JEA* 47 (1961) 161.

97 *NBD* 1353; *He Swore an Oath*, 82–83.

98 Ibid., 83.

99 The same formulas can be found in Papyrus Kahun from the Twelfth Dynasty, cf. Francis L. Griffith, *Hieratic Papyri from Kahun and Gurob*, vols. 1–2 (London: EEF 1898).

100 Alan Gardiner, *Egyptian Grammar* (London: Oxford University Press, 1969) §377.

101 Hayes, *Papyrus of the Late Middle Kingdom,* 102.

102 Ibid., pl. 8, l. 1; similar pattern is l. 8.

103 Ibid., pl. 9, l. 18.

104 Ibid., l. 19.

105 Ibid., pl. 11, l. 51.

106 Ibid., l. 58.

107 Schulman, *SAK* 2 (1975) 241.

108 See Gardiner, *Egyptian Grammar*, §§112, 511.1.

109 *He Swore an Oath*, 84.

110 See his technical discussion of the linguistic matters in ibid., 84–85, and the notes.

111 Kenneth Kitchen, *Pharaoh Triumphant: The Life and Times of Ramesses II* (Warminster: Aris and Phillips, 1982) 88.

112 *Wb*, vol. 1, 516.

113 Redford, "Pharaoh," *ABD*, vol. 5 (1992) 288–289.

114 *DLE*, vol. 1 175–176.

115 Kenneth Kitchen, "Pharaoh," *ISBE*, vol. 3, 821.

116 *Wb*, vol. 3, 395. Erman and Grapow did place a question mark after the Hebrew word *ḥarṭôm*. Yahuda recognized the problem with Egyptian *ḥr* becoming Hebrew *ḥar* and thus opted for *ḥry*.

117 KB, 333; Vergote, *Joseph en Égypte*, 66–73.

118 Alan Gardiner, *Ancient Egyptian Onomastica* (Oxford: Oxford University Press, 1947) 56*; Jan Quaegebeur, "The Egyptian Equivalent of Harṭummîm," in Israellit-Groll, ed., *Pharaonic Egypt*, 164.

119 Ibid., 165.

120 Redford, *The Biblical Story of Joseph*, 203–204.

121 Quaegebeur, in *Pharaonic Egypt*, 166–167, documents this influence.

122 Ibid.

123 Ibid., 167–169.

124 Ibid., 169.

125 Ibid., 164–165. See A, H Gardiner, "The House of Life," *JEA* 24 (1938) 157–199; Labib Habachi, "The 'House of Life' at Bubastis," *CdÉ* 46 (1971) 59–71.

126 "Interpreters of Dreams in Ancient Egypt," *JEA* 4 (1917) 252.

127 "An Alternative Etymology of the Bohairic Word for 'Interpreter of Dreams,'" *JEA* 50 (1964) 184.

128 Alan Gardiner, *Hieratic Papyri in the British Museum,* 3 Series, Chester Beatty Gift, vol. 1, text (London: British Museum, 1937) and I. E. S. Edwards, *Hieratic Papyri in the British Museum,* 4 Series, vol. 1, text (London: British Museum, 1960).

129 J. G. Griffiths has made the ingenious suggestion that the Jewish synagogue had its origins in Egypt and was greatly influenced by the institution of the pr ꜥnḫ in "Egypt and the Rise of the Synagogue," *JTS* 38 (1987) 1–15.

130 Ibid., 8.

131 "A Ramesside Grammar Book of a Technical Language of Dream Interpretation," in Israellit-Groll, ed., *Pharaonic Egypt,* 116.

132 *The Biblical Story of Joseph,* 205–206. No "birthday of the King" is attested in Siegfried Schott's *Altägyptischen Festdaten* (Wiesbaden: Akademie der Wissenschaft und Literatur, 1950).

133 Ibid., 206.

134 "The Birthday of Pharaoh," *Wepwawet* 1 (1985) 22.

135 "Hitherto Unnoticed Evidence Regarding Copper Works of Art of the Oldest Period of Egyptian History," *JEA* 1 (1914) 233.

136 Boddens-Hosang, *Wepwawet* 1 (1985) 22.

137 Arthur Weiser, *The Psalms: A Commentary* (Philadelphia: Westminster Press, 1962) 109–110; Mitchell Dahood, *Psalms I, 1–50* (Garden City, N.Y.: Doubleday, 1966) 7; A. A. Anderson, *The Book of Psalms I, 1–72* (Grand Rapids, Mich.: Eerdmans, 1972) 63; Peter Craigie, *Psalms 1–50* (Waco: Word, 1983) 64–65.

138 Leslie C. Allen, *Psalms 101–150* (Waco: Word, 1983) 81; *TDOT,* vol. 6, 80.

139 By this suggestion I do not mean that the Egyptian and Israelite concepts of divine kingship were the same. While there are some biblical scholars who believe that the idea of divine descent was at work in Israel, others have rejected it. See Keith Whitelam, "King and Kingship," in *ABD,* vol. 4 (1992) 45 for a review of this debate. I think Whitelam is right in suggesting the "sonship" of the Israelite king derives from the anointing ceremony where symbolically the spirit of God (*rûaḥ 'elōhîm*) came upon the king (ibid., 45–46; cf. 1 Sam. 10:1, 6; 16:13). These ideas are further developed in two articles currently in preparation by me: "The King as God's Son in Egypt and Israel" which will appear in the Ronald J. Williams *Gedankschrift* (Toronto: *JSSEA*) and a variation on this paper in *Bible Review* 13 (August 1997). The former discusses the views of Posener and others who reject Frankfort's understanding.

140 *Psalms 1–50,* 67.

141 Conveniently brought together by Othmar Keel, *Symbolism of the Biblical World* (New York: Seabury Press, 1978) 247–268. I would like to gratefully acknowledge the helpful discussions with my colleague, Dr. Andrew Hill, on this matter.

142 Lanny Bell, "Luxor Temple and the Cult of the Royal Ka," *JNES* 44 (1985) 258, 267. I am grateful to Professor Bell for giving me an offprint of this article some years ago and for the conversations we have had on the cult of the royal *ka.*

143 Henri Frankfort, *Kingship and the Gods* (Chicago: University of Chicago Press, 1948) 101–109; Bell, *JNES* 44 (1985) 257–260.

144 John Wilson, *The Culture of Egypt* (Chicago: University of Chicago Press, 1951) 46, 88; Frankfort, *Kingship and the Gods,* 102–103; Gardiner, *Egyptian Grammar,* 74.

145 For another reference in the Bible to the Israelite king being the son of Yahweh, see 2 Sam. 7:14.

146 See Sethe, *JEA* 1 (1914) 233.

147 *History and Chronology of the Eighteenth Dynasty of Egypt* (Toronto: University of Toronto Press, 1967) 3 – 27.

148 Frankfort, *Kingship and the Gods,* 101 – 109.

149 Redford, *History and Chronology,* 17 – 22.

150 Ibid., 27.

151 *Urk.* IV, 648.9.

152 *Wb,* vol. 3, 58.

153 Redford, *History and Chronology,* 25 – 27.

154 *Urk.* I, 83. References to the "king's appearance" in the Palermo Stone, which span Dynasties 1 – 6, are thought to be commemorations of special "appearances" of the king on cultic occasions and not the accession anniversary since they are found sporadically in the year boxes and not annually, as might be the case with the accession feast (Redford, *History and Chronology,* 22).

155 Redford has gathered these in ibid., 26. I am unable to add to these.

156 Redford's nos. 98 and 100.

157 In the Mesopotamian legal tradition going back to the Old Babylonian period (eighteenth and seventeenth centuries B.C.), proclamations of justice (*mišarum*), often including cancelations of debts, could be issued during the king's first year. Such edicts, apparently, served as the basis for later law codes. See J. J. Finkelstein, "Ammiṣaduqa's Edict and the Babylonian 'Law-Codes,'" *JCS* 15 (1961) 91 – and *ANET,* 526.

158 *Joseph en Égypte,* 124 – 134.

159 *The Biblical Story of Joseph,* 208 – 213.

160 Ibid., 215, 221 – 222.

161 Ibid., 224.

162 *Oriens Antiquus* 12 (1973) 240.

163 Ibid.

164 Ibid.

165 Ibid., 241.

166 KB, 1013; *Wb,* vol. 4, 295. The absence of the ר in Hebrew is owing to the fact that as early as the Middle Kingdom, final *rs* in Egyptian were quiescing (i.e., not being vocalized).

167 *The Eerdmans Analytical Concordance to the Revised Standard Version,* ed. R. E. Whitaker (Grand Rapids, Mich.: Eerdmans, 1988) 627.

168 For a recent argument favoring a Late Bronze dating for the tabernacle and the Pentateuch narratives relating thereto, see Kitchen, "The Tabernacle—A Bronze Age Artefact," *Eretz-Israel* 24, Avraham Malamat Volume (1993) 119*– 129*.

169 *HTR* 60 (1967) 117 – 121.

170 *Oriens Antiquus* 12 (1973) 241.

171 Ibid., 240 – 241.

172 Redford, *The Biblical Story of Joseph,* 225 – 226.

173 Ibid., 217.

174 *Urk.* IV, 3.15; see also 5.1 where he is decorated a second time.

175 William Ward, *Index of Egyptian Administrative and Religious Titles of the Middle Kingdom* (Beirut: American University Press, 1982) and Stephen Quirke, "The Regular Titles of the Late Middle Kingdom," *RdÉ* 37 (1986) 107 – 130.

176 Yahuda, *The Language of the Pentateuch,* 21 – 23; Janssen, *JEOL* 14 (1955-56) 67.

177   William Ward, "The Egyptian Office of Joseph," *JSS* 5 (1960) 144–150; Kitchen, "Joseph," *ISBE*, vol. 2, 1128.

178   *The Duties of the Vizier: Civil Administration in the Early New Kingdom* (London/ New York: Kegan Paul International, 1988). See also David Lorton's comments arising from van den Boorn's monograph, "What was the PR-NSW and Who Managed it? Aspects of Royal Administration in 'The Duties of the Vizier,'" *SAK* 18 (1991) 291–309.

179   Ward, *JSS* 5 (1960) 145–150.

180   The biography of Weni, the Sixth Dynasty official from Aswan is often cited as such an example in Egypt. In Israel an example is David's rise from shepherd to king. In Mesopotamia, Sargon of Akkad is portrayed as a man from humble origins who became king of the first unified empire in that region.

181   Jaroslav Černý, "Egypt from the Inception of the Nineteenth Dynasty to the Death of Ramesses III," *CAH*, vol. 2, pt. 2, 237-238.

182   *Egypt of the Pharaohs* (London/New York: Oxford University Press, 1962) 277.

183   *CAH*, vol. 2, pt. 2, 238.

184   Nina de Garis Davies and Alan Gardiner, *The Tomb of Amenemhet*, no. 82 (London: EEF, 1915) 32; Thomas Schneider, *Asiatische Personennamen in des Neuen Reiches*, *OBO* 114 (Freiburg: Universitätsverlag, 1992) 71.

185   Alain Zivie, "Tombes rupestres de la falaise du Bubastieion à Saqqarah—Campaigns 1980–1981," *ASAE* 68 (1982) 63–69 and *Découverte à Saqqarah: Le Vizir oublié* (Paris: Alain Zivie, 1990) 93–181.

186   W. F. Albright, "Northwest-Semitic Names in a List of Egyptian Slaves from the Eighteenth Century B.C.," *JAOS* 74 (1954) 225; Hayes, *Papyrus of the Late Middle Kingdom*, 94; Georges Posener, "Les Asiatics en Égypte sous les XIIᵉ et XIIIᵉ Dynasties," *Syria* 34 (1957) 148.

187   Schneider, *Asiatische Personennamen*, 66–68. Schneider considers the posibility that ʿpr might be a writing for the Semitic ʿbd, "servant," a postion shared by James Hoch (*Semitic Words in Egyptian Texts of the New Kingdom and Third Intermediate Period* [Princeton: Princeton University Press, 1994] 64). While this is possible, I am not convinced. The Egyptian writing system was perfectly capable of writing Semitic ʿbd, and this name is attested in Egypt (see Hoch's entry no. 69).

188   W. K. Simpson, "The Hyksos Princess Tany," *CdÉ* 68 (1959) 237-238.

189   Helmer Ringgren, *Religions of the Ancient Near East* (London: SPCK, 1973) 127–132.

190   Hayes, *Papyrus of the Late Middle Kingdom*, 96

191   These transcriptions were provided by Zivie since the texts of the tomb were not fully published in his monograph.

192   Schneider, *Asiatische Personennamen*, 243–244.

193   Zivie, *Découverte à Saqqarah*, 152.

194   Amihai Mazar, *Archaeology of the Land of the Bible 10,000 –586 B.C.E.* (New York: Doubleday, 1990) 277-279; Rivka Gonen, *Burial Patterns and Cultural Diversity in Late Bronze Age Canaan*, *ASOR* Dissertation Series, vol. 7, (Winona Lake, Ind.: Eisenbrauns, 1992) 9, describes multiple interments as "an indigenous burial custom in Canaan" that began in the Middle Bronze and continued into the Late Bronze Age.

195   The use of the clay coffins in Philistia (e.g., Deir el-Balaḥ) is likely an attempt to copy the Egyptian practice by locals who had close ties to Egypt.

196   C. W. Goodwin, "De la longévité chez les Égyptiens," in F. Chabas, *Mélanges égyptologiques*, 2ᵉ séries (Châlon-sur-Saône: J. Dejussieu 1864) 231–237.

197   The only other example of this figure applied to a biblical character is Joshua

(Josh. 24:29; Judg. 2:8), but it must be recalled that according to biblical tradition, he was born in Egypt, which might explain the application of the Egyptian ideal to this Israelite hero.

198 Moses' age at death is 120, which may symbolize 3 x 40, i.e., the time span of three generations.

199 *RB*, 79.7.

200 "On the Ideal Lifetime of the Egyptians," *OMRO* 31 (1950) 33–41.

201 Ibid., 41.

202 Schulman, *SAK* 2 (1975) 242.

203 Ibid., 236.

204 *The Biblical Story of Joseph*, 241–242.

205 Schulman, *SAK* 2 (1975) 243.

206 Ibid.

207 Thompson, *Origin Tradition*, 63, similarly, see 133.

208 *Prologue to History*, 2–3.

209 See my critique of *In Search of History* in chap. 1, §3.

210 Van Seters, *Prologue to History*, 312.

211 Ibid.

212 David Hackett Fischer, *Historians' Fallacies* (New York: Harper and Row, 1970) 47–48. See above, in chap. 2, §II.

213 *From Canaan to Egypt: Structural and Theological Context for the Joseph Story*, *CBQ* Monograph Series, vol. 4 (Washington, D.C.: 1976) 4.

214 Siegfried Herrmann, *Israel in Egypt* (London: SCM, 1973) 32. He believes in a Ramesside setting, but the final form of the story occurred in the Davidic-Solomonic era (33).

215 *Prologue to History*, 332.

216 In *Pharaonic Egypt*, 166.

217 *Origin Tradition*, 193–194.

218 On Garbini, see discussion in chap. 1, §3.

5

ISRAELITES IN EGYPT

> These are the names of the sons of Israel
> who came to Egypt with Jacob, each with
> his household
>
> Exod. 1:1

I. Exodus 1 – 14: Literary Considerations

The Joseph story serves to explain the circumstances under which the family of Jacob entered Egypt with its flocks and herds, as aliens settling in the northeast Delta, the land of Goshen (cf. Gen. 47). There is no attempt to explain the amount of time that elapsed from Joseph's death (Gen. 50:25 – 26) until the opening of the book of Exodus, from the "good old days" under Joseph to the oppression that begins in Exodus 1. It is widely recognized that Exodus 1:1 – 7 serves as a bridge connecting the story of Joseph and the eisodos to that of Moses and the exodus.[1]

For over a century, source critics have viewed the composition of Exodus 1 through 14 as a combination of the earlier J and E sources with insertions and editorial work by the Priestly writers in the fifth century B.C.[2] During the 1980s serious criticism against this dominant view began to appear, and new literary approaches were advanced.[3]

Recent literary readings of the Exodus narratives reveal that 1:1 through 2:25 contains "key words" that are at work within smaller units and are matched with the same words in the final section of the Exodus narratives (13:17 – 14:31).[4] Charles Isbell's reading of the text shows that some passages, such as 2:23 to 25 (thought by most biblical scholars to be P's addition), "dovetails so nicely with the general structure determined so far by 'J' and 'E' as well as with several JE blocks of material soon to follow."[5] Isbell observes that "the story lines often cross the boundaries commonly set down by source analysis."[6] These observations show that the linguistic and literary criteria used in the past to identify different sources can no longer be sustained.[7] The thematic and stylistic unity of the opening two chapters of Exodus has been reinforced in a subsequent, more detailed study by Gordon Davies.[8] Similarly, G. Fischer discovered that Exodus 3 and 4 also displayed a thematic coherence and literary unity.[9]

Thomas Thompson has recently rejected the traditional source-critical analysis of Genesis and Exodus because it is "no longer sufficient to maintain such a radical interpretation of narrative, one which carries us so far from any immediate reading of the text. Differences in divine names, places names, references to individuals and groups, even differences in style and language, while often giving evidence for lack of homogeneity in the tradition, do not justify the positing of distinct documents, separated by centuries."[10] Rather, he considers this body of literature to be a "traditional complex-chain narrative" that is "an ancient narrative genre, a specific type of oral or literary unit. It has its own beginning and end, its own theme, and its own plot-line (i.e. its own developmental direction), which enables it to exist as a literary entity, and to have a life of its own, independent of both its context and the narrative materials from which it formed. The traditional complex-chain narrative is not an editorial or redactional structure, but a type of literature in its own right: one of the ways in which ancient Israel told long stories."[11] For Thompson, the Exodus narrative is one such "chain-narrative," running from Exodus 1:1 to 15:21, made up of connecting episodes. On the literary level, I find Thompson's theory quite plausible.[12]

While new literary readings of Exodus 1 to 14 are revealing a literary unity, against the more fragmented picture offered by source critics, other scholars now see folklorist, mythic, and legendary influences that once again cast a pall over the historical dimensions of the text. For instance, Thompson frequently uses the term "historiography" to describe the Exodus narratives, while he considers the units to be made up of "ahistorical folk tradition[s]" and "popular folklore and folk history of the time, arranged to make a fundamental affirmation about their already existent self-identity as a nation of *gerim* [sojourners], led by God."[13] Similarly, Niels Peter Lemche assumes that the sojourn and exodus story is legendary and concludes that the material is devoid of historical value. He asserts: "It is generally acknowledged by scholars that the traditions about Israel's sojourn in Egypt and the *exodus* of the Israelites are legendary and epic in nature. The very notion that a single family could in the course of a few centuries develop into a whole people, a nation, consisting of hundreds of thousands of individuals, is so fantastic that it deserves no credence from a *historical* point of view."[14]

Bernard Batto and Gösta Ahlström have renewed interest in the mythological character of the sea-crossing story (see below, chap. 9).[15] For Batto, the Priestly writers historicized the mythic exodus event. Samuel Loewenstamm also holds to the "historicization of myth" in Exodus, while at the same time maintaining an essential historicity, especially in the oppression narratives.[16] On the contrary, Donald Redford responds to Ahlström and those who see a Canaanite/Mesopotamian mythology at work in Exodus, declaring, "This is a curious resort, for the text does not look like mythology." He thinks the proposal of later historicizing of myth is "more ingenious than illuminating."[17] Ramesses II in the battle of Kadesh employed considerable mythic language, notes Redford, to describe a historical event not even the most radical historical minimalist would deny.[18]

As will be argued in more detail below (chap. 9, §VI), the use of mythological language and images in a Hebrew narrative does not mean that a fictitious event is being described. In the end, those who consider the Exodus stories to be historicized myths, folklorist tales, or legends rest on assumptions about the nature of the literature that cannot be proven.

II. A Change in Fortunes

After an undisclosed period of tranquillity and tribal fertility, a radical change occurred when "there arose a new king over Egypt who did not know Joseph" (Exod. 1:8). Unfortunately, this pharaoh, like those who followed in Exodus, is anonymous. This silence is used as evidence for the mythic or legendary nature of the exodus narratives, while for others it demonstrates that the Hebrew writers were not really interested in history or simply did not know the facts.[19] The absence of the pharaoh's name may ultimately be for theological reasons, because the Bible is not trying to answer the question "who is the pharaoh of the exodus" to satisfy the curiosity of modern historians; rather, it was seeking to clarify for Israel who was the God of the exodus. In Exodus 5:1, Moses and his brother Aaron approach Pharaoh with the request, "Let my people go." To which the obdurate monarch responds, "Who is Yahweh that I should hear his voice and let Israel go? I do not know Yahweh."[20] Pharaoh not only rejects Moses' petition, but denies knowledge of Yahweh. This rebuff sets the stage for the subsequent series of plagues in which Yahweh demonstrates who he is, both to Pharaoh and to Israel (Exod. 7:5; 9:29; 14:17–18, 31; on the plagues see chap. 6).

Another factor that might account for the absence of Pharaoh's name in the exodus narratives is that it was normal in New Kingdom inscriptions not to disclose the name of Pharaoh's enemies. Several examples of this practice will suffice to illustrate this point. Thutmose III's campaign against the rebellious coalition at Megiddo was fomented by the king of Kadesh (on the Orontes) who is named "that wretched enemy of Kadesh" (ḫrw pf ḫs n kdšw) or simply "that wretched enemy" in the Annals of Thutmose III[21] and in the Gebel Barkal stela.[22] Even when reviewing the booty taken from this battle, the scribes do not name the king whose possessions the Egyptians captured: "the fine chariot made of gold belonging to the prince (wr) of [Megiddo]," "the fine mail armor of that enemy (i.e., the king of Kadesh)" and "the fine mail armor of the prince of Megiddo."[23]

The Amada stela of Amenhotep II reports on the king's successful battles against some Nubian tribes. "Seven chieftains" from Tekhsy were slain and their bodies unceremoniously tied upside down on the king's bark as he returned to Egypt. Subsequently, six of the enemies were displayed on the walls of Thebes, while the seventh was returned south to Napata for the same treatment.[24] Once again, none of the names of the Nubian chieftains are recorded. In Amenhotep II's Memphis stela reference is made to campaigns in Edom, Canaan, and Syria. Foreign kings who are defeated, deposed, or killed are unnamed.[25] Mention is also made of the chieftains of Naharin (the land east of the Euphrates), Khatti (the Hittites), and Babylon.[26] Despite the fact that these were rather prominent kings, their names are not given. This large stela, and its close match from Karnak, contains extensive documentation of cities and regions attacked. However, only the names of two minor chieftains, Inka of Hetjera and Kaka of Giboa-Saman are recorded.[27] What is different with these two is that they surrendered to Amenhotep, and Kaka was taken to Egypt along with his family as prisoners of war. It thus appears that in the Eighteenth Dynasty, as a rule, Pharaoh's enemies were not usually named unless they were taken captive.

The same practice continues in the Ramesside era. The Karnak reliefs of Seti I show him vigorously battling various enemies. Against the Libyans he is depicted trampling on a chieftain while about to dispatch another with a javelin. Between the two scenes, the inscription reads "smiting the Chieftains of Tehenu" -skr wrw nw thnw.[28] Against the Hittites, the chariot driving Seti fires arrows at the fleeing Hittite king.[29] The twenty lines of text over this relief describe the battle in general terms, but do not mention the name of the depicted Hittite foe.

Ramesses II had extensive reports of his battle at Kadesh against a coalition headed by the Hittite king Muwatallis inscribed on several temples. Throughout the "Bulletin" and "Poem," the expressions "the enemy from Khatti" and "the wretched chief of Khatti" are used throughout, just as in the Eighteenth Dynasty.[30] Lesser kings are also dubbed "the chief of Arzawa," "the chief of Irun," "the chief of Carchemish, the chief of Karkisha," and a simpler form "he of X (i.e., individual's homeland)" is used of the leaders of Masa, Luka, Dardany and Khaleb.[31] In the Merneptah (Israel) stela, the primary focus is on the Libyan invasion. The chieftain is called "the wretched chief" and "the Libyan enemy" throughout the battle report until the point when he is taken prisoner.[32] Only then is his name, Merey, disclosed.[33]

What can be concluded from the normal Egyptian scribal practice of omitting the names of Pharaoh's enemies? Surely historians would not dismiss the historicity of Thutmose III's Megiddo campaign because the names of the kings of Kadesh and Megiddo are not recorded. It seems unlikely that Thutmose and his scribes were not aware of their enemies' names. No one denies that there was a battle at Kadesh between the forces of Ramesses II and Muwatallis because the latter's name does not appear in Egyptian record's of the event. We cannot think the names were omitted because these documents were written by later historians who were ignorant of the details they wrote about because the texts cited above all come from dated documents written during the lifetimes of the kings whose actions are recorded. In the few cases where an enemy's name is divulged, it seems to have been because that chieftain or king was captured and taken prisoner.

In contrast with the Egyptian scribal practice of omitting the names of Pharaoh's royal enemies, Assyrian rulers from the second through the first millenniums are meticulous in reciting the names of their enemies. The same is true of Babylonian and Aramean inscriptions. One need only to scan the two volumes of

Luckenbill's *ARAB* or Pritchard's *ANET* to see the difference between the Egyptian and Assyrian practices. This difference is especially true in Neo-Assyrian annals during the period (ninth through seventh centuries B.C.) when the Old Testament books of Genesis through Joshua were being written, according to many biblical scholars. And yet the New Kingdom Egyptian practice of omitting a king's name is followed in Exodus, rather than the Assyrian tradition of naming monarchs that dominates the first millennium.

The history of the Israelite monarchy in Kings and Chronicles, which spans the first half of the first millennium, faithfully mentions the enemy kings of Israel and Judah's by name: Shishak/Sheshonk I (1 Kings 14:25; 2 Chron. 12:5,9); Neco II (2 Kings 23:29–35; 2 Chron. 35:20); Hophra (Jer. 44:30) of Egypt; Tiglath-pileser III (2 Kings 15:29); Shalmaneser V (2 Kings 17:3); Sargon II (Isa. 20:1); Sennacherib (2 Kings 18:13 – 19:36); and Esarhaddon (2 Kings 19:37) of Assyria.[34] The Hebrew scribal tradition at work in Kings and Chronicles reflects the contemporary Neo-Assyrian counterpart, against the New Kingdom Egyptian custom in Genesis and Exodus. For the Third Intermediate Period (ca. 1100–525 B.C.), there are a limited number of inscriptions dealing with Egypt's wars. One of the most celebrated is the great Piankhy stela recounting his invasion of Egypt to subdue the Delta king, Tefnakht.[35] While Piankhy was a Kushite, he and his successors were thoroughly Egyptianized, and they considered themselves to be legitimate pharaohs.[36] This record details the names and offices of the various petty kings, officials, and priests who had sided with him. This practice of naming seems to be a late development in Egyptian history, similar to the Mesopotamian practices of the first millennium and a sharp contrast from the custom found in the Empire period.

What possible rationale is there for the deliberate omission of the names of Pharaoh's enemies in New Kingdom texts? Could it be a literary counterpart to the practice of excising the names from inscriptions and defacing the images of one's enemies? Alan Schulman has called this practice *damnatio memoriae*.[37] Distinguished from the royal practice of usurpation, *damnatio memoriae* required defacing both the image and name of the individual whose memory and very existence were being magically annihilated. In the case of battle reliefs where, for instance, Seti attacks the Libyan chieftain or the Hittite king, they are shown shot with arrows and about to be killed by Pharaoh's blow. And the names are not recorded.

A variation on the *damnatio memoriae* practice is the Execration Texts. Beginning in the Old Kingdom, names of Egypt's enemies, real or potential, including nations, tribes, and foreign kings, were written on jars or anthropoid figurines and then smashed so as to magically destroy those enemies.[38] Provisionally, it might be suggested that the practice of ignoring the name of Pharaoh's enemies in royal inscriptions was intended to destroy magically Egypt's enemies in a similar way. An alternative explanation for the practice of omitting the names was as a sign of contempt for one's enemy.

The omission of Pharaoh's name in the exodus story, I suggest, was deliberate. For the Hebrew writer, there was good theological reasons for this silence: the reader learns of the name of God Yahweh and his power as the Exodus story unfolds, whereas his arch-rival, Pharaoh, remains anonymous—a nice piece of irony.

III. The Oppression of the Hebrews

The new, paranoid pharaoh began a program of forced labor for the Israelites, making bricks for building projects and "all kinds of work in the field" (Exod. 1:11–14). This scenario has long been considered to have a ring of truth even for more skeptical scholars.[39] Sir Alan Gardiner, the renowned twentieth-century Egyptologist and usually a sharp critic of the historical value of the Old Testament, considered the Exodus narratives to be "no less mythical than the details of the creation as recorded in Genesis," but in the same essay concedes "that Israel was in Egypt under one form or another no historian could possibly doubt; a legend of such tenacity representing the early fortunes of a peoples under so unfavourable an aspect could not have arisen save as a reflexion, however much distorted, of real occurrences."[40] For Martin Noth as well, the forced labor "corresponds with an actual historical situation."[41] Naturally, those opting for more revisionist reconstructions of Israel's origins, especially those holding to the idea that Israel arose as an indigenous Canaanite people, reject the Egyptian sojourn altogether (see chap. 2, §1).

There is no doubt that there was a significant Semitic population throughout Egypt during the New Kingdom (see chap. 3). Because of the preponderance of epigraphic evidence for a Syro-Palestinian presence in Egypt from the mid to late second millennium B.C., even the most skeptical historian cannot dismiss the fact that both the Bible and Egyptian sources agree on this situation.[42] Even as far south as Thebes there was a significant number of Semitic-speaking people during the Empire period.[43] The names of Semites have even turned up among the workers of Deir el-Medineh in western Thebes.[44] While Semites could rise to places of significance in Egyptian society and in the court,[45] the concern here is to examine the evidence for forced labor among this population in Egypt.

Biblical scholars have long been familiar with the scene of laborers at work making bricks from the tomb of Rekhmire, the vizier of Thutmose III (ca. 1479–1425 B.C.; figs. 8 and 9). The adjoining text indicates that these workers were taken as prisoners of war (*skr ᶜnḥw*) from the king's campaigns in the south lands (i.e., Nubia) and north lands (i.e., Syria-Canaan).[46] Taking prisoners of war from western Asia during the Empire period is well attested in private and royal monuments. During the earliest campaigns in the Levant, military officers such as Ahmose, son of Ibana, report on personally capturing prisoners who were in turn given to them by the monarch. General Ahmose claims that he received four slaves from the battle for Avaris, two from Sharuhen, and he captured a charioteer in Thutmose I's Euphrates campaign. The charioteer would likely continue his military career in the Egyptian army, and hence was not given to Ahmose, who was instead decorated with the "gold of valor."[47] In the same biography, Ahmose boasts of his pharaoh's victories: "countless were the prisoners-of-war which his majesty brought from his victories (in Naharin)."[48] Another early Eighteenth Dynasty military officer, Ahmose Pen-Nekhbet, mentions the capture of a great number of prisoners of war by Thutmose II while fighting Shasu (a bedouin), probably in the northern Sinai and Negev region of Canaan.[49]

Later monarchs often recorded the numbers of prisoners taken. Thutmose III is credited with seizing 340 prisoners from the battle at Megiddo.[50] His annals provide documentation of prisoners of war and men and maidservants brought to Egypt from the Levant: year 30 brought thirty-six men and 181 male (hm) and female (hmt) servants; year 31, 492 prisoners of war; year 33, sixty-six male and female servants with their children and 513 male and female servants as tribute from Retenu; year 34, 602 male and female servants as tribute from Retenu; year 38, fifty prisoners of war and 522 male and female servants as tribute from Retenu.[51] In short, during nearly twenty years of recorded annals, which are by no means complete, thousands of people from Canaan and Syria were transported to Egypt as prisoners of war or as gifts from various kings.

While no extensive annals have survived for Thutmose III's successors, a number of inscriptions bear witness to a continuation of the policy of deporting Semitic-speaking peoples from western Asia to Egypt. Amenhotep II's year 7 Memphis stela recounts the king's first two sorties into the Levant. Figures given for captured peoples are 550 Maryanu (elite Hurrian warriors), 240 wives of Maryanu, 640 Canaanites, 232 children of princes, 323 daughters of the princes, 270 concubines of the princess, with the total being 2,214 individuals.[52] The numbers from his second campaign are even higher: 127 chieftains of Retenu, 179 chieftain's brothers, 3600 ʿApiru, 15,200 Shasu-Bedouin, 36,300 Syrians (h3rw), 15,070 from Nagasu, and their families 30,652, with a grand total of 89,600.[53] Interestingly, the figure given for the total is incorrect. Adding all the individual figures, the sum is actually 101,128.[54] Because this total is so high, its reliability might be questioned. However, the figures do not fit typical Egyptian hyperbolic language of capturing hundreds of thousands and myriads. Consequently, for they have not been dismissed as deliberate exaggerations, nor have Egyptologists denied the historicity of the campaigns because of the large total.

One suggestion is that the figures on the Memphis stela represent the grand total for all campaigns up to the time of the stela.[55] J. J. Janssen thought the figures might belong to a census of the region, which would mean they were not deportees to Egypt.[56] Alternatively, Amin Amer proposed that the figures should be taken seriously and reflect a shift in policy from a selective deportation used by Amenhotep II's predecessors to mass deportation.[57] He compares this practice to that used by the Hittite monarch Mursilis II and Middle and Neo-Assyrian kings. The remainder of the Eighteenth Dynasty saw only limited Egyptian military activity in Canaan and Syria, a testimony to Thutmose III and Amenhotep II's effectiveness in controlling the lands from Egypt to the Euphrates, and perhaps because of Amenhotep's mass-deportation program to break down resistance.[58]

The Amarna period may have seen a relaxation of Egypt's grip in western Asia, though General Horemheb led a campaign against the Hittites in Syria, either under Akhenaten or Tutankhamun, that may have involved some battles in Semitic-speaking lands.[59] Seti I campaigned vigorously in Canaan, as his panoramic reliefs at Karnak illustrate.[60] One scene shows the king returning to Egypt with a band of Shasu as prisoners of war (fig. 10).[61] There is a notice in Papyrus Leiden 348 from the reign of Ramesses II of "the ᶜApiru who are dragging stone to the great pylon of [text broken] Raᶜmesse-miamun, Beloved of Maᶜet."[62] The lacuna in this line deprives us of the full name of the structure. Ricardo Caminos does not think the words for "temple" would be a good fit, and there is no known temple by that name. However, he notes that the epithet "Beloved of Maᶜet" is associated with a palace.[63] A close parallel to this text is found in the damaged Papyrus Leiden 349, which again mentions ᶜApiru engaged in state service.[64]

This brief review amply shows that from the early part of the Eighteenth Dynasty until the accession of Ramesses II (when many date the exodus), Egypt was teeming with Semitic-speaking peoples. The presence of the Israelites in this mix during the New Kingdom, then, is very plausible. It is true that the Hebrew Scriptures are concerned with what happened to one particular group, the Children of Israel. Though not brought to Egypt as trophies of war, it is clear that once the policy of employing prisoners of war in labor projects was introduced, the Israelites and other Semites already living in Egypt were treated likewise. The biblical writer hints that he was aware of other people who shared in the arduous labor regimen. When describing the departure from Egypt, Exodus 12:38 notes: "A mixed multitude (ᶜēreḇ raḇ)also went up with them," which is understood to refer to other enslaved workers who joined the Israelites in their flight from Egypt.[65]

What became of the tens of thousands of Semites when brought to Egypt from western Asia? The majority of them did not become the possession of private citizens; rather, they were subjects of the crown or could be assigned to particular temple estates, while those with military connections were integrated into the Egyptian army. During the Amarna period, men from the Levant appear in reliefs from Akhenaten's Theban temples as a part of the police force.[66]

The Rekhmire scene reflects the plight of the majority of deportees. The workers in this scene are shown in the various stages of brick making; scooping water, mixing the water and soil to make mud, forming the bricks, and carrying dried bricks to the place where they were to be used. The adjoining scene shows that the bricks were being used for ramps to facilitate the construction of the temple Akh-menu at Karnak (ipt swt). Behind the first pylon (south side) at Karnak, one can still see the remnants of such a construction ramp that was never dismantled.[67] Papyrus Anastasi I contains a mathematical problem designed to calculate the number of bricks need to build a construction ramp 730 cubits long, fifty-five cubits wide, and reaching sixty cubits in height.[68] Thousands of bricks would be required for building temples and other major structures that utilize massive stones.

Relevant to the Exodus narratives, this scene demonstrates that prisoners of war beginning in the Eighteenth Dynasty were engaged in brick-making work. Second, Semitic-speaking peoples were employed in connection with building projects for the state. Third, stick-wielding Egyptian "overseers" are shown ready to strike slothful workers.

On this third point, it will be recalled that "taskmasters" (śārê massîm/ nōgᵉśîm- Exod. 1:11; Exod. 3:7, 5:6, 10, 13) were appointed to enforce the work. Kenneth

Kitchen has shown that these two terms reflect the "two-tier" labor system known in Egypt, the *nōgᵉśîm* being a more junior officer.[69] His study also demonstrated that as early as the Old and Middle Kingdoms, targets and quotas for brick making were established by the higher officials but there were rarely reached. The Louvre Leather Roll actually records the amounts of the shortfall.[70] This scenario is not unlike the situation with the Hebrews in Exodus 5:7 and 8: "You shall no longer give the people straw to make bricks, as heretofore; let them go and gather straw for themselves. But the number of bricks which they made heretofore you shall lay upon them, you shall by no means lessen it." Occasionally in Egypt, however, an official could boast to his superiors concerning his workers, "they are making their quota of bricks daily" (*st ḥr irt t3y.sn ipt m mnt*).[71] A factor that could reduce or halt brick production was the absence of straw, to strengthen the bricks.[72] In Papyrus Anastasi 4 an official filed a complaint with his superiors: "I am staying at Kenkenento, unequipped, and there are neither men to make bricks nor straw in the neighborhood."[73] In Exodus 5, Israel's oppression reached its climax when Pharaoh doubled the daily quotas while expecting the Israelites to find their own straw. Additionally, from the Louvre Roll it is evident that special religious holidays were granted to the workers, and work rosters from the workmen's village of Deir el-Medineh report men being off work "to offer to their god."[74] This latter point seems to indicate that Moses' request for the Israelites to have time off to worship Yahweh was not unprecedented and may have been standard procedure (Exod. 5:1).

The majority of textual evidence considered in Kitchen's studies, especially the Anastasi Papyri, the Deir el-Medineh materials, and the Louvre Roll, date to the Ramesside era. Together they attest to the very scenario portrayed in the Exodus narratives: a two-tiered administrative structure, the assignment of sometimes unattainable quotas, the problems of making bricks without straw, and the issue of allowing time off from work to worship one's deity.

In addition to "hard service in mortar and brick," Exodus 1:14 also reports that the Hebrews were also forced to do "all kinds of work in the field." It has long been known from New Kingdom tomb paintings that foreigners are shown at work in various agricultural enterprises. In a recent study of these scenes from Theban and other Upper Egyptian tombs, Ellen Morris has demonstrated that Semites were active in agricultural work during the mid-Eighteenth Dynasty.[75] She observes that beginning with the reign of Thutmose III when deportations of prisoners of war from the Levant began is the time when Semitic farm workers appear in the scenes and notes that "the prisoners of war, as well as many peoples received as part of the yearly Syrian tribute, were looked upon as crown property."[76] Hence, these captives could be assigned to whatever tasks Pharaoh and his officials desired. Farming, fowling and vine tending, and pressing grapes are among the most common agricultural labor done by these prisoners. The text accompanying the wine pressing scene in the tomb of Intef at Thebes, Morris observes, specifically identifies the workers as Apiru (i.e., *ḥabiru*). Her investigation of Upper Egyptian tombs of the mid-Eighteenth dynasty shows that indeed prisoners of war from Canaan and Syria were engaged in agricultural work for the state. The same scenario was undoubtedly true in the Delta, if not on a wider scale given the greater amount of land that was farmed in the north. Once again, Exodus portrays the Israelites doing the same sort of work, agricultural in this case, that other Semitic speaking prisoners of war were forced to do for the state.

IV. Exodus 1:11: The Identification of "Store-Cities"

Israel's brick-making endeavor, Exodus 1:11 states, was connected to the building of "store-cities, Pithom and Raamses." Some have wrongly concluded that by the term "store-cities" (ʿārê miskᵉnôṯ) that these were major cities. For instance, Lemche asserts, "According to Exod 1:11, Pithom should be regarded as a city comparable to Ramses." Yet the text offers no information about the size of the cities, nor that the two are comparable. Since the expression "store-cities" is a Hebrew one, how it was understood in an Israelite setting is essential to understanding the meaning of Exodus 1:11. The other occurrences of "store-cities" in the Hebrew Bible are found in the context of Solomon's building projects (1 Kings 9:19; 2 Chron. 8:4, 6) and those of King Jehoshaphat (2 Chron. 17:12). The purpose of the tripartite, pillared halls found in Iron II contexts at sites such as Megiddo, Hazor, and Beer Sheba has been hotly contested. They were originally thought to be stables,[77] and some scholars still hold to this understanding,[78] while Syro-Palestinian archaeologists now seem to prefer to interpret them as storehouses.[79] Assuming that the tripartite pillared buildings are the ʿārê miskᵉnôṯ of Kings and Chronicles, they occupy a relatively small area within the fortified cities.[80] The Israelite cities of Megiddo, Hazor, and Beer Sheba also contained administrative buildings, temples, palaces, and possibly stables. With this reality in mind, it would be wrong to envision the ʿārê miskᵉnôṯ of Exodus as massive storage facilities the size of a city any more than one would consider Megiddo a city purely for storage. As in the Iron II Israelite cities, the Egyptian storage units were closely associated with administrative centers and temples.

A good example of the latter from the New Kingdom is the Ramesseum, Ramesses II's mortuary temple in western Thebes (fig. 11). It was made of stone masonry and surrounded by more than 160 vaulted storage chambers and various ancillary rooms, all made of mud brick (fig. 12).[81] The subsidiary structures housed the temple staff and various workshops that supported the temple economy.[82] Surrounding the entire complex was a massive mud-brick enclosure wall.

Palaces of the New Kingdom were built along a similar plan, as revealed by the earlier Eighteenth Dynasty one at Deir el-Ballas (fifty km north of Thebes) and the Malkata palace of Amenhotep III in western Thebes.[83] They were entirely constructed of mud brick, as was usual for domestic architecture throughout pharaonic Egypt.[84] Regardless of where the "store cities" were located for which the Israelites are reported to have made bricks, New Kingdom Egyptian palaces and temples both had large storage installations constructed of brick. It is most probable that such features stand behind the ʿārê miskᵉnôṯ of Exodus 1:11.

Raamses/Ramesses[85]

Many years ago, Sir Alan Gardiner surveyed the various Egyptian toponyms with the Pharaonic name Ramesses in order to determine which one might be equated with Raamses of Exodus 1:11.[86] Thanks to the ambitious building ventures of Ramesses II, a number of sites bore his name, stretching from "The Dwelling of Ramesses," situated somewhere in northern Sinai, to Abu Simbel in the south.[87] The full name of the Delta residence of the Nineteenth and Twentieth Dynasties was "House of Ramesses Beloved of Amun, Great of Victories" (*pi-rᶜ mss sw mry imn ᶜ3 nḫtw*).[88] Built by Ramesses II in the early years of his reign, Pi-Ramesses flourished through the reign of Ramesses VI (1143–1136 B.C.), when it was abandoned owing to the westward migration of the Bubastite branch of the Nile. Gardiner eliminated the southern sites and the one in Sinai as the capital because they were not in the Delta (texts clearly placed it next to the Nile). In his study of 1918, he concluded that Pelusium (Tell Farama) was Ramesses, against Flinders Petrie's position that it was located in the Wadi Tumilat at Tell el-Retabeh (fig. 2).[89] Later on, Gardiner rejected Pelusium in favor of Tanis,[90] in the light of French excavations at San el-Hagar by Pierre Montet.[91] The impressive Ramesside remains at Tanis led generations of Egyptologists and biblical scholars to identify this site with Pi-Ramesses and the biblical Raamses/Ramesses.[92] There was no doubt that the statues, obelisks, and monumental stones that made up the central temple complex were from Pi-Ramesses. The problem remained, however, that no ceramic or stratigraphic evidence for the Ramesside period had appeared at Tanis.

Meanwhile, Mahmud Hamza had been digging a rather unglamorous site at Qantir near the town of Fakus and the site of Tell el-Dabᶜa in the northeastern Delta (fig. 2).[93] There he found the foundations of a royal palace and some inscribed Ramesside remains, including hieratic ostracons bearing the name Pi-Ramesses, which led him to suggest that this site was the Delta residence of the Ramessides.[94] An important study by William Hayes of glazed tiles from Qantir led him to support Hamza's identification.[95] Subsequent work at the site by Labib Habachi[96] and Shehata Adam[97] has resulted in the virtual unanimous conclusion that Qantir is Pi-Ramesses.[98] As a consequence of the certainty of this identification, a number of Bible atlases now show Raamses/Ramesses at Qantir, not at Tanis.[99] Archaeological work at Qantir was recently renewed and is ongoing under the directorship of Edgar Pusch, the German Egyptologist.

With the location of Pi-Ramesses now certain, it might be thought that there would be little doubt that this site is the same as Raamses/Ramesses of the Exodus narratives. However, over thirty years ago, Donald Redford questioned the equation on linguistic grounds.[100] He rightly noted that the absence of the element *pi* requires an explanation, since it was present in the spelling of Pithom in Exodus 1:11. Redford also thought it was problematic that the sibilants in Egyptian "Ramesses" should appear in Hebrew as *ss* and not *šš*. He suggested that the vocalization better adheres to "post-Saite times" (i.e., late sixth century onward), and that the toponyms were thus late insertions into the text of Exodus 1.[101] Redford's concerns were thoroughly answered by the late Wolfgang Helck, who showed that there are New Kingdom examples of the writing of the capital city without the initial *pi*.[102] He also showed that Redford's concern over the use of different sibilants was unwarranted.[103] The normal writing for Egyptian *š* in Hebrew is *samek*, as demonstrated by the following Egyptian names when transliterated into Hebrew: Pibeseth (Ezk. 30:17) for *pr bstt*; Phineas (Exod. 6:25; Num. 25:7, 11) for *p3 nhsy*; Tehpenes (1 Kings 11:19) for *t3 h(mt) p3 nsw*, Tahpanhes (Jer. 2:16; 43:7–9; 44:1, 14) for *t3 h(wt)-p3 nhsi*; and Pathros (Isa. 11:11; Jer. 44:1, 15; Ezek. 29:14, 30:14) for *p3 t3 rsy*.[104] If these Egyptian words reflect the Hebrew writing of Egyptian *s* as Hebrew *samek*, then Raamses/Rameses of the Pentateuch does corresponds to Egyptian (Pi)-Ramesses.

Redford's rejection of the equation of biblical Raamses with Pi-Ramesses and his identifying it with a later cultic center is called "untenable" by Uphill. He observes that of the six toponyms that employ the name of the great pharaoh, only one, "the Dwelling (*t3 ʿt*) of Ramesses" is even close enough to the northeast Delta to have been a candidate. While it is thus beyond the borders of Egypt,[105] this location is the first stop on the coastal highway after Tjaru.[106] Consequently, Uphill believes that identifying Pi-Ramesses with Raamses/Rameses of Exodus is undeniable.

For the past thirty years, no one has seriously challenged the Raamses/ Pi-Ramesses equation. But now Lemche has once again attempted to cast doubt on this identification.[107] While he does not mention Redford's earlier work, nor Helck's refutation of it, he nevertheless comes to a similar conclusion that the name Raamses does not reflect the Delta capital of the Ramessides, but a later application of the name Pi-Ramesses to Tanis. The basis for his conclusion is a comment by Edward Wente that as a result of the transferal of much of Pi-Ramesses superstructure to Tanis in Dynasty 21, "post-exilic Jewish scholars in Egypt, seeking to localize events of the Exodus, were misled about the location of Piramesse in assuming that the newly created cults of the gods of Rameses at Tanis and Bubastis could serve to identify the site of the Ramesside capital."[108]

There is no question that Psalm 78:12 and 43 used the contemporary first-millennium name "field of Zoan" for the Egyptian *šht dʿnt* since the area that had been dominated by Pi-Ramesses from around 1300 to 1100 B.C. was replaced by nearby Tanis in the subsequent period. But never in Egyptian texts is Tanis (the Hellenized form of Egyptian *dʿnt*) ever called Pi-Ramesses.[109] In fact, *šht dʿ* occurs (written with the city determinative) on an offering list from the Ptah temple in Memphis during Ramesses II's reign, demonstrating that the Egyptians understood Tanis to be different from Pi-Ramesses.[110] Simply put, there is no evidence of transferring the name of the Ramesside capital to Tanis. Thus, Lemche's reasons for trying to associate Raamses of Exodus 1 with Tanis in the late period has no basis in fact. If the writer of Exodus truly understood Raamses of Exodus 1:11 to refer to Tanis (as author of Ps. 78 thought), then why did he not simply write the Hebrew equivalent, Zoan? Clearly the Pentateuchal references all agree that the place where the Hebrews were engaged in forced labor and from which they left Egypt was Raamses/Rameses, not Tanis/Zoan. These factors lead to the undeniable conclusion that the absence of Tanis in the toponymy of the sojourn and exodus narratives shows that the Israelites remember (Pi)-Ramesses as the place they associated with their bondage and the starting point of the departure from Egypt. Furthermore, the appearance of Raamses/Ramesses in the Exodus narrative strongly suggests that the tradition likely came from the period when the Ramesside capital flourished, between 1270 and 1100 B.C.

In its day, Pi-Ramesses was comparable to the largest cities in the ancient Near East. Eric Uphill has declared that it "was probably the vastest and most costly royal residence ever erected by the hand of man. As can now be seen its known palace and official centre covered an area of at least four square miles, and its temples were in scale with this, a colossal assemblage forming perhaps the largest collection of chapels built in the pre-classical world by a single ruler at one time. Yet today not even one site or set of foundations can be clearly enough recognized to give even a rough plan."[111] Compared to the great capitals of the ancient Near East, like Nineveh and Babylon which cover areas of 1,800 and 2,250 acres respectively, Pi-Ramesses covered 2,500 acres.[110] With the palace and the major temples, hundreds of storage facilities like those at the Ramesseum would have required vast quantities of brick.

Pithom

The second toponym in Exodus 1:11 is unquestionably the Hebrew writing for Egyptian p(r) itm: house or domain (i.e., estate) of the god Atum.[113] As with the location of Raamses, Pithom, too, has been identified with different sites around the Delta and Wadi Tumilat.[114] There is nothing in the Bible or from Egyptian sources to suggest that Pi-Ramesses and Pithom were closely related or approximately situated. Edouard Naville was among the first to suggest that Pithom was located at Tell el-Maskhuta, based on his excavations there.[115] Petrie followed Naville, but went further to hypothesize that the sites of Tell el-Retabeh and Tell el-Maskhuta, about fourteen kilometers apart within the Wadi Tumilat, were Ramesses and Pithom respectably.[116] However, Petrie's idea that the Delta Residence was to be found at Retabeh never caught on. Thus, the door opened for it to be considered as Pithom. Gardiner argued forcefully for equating Retabeh with Pithom,[117] a position followed by many others.[118]

The ancient name of Retabeh remains uncertain. Petrie discovered several blocks and fragments at Retabeh containing inscriptions that called Atum "the Lord of Tjeku," along with a scene portraying the deity viewing Ramesses II smiting an Asiatic (fig. 14).[119] He also uncovered earlier materials, including Eighteenth Dynasty architectural remains, scarabs bearing the names of Thutmose III and Amenhotep III, and Middle Kingdom and First Intermediate period scarabs, notably a seal with the name Neb-kau Khety (Tenth Dynasty)[120] and a scarab with the cartouche of Amenemhet I (Twelfth Dynasty).[121] Additionally, remains of a New Kingdom period temple were also uncovered by Petrie.[122]

It is clear, then, that Tell el-Retabeh had a long history owing to its strategic placement in the Wadi Tumilat. None of this evidence positively identifies it as Pithom of Exodus 1:11, but the epigraphic evidence shows that Atum enjoyed a special position at this site and in the surrounding region, perhaps even being the patron of Petrie's temple. The name Pithom may have survived as the Hellenized form Patoumos in Herodotus (2.158), a settlement by which the Neco canal apparently passed.[123]

One problem with identifying Pithom with Tell el-Retabeh is that Naville also discovered some Ramesside blocks at Tell el-Maskhuta where Atum is named as lord of that area.[124] These blocks appear to have been brought there (from Retabeh?) during a later building phase. Alan Lloyd has argued for locating Herodotus's Patoumos at Maskhuta rather than at Retabeh,[125] but his position was based largely upon classical sources and prior to the recent excavations at Tell el-Maskhuta. John S. Holladay showed that there was an occupational hiatus from the Middle Bronze IIB down to the Saite period when Neco II began excavating the Red Sea canal.[126] Van Seters is convinced that Maskhuta is Pithom because it would confirm his view that the biblical story is a sixth-century fabrication because of the absence of New Kingdom remains.[127] However, he gives no reason for rejecting Retabeh as Pithom's location. If there was a New Kingdom settlement at Tell el-Maskhuta, it has not yet been found. Where the several military installations of Tjeku (Succoth) referred to in the Anastasi Papyri were located remains a problem, although Retabeh may certainly have been home to one of the fortified installations.[128] Based on the current textual and archaeological evidence, Tell el-Maskhuta ought to be identified with Egyptian Tjeku (biblical Succoth), which was principally known as a region, not a city in the New Kingdom.[129] It does not seem to have been Pithom.

Hans Goedicke, who directed excavations at Tell el-Retabeh in the late 1970s, has concluded that it was an important defensive site during Ramesses II's reign for the protection of Egypt's borders.[130] Because of Holladay's findings at Tell el-Maskhuta and his own work at Tell el-Retabeh, Goedicke is convinced that "There was only one major settlement in the eastern Wadi Tumilat during the New Kingdom, and that has to be equated with Tell el-Rataba."[131] He further believes that Pithom of the Exodus tradition derives from the name of the temple at this site. Papyrus Anastasi 6, which mentions the Edomite bedouin being permitted to "pass the fortress of Merneptah-hetep-hir-maat which is in Tjeku," also names the place where the flocks were watered as "the pools of Pe(r)-Atum" –brkt n(t) pr-itm.[132] Goedicke claims that the use of Pithom in Exodus is "anachronistic," because only in the late period is Pithom a place-name.[133] But this assertion is unwarranted because, as shown, the "store cities" are in reality storage facilities attached to temples or palaces and not sprawling urban-sized magazines. Pithom need only be the name of the temple (with its associated pools)[134] for which the Israelites made bricks some time in the New Kingdom, and *not* the name of the city per se. Pe(r)-Atum of Papyrus Anastasi 6, a temple in the Wadi Tumilat and likely at Retabeh, admirably fits the biblical usage of Pithom and ᶜārê miskᵉnôt. While Goedicke's excavations have yielded New Kingdom materials, regrettably for the present study, publication of this material is yet to appear.[135]

An alternative suggestion for the location of Pithom was made nearly thirty years ago by Eric Upill. He argued that since Pithom was clearly the Hebrew writing for *P(r) itm* and because Heliopolis was the most important cult center for the worship of the Sun-god, Atum, it should be considered as a candidate for Pithom.[136] In support of his proposal, Uphill notes that there were massive building projects undertaken by Seti I and Ramesses II, including great numbers of storage facilities and a massive enclosure wall surrounding the temple complex measuring around fifteen meters in thickness.[137] While this hypothesis is intriguing and has some merit, the problem remains that neither the city of Heliopolis nor its temple is ever called *p(r)-itm* in Egyptian texts.[138] Rather, the city is known as *iwnw* from the Old Kingdom onward,[139] and this name carries over into Hebrew as *'ōn* in the Old Testament (Gen. 41:45; Ezek. 30:17). Thus the Hebrew historian(s) knew the Egyptian name *iwnw* and likely would have used *'ōn* had Heliopolis been the site in question.

If indeed Retabeh is Pithom of Exodus 1:11, it apparently was bypassed in the route described in 12:37 and Numbers 33:5–6 since no other site is mentioned between the starting point at Raamses and Succoth.[140] This could imply that the Hebrews who worked at Pithom in Exodus 1 were not situated there permanently, or they met up with the Raamses group at Succoth.

The Land of Goshen

Goshen (*gōšen*) is the name of the area where the family of Jacob settled in Egypt at Joseph's suggestion because it was near the capital where he served Pharaoh (Gen. 45:10). Joseph's proposal was subsequently endorsed by the king (Gen. 47:6). It is clear from the ten occurrences of "Goshen" in Genesis that it is an area within Egypt. It is further equated with "the Land of Rameses" in Genesis 47:11.[141] In the book of Exodus, Goshen occurs just twice as the place where the Israelites resided (8:22; 9:26).

The equation of the Egyptian term *Gsm.t* with Hebrew Goshen has been rejected on linguistic grounds.[142] Hence, the origin of the word must be discovered elsewhere. The LXX of Genesis 45:10 and 46:34 reads "Gesem of Arabia," which suggests that there might be a possible association between the Qederite-Arabic name and the Hebrew *gōšen*.[143] For Redford, this Qederite influence in the eastern Delta began in the aftermath of the Assyrian king Esarhaddon's invasion of Egypt in 671 B.C. and down through the Persian period.[144] It is the Qederite dynastic name, Geshem, that influenced the name in the Pentateuch and, in Redford's estimation, helps date the Exodus narratives. While this suggestion is certainly plausible, it is curious that other biblical writers from the sixth century —such as Jeremiah and Ezekiel, who refer to geographical terms in Egypt—do not use the name "Goshen." This observation is significant since Jeremiah actually traveled to Egypt after 586 B.C., passing through the northeastern Delta and visited Tahpanhes (Jer. 43:7, 13; 44:1). Likewise, Psalms 78, 135, and 136, which deal with the sojourn and exodus, do not us the term "Goshen," even though these Psalms date to the first millennium B.C. The absence of Goshen in clearly datable first-millennium texts undermines the argument that its presence in the exodus narratives is indicative of a date in the seventh or sixth centuries.

Even if we allow that Goshen is Hebrew writing for the Qederite-Arabic Geshem, this need not mean, as Redford claims, that its use in the Pentateuch points to a sixth-century origin for the Exodus story. The usage could indicate only the later modernization of the text. The use of Rameses in Genesis 47:11 instead of Goshen demonstrates that the two were understood interchangeably, and Rameses points to the Nineteenth and Twentieth Dynasty as the period when these narratives were written or edited. It is easier to explain the presence of a single later term or toponym in an earlier text than to account for a name that has been out of circulation for centuries when it appears in a late text. Methodologically, when dating a piece of literature that has had a long transmission, one should not automatically date the origin of the text by the presence of later editorial additions. Indeed, the anomalies need to be explained. At the same time, early indicators (e.g., the appearance of Ramesses in Genesis and Exodus) cannot be summarily dismissed as cases of archaizing or ignored, but must be seriously considered as evidence pointing to the date of the events described, when they were initially recorded or an editorial stage in the process of transmission. The use of Rameses and Raamses in the text of Genesis and Exodus long after the Delta Capital had been abandoned around 1100 B.C. makes little sense.

V. Issues in Chronology

The notice of a new pharaoh in Exodus 1:8 does not necessarily mean that the specific king under whom Joseph served (Gen. 45) had died; rather, it likely signals a dynastic shift, the end of one era and the introduction of another.[145] For those who hold to a historical sojourn and exodus, there has been considerable debate over the past century over the dating of the rise of the new pharaoh, the oppression of the Hebrews, and their subsequent departure from Egypt.

From the Egyptian standpoint, two plausible scenarios are suggestive. First, the new king would allude to the Eighteenth Dynasty ruler Ahmose I who succeeded in expelling the Hyksos after a protracted period of time in which his predecessors Seqenenre-Tao II and Kamose had also engaged the Hyksos-controlled areas of Egypt. With the foreign rulers dislodged from Avaris and their control over the Delta and parts of middle Egypt, the Hebrews would have found themselves in the unenviable position of being too closely associated with Semitic rulers to be ignored. The new kings from distant Thebes would not have been aware of Joseph and his contributions to the northern court in the preceding era. Moreover, an association of the Hebrews with their fellow Semites who had ruled Lower Egypt might explain the hostile treatment and the paranoid Pharaoh's statement "if war befall us, they join our enemies [the recently departed Hyksos] and fight against us" (Exod. 1:10).[146] The major problem with this reconstruction has been a lack of evidence for major building activity in Qantir/Tell el-Dabᶜa region until the very end of the Eighteenth Dynasty under Horemheb. But this all changed in the early 1990s when the Austrian team at Tell el-Dabᶜa uncovered the first structure from that time. Manfred Bietak has identified this structure as a citadel built within the old city of Avaris, and he dates it to the very beginning of the Eighteenth Dynasty. The fortification appears to have been built as a base of operation for launching the military campaigns of Ahmose and his successors into Canaan and Syria. Analysis of the ceramic remains from nearby storage facilities point to the time of Thutmose III (1479–1425 B.C.).[147] From excavations during the 1995 season, additional early Eighteenth Dynasty structures have been uncovered to the southwest of the citadel. Bietak believes that these are storage facilities, possibly connected to an adjacent temple that is yet to be uncovered.[148]

This unexpected development means that for the first time there is evidence of substantial building in brick in the Avaris/Pi-Ramesses region immediately following the departure of the Hyksos and a continued presence in the area until the midpoint of the Eighteenth Dynasty. Could the construction associated with Ahmose's fort and associated facilities mark the beginning of the Israelite oppression and brick making referred to in Exodus 1? If so, then the name "Raamses" would have to be understood as a later gloss from the Ramesside period.

The second scenario correlates the beginning of the oppression of the Hebrews with the renewed interest in the northeast Delta beginning with Horemheb (1323–1295 B.C.), continuing under Seti I (1294–1279 B.C.) and reaching its peak under Ramesses II (1279–1213 B.C.). Prior to the discovery of an early Eighteenth Dynasty fort, it was thought that Avaris had been largely abandoned, even though the expulsion of the Hyksos may not have entailed the forced removal of all the Semites living in the Delta. Rather, a selective group made up of the military and political elite would have been forced out of Egypt.[149] As for what happened in the area surrounding Avaris, T. G. H. James has suggested that "nothing is known of the clearance of the rest of the Delta. Possibly no large-scale military operations were needed to secure the allegiance of the whole area to the new Egyptian king."[150] The new fort, while serving as a base for military operations in the Levant could also have had the second purpose of keeping an eye on the remaining Semitic population of the area. Further, the temple of Seth continued in use through the Eighteenth Dynasty until the time of Horemheb when renovations were undertaken, perhaps in conjunction with the celebration of the quadricentennial of the beginning of the Seth cult commemorated by the "400 Year Stela."[151] It is quite possible, then, that the Hebrews were among the remaining population of the northeast Delta after Ahmose's campaigns. Seti I had a palace built at nearby Qantir,[152] around which his son, the Great Ramesses, later built his vast city Pi-Ramesses, all within the shadows of the Hyksos capital of Avaris (fig. 13). According to this second scenario, the Hebrews would have lived peacefully in the region until Horemheb's building activities required the use of forced labor. Ramesses II's massive construction projects, particularly the building of Pi-Ramesses, would have necessitated even more laborers, a need that would coincide with the height of the Israelite oppression as reflected in Exodus 2 and 5.

Even at the outset of this century, Flinders Petrie could write, "The question of the period of the Exodus has long been the subject of discussion."[153] In the decades since, even more discussion of the dating problem has occurred.[154] The discussion has now turned to whether there ever was a sojourn and exodus, which makes the question of when seem a bit trite. It is not my intent to get embroiled in the history and details of this chronological debate, but a brief sketch of some the problems is unavoidable since the chronology cannot be ignored when asking historical questions.

The first problem is that the biblical and archaeological data can be read in different ways, thus producing varying results. The biblical data is complicated by interpretive concerns: Should the numbers be read literally, figuratively, or dismissed as fictitious creations? Given differences in the biblical manuscript traditions, which should be followed?

When the Merneptah stela was discovered, a number of scholars believed that the reference to Israel was an allusion to the exodus event under that monarch, late in the thirteenth century,[155] even though a straightforward reading of the text precludes this interpretation. This position was widely held in the first quarter of this century, but was seriously challenged by James Jack, who argued for a mid-fifteenth-century date based on biblical data and what he believed to be corroborating Egyptian evidence. Based on the Masoretic text of 1 Kings 6:1, which dates the departure from Egypt at 480 years before Solomon's fourth regnal year, Jack concluded that 1445 B.C. was the exodus date since Solomon's accession date, 970 B.C., could be securely fixed (his fourth year being 966/7), thanks to synchronisms between biblical and Assyrian texts.[156] This date is supported by the statement in the historical retrospective of the judge Jephthah. Toward the end of the Judges period, probably early in the eleventh century, the Ammonites were making hostile moves on Israelite territory in Gilead (Transjordan). Against the Ammonites' aggressive moves, Jephthah argued for Israel's right to the land because they had occupied it for three hundred years (Judg. 11:27). Taking 1100 as an approximate date for Jepthah's activities, three hundred years earlier would place the taking of the Transjordan under Moses (Num. 21) around 1400 B.C., about forty years after the departure from Egypt to allow for the time in the wilderness.[157]

One problem with accepting the Hebrew manuscript tradition of 1 Kings 6:1 is that the LXX has a variant reading for the 480 figure of 440 years. If the LXX figure is followed, a date closer to 1400 for the exodus would result, and the arrival of the Israelites in Canaan would date to 1360–1350 B.C. This slightly later date would place the Israelites in Canaan during the stormy days of the Amarna period when internal strife existed, as revealed in the Amarna correspondence.

Those wishing to identify the Hebrews with the troublesome *ḥabiru* would find the military exploits of Joshua and those of the *ḥabiru* occurring in the same general area in the middle of the fourteenth century. At an earlier date, identifying the *ḥabiru* with the Hebrews was common,[158] but in recent decades, the association has been discouraged, largely because *ḥabiru* is now understood to be a sociological term, not indicative of any one particular ethnic group.[159] More recent studies consider the *ḥabiru* to be more specifically groups of refugees who lived out of reach of urban, settled areas, who nevertheless preyed upon such states.[160] This generally accepted meaning need not preclude the term *ḥabiru* from being applied to the Hebrews who were dislocated in Egypt and then again when they returned to Canaan. A few scholars have lately reconsidered the association of the Hebrews and the *ḥabiru*. Lemche, as noted above (chap. 1, §I), believes the Israelites were *ḥabiru*, displaced Canaanites moving from one area of the Levant to another. Ahlström also allowed for a possible connection between the Israelites who occupied the hill country and the *ḥabiru*.[161] The appearance of 3600 captured ʿprw (Egyptian for *ḥabiru*), a rather large figure, in the Memphis stela of Amenhotep II,[162] suggests that the *ḥabiru* were more than just small marauding bands. Listing the ʿprw/*ḥabiru* alongside other ethnic groups from Hurru, Retenu, and the Shasu suggests that the Egyptians may have viewed the *ḥabiru* as a distinguishable ethnic group.

Dating the period of the oppression and exodus to the fifteenth century B.C. has largely been replaced in favor of a thirteenth-century date, although a few adherents to the earlier date have followed Jack's thesis.[163] Naturally, those who opt for a thirteenth-century Israelite exodus and entry into Canaan have to reject the *ḥabiru* association in the Amarna letters for chronological reasons.

How then is the 480-year figure treated by scholars who reject it as a literal number? Petrie suggested that the number might have resulted from tallying up the duration of the Israelite judges from Saul back to Joshua.[164] However, as Jack showed, if all the periods are added together, such as the forty years in Sinai, the lengths of the judges, and periods of peace between judges, plus the length of David's reign, the total is 534 years. On top of this figure, the duration of Joshua's leadership in Canaan and the length of Saul's kingship, which are not preserved, bring the total close to six hundred years.[165]

Another solution, which is widely held by biblical scholars, is to regard the 480 figure as a number that symbolizes twelve times forty, with forty representing a generation.[166] With a generation being closer to twenty-five years, twelve times twenty-five gives three hundred years; when added to Solomon's fourth year, the exodus falls within the reign of Ramesses II around 1267. The reference to the store-city of Raamses in Exodus 1:11 is viewed as additional support for placing the oppression period in Egypt's Nineteenth Dynasty. Furthermore, the thirteenth-century dating squared nicely with the so called "archaeological date" (ca. 1230-1220 B.C.) of the conquest of the Albright-Wright school. The archaeological evidence for the settlement of Israel in Canaan, according to Israel Finkelstein (see chap. 2), dates to the late thirteenth century or early in the twelfth. Finkelstein's conclusions do not necessarily contradict an exodus in the Ramesside period.

There are, however, two obstacles for interpreting the 480 number as a symbolic number for twelve generations: 1) the genealogical lists from the exodus period to Solomon's day do not add up to twelve or eleven (if the LXX reading symbolizes eleven times forty);[167] 2) there is no evidence elsewhere in the Bible for using a large figure to symbolize a number of generations.[168]

An even later date, in the twelfth century, has been advanced for the exodus and conquest by Gary Rendsburg.[169] He would place the departure from Egypt during the reign of Ramesses III. Rendsburg considers the mention of Raamses in Exodus 1:11 to reflect the oppression under the early Nineteenth Dynasty pharaohs. Rather than interpreting the reference to Philistia in Exodus 13:17 as an anachronistic or a later gloss, he takes it to refer to the Sea Peoples's invasion of Egypt on the Mediterranean coast. This was the warfare the Israelites feared that led them to take a more southerly route of departure.[170] Additionally, Rendsburg examines the archaeological record, and finds that some of the sites associated with the Israelite conquest in Joshua also have destruction levels in the mid-12th century.[171] A third line of argumentation he develops to support his 12th century date is genealogical evidence.[172]

Rendsburg is to be commended for taking the biblical data seriously. However, the reference to Philistia and the mention of "war" in Exodus 13:17 can be understood differently in view of fresh archaeological work in north Sinai (see chap. 8, §IV, and chap. 9, §II). The most significant problem for the twelfth-century reconstruction is the reference to Israel in the Merneptah stela, which dates to the end of the thirteenth century. Rendsburg offers two strained explanations. First, he suggests a novel but completely unparalleled suggestion that "Israel" refers to Israelites enslaved in Egypt. I am not aware of any New Kingdom text where a monarch includes a conquered people who lives within Egypt in the context of a report on the fruits of a foreign campaign. The geographical context of Merneptah's campaign is clearly Canaan and Syria. Why bother mentioning a people already residing in Egypt? Alternatively, Rendsburg proposes the old idea that not all the Israelite tribes were in Egypt,[173] but this position finds no support in the biblical or archaeological record. In the end, his attempt to reinterpret the Merneptah stela in order to make the Egyptian evidence fit the twelfth-century date is simply unconvincing. It would seem better to admit that the Merneptah stela precludes an exodus date after 1200 B.C. and work backwards from there.

It is clear that even after over a century of academic inquiry into the date of the exodus, we are no closer to a solution today. For those who reject the historicity of the Israel in Egypt and exodus narratives, to investigate the chronology is ludicrous. But for those who take the events seriously, the quest remains an intriguing investigation of the biblical and archaeological data. If there is a prevailing view among historians, biblical scholars, and archaeologists, an exodus in the Ramesside era (1279–1213 B.C.) is still favored. The Merneptah stela (ca. 1209/8 B.C.) serves as a *terminus ad quem* for arrival of the Israelites in Canaan. The question remains: How long had they been there prior to Merneptah's time?

Notes

1 Umberto Cassuto considered this unit a transitional one "to link the two books together" (*A Commentary on the Book of Exodus* [Jerusalem: Magnes, 1951]; trans. Israel Abraham, English edition, 1967 7); for Martin Noth, this paragraph was P's editorial work, linking the two books (*Exodus* [Philadelphia: Westminster Press, 1962] 20); similarly, see J. Philip Hyatt, *Exodus* (London: Marshall, Morgan, and Scott, 1971) 57; for Moshe Greenberg (*Understanding Exodus* [New York: Behrman House, 1969] 18) and Brevard Childs (*Exodus* [Philadelphia: Westminster Press, 1974] 1–2) this introductory paragraph recapitulates the preceding story in Genesis. Thomas Thompson also follows this thinking, remarking that "The introduction in Exod 1.1–16.8 does not present the beginning of a new narrative so much as it establishes continuity with the preceding narrative from Genesis" (*The Origin Tradition of Ancient Israel*, vol. 1: *The Literary Formation of Genesis and Exodus 1–23, JSOT* Supp. Series, vol. 55 [Sheffield: Sheffield Academic Press, 1987] 133. Similarly, Gordon F. Davies contends that the genealogy in Exod. 1:1–4 can "be profitably understood as a line in a chain of genealogies in Genesis 12–50" (*Israel in Egypt: Reading Exodus 1–2, JSOT* Supp. Series, vol. 135 [Sheffield: Sheffield Academic Press, 1992] 24.

2 Gerhard von Rad, *Genesis: A Commentary* (Philadelphia: Westminster Press, 1961) 23-27; Noth, *Exodus*, 12-18.

3 See discussion in chap. 1, §I.

4 Charles Isbell, "The Structure of Exodus 1:1–14," in *Art and Meaning: Rhetoric in Biblical Literature*, ed. D. J. A. Clines, David Gunn, and A. J. Hauser (Sheffield: Sheffield Academic Press, 1982) 37–61.

5 Ibid., 51.

6 Ibid., 56.

7 Another recent study that argues for the literary unity of Exodus 1 – 2 is Donald W. Wicke, "The Literary Structure of Exodus 1:2 – 2:10," *JSOT* 24 (1982) 99 – 107.

8 *Israel in Egypt* 13 – 181

9 *Jahwe unser Gott: Sprache, Aufbau und Erzähltechnik in der Berufung des Mose (Ex. 3–4)*, OBO 91 (Freiburg: Universitätsverlag, 1989).

10 *Origin Tradition*, 155.

11 Ibid., 156 – 157.

12 For my critique of dating the Genesis and Exodus material, see chap. 4, n. 60.

13 Ibid., 39, 195. Dorothy Irvin has also argued for the folklorist character of the Pentateuchal narratives, see "The Joseph and Moses Narratives," in *Israelite and Judaean History*, ed. John Hayes and J. Maxwell Miller (Philadelphia: Westminster Press, 1977), §3. See also her subsequent larger study, *Mytharion: The Comparison of Tales from the Old Testament and the Ancient Near East*, AOAT, vol. 32 (Neukirchen: Neukirchener Verlag-Vluyn, 1978). See my critique of her approach in chap. 4, §I.

14 *Ancient Israel: A New History of Israelite Society* (Sheffield: *JSOT* Press, 1988) 109.

15 See Batto's *Slaying the Dragon: Mythmaking in the Biblical Tradition* (Louisville: Westminster/John Knox Press, 1992), esp. chap. 4 – 5.

16 *The Evolution of the Exodus Tradition* (Jerusalem: Magnes Press, 1992) 291 – 292, 23 – 30.

17 *Egypt, Canaan, and Israel in Ancient Times* (Princeton: Princeton University Press, 1992) 409.

18 Ibid.

19 Implied in Donald Redford, "An Egyptological Perspective on the Exodus Narrative," in *Egypt, Canaan and Israel: Archaeological and Historical Relationships in the Biblical Period* (Tel Aviv: Tel Aviv University, 1987) 257; John Van Seters, "Moses," *The Encyclopedia of Religion*, vol. 10, ed. M. Eliade (New York: Macmillan, 1987) 115; Hyatt, *Exodus*, 58.

20 Translation is my own.

21 *Urk.* IV, 648.14, 649.5, 661.15.

22 *RB*, 59.10 – 11.

23 *Urk.* IV, 663.14 – 15, 664 3 – 4.

24 Ibid., 1297 – 1298.

25 Ibid., 1300 – 1309.

26 Ibid., 1309.

27 Ibid., 1303, 1308.

28 The Epigraphic Survey, *Reliefs and Inscriptions at Karnak*, vol. 4: *The Battle Reliefs of King Sety I* (Chicago: Oriental Institute, 1986), pl. 27, 29.

29 Ibid., pl. 33 – 34. While the text does not specifically identify the escaping Hittite as Seti's counterpart, his large size compared with other Hittite charioteers in the scene suggests that he is the leader (ibid., 104).

30 KRI, vol. 2, 2 – 124.

31 Ibid., 50 – 51.

32 Ibid., vol. 4, 14 – 15.

33 Ibid., 16.4 – 5, 17.6 – 7.

34 One could add Zerah the Kushite (1 Chron. 14:9), although he was probably a mercenary general. Cf. Kenneth Kitchen, *The Third Intermediate Period in Egypt (1100–650 B.C.)*, 2d ed. (Warminster: Aris and Phillips, 1986) 309.

35 Nicolas Grimal, *La Stèle Triomphale De Pi(ʿankhy) Au Musée Du Caire*, JE 48862– 47089 (Cairo: IFAO, 1981). For a translation, see Miriam Lichtheim, *Ancient Egyptian Literature*, vol. 3 (Berkeley and Los Angeles: University of California Press, 1980) 66 – 84.

36 Kitchen, *Third Intermediate Period*, chaps. 22, 23; Nicolas Grimal, *A History of Ancient Egypt* (Oxford: Blackwell, 1992) 334–341.

37 "Some Remarks on the Alleged Fall of Senmut," *JARCE* 8 (1969–1970) 29–48.

38 Barry Kemp, *Ancient Egypt: A Social History* (Cambridge: Cambridge University Press, 1982) 134, 141–143.

39 J. Maxwell Miller and John H. Hayes, *A History of Ancient Israel and Judah* (Philadelphia: Westminster Press, 1986) 67.

40 "The Geography of the Exodus," in *Recueil d'études égyptologiques dédiées à la mémoire Jean-François Champollion* (Paris: Bibliothèque de l'école des hautes études, 1922) 204–205.

41 Noth, *Exodus*, 20.

42 Thompson, in *Israelite and Judaean History*, 155–157; Redford, *Egypt, Canaan and Israel*, 144–148.

43 For a comprehensive study of Semitic names in Egypt during the New Kingdom, cf. Thomas Schneider, *Asiatische Personennamen in des Neuen Reiches*, OBO 114 (Freiberg: Universitäts Verlag, 1992).

44 William Ward, "Foreigners Living in the Village," in *Pharaoh's Workers: The Villagers of Deir el Medina*, ed. L. H. Lesko (Ithaca: Cornell University Press, 1994) 61–85.

45 See chap. 4, §III.

46 Norman de Garis Davies, *The Tomb of Rekhmire at Thebes* (New York: Metropolitan Museum of Art, 1943) 47, pl. 56, 57. Throughout this section I translate the expression *skr ʿnḫ(w)*, literally "living smitten ones," as "prisoner(s) of war."

47 *Urk.* IV, 4.11–13, 4.16–5.2, 9.17–10.3; for translation, cf. Lichtheim, *Ancient Egyptian Literature*, vol. 2, 12–14.

48 *Urk.* IV, 9.14.

49 Ibid., 36.13.

50 Ibid., 663.6.

51 Ibid., 690.7, 691.2, 698.7, 699.5, 706.4, 717.1, 10.

52 Ibid., 1305.5–8. The actual total of these numbers 2,255. Why 2,214 is given is unclear. For a translation of this stela, cf. Barbara Cumming, *Egyptian Historical Records of the Later Eighteenth Dynasty*, fasc. 1 (Warminster: Aris and Philllips, 1982) 31–31 and *ANET*, 245–247.

53 *Urk.* IV, 1308.19–1309.5.

54 John Wilson made this observation in *ANET*, 247, n.48. Anthony Spatinger believes these figures are exaggerated in order to make a relatively small military operation look more impressive ("The Historical Implications of the Year 9 Campaign of Amenophis II," *JSSEA* 13 no. 2 (1983) 89–101).

55 Elmar Edel, "Die Stelen Amenophis II. aus Karnak und Memphis," *ZDPV* 69 (1953) 97–176. Gardiner concurs with Edel's position, *Egypt of the Pharaohs* (New York: Oxford University Press) 203.

56 "Eine Beutliste von Amenophis II. un das Problem der Sklaverei im alten Aegypten," *JEOL* 17 (1963) 141–147.

57 "Asiatic Prisoners Taken in the Reign of Amenophis II," *Scripta Mediterranea* 5 (1984) 27–28.

58 Ibid.

59 Alan R. Schulman, "Hittites, Helmets and Amarna: Akhenaten's First Hittite War," in *The Akhenaten Temple Project*, vol. 2, ed. D. B. Redford (Toronto: University of Toronto Press, 1987) 53–79.

60 Epigraphic Survey, *Battle Reliefs of King Sety I.*

61 Ibid., pl. 6.

62 Ricardo Caminos, *Late-Egyptian Miscellanies* (London: Oxford, 1954) 491.

63 Ibid., 494.

64 Ibid., 493; KRI vol. 3, 250–251.

65 Noth, *Exodus*, 99; Hyatt, *Exodus*, 139; Nahum Sarna, *Exploring Exodus* (New York: Schocken, 1986) 91–96.

66 Donald Redford, "Foreigners (Especially Asiatics) in the Talatat," in *Akhenaten Temple Project*, 13–27.

67 The first pylon, though not inscribed, is thought to date to the Twenty-fifth (Kushite) Dynasty, but this is by no means certain. Cf. Jill Kamil, *Luxor: A Guide to Ancient Thebes*, 3d ed. (New York: Longman House, 1983) 39.

68 Alan H. Gardiner, *Egyptian Hieratic Texts*, vol. 1, pt. 1 (Leipzig: Hinrichs, 1911) 16–17, 25.

69 "From the Brickfields of Egypt," *TB* 27 (1976) 143–144; see also James Hoffmeier, "Taskmaster," *ISBE*, vol. 4, 737.

70 Kitchen, *TB* 27 (1976) 141–142; *RITA*, vol. 2, 520–522.

71 For the text, see *LEM*, 30–31, and translation, Caminos, *Late-Egyptian Miscellanies*, 106.

72 Charles F. Nims, "Bricks Without Straw," *BA* 13 no. 2 (1950) 22–28.

73 *LEM*, 48; Caminos, *Late-Egyptian Miscellanies*, 188.

74 Kitchen, *TB* 27 (1976) 145–146. For additional references, see Kitchen, *Ancient Orient and Old Testament* (Downers Grove, Ill.: IV Press, 1966) 156–157.

75 Her paper "The Consequences of Conquest: A Foreign Population's Entrance and Acculturation into Ancient Egyptian Society," was presented at the Society of Biblical Literature annual meeting in New Orleans on November 26, 1996. I appreciate her sending me a pre-publication copy of her paper.

76 Ibid.

77 R. S. Lamon and G. M. Shipton, *Megiddo*, vol. 1 (Chicago: University of Chicago Press, 1939) 32–47, figs. 49–53. In recent years, the dating of the "stables" has been shown to be from the ninth century, not the tenth. Subsequently, Graham Davies has demonstrated that the outline "stables" of the Solomonic era are actually visible in the floor of the ninth century level ("Solomonic Stables at Megiddo After All?" *PEQ* 120 [1988] 130–141).

78 John S. Holladay, "The Stables of Ancient Israel: Functional Determinants of Stable Construction and the Interpretation of Pillared Building Remains of the Palestinian Iron Age," in *The Archaeology of Jordan and Others Studies, Presented to Siegfried H. Horn*, ed. L. T. Geraty and L. G. Herr (Berrien Springs, Mich.: Andrews University Press, 1986) 103–165; Gabriel Barkay, "The Iron Age II–III," in *The Archaeology of Ancient Israel*, ed. Amnon Ben-Tor (New Haven: Yale University Press, 1992) 314.

79 James B. Pritchard, "The Megiddo Stables: A Reassessment," in *Near Eastern Archaeology in the Twentieth Century*, Nelson Glueck volume, ed. J. A. Sanders (Garden City, N.Y.: Doubleday, 1970) 268–276; Yigael Yadin, *Hazor: The Schweich Lectures 1970* (London: Oxford University Press, 1972) and "The Megiddo Stables," in *Magnalia Dei: The Mighty Acts of God*, ed. F. M. Cross et al. (Garden City, N.Y.: Doubleday, 1976) 55–107; Zev Herzog, "The Storehouses," in *Beersheba I*, ed. Y. Aharoni (Tel Aviv: Tel Aviv University, 1986). Amihai Mazar has tried to mediate the situation by noting that both positions make sense; hence he wonders if the pillared buildings were both stables and storehouses depending upon the community's need at a given time. See *Archaeology of the Land of the Bible 10,000–586 B.C.E.*, [New York: Doubleday, 1990) 476–478.

80 In order to visualize the actual space occupied by the pillared halls, see the aerial photograph of Megiddo in Lamon and Shipton, *Megiddo*, fig. 114, and the drawing in Graham Davies, *Megiddo: Cities of the Biblical World* (Grand Rapids, Mich.: Eerdmans, 1986) 79.

81 J. E. Quibell, *The Ramesseum* (London: Egyptian Research Account, 1896) plate 1.

82   For this situation in the Ramesside period, see Kenneth Kitchen, *Pharaoh Tri-umphant: The Life and Times of Ramesses II* (Warminster: Aris and Phillips, 1982) 154–156.

83   W. Stevenson Smith and W. Kelly Simpson, *The Art and Architecture of Ancient Egypt* (New York: Penguin, 1981) chap. 15.

84   A. J. Spencer, *Brick Architecture in Ancient Egypt* (Warminster: Aris and Philips, 1979) 94–103.

85   The different spelling of the English reflects variant vowel pointing of this name in the Masoretic text. These minor variations do not mean that different toponyms are intended.

86   "The Delta Residence of the Ramessides," *JEA* 5 (1918) 127–171.

87   Ibid. The Amara West temple was situated even further south, cf. H. W. Fairman, "Preliminary Report on the Excavations of Amara West, Anglo-Egyptian Sudan, 1938–9," *JEA* 25 (1939) 139–144 and "Preliminary Report on the Excavations of Amara West, Anglo-Egyptian Sudan, 1947–8," *JEA* 34 (1948) 3–11.

88   Professor Kitchen tells me that the epithet ꜥꜣ nḫtw, "Great of Victories" was applied up to year 21, after which kꜣ ꜥꜣ n pꜣ-rꜥ ḥr ꜣḫty, "Great soul of Pre-Harakhty," replaces it.

89   W. M. F. Petrie, *Hyksos and Israelite Cities* (London: British School of Archaeology in Egypt, 1906) 28–34 and *Egypt and Israel* (London: Society for Promoting Christian Knowledge, 1912) 29, 33.

90   A. H. Gardiner, "Tanis and Pi-Raꜥmesse: A Retraction," *JEA* 19 (1933) 122–128.

91   *"Tanis, Avaris et Pi-Ramses,"* RB 39 (1933) 191–215; *Le Drame d'Avaris: Essai sur la penetration des Semites en Egypte* (Paris: Geunther, 1941).

92   On the work at Tanis, see Pierre Montet, *La Necropole royale de Tanis I–III* (Paris: 1947–1960) and *Les Énigmes de Tanis* (Paris, Centre National de la Recherche Scientifique 1952).

93   "Excavations of the Department of Antiquities at Qantîr (Faqûs District) (Season, May 21st – July 7th, 1928),"*ASAE* 30 (1930) 31–68.

94   Ibid., 43–45.

95   *Glazed Tiles from a Palace of Ramesses II at Kantir* (New York: Metropolitan Museum of Art, 1937).

96   "Khataꜥna-Qantir: Importance," *ASAE* 52 (1954) 443–559.

97   "Recent Discoveries in the Eastern Delta," *ASAE* 56 (1959) 301–324.

98   Manfred Bietak, *Tell el Dabꜥa II* (Vienna: Verlag der österreichischen Akademie der Wissenschaaften) and *Avaris and Piramesses: Archaeological Exploration in the Eastern Nile Delta* (London: Oxford University Press, 1986) 226–231. Gardiner, after first suggesting Pelusium and then Tanis were Pi-Ramesses, came to agree that Qantir was the site by the late 1940s, cf. *AEO*, vol. 2, 171*-175*. John Van Seters, *The Hyksos: A New Investigation* (New Haven: Yale University Press, 1966) 127–151; Kitchen, "Raamses," *NBD*, 1006; Eric Uphill, "Pithom and Raamses: Their Location and Significance," *JNES* 27 (1968), 291–316 and *JNES* 28 (1969) 15–39 and *The Temples of Per-Ramesses* (Warminster: Aris and Phillips, 1984), Edgar Pusch, "Pi-Ramesses-Beloved-of-Amun, Headquarters of Thy Chariotry," in Pelizaeus-Museum Hildesheim Guidebook (Mainz: Verlag Philipp von Zabern, 1996) 126–144.

99   *ABL*, 10; *OBA*, 58–59 (this represented a change from Tanis to Qantir in its 3d edition, 1984); *NBA*, 31; *HAB*, 57; *NIVAB*, 89.

100   "Exodus I 11," *VT* 13 (1963) 408–418.

101   Ibid., 412–415; to a certain extent he has renewed this contention in *Egypt, Canaan, and Israel,* 138–139.

102   *"Ṯkw und die Ramses-Stadt,"* VT 15 (1965) 35–48. Redford offered a brief

rebuttal of Helck's article in a footnote in "The Literary Motif of the Exposed Child (cf. Ex. ii 1-10)," *Numen* 14 (1967) 221-222 n.52.

103 Ibid., 42-47. More on the problem of sibilants when the name of Moses is discussed (chap. 6, §III).

104 Many years ago, T. J. Meek recognized that a number of personal names of Levites in the Pentateuch were of Egyptian etymology. Cf. "Moses and the Levites," *AJSL* 56 (1939) 113-120. Professor Kitchen has discussed the problem of the sibilants and has also cited some of these examples in his paper "Raamses, Succoth and Pithom" which was presented at the symposium "Who Was the Pharaoh of the Exodus?" held in Memphis, Tenn., April 1987. The papers were never published as planned. I am grateful to Professor Kitchen for giving me a copy of this paper for citation here.

105 *Temples of Per-Ramesses*, 3.

106 In Seti I's relief at Karnak it is called the "Dwelling of the Lion" while it is called "the Dwelling of Sese" in Papyrus Anastasi 1. See Alan Gardiner, "The Ancient Military Road Between Egypt and Palestine," *JEA* 6 (1920) 213. Sese is an abbreviation for Ramesses. Ibid., 103.

107 "Is It Still Possible to Write a History of Ancient Israel?" *SJOT* 8 (1994) 165-190.

108 "Rameses," *ABD*, vol. 5 (1992) 617.

109 *AEO*, vol. 2, 199-201, 171-175.

110 KRI, vol. 2, 490.8-10, and *RITA*, vol. 2, 310. I am indebted to Professor Kitchen for this reference.

111 *Temples of Per-Ramesses*, 1. For a rough plan, see Bietak, *Tell el Dabᶜa II*, or Kitchen, *Pharaoh Triumphant*, 123.

112 Ibid., 227.

113 Redford, *VT* 13 (1963) 403.

114 For a recent survey of the problems surrounding the location of Pithom, see Edward Bleiberg, "The Location of Pithom and Succoth," in *Egyptological Miscellanies*, ed. J. K. Hoffmeier and E. S. Meltzer, *Ancient World* 6 (1983) 21-27.

115 *The Store City of Pithom and the Route of the Exodus* (London: Egypt Exploration Society, 1883) 9, 21.

116 *Hyksos and Israelite Cities*, 28-34.

117 *JEA* 5 (1918) 242-271.

118 T. E. Peet, *Egypt and the Old Testament* (Liverpool: University of Liverpool, 1924) 67-69; Redford, *VT* 13 (1963) 407-408; T. O. Lambdin, "Pithom," *IDB*, vol. 3, 821; Kitchen, "Raamses, Succoth and Pithom."

119 *Hyksos and Israelite Cities*, pl. 30-31. For a detailed discussion of Tjeku, see chap. 8, §II.

120 For a discussion of the historical implications of this earlier material, see chap. 3, §II.

121 Petrie, *Hyskos and Israelite Cities*, pl. 32A, 33, 34.

122 Ibid., pl. 35, 35A.

123 For equating Patoumos with Pithom, see Alan B. Lloyd, "Necho and the Red Sea: Some Considerations," *JEA* 63 (1977) 142 n.1.

124 Naville, *The Store City of Pithom*, pl. 3A. Additionally, see PM, vol. 4, 52-55.

125 *JEA* 63 (1977) 142 n.1.

126 For further discussion of this site, see chap. 3, §II.

127 *Encyclopedia of Religion*, vol. 10, 116.

128 Major walls surrounding the site were mapped by Petrie, *Hyksos and Israelite Cities*, pl. 35.

129 For a discussion of the textual evidence concerning Tjeku and its association with biblical Succoth, see chap. 8, §II.

130 "Ramesses II and the Wadi Tumilat," *VA* 3 (1987) 13–24.

131 "Papyrus Anastasi VI 51–61," *SAK* 14 (1987) 93.

132 *LEM*, 77. Translations in Caminos, *Late Egyptian Miscellanies*, 293; *ANET*, 259.

133 *VA* 3 (1987) 94.

134 Redford has discouraged identifying Pe(r) Atum of Pap. Anastasi 6 with Pithom of Exodus 1:11 on the grounds that the pools "are here located in *Tjkw*, and not necessarily the 'House of Atum' itself" (*Egypt, Canaann and Israel,* 141). However, Goedicke's discovery of a depression on the north side of the site, measuring 120 by 80 meters and thought to be an ancient pond, indicates that this feature belonged to the nearby temple of Atum (*SAK* 14, 96). Thus, a reference to the pools of Pithom in Tjeku makes very good sense. Kitchen wonders if "three Waters of Pharaoh" in Tjeku mentioned in Deir el-Medineh ostracon (no. 1076) "is reminiscent of the pools of Pithom" in Pap. Anastasi 6, 56–57 (in "Raamses, Succoth and Pithom").

135 My colleague Alfred Hoerth, who was a member of the excavation team, has kindly furnished this information.

136 *JNES* 27 (1968) 291–316, 28: 291–316.

137 Ibid., 27: 294–296.

138 Redford, "Heliopolis," *ABD*, vol. 3, 122–123.

139 *Wb*, vol. 1, 54.

140 This point has been observed by Kitchen (*ABD*, vol. 2, 703) and George Kelm, *Escape to Conflict* (Fort Worth: IAR Publications, 1991) 73. On the other hand, if Pithom is not Retabeh in the Wadi Tumilat, then the absence of its mention in the Raamses-Succoth sequence might be further explained.

141 The appearance of Rameses in the Joseph story need only be ascribed to the time of authorship (or subsequent editorial activity) and not the historical setting of Joseph. To explain this difference as the difference between J and P is not convincing.

142 Joseph Vergote, *Joseph en Égypte* (Louvain: Publications Universitaires, 1959) 184–186; Kitchen, "Goshen," *NBD*, 435; William Ward, "Goshen," *ABD*, vol. 2, 1076.

143 I. Rabbinowitz, "Aramaic Inscriptions of the Fifth Century B.C.E. from a North-Arab Shrine in Egypt," *JNES* 15 (1956) 1–9.

144 In *Egypt, Canaan, and Israel,* 139–140.

145 Ronald Clements, *Exodus* (Cambridge: Cambridge University Press, 1972) 7; Hyatt, *Exodus*, 58; Jack Finegan, *Let My People Go: A Journey through Exodus* (New York: Harper and Row, 1963) 21. Surely if this pharaoh was the immediate successor of the pharaoh whom Joseph served he would have known the Hebrew official, as probably his grandson would have.

146 Sarna, *Exploring Exodus,* 7–14.

147 Manfred Bietak et al., "Tell el-Dabᶜa—ᶜEzbet Helmi Vorbericht über den Grabungspltz H/I (1989-1992)," *ÄL* 4 [1994] 32–38. Professor Bietak presented an update on the work in this area through the 1995 season at the International Congress of Egyptologists held in Cambridge, England, in September 1995. I am grateful to him for personally discussing these important discoveries with me on that occasion. Irmgard Hein, the ceramic specialist working with this material, also reported on her analysis at the 1995 congress. See her preliminary report in "Erste Beobachtungen zur Keramik aus ᶜEzbet Helmi," *ÄL* 4 (1994) 39–43. She told me that she believes some of the material could be as late as the time of Amenhotep II.

148 Manfred Bietak, *Avaris: The Capital of the Hyksos* (London: The British Museum, 1996) 68–69.

149 Furthermore, the fact that King Ahmose pursued the Hyksos to the Canaanite city of Sharuhen suggests that the entire Semitic population of the Avaris region could not have been besieged within its walls, given the vast differences in scale between the two.

150 "Egypt: From the Expulsion of the Hyksos to Amenophis I," *CAH*, vol. 2, pt. 1, 295.

151 Bietak, *Avaris and Piramesse*, 266–271 and "Zur Herkunft des Seth von Avaris," *ÄL* 1 (1990) 9–16. Hans Goedicke argues that since the Seth cult predates the coming of the Hyksos, the stela does not commemorate the beginning of the Seth temple at Avaris. Cf. "The '400-Year Stela' Reconsidered," *BES* 3 (1981) 25–42.

152 Raymond Faulkner, "Egypt: From the Inception of the Nineteenth Dynasty to the Death of Ramesses III," *CAH*, vol. 2, pt. 2, 222; Bietak, *Avaris and Piramesse*, 229.

153 Petrie, *Egypt and Israel*, 37.

154 See James W. Jack, *The Date of the Exodus in the Light of External Evidence* (Edinburgh: T and T Clark, 1925) and John J. Bimson, *Redating the Exodus and Conquest* (Sheffield: *JSOT* Press, 1981). William H. Stiebing, Jr., *Out of the Desert?* (Buffalo: Prometheus Books, 1989) contains a good review of the different positions.

155 Petrie, *Egypt and Israel*, 37–38; Samuel R. Driver, *The Book of Exodus* (Cambridge: Cambridge University Press, 1911) xxx.

156 *Date of the Exodus*, 199–202.

157 While the number forty is regarded as a symbolic one in the Bible, the tradition of the forty years in Sinai seems to be literal in view of Deuteronomy 2:14, which states, "the time from our leaving Kadesh-Barnea until we crossed the brook Zered was thirty-eight years." The two years required to reach the figure of forty come from the time at Mt. Sinai and the period to reach Mt. Sinai from Egypt. These time periods are spelled out in Exodus 19:1, which allows three months from the exodus to the arrival at Mt. Horeb/Sinai, and Numbers 10:11 reports that the departure from Sinai occurred "in the second year, in the second month, on the twentieth day of the month." Kitchen believes that in this case the forty-year figure cannot "be dismissed as a meaningless round figure" (*Ancient Orient*, 60). Could it be from this forty-year period in which all those who had been born in Egypt and were over twenty died (Num. 14:26–35) that the symbolic number originated and became the figure that represented a generation?

158 E.g., Jack, *The Date of the Exodus*, 128–141. While George Mendenhall did not make a direct correlation between the *habiru* of the Amarna letters and the Hebrews of Joshua, he nevertheless allowed for the possibility that Hebrews could be classified as *habiru*—i.e., individuals or a group who have disassociated themselves from their former societal obligations and status. "The Hebrew Conquest of Palestine," *BA* 25 no. 3 (1962) 66–87.

159 Moshe Greenberg, *Hab/piru* (New Haven: AOS, 1955).

160 Giorgio Buccellati, "ᶜapiru and Munnabtutu—the Stateless of the First Cosmopolitan Age," *JNES* 36 (1977) 145–147; Jean Bottéro, "Entre nomades et sédentaires: Les Habiru," *Dialogues d'histroire ancienne* 6 (1980) 201–213.

161 *Who Were the Israelites?* (Winona Lake, Ind.: Eisenbrauns, 1986) 15.

162 *Urk.* IV, 1309.1.

163 Bimson, *Redating the Exodus and Conquest*, chaps. 1–3; Charles F. Aling, *Egypt and Bible History* (Grand Rapids, Mich.: Baker, 1981) chaps. 4–5; William Shea, "Exodus, Date of the," *ISBE*, vol. 2, 230–238.

164 *Egypt and Israel*, 38.

165 Jack, *Date of the Exodus* 211–212. The duration of Saul's reign and age at accession is a problem owing to these figures having been lost in the transmission of the

Hebrew text. Consequently, the LXX has different readings and some manuscripts omit I Sam. 13:1 altogether.

166 Siegfried Herrmann, *Israel in Egypt* (London: SCM Press, 1973) 48–49; John Bright, *A History of Israel* 3d ed. (Philadelphia: Westminster Press, 1981) 123; Kenneth Kitchen, "The Exodus," *ABD*, vol. 2, 702.

167 For a recent study of early Israelite genealogies, see Gary Rendsburg, "The Internal Consistency and Historical Reliability of the Biblical Genealogies," *VT* 40 (1990) 185–205. His study deals mostly with genealogies from the sons of Jacob to the figures around the exodus period. The genealogies in 1 Chron., Rendsburg, like many others, believes are somewhat artificial and elongated and not completely trustworthy for historical reconstruction.

168 Some might argue that the 430-year figure, representing the duration of Israel's sojourn in Egypt, in the Masoretic text of Exodus 12:40 corresponds in some way to the fourth generation in Genesis 15:16. It was Albright who suggested that *dôr* (generation) could signify a life span, with one hundred years being a rounded-off number. Thus four *dôr* and four hundred years might be two different methods of reckoning the same time span as in Genesis 15:13, 16 ("Abram the Hebrew: A New Archaeological Interpretation," *BASOR* 163 [1961] 50–51). A number of scholars have followed Albright's hypothesis: Kitchen, *Ancient Orient,* 54; Victor Hamilton, *The Book of Genesis Chapters 1–17* (Grand Rapids, Mich.: Eerdmans, 1990) 436.

169 "The Date of the Exodus and the Conquest/Settlement: The Case for the 1100s," *VT* 42 (1992) 510–527.

170 Ibid., 521.

171 Ibid., 513–516.

172 Ibid., 521–524 and *VT* 40 (1990) 185–205.

173 Ibid., 519.

6

MOSES AND THE EXODUS

> Moreover, the man Moses was very great in
> the land of Egypt, in the sight of Pharaoh's
> servants and in the sight of the people
>
> Exod. 11:3

I. Moses and Recent Scholarship

No figure casts a greater shadow in the pages of the Old Testament than Moses. While the Exodus narratives clearly attribute the "signs and wonders on the land of Egypt" (Exod. 7:3) to God, Moses is portrayed as the human agent through whom they were effected, resulting in the liberation of the Israelites from Pharaoh's clutches. Because of his role in Israel's exodus from Egypt and his receipt of divine laws at Sinai, Moses has had a unique status throughout Jewish and Christian canonical and noncanonical literature.[1] Because Moses appears in the Pentateuch as "larger than life" and able to execute what seems to modern readers to be fantastic miracles, from turning the Nile to blood to dividing the waters of the "Red" Sea, questions about the man and the events have been raised by the post-Enlightenment rationalist scholarship that still dominates the academy.[2] One of the results of the nineteenth- and twentieth-century scholarly preoccupation with the quest for Pentateuchal sources and the history of the traditions,[3] is a renewed skepticism about the historicity of the stories and the person of Moses himself. Martin Noth, for instance, after studying the Moses narratives in the Pentateuch, concluded that the lone historical tradition is the death and burial of Moses in Deuteronomy 34.[4] John Van Seters goes a step further, dogmatically asserting, "The quest for the historical Moses is a futile exercise. He now belongs only to legend."[5] The historicity of the Moses narratives is further questioned by those who treat the narratives as "folktales."[6] In the 1990s a deconstructed Moses appears who, in the view of Robert Coote, "might have had an Egyptian name simply because he was an Egyptian, ambitious, adventuresome prince or tribal renegade of the Nile. . . . Moses played a double role of loyal ally and rebel to pharaoh."[7]

Introducing Moses and the events of Exodus 2 through 14 in this negative manner should by no means be interpreted as reflecting the unanimous view of biblical scholars and archaeologists over the past decades. In fact, many have taken a positive view of the historicity of the Exodus narratives and the person of Moses,[8] a position with which I have been sympathetic.[9]

II. The Birth of Moses

When Pharaoh's strategy of pressing the Israelites into hard labor failed to reduce the burgeoning Israelites, he ordered the Hebrew midwives to kill all male babies (Exod. 1:15-16). But they refused to go along with the king's barbarous decree on moral grounds (Exod. 1:17). This failure resulted in yet another directive to his own people to cast Hebrew baby boys into the Nile (Exod. 1:22). It is in this context that the birth of Moses is set (Exod. 2:1-2). After three months of hiding her baby boy, Moses' mother made a basket of rushes, placed it with the baby in the Nile by the water's edge to see what fate would befall the babe. In an ironic twist, a princess discovers the endangered child and decides to adopt him as her own, at which time the name Moses is given (2:5-10).

This intriguing story has attracted much comparative interest because of similarities with the so-called "Legend of Sargon." Although set in the life of King Sargon of Akkad (2371-2316 B.C.), the surviving fragments of the tale are Neo-Assyrian and Neo-Babylonian in date (seventh to sixth centuries B.C.).[10] In this text, Sargon claims that his mother was an *entu* (priestess), but his father was unknown. Perhaps because she was to remain sexually chaste in her role as *entu*, she sought to cover up this birth by placing the baby in a reed basket, waterproofed with bitumen and set adrift in the Euphrates. Subsequently, the basket was found by Akki, the gardener of the goddess Ishtar who reared the baby. In adulthood, Sargon became the great king of Sumer and Akkad.

In a very thorough study, Donald Redford collected all the known tales using the "exposed child" motif from the ancient Near East.[11] In all thirty-two examples were produced, which he divided into three categories based upon the reason for the exposure: 1) the child is exposed owing to shameful circumstances; 2) a king or some powerful figure is trying to kill the child who poses a threat to his rule or dynasty; and 3) a massacre is introduced that threatens the life of the child along with others.[12] According to Redford's scheme, the Sargon legend fits into the first class, whereas the Moses birth story fits into the third.[13] Placing the two tales in very different circumstances illustrates that while there are some intriguing similarities between the two, there are fundamental differences. Hence, he concludes "they are not true parallels."[14] Brian Lewis likewise sees significant differences between the two stories and yet believes that the exposed-child motif influenced the writer(s) of the Moses birth story who introduced innovations to it.[15] Earlier on, Martin Noth also believed that influence of the Mesopotamian exposed-child motif on the Moses story could "hardly be doubted."[16] Similarly, John Van Seters has recently come to the same conclusion.[17] Lewis agrees with Hugo Gressman in believing that this episode was a legend that was added in the latest stages of the evolution of the Moses tradition.[18] In attempting to further develop the literary form of the Moses birth narrative, Childs concluded that it was "a historicized wisdom tale" like the Joseph story.[19] Redford's thoughtful critique of von Rad's old idea that the Joseph story was a wisdom tale is equally valid for Childs's proposal that the Moses birth pericope is a wisdom piece.[20]

While many distinguished scholars have been convinced of some sort of literary dependence of the Moses story on the Sargon legend, there are a significant number who have questioned this connection. Morton Cogan has shown that the Hebrew word *hašliyk* is the technical term for "expose," as in the case of Jeremiah's abandonment (Jer. 38:3 – 8) or Joseph's being thrown into a pit (Gen. 37:22).[21] He argues that the Akkadian counterpart is *nadû*, which is used in the case of Sargon. Cogan, however, notices that the term *hašliyk* is not found in Exodus 2:1 through 10, which significantly undermines the theory that the Moses story is associated with the exposed-child motif. The important differences between the two stories led John Durham to state that "as intriguing as these parallels certainly are, however, too strict a dependence upon them as Vorlagen must be avoided. There can be no question, certainly, of any exposure of the infant Moses. For one thing, there is not even a suggestion here of the divine rescuer so essential in the exposure-of-the-infant-hero motif. For another, the exposure of Moses by a Hebrew woman, and by his own mother at that, would turn a positive story, in this context, into a negative nonsense."[22] Tremper Longman III, in a recent study of the genre "fictional Akkadian autobiography" comes to a similar conclusion about the proposed relationship between the two birth stories after reviewing details of both: "Thus while there is a definite similarity between Exodus 2 and the Sargon Birth Legend, the differences in detail between them caution against a too easy identification of the two and against the idea that the Moses story is borrowed directly from Akkadian literature."[23] A further problem for those wishing to find a correlation between the Sargon legend and the Moses birth story is, as noted above, that the earliest surviving copies of the Sargon text date from Neo-Assyrian or later times. This factor, along with others, suggests that the legend may have been recorded by (or for) the late eighth century B.C. Assyrian king, Sargon II, who took the name of his great Akkadian forebear and identified himself with that monarch.[24] This possibility diminishes the case for the Sargon legend influencing Exodus because, if we allow that J or E (usually dated to the tenth and eighth centuries respectively) is the source behind Exodus 2:1 through 10,[25] and follow the traditional dating for these sources, both would predate the reign of Sargon II (721 – 705 B.C.).[26]

Alternatively, some scholars have looked to Egypt to find a literary prototype for the Moses birth story. The myth of Horus, which some cite, contains an episode in which Horus is born in the marshland of the Delta where he was hidden from his avenging uncle Seth by his mother Isis.[27] Moshe Greenberg finds this parallel so compelling that he states, "In view of this, the derivation of Moses' birth-story from Mesopotamia seems uncalled for."[28] Despite Greenberg's enthusiasm for associating the Horus myth with the Moses tale, this identification has by and large been rejected. J. Gwyn Griffiths, for instance, opines that "points of broad similarity in the two stories do not count for much."[29] Redford also rejects an Egyptian background to the biblical story because the closest Egyptian parallels derive from the Greco-Roman period, claiming that "the narrative of Exodus 2 still finds its closest parallel in the Sargon legend" and "that the literary tradition [is] at home in the plain of the Tigris-Euphrates."[30]

I concur with those who reject associating the Horus myth with the Moses birth story, largely on the dissimilarity of detail and the fact that the surviving Egyptian sources, as Redford noted, were of Greco-Roman date, too late to be seriously considered as influences on the Hebrew author. In the end, the reason for the multitude of stories from across the Near East and Mediterranean of casting a child into the waters is that it may reflect the ancient practice of committing an unwanted child, or one needing protection, into the hands of providence. A modern parallel would be leaving a baby on the steps of an orphanage or at the door of a church.[31]

III. Egyptian Elements in Exodus 2:1–10

While scholars have been concerned with assessing the merits of a Hebrew borrowing of a literary motif from Mesopotamia or Egypt, they have missed the small details in the text that are undeniably Egyptian. Over eighty years ago Gressmann observed the presence of general features reflecting Egyptian local color in Exodus 2.[32] In fact, a careful reading of the Hebrew text of the birth narrative reveals that a number of words used are of Egyptian origin. Verse 3 contains a significant cluster: "And when she could hide him no longer she took for him a *basket* made of *bulrushes*, and daubed it with bitumen and *pitch*; and she put the child in it and placed it among the *reeds* at the *river's brink*." The italicized words are of certain or possible Egyptian etymology, a detailed discussion of which follows.

1. "Basket" is Hebrew *tēbat* (תֵּבַת) and derives from the Egyptian word *ḏb3t*. This etymology has been recognized both by Hebraists[33] and Egyptologists.[34] Egyptian *ḏb3t* means "box," "coffin," and "sarcophagus," and is attested as early as the Middle Kingdom and continues into Coptic (B) as *taibi* (ⲧⲁⲓⲃⲓ)[35] and survives into Egyptian Arabic as *tabût*, where it has the same range of meanings.[36] While some commentators on Exodus have acknowledged that the Egyptian root is behind the Hebrew word,[37] amazingly, most recent works have omitted this detail in favor of discussing theological and salvific significance of this term because it is also used for Noah's ark.[38] The two "arks" were employed to save Noah, his family, Moses, and by extension, the Hebrew people.[39] The fact that *tēbat* occurs nowhere else in the Old Testament strongly suggests that a thematic relationship between the stories and choice of terms existed. Be that as it may, the Egyptian etymology of this key word cannot be overlooked.

2. *Gome'* (גֹּמֶא) is the Hebrew word translated "bulrushes" (KJV, RSV) or "papyrus" (JB) in English versions. Back in 1911, Driver wrote that *gōme'* was a word of "uncertain" derivation.[40] Nahum Sarna has recently written that the Hebrew

word "may well be of Egyptian derivation,"[41] but most commentators of Exodus have either ignored or been unaware of the word's Egyptian etymology. I think the certainty is stronger than Sarna's cautionary acceptance of this association. The Egyptian word *ḳm3*, meaning "papyrus," is the word rendered *gōme'* in Ex- odus 2:3. This etymology is recognized by Hebrew lexicographers Koehler and Baumgartner,[42] and discussed in other linguistically oriented studies.[43] In the 1920s when the *Wörterbuch der Ägyptischen Sprache* was being compiled, Erman and Grapow could trace occurrences of *ḳm3* only to the Twenty-first Dynasty.[44] However, examples from the Ramesside period have subsequently been docu- mented. In Papyrus Lansing it is written as *ḳmy*, where as in Papyrus Anastasi 4 it appears as *gmy*, illustrating the *ḳ* and *g* interchange reflected in the Hebrew writ- ing of *gōme'*.[45] Clearly *gōme'* is semantically and linguistically related to the Egyptian *ḳm3*.

3. The word *zāpet* (זֶפֶת), "pitch," appears only in Exodus 2:3 and Isaiah 34:9 in the Hebrew Bible, and cognates are restricted to Syriac and Arabic.[46] There is an Egyptian word, *ḏft*, a type of oil, recorded only once in a Ramesside-period text.[47] However, Egyptian *ḏ* should appear in Hebrew as a *ṣ* (*tsadeh*), not a *z* (*zayin*), which renders this equation unlikely. Another possible root is *śft*, which has been translated as "resin" and "oil" and is attested in more than one Rames- side text,[48] as well as in Old and Middle Kingdom inscriptions.[49] This etymol- ogy is somewhat problematic because normally the Egyptian *ś* does not appear in Semitic as *zayin*. On the other hand, if the words derive from a common Afro- Asiatic root, then the difficulty of associating Hebrew *zpt* and Egyptian *śpt* is re- moved.[50]

4. *Sûp* (סוּף) is the word rendered "reeds," which is unquestionably the Egyptian word *ṯwfy*. The Egyptian etymology of this word is well established and fully treated below in connection with the discussion of the Red Sea/Reed Sea prob- lem (see chap. 9, §III). There may be a symbolic connection between the reedy waters in which the baby Moses' basket was placed and Israel's salvation at the Sea of Reeds. In both cases, pharaoh's plans to destroy the Hebrews were thwarted and an unexpected escape resulted in the reedy waters of the Nile for Moses (Exod. 2) and for the Israelites of the Sea of Reeds (Exod. 14).

5. The "river" in this Egyptian setting is obviously the Nile. But the normal He- brew word for river, *nāhār*, is not used here. Rather, the word *hayᵉ'ōr* (הַיְאֹר) ap- pears, which is a transliteration of the Egyptian *itrw*, the word for the Nile.[51] The absence of the *t* in the Hebrew writing presents no problem because the Hebrew spelling, in fact, reflects the Egyptian vocalization beginning in the Eighteenth Dynasty.[52] The omission of the *t* is also witnessed in the Akkadian writing of *itrw* as *ia'uru*, and this is also the vocalization that survives into Coptic as ⲓⲟⲣ (*ior*).[53] Not surprisingly, the Egyptian word for the Nile is used in this story.

6. The word *śāpāh* (שָׂפָה) the river's "brink" or bank is related to the Egyptian word *spt*. In Hebrew, Ugaritic, and Akkadian,[54] as well as Egyptian, *śāpāh/spt* means both lips and riverbank.[55] It appears that *śāpāh* is a Semitic cognate, rather than a later loanword per se, since it is found in Egyptian as early as the Old Kingdom Pyramid Texts (e.g., PT 469a). In other words, it was a part of the inherited Se- mitic stratum of the Egyptian language.[56] This may explain why the Hebrew *ś* is written instead of the expected *s*. While there are a number of other Hebrew words for edge or bank of a river (e.g., *yād, peh/pānîm, gādāh,* and *qāṣeh*), it is nev- ertheless one of the words commonly used in Egypt for the Nile's edge, *spt*, that is written in Exodus 2:3 (and 7:15) as well as in the Joseph story in Genesis 41:3

and 17.[57] In view of the fact that four other words could have been used in Exodus 2:3, the choice of term used in Egypt cannot be coincidental.

Exodus 2:3 contains the central elements of the Moses birth narrative that are so commonly compared with the Sargon legend. Yet we see that this verse contains no less than six words used in Egypt during the New Kingdom. "River," "basket," and "reeds" occur again in 2:5, as does "Pharaoh" (which is repeated in 7, 9, and 10), which is of unquestioned Egyptian origin (see chap. 4, §III). How is the presence of Egyptian terms in the narrative to be explained, especially if the motif was borrowed from Mesopotamia? This significant concentration of Egyptian terms militates against the Mesopotamian connection. Hence, I am inclined to agree with Sarna's contentions that "the supposed affinities between this folkloristic composition [i.e., the Sargon legend] and our Exodus narrative are fanciful."[58] It seems that the Egyptian setting of the story is itself responsible for the Egyptian features in the pericope. Furthermore, it seems unlikely that a scribe during the late Judaean monarchy or the exilic period (or later) would have been familiar with these Egyptian terms. Even if that possibility is allowed, in a period when Assyria and Babylon overshadowed Hebrew thought, the inclusion of these Egyptian features would serve no purpose. Consequently, the birth narrative of Exodus 2 must at least date back to the time of Solomon, when close political and cultural ties with Egypt existed,[59] or even earlier.

IV. The Name of Moses

Providentially for baby Moses and his family, an unnamed daughter of Pharaoh passed by the shore, noticed the basket, found the Hebrew baby in it, and arranged for his mother to nurse him (Exod. 2:5–9). Verse 10 reads: "And the child grew, and she brought him to Pharaoh's daughter, and he became her son; and she named him Moses, for she said, 'Because I drew him out of the water.'" Two problems emerge from the naming of Moses: First, the root of the name *mōšeh* (מֹשֶׁה); and second, who names the child, the mother or the princess?

There is widespread agreement that at the root of the name of the great Hebrew leader is the Egyptian word *msi*,[60] which was a very common element in theophoric names throughout the New Kingdom (e.g., Amenmose, Thutmose, Ahmose, Ptahmose, Ramose, Ramesses).[61] Even Van Seters acknowledges that "few would dispute . . . it derives from the Egyptian verb *msy* ("to give birth") a very common element in Egyptian names."[62] He cautions against allowing historicity to be assumed from this factor alone, maintaining it only shows "the name's appropriateness to the background of Israel's sojourn in Egypt" and "a name by itself, however appropriate to the time and events described, does not make a historical personality."[63] Of course, his observation is correct. However, given the authenticity of the name and because it does fit a New Kingdom setting, one wonders how Van Seters can be so certain that the story is legend, especially a much later one, given the authenticity of this important detail?

While the acceptance of the word *msi* as the root for Moses' name is overwhelming among scholars of the Pentateuch, problems remain. Above (cf. chap. 5, §IV), it was argued that Egyptian toponyms with s were typically represented in Hebrew by the s (*samek*) and not š (*shin*) as Redford expected should be the case. If the names Moses and Raamses both contained the Egyptian root *msi*, one would expect the two words to be represented by the same sibilant, when in fact they are not. This complication was recognized and addressed many years ago in Griffiths's seminal study of the name of Moses.[64] He believed it was inadequate to explain the difference as a case of "the looseness" in the treatment of sibilants going between the two languages. Rather, he argued: "A distinction should be made, at any rate, between names which are transliterated from Egyptian into Hebrew or vice versa for a temporary purpose and those which find a permanent place in the second language and hence get a chance to develop and change according to the nature of this language."[65] Building upon Griffiths's suggestion, perhaps the distinction could be further clarified. Generally, personal names are more temporal in nature when borrowed into another language than toponyms, which tend to be more permanent. Griffiths has gathered examples of Egyptian personal names with Egyptian s that are transliterated into Semitic languages by the expected š, including a Middle Babylonian writing of *riʒmašeš* for *Rᶜ-ms-sw*, Ramesses.[66] In the fourteenth century B.C. Amarna Letters,[67] names of Egyptian officials with the *msi* plus divine name formula are found on numerous occasions, and the Egyptian s is regularly represented by the Semitic š (e.g., Amanmašša = Amenmesse [EA, 113:36, 43], Haramassi = Hormesse [EA, 20:33, 36; 49:25]; Tahmašši = Ptahmasse [EA, 265:9]).

While this sibilant correspondence occurs most frequently when transliterating Egyptian personal names into Semitic, there are exceptions. Some cases of Egyptian names with s appearing as s in Semitic texts were documented by Griffiths: Isis = ʾs; Osiris = ʾwsri.[68] Wolfgang Helck has also shown that the "rule" that the Egyptian s should always appear in Semitic as š is not consistent.[69] A factor not considered by Griffiths for why there is an inconsistency in how Egyptian sibilants are written in Semitic languages is the existence of dialectical differences within the Near East. The well-known story in Judges 12:4 through 6 illustrates the problem of vocalizing sibilants even between Israelite tribes. The defeated Ephraimites are reported to have fled from Gilead (Transjordan) for the fords in the Jordan River to return to their territory when they were stopped by Jephthah's troops. After denying they were Ephraimites (the enemy), the Israelites from Gilead demanded of each man, "'say Shibboleth,' and he said 'Sibboleth,' for he could not pronounce it right; then they seized him and slew him" (12:6). The former word is written with a *shin* while the latter with a *samek*. Clearly, dialectical difference between Israelites (and their Semitic-speaking neighbors) means that rigid rules about sibilants (and other letters) passing between different languages or even between Semitic languages are difficult to maintain. These considerations show that we cannot always expect sibilants going between Egyptian and Semitic languages conform to rigid rules set by modern linguists. Consequently, Hebrew *mōšeh* may well correspond to Egyptian *msi*.

An alternative approach is taken by Kitchen, who suggests that the woman who names the baby in Exodus 2:10 might be the mother, Jochebed, and not the princess.[70] Indeed Hebrew *wattiqrā'* ("she named") is somewhat ambiguous, and Cassuto,[71] like Kitchen, believed the speaker is the mother. Thus, Kitchen reasons, if the mother is naming the child, the name might be derived from the Hebrew root *māšā* and would have played nicely on the Egyptian word *msi*. This suggestion is certainly an intriguing possibility, but the reason given for the name—"because I drew him out of the water"—seems to refer to the actions of the princess (2:5–6) since the mother was not present then, only the sister. This consideration might favor the daughter of pharaoh as the one who named Moses.

Regardless of whether Griffiths or Kitchen is correct, both agree that the Egyptian word *msi* is some how involved in the naming. The Hebrew *mōšeh* is actually the active voice, not the expected passive *māšûy* ("one who is drawn out"),[72] a form in which *mōšeh* might constitute wordplay on *môšîaᶜ*, "savior, deliverer."[73] Furthermore, the active form also corresponds to the Egyptian word *mōse*, meaning "son" or "child," another pun on the same name.[74] Before becoming Israel's deliverer, Moses was a foster son of the princess.

V. Moses in Pharaoh's Court

For some, the whole notion of Moses being reared in the Egyptian court seems like a legendary feature. But a closer look at the royal court in the New Kingdom suggests otherwise. Thutmose III (1457–1425 B.C.) initiated the practice of bringing the princes of subject kings of western Asia to Egypt to be trained in Egyptian ways so as to prepare them to replace their fathers upon their death. This policy is laid out in the following text which deals with the tribute from Retenu (Syria-Palestine): "Now the children of the chieftains and their brothers are brought in order to be hostages of Egypt. Now if anyone of these chieftains die, then his majesty will have his son go to assume his throne."[75] References to the presence of the sons of Syro-Canaanite kings in Pharaoh's court and possible allusions to the inauguration of the practice by Thutmose III are found in some of the Amarna letters. Aziru of Amurru, in order to show his loyalty to Egypt says, "I herewith give [my] sons as 2 att[endants] and they are to do what the k[ing, my lord] orders" (EA, 156:9–14).[76] Meanwhile, Arasha of Kumidu claimed: "Truly I send my own son to the king, my lord" (EA, 199.15–21).[77] Jerusalem's king, Abdu-Heba, maintains that his legitimacy as king was due to his appointment by Pharaoh, stating "neither my father nor my mother put me in this place, but the strong arm of the king brought me into my father's house (EA, 286.10–15)."[78] From this statement it might be inferred that Abdu-Heba had been a prince schooled in Egypt before his appointment to the kingship of Jerusalem.

Perhaps in the absence of a son, or one old enough to be sent to Egypt, a king's brother might be sent to Egypt instead, as Biryawaza of Damascus reports: "[I] herewith [s]end [m]y brother [t]o you" (EA 194.28-32).[79] In addition, the Amarna Letters, and other New Kingdom documents, abound with references to daughters of kings from the Levant, Anatolia, and Mesopotamia going to Egypt to marry the pharaohs to seal a diplomatic marriage.[80]

Thus, foreign princes and princesses were no strangers to the Egyptian court of New Kingdom. Among the titles of Akhenaten's vizier, the Semitic-named Aper-el, recorded in his recently discovered tomb at Saqqara is ḥrd n k3p, "child of the nursery." The k3p seems to have been connected to the palaces of Egypt and appears to have had an educational component to them, the mnᶜ or mnᶜt being the tutor.[81] Little is known about this institution in the Middle Kingdom, but it flourished in the New Kingdom and was open to foreigners, Nubians and Semites alike.[82] In a study of the children of the nursery during the Eighteenth Dynasty, Betsy Bryan observes that among them "were also children of foreign rulers who were sent or taken as hostages to Egypt to be 'civilized' and then returned to rule as vassals."[83] She also points out that some of the children of the nursery went on to be court officials, with a few attaining high positions in the government. Aper-el was an alumnus of the k3p, a foreigner, too, who reached the highest administrative post in the land after he or his father came to Egypt as part of the Egyptian program for maintaining its Asian empire.

According to Bryan, nurseries were located "throughout the country" wherever there were royal residences, and thus the ḥrdw "were raised in the confines of palaces within Egypt," and they "obviously had advantages not available to many."[84] The picture of Moses in Exodus 2 being taken to the court by a princess where he was reared and educated is quite consistent with the emerging information about the k3p in the New Kingdom, the only period for which there is evidence of foreigners being included in this royal institution.[85]

VI. Moses the Refugee

In adulthood, Moses is portrayed as leaving the comfort of the court to see the plight of his people (Exod. 2:11). As a Hebrew attached to the court, Moses may have been acting in some official capacity.[86] Upon seeing an Egyptian official beating a Hebrew, Moses retaliated, killing the Egyptian, which led him to flee from Pharaoh's anger (Exod. 2:12–15). Moses' flight took him to the land of Midian, generally thought to be in northern Arabia, on the east side of the Gulf of Aqaba.[87] One reason for not stopping in Sinai to hide out is that throughout the New Kingdom the Serabit el-Khadim area was regularly frequented by Egyptian mining expeditions.[88]

Biblical scholars have long accepted the early origins and authenticity of the Midian episode in Moses' life.[89] Not surprisingly, Van Seters has challenged this long-held stance, arguing that J borrowed the motif of the political fugitive from 1 Kings 11:14–22 and applied it to the Moses story.[90] While the comparison of the Moses story to the Hadad the Edomite episode is novel,[91] the parallels seem banal. In point of fact, Van Seters needs the dependency of the Moses story on that of Hadad in order to defend his idiosyncratic thesis that the Deuteronomic History (which includes 1 and 2 Kings) predates J.[92]

Another literary parallel to the Midian pericope is the Egyptian "Tale of Sinuhe," which was written some time in the Twelfth Dynasty, but continued in circulation down into the Nineteenth Dynasty, the Ramesside age.[93] The main points of the story are:

1. Sinuhe flees Egypt fearing Pharaoh's wrath over events surrounding the assassination of his predecessor, King Amenemhet I.
2. He lives a life as a tent-dwelling Bedouin in Syria-Canaan where he is taken in by a friendly chieftain and married to his eldest daughter.
3. At Pharaoh's directive, Sinuhe returns to Egypt to stand before his sovereign.

These same features are found in the story of Moses in Exodus.

1. Moses flees Egypt fearing Pharaoh's death sentence for killing the Egyptian official (Exod. 2:11-15).
2. He lives among the seminomadic herdsmen of Midian, marrying a daughter of the priest of Midian (Exod. 2:16-22).
3. At God's instruction, he returns to Egypt to stand before Pharaoh (3:10, 4:18-5:1).

These striking similarities between the main elements in the stories of Sinuhe and Moses have, surprisingly, not attracted the attention of biblical scholars.[94] A notable exception is a study by J. Robin King that identifies ten narrative steps in the "Tale of Sinuhe" that serve as the model for other later literary works.[95] While the ten steps do not perfectly fit the Moses story because of the inclusion of the birth narrative in 2:1 through 10, King recognizes the presence of the general outline of the Sinuhe narrative structure in Exodus 2 through 5.[96] King's citations of where this structure is found in sources from the second and first millenniums B.C. span across the Near East because this "structure is one version of an ancient Near Eastern oicotype specifically designed to narrate stories of divine politics and reconciliation."[97]

Whether or not this literary structuring is in the view of the author(s) of Exodus 2 to 5 is difficult to say. The number of stories of political figures fleeing one land for another from the ancient Near East, including the Moses story, may reflect upon the political realities of that region and the hospitality that could be shown by a host tribe, nation, or king.[98] As noted above (chap. 5, §II), since all the other examples of the narrative-step structure cited by King were applied to the stories of well-known historical figures (e.g., Hattusilis, Idrimi, Esarhaddon, and Nabonidus), it would be illogical to dismiss Joseph as a historical figure because of the use of this literary pattern. The same argument holds true for Moses in Exodus.

The chronological datum offered in the Bible for the length of Moses' stay in Midian is ambiguous. A brief obituary of the pharaoh from whom Moses fled states, "In the course of those many days the king of Egypt died" (Exod. 2:23). When the expression "many days" is used in Deuteronomy 1:46 it refers to the period of Israel's stay at Kadesh Barnea, which was considerable. In any event, Moses remained long enough to marry and have two children prior to his return to Egypt (Exod. 2:22; 18:3-4), which may only have been a few years.

VII. Moses before Pharaoh: The Plagues

Moses stood before Pharaoh in order to secure the temporary release of the Israelites in order to have a religious retreat in the wilderness. Since we have seen that Egyptian laborers were given time off from work for religious observances, Moses' appeal seems a reasonable one. Whatever hopes for a speedy release of the Hebrews seemed dashed by Pharaoh's rejection,[99] and a contest of wills and clash of religious ideology follows; namely, the plagues, "signs in Egypt (Ps. 78.43).

The Plagues Cycles: Literary Considerations

Since the days of Wellhausen, the plagues narrative has been considered a composite of J, E, and P sources by many biblical scholars.[100] One of the main criteria for distinguishing J from E has been the use of Yahweh and Elohim. However, in the passages assigned to E by Hyatt (9:22–23a, 35; 10:12–13a, 20–23, 27),[101] and Childs (7:15b, 17b, 20b, 23; 9:22–23a, 24a, 25a, 35a; 10:12–13a, 15, 20, 21–23, 27; 11:1–3),[102] the divine name is written and not Elohim. In fact, Elohim never stands alone in the plagues cycle.[103] Because of this problem, Noth argued that J and E were nearly indistinguishable, concluding that a JE source, supplemented by P, was used in these narratives.[104] Georg Fohrer disagreed with Noth, preferring the three-source hypothesis, believing that a redactor removed the classical differences between J and E.[105] For Ronald Clements, that redactor is the Deuteronomist.[106] Because Van Seters rejects the existence of an independent E source, he considers J and P to be present, with P supplementing the primary J material.[107] This conclusion, of course, would imply that P is the redactor. These hypothetical analyses demonstrate the disarray in the source-critical camp that has existed for some years now. No wonder Thomas Thompson has recently labeled source-critical orthodoxy as "no longer sufficient" to explain the narratives in Genesis and Exodus.[108] Instead, he considers 5:1 to 13:16 to be a single "complex-chain narrative."[109]

Complicating the questions surrounding the nature of the plagues narrative is the relationship between Exodus 7:14 to 12:44 and references to the plagues in Psalms 78 and 105.[110] The Psalms do not recite all ten of the plagues enumerated in Exodus, nor are they written in the same sequence.[111] Too much has been made of these differences. For instance, Psalm 78 has the rebellion in the wilderness (40–41) preceding the plagues (44–51). Surely the Psalmist was not so misguided in recalling Israel's traditions to think that the wilderness experience occurred prior to the exodus event. Commenting on the variations between the Psalms and Exodus, Leslie Allen suggests that they "reflect only a free handling of the source material,"[112] or what I have called "liturgical license" on the part of the Psalmists.[113] The purpose behind the sequence reported in Psalm 78, it appears, was not accidental or the result of an erroneous source; rather, it was deliberate, to demonstrate that in the wilderness the Israelites had so quickly forgotten the events of the plagues that should have sustained them during the trials in Sinai. Because of the liturgical and didactic nature of the plague stories in the Psalter, they should not be used to reconstruct the sequence in Exodus, nor can they be used to isolate sources behind the Pentateuch.

In their present form, the nine plagues of Exodus constitute a literary unity comprised of three parallel cycles, with the tenth plague functioning as the climax.[114] Samuel Lowenstamm believes that the significance of the tenth plague lies in the nature of the number ten being "a typological number—if not a climactic one, at least expressing completeness."[115] In order to illustrate the literary structure of Cassuto and Sarna, the latter's chart is reproduced as Table 6.1.[116]

When the plagues narrative is viewed in this broad literary manner, a tightly woven, elegant tapestry appears. If this is simply the hand of the redactor who brought together divergent traditions, it must be asked "if it is possible any longer to isolate the threads that have been so thoroughly reworked."[117] Consequently, a number of scholars argue that the text in its present form must be treated as a unit, whatever its prehistory.[118]

The Phenomena of the Plagues

Because of their penchant for identifying sources behind the final form of the narrative, biblical scholars have failed to consider the nature of the sequence of the plagues. Nearly ninety years ago Flinders Petrie observed, "The order of the plagues was the natural order of such troubles on a lesser scale in the Egyptian season, as was pointed out long ago."[119] Petrie thought that the bloodlike waters of the Nile were the result of stagnating conditions that occurred just prior to the beginning of the inundation, when water levels were at their lowest.

Greta Hort took the opposite tack. She hypothesized the "plague" resulted from a high Nile because the four conditions describing the water in Exodus 7:20 to 24 could only be met during the inundation.[120] The Nile rises in July and August, crests in September,[121] and usually is reddish in appearance owing to the presence of *Roterde*, particles of soil, suspended in the water. In Exodus, the Nile is described by the blood-red color (7:20); the death of its fish (7:21a); its foul smell; and its undrinkable state (7:21c). Hort maintains that only one scenario could result in these four conditions: the presence of millions of flagellates (*Euglena sanguinea* and *Haematoccus pluvialis*) in the floodwaters.[122] Probably originating in Lake Tana, Ethiopia, the flagellates flowed to Egypt via the Blue Nile and would account for the reddish color and the putrid smell. During the darkness of night, flagellates require higher amounts of oxygen, whereas during the day they give off an abundance of oxygen. This fluctuation, Hort explains, would cause the death of fish, which need constant amounts of oxygen. She further argues that the following five plagues came as a consequence of the first.[123] Frogs, the second plague, are known to invade the land toward the end of the Nile's inundation in September and October. It is reported in this case (Exod. 7:25) that a week separated the first and second plague, suggesting a connection between the two, Hort avers. The sudden death of the frogs (Exod. 8:13), she believes, was because of contamination caused by *bacillus anthracis* from the decomposing fish.[124]

The identity of the insect (*kinnîm*) involved in the third plague has been disputed by scholars. "Gnats" is a common translation (RSV, NAS, NIV),[125] while "lice" is also suggested (KJV).[126] A number of commentators have understood "gnats" to mean a type of mosquito,[127] an interpretation accepted by the Jerusalem Bible and Hort.[128] The flood season in Egypt always brought with it mosquitoes that could quickly reproduce in the pools and puddles left by the retreating Nile. The "flies" (*ᶜārōḇ*) of the fourth plague may have been dog flies, known for their

TABLE 6.1

The Plague		Exodus Source	Fore-warning	Time of Warning	Instruction Formula	Agent
First	1. Blood	7:1 14	yes	"in the morning"	Station yourself	Aaron
Series	2. Frogs	7:25 – 8:11	yes	none	Go to Pharaoh	Aaron
	3. Lice	8:12 – 15	none	none	none	Aaron
Second	4. Insects	8:16 – 28	yes	"in the morning"	Station yourself	God
Series	5. Pestilence	9:1 – 7	yes	none	Go to Pharaoh	God
	6. Boils	9:8 – 12	none	none	none	Moses
Third	7. Hail	9:13 – 35	yes	"in the morning"	Station yourself	Moses
Series	8. Locust	10:1 – 20	yes	none	Go to Pharaoh	Moses
	9. Darkness	10:21 – 23	none	none	none	Moses
Climax	10. Death of Egyptian Firstborn	11:4 – 7 12:29 – 30	yes	none	none	God

vicious biting, based on the LXX reading *kunómuia*. Hort considers the quick out-break of this plague to be consistent with this type of mosquito and believes it was the cause of the sixth plague.[129] The fifth plague (*deber*) affected field animals (Exod. 9:3) and is thought to be a "murrain" (KJV, RV), a "deadly" (JB), "severe" (RSV), or "terrible" (NIV) plague.[130] Hort maintained that this plague resulted from anthrax spread inland by the frogs associated with the second plague. "Boils" is a common understanding of *šeḥîn* (KJV, RSV, NAS, NEB, JB), which makes sense in the light of the meanings of Ugaritic *šḥn* ("burn") and Akkadian *šaḫānu* ("grow hot"), which would be consistent with an infection.[131] This plague specifically hit animals and humans alike (Exod. 9:9), and, based on a statement in Deuteronomy 28:35, it appears that this plague primarily affected the lower extremities of people. To Hort this is a clue that it was a fly, *Stomoxys calcitrans*, which carried anthrax, rather than wasps, another common carrier of anthrax that typically attacks the head area.[132] Moreover, she contends that the flies that were the pest of the fourth plague were responsible for the boils of the sixth plague.[133] The infection would have been passed on by the flies biting humans and other animals after coming in contact with rotting, dead animals (the result of the fifth plague).[134]

According to Hort's scheme, the first six plagues form a natural sequence of interdependent events resulting from a high Nile infected by flagellates, whereas plagues seven through ten were not connected to the first six. Hail, thunder, and lightning, the seventh plague (Exod. 9:23) not only caused damage to crops (Exod. 9:25, 31 – 32), but was a source of terror to the Egyptians since hail is uncommon in Egypt. Violent rainstorms do strike Egypt from time to time, with several devastating examples occurring in recent years. The note in 9:31 that "the flax and barley were ruined" by the hail is interesting in that these two crops are known to have grown together as paintings from the mid Eighteenth Dynasty tomb of Paheri at el-Kab depict the harvesting of barley and the pulling of flax occurring in adjacent fields.[135] While this scene illustrates that these two crops did in fact grow side by side at the same time, their harvest was not necessarily concurrent since flax can be pulled at different stages in development depending on its use.[136] From the period A.D. 1000 to 1800, wheat and flax are known to have overlapped, and the statement that the wheat was not destroyed because it would have appeared after the plague of the hail (Exod. 9:32) is also consistent with the agricultural growth and harvest pattern over the past one thousand years; wheat, although planted before the other two, was harvested a month and a half to two months after the barley.[137] Barley and flax are among the first crops planted and harvested after the inundation.[138] This information lends further support to Hort's thesis that the first six plagues are connected to the inundation, and those that followed occurred over several following months. This attention in Exodus 10:31 and 32 to the period when crops matured shows that the writer of these narratives had an excellent knowledge of the Egyptian agricultural calendar. The presence of this type of information could hardly be the guesswork of an author removed by a great amount of space and time from the events.

The eighth plague offers no particular problem from a phenomenological perspective since locust plagues were known throughout the ancient Near East and Africa as a particularly feared bane, even in modern times. A press report several years ago began with the following ominous description: "Billions of locusts are moving across North Africa in the worst plague since 1954, blotting out the sun and settling on the land like a black, ravenous carpet to strip it clean of vegetation."[139] The locusts, the report continued, could cover 150 square miles at a time, with a quarter million per acre, devouring one hundred thousand tons of vegetation each time the horde landed. This particular horde began in the Red Seas region of Sudan and moved through Chad, Libya, Tunisia, Algeria, and Morocco. Exodus 10:13 has the locust swarms being blown in by an east wind, which might be from the southeast since the Hebrews did not use more specific directions than the four cardinal points,[140] and locusts hordes that hit north Africa generally do originate in the Sudan area.[141]

The final plague in the third series, three days of darkness (Exod. 10:21–23), has long been associated with the desert sandstorms, *khamsins* common to Egypt in March.[142] The minute particles of sand transported by the *khamsins*, coupled with the extreme heat, make these desert storms most uncomfortable. I can attest to the discomfort of this phenomenon: in 1967 I traveled by train from Minya to Cairo (about 275 kilometers or 170 miles) and throughout this trip, the Nile Valley was blanketed by a brownish cloud that literally could be felt, a point noted in Exodus 10:21. In the mid-afternoon hours, cars drove with lights on. Again in March of 1995, a *khamsin* covered Egypt from South of Luxor to north of Cairo throughout the day, grounding planes. Finally at 11:00 P.M. our plane could depart Luxor for Cairo. *Khamsins* can last up to two or three days.

While there has been widespread support for interpreting the ninth plague as a sandstorm, there have certainly been those who reject this association. Noth, for instance, thinks the connection is "not very probable."[143] Likewise, Hyatt consers the *khamsin* explanation to be unlikely, since the degree of darkness described in Exodus is not consistent with that caused by a *khamsin*.[144] Hort, however, observes that in the aftermath of the damage to crops caused by the earlier plagues, even more dust would have been swept up by the storms, making the clouds of dust thicker and darker.[145] Those who reject the *khamsin* hypothesis have probably not endured a searing dust storm so well known to Egyptians.

Hort's scenario for explaining the phenomena of the plagues, I believe, is compelling indeed. However, D. J. McCarthy rejected her approach on the grounds of differences in the sequence of plagues in the Exodus and Psalms traditions, stating that there was no attempt to mirror reality in the "sequence of these episodes."[146] He believes that the protracted process of oral and literary composition gave rise to these inconsistencies and militates against a naturalist interpretation. In view of the literary considerations reviewed above and the fact that Hort's thesis works logically and moves with Egyptian seasonal changes, is it just coincidence that the redactor organized the divergent, even supposedly contradictory, traditions into a form that makes perfect sense in an Egyptian setting?

Following Hort's thesis, the first nine plagues are natural occurrences known to Egypt, albeit magnified and occurring in close proximity, but the tenth plague, because of its selective nature, cannot be linked to any particular disease. Sarna offers a salient assessment of the plagues on Egypt: "From a theological perspective, they are instances of God's harnessing the forces of nature for the realization of His own historical purpose. The tenth and final visitation upon the pharaoh and his people is the one plague for which no rational explanation can be given. It belongs entirely to the category of the supernatural."[147]

In response to the crisis in Egypt over the plagues, the magicians (*ḥarṭummîm*)[148] declared, "This is the finger of God" (Exod. 8:19 [Heb. 15]). This statement indicates that the Egyptians recognized these events, despite their natural appearance, to be of divine origin. The expression "the hand or finger of a deity" has particularly been linked to plagues.[149] For both the Egyptians and the Israelites, the world in which they lived was not divided into dichotomous categories such as church and state or natural and miraculous. Rather, these concepts were dynamically interrelated; all the forces of nature were divinely controlled.[150] Consequently, the plagues need to be considered from the perspective of the Egyptian worldview.

The Plagues from an Egyptian Religious Perspective

The Bible itself makes the claims that "on all the gods of Egypt I will execute judgments" (Exod. 12:12) and "upon their gods also the LORD executed judgments" (Num. 33:4). Based on these statements, some have tried to make a correlation between each plague and a particular Egyptian deity or religious institution.[151] For instance, Charles Aling says the first plague, "is quite obviously an attack against the Nile god, Hapi."[152] In point of fact, Hapi is only associated with the inundation, and is not a Nile god.[153] In the past, it was common to refer to the obese fecundity figures as "Nile gods"; it is now clear, however, that these strange figures are personifications of fertility.[154] If Hort is correct in believing that the first plague coincided with the beginning of the inundation, it might be possible to draw a connection with Hapi. Alternatively, the annual flooding of the Nile was also associated with the resurrection of Osiris.[155] Thus, the bloodlike waters might signal his death rather than his resuscitation, death for Egypt's agriculture rather than verdant fields,[156] a frightful prospect for the Egyptians.

The suggestions that other plagues that afflicted animals such as frogs (associated with the goddess Hekat) and cattle (cows with Hathor; bulls with Apis) were an affront to the animals associated with those deities is problematic because the Egyptians did not look at a frog and consider it a manifestation of Hekat, nor treat a cow with special respect because of the link with Hathor. During the period when the cult of Apis was maintained in Memphis (from ca. 1400 B.C. through the late period), only one special bull was associated with Apis, received special treatment, and was mummified and buried at Saqqara. The Egyptians were not like the Hindus, who consider animals sacred and hence are vegetarians. Bovines were eaten throughout Egyptian history, and the sacrifice of bulls was, indeed, an important component of the funerary ritual.[157] Consequently, the notion that particular animals and their corresponding deities are under attack with the various plagues must be dispelled.

The seventh plague is described as a violent lightening, thunder, and hail storm (Exod. 9:22 – 24). Thunderstorms were especially feared in Egypt and thought to be wonders or miracles. In an Eleventh Dynasty quarry inscription from the Wadi Hammamat in the eastern desert of Upper Egypt, a rain storm is described as a divine manifestation: "Rain was made, the forms of this god (Min) were seen, his power was given to the people, the highland was turned into a lake."[158]

The belief that rain and storms were the result of divine activity is reflected in a stela erected at Karnak during the reign of Ahmose (ca. 1538 B.C.). A devastating storm struck Egypt, according to this text, a storm thought to be associated with the cataclysmic eruption of the Aegean island of Thera (Santorini) by Karen Foster and Robert Ritner.[159] Ritner's new translation of the Ahmose text reveals the religious understanding of and the fearful response to this extraordinarily powerful storm in Egypt.[160]

8. The gods [caused] the sky to come in a tempest of r[ain], with darkness in the western region and the sky being

9. unleased without [cessation, louder than] the cries of the masses, more powerful than [. . .], [while the rain raged(?)] on the mountains louder than the noise of the

10. cataract which is at Elephantine. Every house, every quarter that they reached [. . .]

11. floating on the water like skiffs of papyrus opposite the royal residence for a period of [. . .] days,

12. while a torch could not be lit in the Two Lands. Then His Majesty said: "How much greater this is than the wrath of the great god, than the plans of the gods!" Then His Majesty descended

13. to his boat, with his council following him, which the crowds on the East and West had hidden faces, having no clothing on them

14. after the manifestation of the god's wrath.

The text continues by reporting that the King went to a temple in Thebes to appear before the golden statue of Amon-Re and appease him with offerings. Subsequently, the restoration of damaged temples and burial complexes throughout Egypt was ordered. Line 13 reflects the fear that awestruck Egyptians felt in the wake of the storm.

In the Exodus story, Pharaoh's response to the thunderstorm is to confess that he and his people were in the wrong, and he implored Moses to intercede with God in order to end the destructive storm (Exod. 9:27–29). It is noteworthy that in the Ahmose text the god's wrath is mentioned twice (lines 12 and 14), and divine intervention is sought.

There is some justification for the view that the ninth plague, the darkening of the sun, is aimed at the Sun-god, Re or Atum. Cassuto noted that in Exodus 10:10, one of the verses introducing the ninth plague, the Hebrew word $r\bar{a}^c\hat{a}$, "evil," plays on Egyptian r^c, the sun.[161] More recently, Gary Rendsburg has extended Cassuto's suggestion to other uses of $r\bar{a}^c\hat{a}$ in the Pentateuch that also play on the Egyptian term r^c.[162] Because of the supreme role of the Sun-god in ancient Egypt, Cassuto's idea, that the obscuring of the sun by Yahweh is making a statement of his supremacy over the premier deity of Egypt, has some merit. However, in Egyptian royal ideology, the king who was the "Son of Re," is also responsible for Egypt's well-being. It is my contention that the plagues story needs to be examined in the light of Pharaoh's role as the god of the Egyptian state.[163]

The Hebrew Scriptures view the plagues as a contest, a divine struggle. The cosmic confrontation is played out with Pharaoh as the representative of Egypt's gods and Moses and Aaron as Yahweh's agents. Exodus 3:19 and 20 and 6:1 declare:

> I know that the king of Egypt will not let you go unless compelled by a mighty hand. So I will stretch out my hand and smite Egypt with all the wonders which I will do in it; after that he will let you go.

> But the LORD said to Moses, "Now you shall see what I will do to Pharaoh; for with a strong hand he will send them out, yea, with a strong hand he will drive them out of his land.

The language of this struggle in the Exodus narratives has a decisive military flavor and the terms "strong hand" ($y\bar{a}\underline{d}$ $h^a z\bar{a}q\bar{a}h$) and "outstretched arm" ($z^e r\hat{o}a^c$ $n^e \underline{t}\hat{u}y\hat{a}$) used in the Pentateuch[164] correspond to the Egyptian terms $hp\check{s}$, "strong arm" and pr-c, "the arm goes forth or is extended" (fig. 15).[165] Evidence that the Hebrew use of $z^e r\hat{o}a^c$ derived from the Egyptian concept of the conquering arm of pharaoh is the use of zu-ru-$u\underline{h}$ in the Amarna Letters of Abdu-Heba of Jerusalem (EA, 286.12; 287.27 & 288.14).[166] Moran renders zu-ru-$u\underline{h}$ as "the strong arm (of the king)"—that is, Pharaoh.[167] In support of this correlation between the Hebrew and Egyptian concepts, Manfred Görg, independently of me, reached the same conclusion in an article published in the same year as my study.[168]

The centrality of Pharaoh in the plagues cycle is further realized when we consider the Egyptian monarch's responsibility to maintain cosmic order, Maat ($m3^ct$), that was established by the creator-god.[169] If there was a failure in the land, $isft$, a state of chaos, was said to prevail. An Egyptian sage named Ipuwer lamented the deteriorated situation when $isft$ reigned:

> Now, Hapy inundates but none plow for him, everyone says,
> "we don't know what has become of the land."
> Indeed, women are barren, none conceive, Khnum does
> not shape because of the condition of the land . . . .
>
> Now the river is (turned to) blood. When people drink of
> it they [shrink] from people and crave water . . . .
>
> Foreign bowmen (Asiatics) have come to Egypt. . . .
> Look, the land is deprived of kingship by a few people
> who ignore tradition . . .
> [////] is the crown of Re, who pacifies the Two Lands.[170]

A note of despair also sounds in the "Prophecy of Neferti," which dates to early in the Twelfth Dynasty (1970–1950 B.C.). Unlike the purely morbid tone of Ipuwer, Neferti's prophecy moves from gloom to glory. This turnabout is the result of the accession of Amenemhet as king. Neferti states:[171]

> The river of Egypt is dry, one can cross the water on foot;
> one seeks water for ships to sail on it,
> its course having become a riverbank (ll. 26–27)
>
> All happiness has gone away, the land is cast down in trouble
> because of those feeders, Asiatics (*sttyw*) who are throughout the land.
> Enemies have arisen in the east, Asiatics have come down to Egypt.
> (ll. 31–33)
>
> Re withdraws himself from mankind. Though he rises at the right time,
> one does not know when noon occurs (ll. 51–52)
>
> Then a king will come from the South, who is called Ameny . . .
> He will take the white crown and will wear the red crown (ll. 58–59)
>
> Then Order (*m3ᶜt*) will come to its [right] place, and Chaos [*isft*] will be
> driven out. (ll. 68–69)

Irregularities in nature abound when cosmic order is gone awry, according to these texts. First the Nile is either extremely low, owing to poor inundations, or in some way is contaminated, and so crops fail. Second, the sun is in some way obscured. Three, kingship that unites and controls the land is missing, and four, foreigners are present in Egypt, contributing to the disruption of order. Neferti announces that when the king politically unites the land and rules according to mythic principle, then chaos is dispelled and order is enthroned.

Because of this association between cosmic order and kingship, Egyptian rulers could take credit for the productivity and well-being of the land. Again, from the Twelfth Dynasty, in stanza 11 of the "Instruction of Amenemhet I" he declares:

> I am the one who made grain, beloved of Nepri (grain deity)
> Hapi honored me on every field.
> No one hungered in my years,
> No one thirsted in them.[172]

In the "loyalist" instruction of a Twelfth Dynasty official named Sehetep-ib-re, the following grand portrait of the king is offered:

> He is Re who is seen by his rays,
> who illuminates the Two Lands more than the Sun-disc (i.e., Aten)
> who makes it healthy more than a high inundation,[173]
> having filled the Two Lands with strength and life.[174]

Associating the king with the Sun-god continues in the New Kingdom. Concerning Ahmose it could be said:

> He is looked upon like Re when he rises,
> like the shining of Aten,
> like rising of Khepri at the sight of his rays on high,
> like Atum in the eastern sky.[175]

Merneptah's accession to the throne upon the death of Ramesses II is celebrated in Papyrus Sallier 1:[176]

> Be joyful the entire land!
> Good times have come.
> The lord (l.p.h. = life, prosperity, and health) has ascended in all lands,
> and orderliness (*mty*) has gone down to its throne.
> The king of Upper and Lower Egypt, lord of millions of years,
> great in kingship just like Horus, Ba-en-Re Mery-Amun (l.p.h.),
> who overwhelms Egypt with festivals,
> the Son of Re who is more excellent than any king,
> Merneptah hetep-hir-maat (l.p.h.).
> Every truthful one (*m3ct*) come and see.
> Truth (*m3ct*) has subdued falsehood (*grg*).
> Evil ones have been thrown [on] their faces.
> All the greedy are ignored.
> The flood arises and does not subside,
> the inundation (*hcpy*) crests.
> The days are extended, the night have hours,[177]
> and the moon comes precisely (i.e. at the right time).
> The gods are satisfied and content.

The sentiment expressed in Neferti is likewise found in this Nineteenth Dynasty hymn. The legitimate king who rules by *m3ct* can expect the Nile to flood properly and bring fertility to the land, and additionally the sun and moon operate according to the created order.

The texts reviewed here, spanning from the Middle through New Kingdoms, illustrate that the king was closely associated with the sun and moon, the inundation and the fertility of the land. Furthermore, the connection between Pharaoh and the gods of Egypt is firmly established. What the plagues of Exodus show is the inability of the obstinate king to maintain *m3ct*. Rather, it is Yahweh and his agents, Moses and Aaron, who overcome in the cosmic struggle, demonstrating who really controls the forces of nature.

The Rod of Moses and Pharaoh's Rule

That the plagues were a direct challenge to Pharaoh's ability to maintain order is further supported when the significance of Moses' rod is considered from an Egyptian perspective. It is when Moses is keeping Jethro's sheep (Exod. 3:1) that we are first introduced to the rod or staff (*maṭṭeh*). God asks Moses, "'what is in your hand?' He said, 'A rod.'" (Exod. 4:2). It is then transformed into a serpent when cast upon the ground. This staff would later be used in the contest between Moses and Pharaoh's magicians (Exod. 7:8–12). Apparently, Moses was carrying a common shepherd's crook.

Throughout Pharaonic history, one of the regular symbols of kingship was a small shepherd's crook. These are ubiquitous in royal statuary and iconography. William Hayes argued that the "adoption of the shepherd's crook as a divine and royal scepter and as a general symbol of authority goes back far into Egypt's pre-history."[178] He finds this emblem in the iconography of the god Andjety, who is associated with shepherds from the eastern Delta. This same crook is attested in Old Kingdom herding scenes, but from the Middle Kingdom onward, two types of crooks are regularly found in scenes where men tend cattle and various types of fowl.[179] In the Middle Kingdom, the long crook is still found in the hand of monarchs (fig. 16), but starting late in the Old Kingdom, this particular crook becomes reduced in size to that of a scepter carried by royalty and divinities (fig. 6). In the Eighteenth Dynasty some high-ranking officials, like the Viceroys of Kush (Nubia) are shown holding this staff, clearly symbolizing authority or perhaps their roles as representatives of the king.[180]

This staff or scepter originates in a pastoral context, as the earliest pictorial evidence suggests.[181] Further support for the pastoral origins is that the word ꜥwt, known as early as the Old Kingdom and the word for small cattle, goats, and herds, is written with hieroglyphs for shepherds staff, ⌐ or ⌐.[182] The shape of the hieroglyph and tomb illustrations of the crook has been confirmed by actual discoveries of this staff from the Middle Kingdom.[183]

In the "Wisdom for Merikare," ca. 2200, humanity is described in the following manner: "Well nourished is mankind, god's flock" (ꜥwt).[184] If humans were considered god's "flock" then the association of the king as shepherd and humans as the flock can easily be made. John Wilson draws upon this idea as a chapter title, "The King as the Good Shepherd," in his classic book, *The Culture of Egypt*.[185] He introduced this chapter by discussing how the role of the king had significantly changed from the Old to Middle Kingdoms.

Several points of Egyptological significance emerge. First, the crook/scepter hieroglyph is used in the writing of *ḥḳꜣ*, meaning "rule" and "ruler," as well as in the word "scepter."[186] Might the staff of Moses in the plague narratives present itself as a challenge to the very rulership of Pharaoh? Second, the Egyptian magicians initially think of Moses as just another magician, until they are unable to duplicate or stop the third plague, gnats. Exodus 8:18 reads: "The magicians tried by their secret arts to bring forth gnats, but they could not. So there were gnats on man and beast. And the magicians said to Pharaoh, 'This is the finger of God.'" B. Couroyer proposed an Egyptian understanding lies at the root of this statement.[187] For him, the finger is God's power manifested through the rod. If Couroyer is correct, then there is additional support for my suggestion that the rod of Moses represented a challenge to Pharaoh's rulership and his ability to maintain order.

A final intriguing point presents itself for consideration. The Egyptian word ḥk3 meant "ruler" and "scepter," while the ḥk3 is the word for magic.[188] The difference between the two is that k is used in the latter and ḳ in the former. A wordplay may well have been involved between the Egyptian words, which would render the differences between ks inconsequential. Perhaps the Egyptian magicians saw the actions of this staff as merely magic at first, but when they could no longer duplicate Moses and Aaron's wonders, they saw it as a divine act. Clearly, Yahweh had shown himself to be the "ruler" of Egypt, and not Pharaoh. It was this same Pharaoh in Exod. 5:2 that said, "Who is the Lord, that I should heed his voice and let Israel go? I do not know the Lord, and moreover I will not let Israel go." The plagues finally convinced this intransigent monarch to let Israel depart (Exod. 12:31–33). But in the final showdown at the sea, God discloses to Moses the rationale for this final act of judgment: "I will harden the hearts of the Egyptians so that they shall go after them, and I will get glory over Pharaoh and all his host, his chariots, and his horsemen. And the Egyptians shall know that I am the Lord, when I have gotten glory over Pharaoh" (Exod. 14:17–18). Indeed, the gods of Egypt and their power are shown to be impotent in the plagues narrative. In the final analysis, however, the "signs and wonders" represent God's triumph over Pharaoh, as is emphasized by the twice repeated claim "I will get glory over Pharaoh."

After being struck with the tenth plague, Passover, in which the eldest sons of Egypt were killed (Exod. 12), the Israelites were permitted to leave their hardship behind and head for the Promised Land. But leaving Egypt across the Delta's marshes and the lakes along the isthmus of Suez and a recently discovered ancient canal along Egypt's border with Sinai posed incredible obstacles for Israel's flight to the land of Canaan.

Notes

1   For a recent review of the ancient and modern literature on Moses, see "Moses" in *ABD*, vol. 4, 909–921.

2   It must be noted that the minimalizing historical tendencies and the rejection of Moses' role in the writing of the Pentateuch predates the Enlightenment. From the early centuries of the Christian Era, gnostic writers started down this road, followed later by scholars such as Thomas Hobbes (1588–1679) and Benedict Spinoza (1632–1677) who laid the groundwork for such thinking. Cf. R. K. Harrison, *Introduction to the Old Testament* (Grand Rapids, Mich.: Eerdmans, 1969) 3–11, for the Enlightenment period up to Wellhausen see 11–18.

3   For a helpful review of much of this literature, see John Van Seters, *The Life of Moses: The Yahwist as Historian in Exodus-Numbers* (Philadelphia: Wesminster/John Knox Press, 1994).

4   *History of Pentateuchal Traditions* (Englewood Cliffs, N.J.: Prentice-Hall, 1972) 156–175.

5 "Moses," *Encyclopedia of Religion*, vol. 10, ed. M. Eliade (NewYork: Macmillan, 1987) 116.

6 Thomas Thompson and Dorothy Irvin, "The Joseph and Moses Narratives," in *Israelite and Judaean History*, ed. John Hayes and Maxwell Miller (Philadelphia: Westminster Press, 1977) 181-203. See my discussion and critique of this study above in chap. 4, §II.

7 *Early Israel: A New Horizon* (Minneapolis: Fortress, 1990) 90-91.

8 E.g., Umberto Cassuto, *A Commentary on the Book of Exodus* (trans. I. Abrahams Jerusalem: Magnes, 1967; orig. Hebrew ed., 1951); *Pierre Montet, Egypt and the Bible* (Philadelphia: Fortress Press, 1968) 16-34; Dewey Beegle, *Moses, the Servant of Yahweh* (Grand Rapids, Mich.: Eerdmans, 1972); Siegfried Herrmann, *Israel in Egypt* (London: SCM, 1973) chap. 4; E. F. Campbell, "Moses and the Foundations of Israel," *Interpretation* 29 (1975) 141-154; W. F. Albright, "Moses in Historical and Theological Perspective," in *Magnalia Dei: The Mighty Acts of God*, ed. F. M. Cross et al. (Garden City, N.Y.: Doubleday, 1976) 120-131; K. A. Kitchen, *The Bible in Its World* (Exeter: Paternoster, 1977); John Bright, *History of Israel*, 3d ed. (Philadelphia: Wesminster Press, 1981) chap. 3; Nahum Sarna, *Exploring Exodus* (NewYork: Schocken, 1986) chap. 2.

9 "Moses," *ISBE*, vol. 3 (1986) 415-425.

10 E. A. Speiser in *ANET*, 119; Brian Lewis, *The Sargon Legend: A Study of the Akkadian Text and the Tale of the Hero Who Was Exposed at Birth*, *ASOR* Diss. Series, vol. 4 (Cambridge, Mass.: *ASOR* Publications, 1980) 1-10.

11 "The Literary Motif of the Exposed Child (cf. Ex. ii 1-10)," *Numen* 14 (1967) 209-228.

12 Ibid., 211.

13 Ibid., 214, 218.

14 Ibid., 219.

15 Ibid., 263-266.

16 *Exodus: A Commentary* (Philadelphia: Westminster Press, 1962) 27.

17 *Life of Moses*, 27-29.

18 *Mose und Seine Zeit* (Göttingen: Vandenhoeck and Ruprecht, 1913) 7-10.

19 "The Birth of Moses," *JBL* 84 (1965) 118-122. Initially, Childs believed that this story derived from E. Later on in his *The Book of Exodus* (Philadelphia: Westminster Press, 1974) 7-8 he shifted towards J as the source.

20 *A Study of the Biblical Story of Joseph*, *VTS*, vol. 20 (Leiden: Brill, 1970) 94-105.

21 "A Technical Term for Exposure," *JNES* 27 (1968) 133-135.

22 *Exodus* (Waco: Word, 1987) 15.

23 *Fictional Akkadian Autobiography: A Generic and Comparative Study* (Winona Lake, Ind.: Eisenbrauns, 1991) 71.

24 Lewis, *Sargon Legend*, 99-107; see also Sidney Smith, "Esarhaddon and Sennacherib," *CAH*, vol. 3, 46, who points out that Sargon II often patterned his activities after those of Sargon the Great.

25 Source critics are divided on this point. Cf. Childs, *Book of Exodus*, 7-8, who favors E, while J. P. Hyatt, *Exodus* (London: Marshall, Morgan, and Scott, 1971) 48, Noth, *Exodus*, 25, and others prefer J.

26 Unless Van Seters's radical downdating of J to the sixth century is correct; cf. *Life of Moses*, 1-3 and his earlier works *Prologue to History: The Yahwist as Historian in Genesis* (Louisville: Westminster/John Knox, 1992) and *Abraham in History and Tradition* (New Haven: Yale University Press, 1977). His reasoning for dating the J materials (if there even is a "J" source) and the evidence he presents is just not compelling, hence I am very skeptical of Van Seters's metachronistic tendencies. Concerning the dating of the the Sargon

legend, it is certainly possible that renewed interest in Sargon the Great by his Neo-Asyrian namesake might have motivated the compostion of the text in its present form from a much earlier antecedent.

27 R. T. Rundle-Clark, *Myth and Symbol in Ancient Egypt* (London: Thames and Hudson, 1959) 186–188.

28 *Understanding Exodus* (New York: Behrman House, 1969), 96.

29 *The Conflict of Horus and Seth* (Liverpool: University of Liverpool Press, 1960), 96.

30 Redford, *Numen* 14 (1967) 224, 227.

31 So suggests R. Alan Cole, *Exodus: An Introduction and Commentary* (Downers Grove, Ill.: IV Press, 1973) 57.

32 Gressman, *Mose*, 7.

33 KB, 1017.

34 *Wb*, vol. 5, 561.

35 Ibid.; Jaroslav Černý, *Coptic Etymological Dictionary* (Cambridge: Cambridge University Press, 1976) 180.

36 Hans Wehr, *Arabic-English Dictionary*, 3d ed. (Ithaca: Spoken Languages Service, 1976) 88.

37 S. R. Driver, *The Book of Exodus* (Cambridge: Cambridge University Press, 1911) 8; Cole, *Exodus,* 57; "Ark of Noah" and "Basket," *IDB*, vol. 1, 222, 364; "Basket," *ISBE*, vol. 1, 437–438.

38 Chayim Cohen is among a select number who questions the Egyptian etymology of *tēbat* ("Hebrew *tbh*: Proposed Etymologies," *JANES* 4 no. 3 [1972] 37–51). He rejects the association with *db3t* because this word is never used for a boat in Egypt. While his reasoning has some merit with the occurrence of the word in the Genesis flood story, it carries little weight in Exodus 2. Moses' mother is simply making a device that will float and preserve the life of the infant. A rectangular, waterproofed basket of reeds would do the job, and this could be *db3t* in Egyptian.

39 E.g., Cassuto, *Exodus*, 18–19; Terence Fretheim, *Exodus* (Louisville: John Knox Press, 1991) 36–41; Hyatt, *Exodus*, 63; Durham, *Exodus*, 16; Childs, *Exodus*, 18–20; R. E. Clements, *Exodus* (Cambridge: Cambridge University Press, 1972), 14–15; and Noth, *Exodus*, 25–26. Surprisingly, even Sarna (*Exploring Exodus*, 28) who normally is careful to identify the Egyptian etymologies in Exodus, appears to have missed this one.

40 *Exodus*, 8.

41 *Exploring Exodus*, 29.

42 KB, 187.

43 Thomas Lambdin, "Egyptian Loan Words in the Old Testament," *JAOS* 73 (1953) 149; "Papyrus," *ISBE*, vol. 3, 651.

44 *Wb*, vol. 5, 37.

45 *LEM*, 110.6, 43.16. Interestingly, these are different copies of the same text, showing that they are one and the same word (cf. Ricardo Caminos, *Late Egyptian Miscellanies* [London: Oxford University Press, 1954] 167). These two writings are very important for showing that *gōme'* derived from Egyptian *km3,* because slightly before Caminos's discussion of these texts, Lambdin had regarded the Hebrew *g* representing Egyptian *k* to be problematic (*JAOS* 73 [1953)] 149). The fact that that *gmy* could be written as a variant writing of *kmy* demonstrates that during the New Kingdom the vocalizations of these two sounds were very close, perhaps indistinguishable. Hence the writing of Egyptian *k* as Hebrew *g* is neither unexpected nor problematic.

46 KB, 263.

47 *DLE*, vol. 4, 159; Caminos, *Late Egyptian Miscellanies*, 209.

48 *DLE*, vol. 3, 41.

49 *CDME*, 225; *Wb*, vol. 4, 118. In the Old Kingdom, it was written as *sft*, but by the Middle Kingdom the *t* was vocalized as *t*.

50 I greatly appreciate the discussion I had with James Hoch concerning the linguistic problems surrounding these words.

51 KB, 358; *Wb*, vol. 1, 146; "Nile," *ABD*, vol. 4, 1108; "Nile," *ISBE*, vol. 3, 536.

52 Kitchen, "Nile," *NBD*, 834; so noted in KB, 358.

53 *ISBE*, vol. 3, 536; *Wb*, vol. 1, 146.

54 KB, 928.

55 *Wb*, vol. 4, 99–100.

56 Egyptian is recognized as having both Semitic and African elements in it, hence the terms Hamito-Semitic or Afro-Asiatic. Cf. Alan Gardiner, *Egyptian Grammar*, 3d ed. (London: Oxford University Press, 1969) 2–4; Jaroslav Černý, "Language and Writing," in *The Legacy of Egypt*, 2d ed, ed. J. R. Harris (Oxford: Clarendon Press, 1971) 197–198; W. V. Davies, *Egyptian Hieroglyphs* (Berkeley and Los Angeles: University of California Press, 1987) 6–8.

57 These are all the cases where the banks of the Nile are mentioned in the Old Testament, except possibly Isaiah 19:7, where the Nile is described as drying up, along with *pî yeôr*, which the RSV translates "brink of the Nile." In my opinion, this expression is better rendered as "the mouth of the Nile." When the annual inundation fails, the northern branches of the Delta recede.

58 Sarna, *Exploring Exodus*, 30.

59 On Solomon's ties with Egypt, see Hoffmeier, "Egypt as an Arm of Flesh: A Prophetic Response," in *Israel's Apostasy and Restoration: Essays in Honor of Roland K. Harrison*, ed. Avraham Gileadi (Grand Rapids, Mich.: Baker, 1988) 79–85; Alberto Green, "Solomon and Siamun: A Synchronism between Early Dynastic Israel and the Twenty-First Dynasty Egypt," *JBL* 97 (1978) 353–367; Donald Redford, "Studies in Relations during the First Millennium B.C. (II), The Twenty-Second Dynasty," *JAOS* 93 (1973) 3–17.

60 Noth, *Exodus*, 26; Clements, *Exodus*, 15; Childs, *Exodus*, 7; Herrmann, *Israel in Egypt*, 43–44; Hyatt, *Exodus*, 65.

61 Hermann Ranke, *Die Ägyptischen Personennamen*, vol. 1 (Glückstadt: J. J. Augustin, 1935) 164–165, shows that the overwhelming majority of *ms*-type names are of New Kingdom date.

62 "Moses," *Encyclopedia of Religion* 10, 115.

63 Ibid.

64 "The Egyptian Derivation of the Name Moses," *JNES* 12 (1953) 225–231. I am grateful to Professor Griffiths, who was kind enough further to discuss the linguistic problem as I was preparing my article "Moses" for *ISBE*, vol. 3.

65 Griffiths, *JNES* 12 (1953) 229.

66 Ibid., 230.

67 William L. Moran, *The Amarna Letters* (Baltimore: The Johns Hopkins University Press, 1992) 380, 382, 384.

68 Griffiths, *JNES* 12 (1953) 229.

69 "*Tkw* und dies Rameses-Stadt," *VT* 15 (1965) 42–47.

70 "Moses," *NBD*, 794.

71 Cassuto, *Exodus*, 20–21.

72 Ibid.

73 E.g., Judges 3:9, 15; KB, 413.

74 Hoffmeier, "Moses," *ISBE*, vol. 3, 417; Ronald Williams, "Egypt and Israel" in the *Legacy of Egypt*, 2d ed., ed. J. R. Harris (Oxford: Clarendon Press, 1971) 262.

75 *Urk.* IV, 690.2 – 5.

76 Moran, *Amarna Letters*, 242. A further allusion to Aziru's son being sent to Egypt is found in EA, 162.42 – 54 (Ibid., 249).

77 Ibid., 276.

78 Ibid., 326.

79 Ibid., 272.

80 For a detailed investigation of this practice, see James Hoffmeier, "The Wives' Tales of Genesis 12, 20 & 26 and the Covenants at Beer-Sheba," *TB* 43 no. 1 (1992) 87 – 99, and A. R. Schulman, "Diplomatic Marriage in the Egyptian New Kingdom," *JNES* 38 (1979) 177 – 193.

81 Erika Feucht, "The Ḥrdw n k3p Reconsidered," in *Pharaonic Egypt: The Bible and Christianity*, ed. Sarah Israelit-Groll (Jerusalem: Magnes Press, 1985) 41 – 44.

82 Ibid., 38 – 44.

83 *The Reign of Thutmose IV* (Baltimore: The Johns Hopkins University Press, 1991) 261. Evidence for the continuity of the institution of the k3p, Nili Fox has recently proposed, is behind the yᵉlādîm in the Jerusalem court from the time of Rehoboam "Royal Officials and Court Families: A New look at the ילדים (yĕlādîm) in 1 Kings 12," *BA* 59 no. 4 [1996] 225 – 232). Fox recognizes the problem presented for a connection between the chronological gap between the last citations of the title ḥrd n k3p, from the late eighteenth Dynasty, and the appearance of the yᵉlādîm at the end of the tenth century in Israel. It is certainly possible that the "Nursery" continued in Egypt into the Ramesside era, but records are simply lacking at the present, or as Fox suggests, the institution was utilized in the Canaanite city-states, Jerusalem being one, from which it carried over to the Davidic court.

84 Ibid.

85 The New Testament records that "Moses was instructed in all the wisdom of the Egyptians" (Acts 7:22). This tradition concerning Moses follows Philo (*De vita Mosis* 1, 5) and is continued in Josephus's *Antiquties* (2:9.7).

86 I suggested this idea some years ago, in "Moses," *ISBE*, vol. 3, 417.

87 *HAB*, 57; *OBA*, 59; *ABL*, 10.

88 Itzhaq Beit-Arieh, "Fifteen Years in Sinai," *BAR* 10 (1984) 26 – 54; "Canaanites and Egyptians at Serabit el-Khadim," in *Egypt, Israel, Sinai: Archaeological and Historical Relationships in the Biblical Period*, ed. Anson Rainey (Jerusalem: Tel Aviv University Press, 1987) 57 – 67; A. H. Gardiner and T. E. Peet, *The Inscriptions of Sinai* (London: Oxford University Press, 1955).

89 Roland de Vaux, *The Early History of Israel* (Philadelphia: Westminster Press, 1978) 330 – 338; Benjamin Mazar, "The Sanctuary of Arad and the Family of Hobab the Kenite," *JNES* 24 (1965) 297 – 303; W. F. Albright, "Jethro, Hobab and Reuel," *CBQ* 25 (1963) 1 – 11.

90 *Life of Moses*, 29 – 33.

91 Some years before Van Seters proposed this connection, Sarna (*Exploring Exodus*, 35) had noticed that the route of Moses' escape is reversed by Hadad in 1 Kings 11.

92 Van Seters, *Life of Moses*. See n.26, above.

93 Miriam Lichtheim, *Ancient Egyptian Literature*, vol. 1 (Berkeley and Los Angeles: University of California Press, 1973) 222 – 223, for a translation, see 223 – 233; *ANET*, 18 – 22; W. K. Simpson, *The Literature of Ancient Egypt* (New Haven: Yale University Press, 1972) 57 – 74.

94 Some with Egyptological training have at least made passing references to Sinue, e.g., Herrmann, *Israel in Egypt*, 45 – 46; Kitchen, "Moses," *NBD*, 796; Hoffmeier, "Moses," *ISBE*, vol. 3, 417. Avraham Gileadi (*The Apocalyptic Book of Isaiah* [Provo: Hebraeus Press,

1982] 173) has recognized a tripartite narrative plot in Sinuhe and several other Egyptian pieces of literature. He uses the labels "trouble at home, exile abroad, and happy home coming." He saw the pattern in the Jacob story in Genesis, but was primarily concerned with applying this tripartite structure to the book of Isaiah. He did not mention Moses' flight to Midian as an example.

95   "The Joseph Story and Divine Politics," *JBL* 106 (1987) 577–594. This important article was discussed in some detail in chap. 4, §II.

96   Ibid., 589–590.

97   Ibid., 594.

98   Suggested by me in "Moses," *ISBE*, vol. 3, 417.

99   For a discussion of Exod. 5:2, see chap. 5, §II.

100   S. R. Driver, *Introduction to the Literature of the Old Testament* (Cambridge: Cambridge University Press, 1913) 24–29; *IDB*, vol. 3, 823; Childs, *Exodus*, 130–142; Clements, *Exodus*, 40–41; Hyatt, *Exodus,* 96–144.

101   *Exodus*, 48.

102   *Exodus*, 131.

103   Hoffmeier, "Egypt, Plagues in," *ABD*, vol. 2, 374.

104   *Exodus,* 9–18.

105   *Überlieferung und Geschichte des Exodus*, BZAW no. 91 (Berlin: *BZAW*, 1961) 60–62.

106   *Exodus,* 4–5.

107   *Life of Moses*, 77–112.

108   *The Origin Tradition of Ancient Israel*, vol. 1: *The Literary Formation of Genesis and Exodus 1–23* (Sheffield: *JSOT* Press, 1987) 155.

109   For a discussion of Thompson's thesis, see chap. 5. §I. For my critique of his dating of the Genesis and Exodus narratives, see chap. 4, n. 60.

110   For discussions of the relationship between these three, see A. Lauha, *Die Geschichtsmotive in den alttestamentlichen Psalmen*, Tom. 56 (Helsinki: AASF Sarja B, 1945) 39–50; B. Margulis, "The Plague Tradition in Ps. 105," *Biblica* 49 (1969) 491–496; S. E. Lowenstamm, "The Number of Plagues in Ps. 105," *Biblica* 52 (1971) 34–38 and *The Evolution of the Exodus Tradition* (Jerusalem: Magnes Press, 1992) 69–102.

111   The table in *IDB*, vol. 3, 823 helpfully lays out the plague sequences in the three different Hebrew accounts.

112   *Psalms 101–150* (Waco:Word, 1983).

113   *ABD* 2, 374.

114   Cassuto, *Exodus*, 92–93; Sarna, *Exploring Exodus*, 73–78.

115   *Exodus Tradition*, 188.

116   Sarna, *Exploring Exodus*, 76.

117   Hoffmeier *ABD* 2, 374.

118   Childs, *Exodus*, 149–151; Rolf Rendtorff, *The Old Testament: An Introduction* (Philadelphia: Fortress, 1979) 149–151; Noth, *Exodus*, 18.

119   *Egypt and Israel* (London: Society for Promoting Christian Knowledge, 1911) 35–36.

120   "The Plagues of Egypt," *ZAW* 69 (1957) 84–103 and *ZAW* 70 (1958) 48–59.

121   This pattern is based on records from the last century prior to the building of the first Aswan Dam and ancient records from the New Kingdom, cf. J. J. Janssen, "The Day the Inundation Began," *JNES* 46 (1987) 129–136.

122   *ZAW* 69 (1957) 94.

123   Ibid., 94–96.

124   Ibid., 98.

125 See also Cassuto, *Exodus*, 49.

126 Clements, *Exodus*, 49.

127 Driver, *Exodus*, 65; Childs, *Exodus*, 156.

128 *ZAW* 69 (1957) 98–99.

129 Ibid., 99–103.

130 KB, 202 renders it "bubo-pest, plague."

131 KB, 960. As a child growing up in Egypt, I had firsthand experience with painful boils, called "Nile Boils" by some Egyptians, but these may not have been the inflictions described in Exodus 9.

132 *ZAW* 69 (1957) 101.

133 Ibid., 99, 101–103.

134 I maintain that the statement "all the cattle of the Egyptians died" (Exod. 9:6) is hyperbolic (Cf. Cassuto, *Exodus*, 111).

135 J. J. Taylor and F. L. Griffith, *The Tomb of Paheri at El Kab* (London: EEF, 1894) pl. 3, 2d register from top.

136 T. G. H. James, *Pharaoh's People* (Oxford: Oxford University Press, 1984) 123.

137 Karl W. Butzer, *Early Hydraulic Civilization in Egypt: A Study in Cultural Ecology* (Chicago: University of Chicago Press, 1976) 49.

138 Ibid.

139 *Chicago Tribune*, 25 March 1988, §1, p. 8.

140 Driver, *Exodus*, 81.

141 Cassuto, *Exodus*, 127. Hyatt (*Exodus*, 124) accepts the easterly direction on the grounds that Arabia and Sinai provide favorable conditions for locusts to breed.

142 E.g., Petrie, *Egypt and Israel*, 36; Driver, *Exodus*, 82–83; Jack Finegan, *Let My People Go: A Journey Through Exodus* (New York: Harper and Row, 1963) 55; Cole, *Exodus*, 101–102; Kitchen, "Plagues of Egypt," *NBD*, 944.

143 *Exodus*, 83.

144 Hyatt, *Exodus*, 126.

145 *ZAW* 70 (1958) 52–53.

146 "Moses' Dealings with Pharaoh: Ex. 7,8–10," *CBQ* 27 (1965) 336–337.

147 *Exodus*, 93.

148 For a discussion of this Egyptian term, see chap. 4, §II.

149 Robert Stieglitz, "Ancient Records and the Exodus Plagues," *BAR* 13, no. 6 (1987) 46-49 and B. Couroyer, "Le 'Doigt de Dieu' (Exode VIII, 15)," *RB* 63 (1956) 481–495.

150 For Egypt, see Henri Frankfort, *Ancient Egyptian Religion* (New York: Columbia University Press, 1948), chaps. 1, 2; Siegfried Morenz, *Egyptian Religion* (Ithaca: Cornell University Press, 1973), chaps. 1, 2. In Israelite thought, see Lev. 26:14–20; Deut. 28:1–24; Ps. 24:1–2; Job 38–41.

151 John J. Davis, *Moses and the Gods of Egypt* (Grand Rapids, Mich.: Baker, 1971); Charles Aling, *Egypt and Bible History* (Grand Rapids, Mich.: Baker, 1981) 103–109; and to a certain extent Sarna (*Exodus*, 78–80), although he recognizes that there is a God-versus-Pharaoh dimension to the plagues story.

152 *Egypt and Bible History*, 106.

153 See my "Plagues of Egypt," *ABD* vol. 2, 376.

154 Cf. John Baines, *Fecundity Figures* (Warminster: Aris and Phillips, 1985) and my review of this book in *JEA* 75 (1989) 255–256 endorsing his conclusions.

155 According to one tradition preserved in the Pyramid Texts, Osiris is drowned in the Nile (PT §§24d; 615c-d; 766d). For a discussion of this tradition, see Griffiths, *Conflict of Horus and Seth*, 4–7. On the association between Osiris and the inundations,

see Henri Frankfort, *Kingship and the Gods* (Chicago: University of Chicago Press, 1978) 190–191.

156 Sarna, *Exodus*, 79; *ABD* II 376.

157 Butchering scenes are common in tombs from the Old Kingdom onward, and "beef" or "leg of beef" is a regular feature of the offering formulas throughout Egyptian history.

158 Translation and discussion in James K. Hoffmeier, *Sacred in the Vocabulary of Ancient Egypt*, OBO 59 (Freiburg: Universitätsverlag, 1985) 224.

159 "Texts, Storms, and the Thera Eruption," *JNES* 55 no. 1 (1996) 1–14.

160 Ibid., 11.

161 Cassuto, *Exodus*, 129.

162 "The Egyptian Sun-God Ra in the Pentateuch," *Henoch* 10 (1988) 3–15.

163 I developed this idea in *ABD*, vol. 2, 376–377 and "Plagues of Egypt" in *The New International Dictionary of Old Testament Theology* (Grand Rapids, Mich.: Zondervan, forthcoming). For the most recent volume on Egyptian kingship, see David O'Connor and David Silverman, *Ancient Egyptian Kingship* (Leiden: Brill, 1995).

164 E.g., Exod: 3:19; 6:6; 13:3, 14, 16; 15:6, 12, 16; 32:11; Deut. 3:24; 6:21; 9:26, 29; 26:8.

165 "The Arm of God Versus the Arm of Pharaoh in the Exodus Narratives," *Biblica* 67 (1986) 378–387.

166 Ibid., 384–385.

167 *The Amarna Letters*, 326, 328, 331. Moran accepts Görg's observations (327, n. 2; see next note), but he apparently missed my *Biblica* article.

168 "'Der Starke Arm Pharaos'—Beobachtungen Zum Belegspektrum Einer Metapher in Palastin und Ägypten," in *Hommages à François Daumas* (Montpellier: Université Paul Valéry, 1986) 323–330.

169 Morenz, *Egyptian Religion*, 12–13; Frankfort, *Kingship and the Gods*, 51–56.

170 Text from A. H. Gardiner, *Adomonitions of an Egyptian Sage* (Leipzig: J. C. Hinrichs, 1909). For a more recent translation, see Lichtheim, *Ancient Egyptian Literature,* vol. 1, 151–156.

171 The translation is based on Wolfgang Helck's critical edition, *Die Prophezeiung des Nfr.tj*, Kleine Ägyptische Texte (Wiesbaden: Otto Harrassowitz, 1970) 16–28. See above, chap. 3, §I.

172 Translation based on the critical edition of Wolfgang Helck, *Der Text der Lehre Amenemhets I. für seinen Sohn*, Kleine Ägyptische Texte (Wiesbaden: Otto Harrassowitz, 1969) 72–73.

173 For translating *ḥ'py '3* as "high inundation," see Janssen, *JNES* 46 (1987) 131.

174 *Les.*, 68.

175 *Urk.* IV, 19.6–8.

176 Text in *LEM*, 86.11–87.2. For other translations, see Caminos, *Late Egyptian Miscellanies*, 324; Adolf Erman, *The Literature of the Ancient Egyptians* (New York: Benjamin Blom, 1971; orig. 1927) 278–279.

177 Literally, "under hours" (*ḥr wnwt*), which Caminos (*Late Egyptian Miscellanies*, 324) understood to mean "the right hours."

178 *The Scepter of Egypt*, vol. 1 (Cambridge, Mass.: Harvard University Press, 1953) 286.

179 Henry Fischer, "Notes on Sticks and Staves," *MMJ* 13 (1978) 7–8.

180 Ibid.

181 Ibid.

182 *WB*, vol. 1, 170; *CDME*, 39. Gustav Jéquier, *Les Frises d'objects des Sarcophages du Moyen Empire*, MIFAO 47 (Cairo: IFAO, 1921) 168–173.

183 Hayes, *The Scepter of Egypt*, vol. 1, 285. Ornamented shepherds' staves were discovered in the tomb of Tutankhamun, cf. Howard Carter and A.C. Mace, *The Tomb of Tut-Ankh-Amen*, vol. 1 (New York: G. H. Doran, 1923), cf. Pl. 69, 70 (possibly), 71B.

184 For the text see Wolfgang Helck, *Die Lehre für Könige Merikare*, Kleine Ägyptische Texte (Wiesbaden: Otto Harrassowitz, 1977) 83.

185 (Chicago: University of Chicago Press, 1951), chap. 6.

186 *Wb*, vol. 3, 170.

187 *RB* 63 (1956).

188 *Wb*, vol. 3, 170–171, 175–176.

7

THE EASTERN
FRONTIER CANAL

Implications for the Exodus from Egypt

> And they set out from Etham, and turned
> back to Pi-ha-hiroth, which is east of Baal-
> zephon; and they encamped before Migdol
>
> Num. 33:7

I. Discovery and Location

In the early 1970s, a team of scientists of the Geological Survey of Israel, while working in the Sinai Peninsula during Israel's occupation of the territory east of the Suez Canal, discovered the remains of what they believed was a canal that ran along Egypt's border with the Sinai (fig. 17).[1] Aerial photography and on-site study led to this identification by the leaders of the team, Amihai Sneh and Tuvia Weissbrod (figs. 18, 19). The width of this canal constantly measures seventy meters at the top and was probably tapered toward the bottom where it is thought to be around twenty meters wide.[2] This makes it wider than the Suez Canal when cut in 1875 by de Lesseps, which was fifty-four meters across at the top and twenty-two at the bottom. The recently discovered channel is calculated to be two to three meters deep.

Two sections of the ancient canal were found east of the Suez Canal. One section, discernible for about six kilometers, runs in an east-west line, starting about fifteen kilometers east-northeast of Qantara. The northernmost portion apparently emptied into the Mediterranean west of Pelusium (Tell Farama). This segment is seven or eight kilometers in length and begins around 31°N, 32°30'E. A nearly twelve-kilometer section, located west of the Suez Canal, appears to have connected Lake Timsah (by present-day Ismailiya) and Lake el-Ballah to the north, was actually discovered over a century ago by the French engineer Linant

164

de Bellefonds.[3] A section of the ancient canal, just north of Ismailiya, is currently being used for irrigation purposes. By simply viewing this part, one can determine that a long history of excavations preceded its usage in the last 150 years (fig. 20). Because he was aware of classical sources that described the Red Sea canal begun by Pharaoh Neco (610–595 B.C.) and completed by the Persian emperor Darius (522–486 B.C.), de Bellefonds thought this canal was the one dating from that period, although he could produce no supporting archaeological evidence. However, because of the similarity of the dimensions of this segment with those further north (which clearly are too far north and east to be the Neco-Darius canal), Weissbrod and Sneh proposed that this third portion was also part of the earlier canal. They suggest it had silted up and was reopened in the first millennium to make the Red Sea canal.[4] Furthermore, because they believed that water ran through it "continuously since Pharaonic time," fed from the southern end of the Bubastite branch of the Nile, they postulated that the canal might have been connected to the Wadi Tumilat.[5] This claim, however, has been questioned.[6] Without offering any evidence or rationale, Karl Butzer theorizes that the head of the canal was the Pelusiac near Tell Defeneh.[7] Eliezer Oren and John Holladay, who have done extensive archaeological survey work in North Sinai and the Wadi Tumilat region, concur with Butzer.[8] Nevertheless, it is clear that at least periodically, especially during flood season, the Wadi served as an overflow channel for the Nile.[9] Also, Herodotus, who visited Egypt within decades of the completion of the Red Sea canal, claims that it passed through the Wadi (II, 158),[10] and Edourd Naville apparently found traces of it.[11] Furthermore, Pierre Montet believed that a series of Ramesses II stelae found along the Wadi Tumilat marked the line of a canal that existed during the Nineteenth Dynasty.[12] Traces of at least two defunct canals through the Wadi Tumilat have been identified,[13] and one still flows through it (fig. 21). Dating these waterways is most problematic, but it is clear that the Wadi Tumilat has enjoyed a long history of canal activity and in prehistoric times apparently had a branch of the Nile flowing through it.[14]

Some might be inclined to think that discovered traces actually belong to the defunct Pelusiac branch of the Nile, known to have passed by Pelusium. However, Sneh and Weissbrod are also credited with the earlier discovery of traces of the Pelusiac branch of the Nile in the area east of the Suez Canal (see fig. 17, which shows their reconstruction of the canal and the Pelusiac).[15] In the 23-kilometer stretch between the Suez Canal and Pelusium, the width of the Pelusiac branch varied in width from eighty to one hundred meters,[16] whereas the canal displayed a constant width of seventy meters.[17] The former is what would be expected from a river, while the latter is consistent with a man-made feature. Moreover, one should expect to find embankment dump from the excavation and dredging of a canal; the reason the line of the canal is visible in the aerial photographs is because of the embankments, whose presence was confirmed after on-ground examination of the canal traces.[18] Additionally, aerial photography reveals that the northernmost segment of the canal and the Pelusiac actually intersect about two kilometers west of Pelusium, demonstrating that the two features could not be confused.[19] However, this point of intersection represents the eastward migration of the Pelusiac, which only reached this point in the first millennium probably after the canal had silted up. In the second millennium, the Nile debouched further to the west and did not intersect with the canal.[20]

Thus, despite the many questions that remain regarding the routing of this waterway and its source of water, it is quite clearly a canal. So confident is Oren of the nature of this feature that he concludes: "The discovery of the Eastern Canal has refuted another erroneous but almost universally accepted hypothesis: that the Pharaonic waterways, i.e., 'the Waters- of -Horus,' the 'Waters of the Sun (Re),' or biblical Shihor, are in fact identical with the Pelusiac arm of the Nile."[21]

In the early 1990s, the risk posed to archaeological sites in north Sinai by the new *As-salaam* canal (being dug from the Nile valley to el-Arish) as part of a massive irrigation project prompted renewed research in this region.[22] An international team of scholars have been undertaking archaeological and geological surveys of north Sinai and has reconfirmed the presence of the canal, although they have added no new information.[23] The focus of the most recent geological survey has been on the route of the Pelusiac branch of the Nile (compare fig. 17 and 22).[24] This geomorphological investigation has the Pelusiac moving in a northeasterly direction from the Nile valley, compared with Sneh and Weissbrod's mapping, which has the Nile traveling nearly straight east toward Pelusium. The difference between the two reconstructions may be due to the fact that the Pelusiac meandered considerably over the millennia, leaving different traces of its path. Consequently, the conflicting results from the two surveys may be explained as identifying portions of the Nile's easternmost branch at various periods in its history.[25]

II. The Purpose and Dating the Canal

Weissbrod and Sneh offered three reasons for the excavating of what they called the Frontier Canal. First and foremost, they believe it was dug for defensive purposes, as well as for irrigation and navigation.[26] By connecting the area from the Wadi Tumilat and Lake Timsah with Lake el Ballah and north to the sea, a formidable defensive barrier against invasion and infiltration would have been created, especially if combined with a network of forts.

The Israeli geologists associated the newly discovered canal with the one shown on a relief of Seti I (ca. 1300 B.C.) at Karnak temple, Thebes (fig. 10).[27] In the midst of the waterway, a hieroglyphic label reads, *t3 dnit*. Sir Alan Gardiner commented on this scene in 1920[28] and noted that the building complex depicted on this relief, to the left of the canal, is labeled *ḥtm n t3r(w)*, "the Fortress of Tjaru." Currently, the earliest known reference to this fort by this name is in the annals of Thutmose III.[29] Throughout the New Kingdom, this site was the departure point of military expeditions from Egypt to the Levant. But its specific location has remained uncertain. Following the earlier suggestions of Carl Küthmann, Gardiner located the Fortress of Tjaru at Tell Abu Sefêh.[30] This identification was not based upon the results of substantial excavations, but relied upon textual references that located it in the Egypt/Sinai border region, and upon two Ramesside-period inscriptions found on the surface.[31] (See chap. 8, §IV.)

Gardiner offered the following description of the Seti Karnak relief: "The fortress lay, as the sculptures show, partly on one side and partly on the other of a canal full of crocodiles, the reedy banks of which suggest that it did not contain flowing water. The name of the canal was *ta-denit*, clearly meaning 'the dividing-waters' and so-called because they sundered Egypt from the desert."[32] The careful investigation of the Seti relief by the University of Chicago's Oriental Institute epigraphic survey, published a decade ago, reinforces Gardiner's earlier observations: "Three rows of Shasu march in front of the chariot towards the border, marked by a canal: crocodiles lurk in its waters, and marshes surrounding it are suggested by reeds lining its edge. A compound is apparently a parade ground, having a gate at either end (east and west) and also a reviewing stand. More extensive buildings can be seen on the Egyptian side across the bridge."[33] The close relationship between the Fortress of Tjaru and the canal supports the hypothesis that the canal had a defensive purpose as an extensive moat. The bridge, of course, was necessary for moving Egyptian troops back and forth across the canal. If the bridge was a permanent fixture, the proximity of the fort would be essential to defend it, and the relief certainly suggests this.

Because they believed the canal depicted at Karnak and the feature they discovered were one and the same, the Israeli geologists reconstructed a section of the canal not visible in their photographs, passing by Tell Abu Sefêh, thinking it was Tjaru. I visited Tell Abu Sefêh in March 1994 and examined the area on the eastern side of the tell to see if any traces of the canal were visible. This area is certainly flat enough for a canal to have passed by this tell and mingled with the sand that now covers the area are traces of darker, apparently alluvial, soil. It would appear that a body of water once covered or passed through this location. I was not able, however, to discover any traces of the canal's embankment during that visit. Later in the spring of 1994, excavations began at Tell Abu Sefêh and immediately clarified the nature of the body of water on the east side of the site. Some preliminary results and historical implications are treated in the next chapter (§IV). It is now clear that this site cannot be Tjaru.

Weissbrod and Sneh believe that the history of the canal might go back before the Nineteenth Dynasty Seti I scene, perhaps even to the Twelfth Dynasty because of the references concerning Sinuhe's journey back from Palestine by boat to Itj-tawy, the capital.[34] The pertinent lines read:

> This humble servant traveled south.
> I stopped right on the Ways of Horus.
> The commander in charge of the frontier patrol
> sent a messenger to the palace to let one (i.e., the king)
> know (of Sinuhe's arrival).
> Then his majesty had a capable overseer of royal domains
> dispatched (with) boats loaded with royal gifts for the Asiatics
> who came with me to accompany me to the Ways of Horus.
> . . . I set out after having set sail, there was kneading (bread) and
> straining (beer) for me until I reached the quay of Itj-tawy.[35]

The impression is that Sinuhe journeyed by boat from the land of Yaa (somewhere in the Levant) to a point called "the Ways of Horus" where a military garrison was stationed. Unlike the New Kingdom, where *w3wt ḥr* is thought to be the name of the military road across northern Sinai, in the Middle Kingdom it appears was the name of the "frontier town" that marked the end of Egypt and the beginning of the road to Palestine.[36] To a certain extent, this interpretation has recently been endorsed by Dominique Valbelle.[37]

From this place, the commander sent a messenger back to Egypt to announce Sinuhe's arrival, prompting Senusert I to dispatch a flotilla bearing gifts for Sinuhe's Asian comrades and to escort him back to the capital. Presumably, his friends who had ferried him to the meeting point in Sinai would have returned north in their boat. While this story may accurately describe boat travel between Egypt and western Asia, the text does not use the words for "river" or "canal" to describe the water route traveled back to the capital. Thus, the evidence from Sinuhe is not specific enough to determine which body of water is meant.

In 1971, just before the discovery of the canal, William Ward argued, based on a statement in the "Wisdom for Merikare" (ca. 2200 B.C.), that a canal was begun by Merikare's predecessor.[38] According to Ward, the king was instructed to dig a canal in the area between the Ways of Horus and Lake Timsah.[39] This could be the section of the canal discovered by the de Bellefonds in the last century and mapped by the Israel Geological Survey (fig. 17).

William Shea concurs with Sneh's suggested connection with "Sinuhe."[40] During the escape from Egypt, Sinuhe states "I reached the Walls of the Ruler which were made to repel Asiatics, to trample the Bedouin."[41] Because "the walls" were manned with troops, Sinuhe had to be very careful. Could there have been a network of forts situated along the canal? Tell el-Herr appears close to the canal on Sneh and Weissbrod's map (fig. 17), and the Fortress Tjaru was situated close to "the canal" according to the Seti I relief.

Shea agreed with the Israeli team that the history of the canal could be traced back to the Twelfth Dynasty. In addition, he introduced Ward's understanding of lines 91 to 98 of "Wisdom for Merikare" to the discussion of dating the newly discovered canal, drawing a connection between it and Khety's instruction to Merikare.[42] Ward interpreted lines 99 to 101 as follows:

> Merikare is to build a canal, presumably from the fortress at Ways-of-Horus southward to Lake Timsah (lines 99ff.). This line of defense, once completed, would be the logical one since it would guard the whole area from the southeastern shore of Lake Manzeleh to Lake Timsah. Its northern terminus would be at the land-route which entered Egypt through Ways-of-Horus and its southern terminus at the entrance to the Wadi Tumilat at Ismailiyah. Precisely this region was the main point of entry for nomads wishing to move out of the desert into the Delta. A fortified canal, half-filled with water, would be an ideal defensive position, easily manned by troops and mobile units of rafts or small boats patrolling the length of the canal.[43]

Ward's interpretation of these lines is uncanny in view of the fact that the canal had not been discovered when his book was published in 1971.

Shea believes that the idea for the canal could go back to "Merikare," and its construction may have begun at that time, but it probably was not completed until the early Twelfth Dynasty (ca. 1900 B.C.).[44] Another possible reason for connecting the canal with the Twelfth Dynasty is the references in Aristotle, Strabo, and Pliny to Sesostris digging a canal. In his *Meteorologica* (1, 14.22–29), Aristotle offers the following tradition regarding the Red Sea Canal or Canal of the Pharaohs, as it has been called: "One of the kings tried to dig a canal to it. (For it would be of no little advantage to them if this whole region was accessible to navigation: Sesostris is said to be the first of the ancient kings to have attempted the work.)"[45] Strabo's report is similar: "The canal was first cut by Sesostris before the Trojan War—though some say the son of Psammitichus [i.e., Neco II], who only began the work and then died—and later by Darieus the First, who succeeded to the next work done upon it" (*Geography* 17. 1,24).[46] Pliny states that "this project was originally conceived by Sesostris King of Egypt," but that Darius and later Ptolemy II also excavated it (*Natural History* 6, 33, 165).[47] The earliest of the classical writers to comment on the Red Sea Canal was Herodotus (2, 158), who visited Egypt in the fifth century B.C. He mentions the role of Neco II and Darius, but makes no reference to Sesostris. Thus, there are three classical writers who trace the origins of the canal to king Sesostris, a king they understood to predate Neco and Darius. The possibility remains that a genuine memory of the canal-excavating accomplishments of one or more of the Sesotrises or Senuserts from Dynasty 12 may be preserved in these classical sources.[48] The late Georges Posener thought these references might be connected with the work of Senusert I or III.[49] Currently, no contemporary Egyptian texts support or deny this tradition.

III. A Possible Connection with Pi-hahiroth of Exodus 14:2

If indeed a canal existed along Egypt's border with Sinai during the New Kingdom, and the evidence does support this view, it seems logical to conclude that it would have been an impediment to the Israelites in their departure from Egypt. Thus it must be asked: Is there any reference or allusion to this canal in the Exodus narratives?

The itinerary of the departing Hebrews from Egypt includes Pi-ha-hiroth in Exodus 14:2 and Numbers 33:7. Scholars have long attempted to find an Egyptian etymology for Pi-ha-hiroth because of the initial element *pi* (i.e., *pr*) is suggestive of Egyptian toponyms such as Pi-Ramesses, Pithom, and Pi-Besethet.[50] Consequently, several Egyptian etymologies have been proposed, *Pi-h(w)t-hr*, "House of (the goddess) Hathor"[51] and *pi-hrt*, "House of Heret," a Semitic deity,[52] being two widely suggested options. The first proposed Egyptian root contains a number of linguistic problems, the most glaring being that *h(w)t* would not become Hebrew *ha*. Second, there are geographical problems. In Papyrus Anastasi 3, 3,[53] there is a town named Pi-Hathor (*pi-h(w)t hr*) that Redford at one point had speculated was behind the biblical toponym.[54] However, Caminos located this town between Tanis and Bubastis,[55] putting it west of Pi-Ramesses, and thus not possibly in the Isthmus of Suez, either in the north or central areas. Redford now rejects correlating this Pi-Hathor with Pi-ha-hiroth because of the geographical problems posed.[56] Concerning the identification *pi-hrt*, while there is a goddess named *ḥrrt*,[57] there is no evidence that this deity had a cult center in the eastern Delta or Isthmus of Suez to warrant a toponym. Clearly, none of the Egyptian roots proposed is very convincing, and none has been widely accepted by either biblical scholars or Egyptologists.

Alternatively, a Semitic etymology has been proposed. As early as 1948, W. F. Albright had suggested that "Pi-ha-hiroth" might derive from a popular Semitic etymology meaning "the Mouth of the Canals," from the Egyptian *Pi Ḥrt* for the Temple of the Goddess *H-r-t*.[58] I believe he was on the right track in translating it as a Semitic term, but wrong on the second part since he could produce no evidence for a temple to this goddess, and nearly fifty years later there is still no textual or archaeological evidence to support this proposal. Subsequently, Henri Cazelles entertained the possibility that a canal was the feature in question, but did not offer any evidence.[59] With the discovery of the canal remains in Sinai, Weissbrod and Sneh also thought that "Pi-ha-hiroth" is a Semitic term for "mouth of the canal."[60] Just recently, Redford has come around to this position, stating: "As transcribed the word resembles a Hebraized form of Akkadian origin, Pi-ḫiriti, 'the mouth of the canal,' which would be an appropriate toponym for the E edge of the heavily canalized E delta."[61] He does not, however, link this canal with the one discovered in the Isthmus of Suez.

A closer examination of Semitic cognates supports the translation, "mouth of the canal(s)." In Mesopotamian texts from as early as the Akkadian period (late third millennium B.C.) *ḫerû* is attested and means "to dig, dig out, dig up" and is applied to rivers and canals.[62] From the Old Babylonian period onward, *ḥarāru* means "to dig (with a hoe)," "to groove," and *ḥarru* means "a water course" or "irrigation ditch."[63] *Ḥerūtu* from the Kassite period (1600–1200 B.C.) is a noun meaning "digging work," and is applied to ditches and canals.[64] It is this form of the word that comes closest to the Hebrew writing *ḥîroṯ*. The root *ḥrt* is found also in Ugaritic, Hebrew, Punic, and Arabic and carries similar meanings.[65] These meanings suggest that a feature which had been dug, like a trench or canal, is behind the heretofore elusive toponym.

The element *ha* would be the definite article in Hebrew, while *pî* would be construct form of Hebrew *peh*, "mouth."[66] There is some support for this interpretation in the LXX of Numbers 33:7, which renders Pi-ha-hiroth as "the mouth (στομα/*stoma*) of Iroth." Furthermore, the Palestinian Targum of Jonathan Ben Uzziel translated the toponym in question "the mouths of Hirathata," but wrongly equated it with Tanis.[67] In English we use the term "mouth" to describe the opening of a river or stream, especially where it pours into a larger body of water. The Hebrew *pî* is used in the same manner in Isaiah 19:7 to describe the mouth of the Nile.

In conclusion, I favor understanding "Pi-ha-hiroth" as a Semitic toponym that is descriptive of a particular area; specifically a point where the Frontier Canal, emptied into the Sea of Reeds (see chap. 8 and fig. 2 for proposed location). As such, the historian should not expect to find the toponym "Pi-ha-hiroth" among the Egyptian onomastics for the eastern frontier of Egypt. According to the Geological Survey of Israel's map of the Eastern Frontier Canal (fig. 17),[68] the canal ran north from Lake Timsah to Lake el-Ballah,[69] and then proceeded in a northeasterly direction from the north side of that lake to the Mediterranean coast, just west of Tell Farama. Thus, there is linguistic evidence to support the suggestion that Pi-ha-hiroth describes a point where a canal opens or empties into a larger body of water, perhaps El-Ballah Lake or Lake Timsah. Now that there is evidence for a canal from Pharaonic times, the reading of Pi-ha-hiroth as the juncture between the canal and one of the lakes in the Isthmus of Suez takes on credibility. But determining which canal mouth and which of the several possible lakes was intended remains unclear, but will be discussed further in the following two chapters.

IV Scientific Investigation of the Canal

A number of intriguing questions remain to be answered about the Eastern Frontier Canal. Reconstructing the entire route of the canal is essential to determine its source or sources. If the canal's purpose was primarily defensive, then to have been effective, it should have had a branch running south from the southern end of Lake Timsah to the Bitter Lakes. During the New Kingdom, a number of forts existed on Egypt's frontier with Asia (see chap. 8). Determining the relationship between forts and the canal (as in the case of Tjaru according to the Seti relief) is another area for investigation. The juxtaposition of the terms "Pi-ha-hiroth" and "Migdol," which means "fortress" or "tower," in Exodus 14:2 and Numbers 33:7 further supports the idea of the close proximity of defense structures to the canal (see chap. 8, §IV).

Given the size of the area involved, the best way to answer some of these questions is to study radar images taken from the space shuttle. Shuttle Imaging Radar (SIR-C) has been used successfully to identify ancient riverine systems in the eastern Sahara.[70] Given the similarity of the feature in the Sinai border region, this technology should be able to provide a clearer picture of the route of the canal, especially in the areas its course has been lost because of erosion or sand and dunes that now cover the area. The importance of SIR-C to this investigation lies in its capability to penetrate the arid desert sand by two to four meters, depending on conditions on the ground. Not only could this technology delineate the missing segments of the canal, it might help identify tells covering forts known to have existed in this region in ancient times that remain undetected by archaeologists.

SIR-C work is a cooperative venture of the Jet Propulsion Laboratory (JPL) in Pasadena, California, and NASA. In 1991 I proposed that JPL radar-image the Isthmus of Suez and northern Sinai area in a future mission. The missions of *Endeavour* of April 9 through 18, 1994, and September and October 1994, were devoted to earth study, including radar-imaging of parts of the Sahara and the Sinai. The April mission, regrettably, missed the critical area in Sinai and the area west of the Suez Canal between Qantara and Ismailiyah by only twenty or thirty kilometers. The subsequent October mission imaged areas even further south. I have been assured in writing that a mission in 1998 or 1999 will include the critical area of Sinai as JPL works towards mapping the entire earth. Thus, we shall have to wait a few more years until the images are available and the questions we have raised might find some answers.

Despite the delay this has caused in my study of this critical region, it appears that the Eastern Frontier Canal was functioning during the New Kingdom. Consequently, it was likely a barrier for the Israelites when departing from Egypt, and may be hinted at in Pharaoh's words spoken just after the text reports the Israelite arrival at Pi-ha-hiroth and "the sea" (Exod. 14:2): "Pharaoh will say of the people of Israel, 'They are entangled in the land; the wilderness has shut them in'" (Exod. 14:3).[71] The geographical problems surrounding the location of the toponyms of Exodus 14:2 are treated in the following chapter.

Notes

1 Amihai Sneh, Tuvia Weissbrod, and Itamar Perath, "Evidence for an Ancient Egyptian Frontier Canal," *American Scientist* 63 (1975) 542–548.

2 Ibid., 543.

3 *Mémoires sur les principaux travaux d'utilité publique executés en Egypte depuis la plus antiquité jusqu' à nos jours*, ed. Arthus Bertrand (Paris: Librairie Scientifique et Maritime, 1872–1873) pl. 3. Others have followed this interpretation of the canal remains north of Ismailiya, e.g., Aly Bey Shafei, "Historical Notes on the Pelusiac Branch, the Red Sea Canal and the Route of the Exodus," *Bulletin de la Societé Royal de Geographie d' Egypte* 21 (1946) 242.

4 *American Scientist* 63 (1975) 546.

5 Ibid., fig. 6 A, and p. 545.

6 Herrmann Kees, *Ancient Egypt: A Cultural Topography* (Chicago: University of Chicago Press, 1961) 113–114; Carol Redmount, "The Wadi Tumilat and the 'Canal of the Pharaohs,'" (*JNES* 54 1995) 127–135.

7 *Early Hydraulic Civilization in Egypt* (Chicago: University of Chicago Press, 1976) 46 n.2. Sneh and Weissbrod had considered this possibility, but preferred a connection via the Wadi Tumilat (*American Scientist* 63 [1975] 543).

8 *Tell el-Maskhuta: Preliminary Report on the Wadi Tumilat Project 1978–1979*, ARCE Reports, no. 6 (Malibu: Undena Publications, 1982) 2–3; "Migdol: A New Fortress on the Edge of the Eastern Nile Delta," *BASOR* 256 (1984) fig. 2, p. 8.

9 See chap. 9, §IV.

10 Cf. Alan Lloyd, *Herodotus Book II, Commentary 99–182* (Leiden: Brill, 1992) 157 and "Necho and the Red Sea: Some Considerations," *JEA* 63 (1977) 142–155.

11 *The Store-city of Pithom and the Route of the Exodus* (London: EEF, 1903) 2.

12 *Géographie L'Égypte Ancienne*, vol. 1 (Paris: Imprimie Nationale, 1957) 218–219.

13 Carol Redmount, *On an Egyptian/Asiatic Frontier: An Archaeological History of the Wadi Tumilat* (University of Chicago: UMI, 1989) 199–200 and "'Canal of the Pharaohs,'" *JNES* 54 (1995) 127–135.

14 K. S. Sanford and W. J. Arkell, *Paleolithic Man and the Nile Valley in Lower Egypt*, Oriental Institute Publication 46 (Chicago: University of Chicago Press, 1939) chap.1. E. M. El Shazly, "The Ostracinic Branch, A Proposed Old Branch of the River Nile," *DE* 7 (1987) 69–78; Redmount, *On an Egyptian/Asiatic Frontier*, 20–21.

15 Amihai Sneh and Tuvia Weissbrod, "Nile Delta: The Defunct Pelusaic Branch Identified," *Science* 180 (1973) 59–61.

16 Ibid., 61.

17 Sneh et al., *American Scientist* 63 (1975) 543.

18 Ibid., 543 – 544.

19 Ibid., 545, fig. 4.

20 Ibid., 544 – 545.

21 Oren, *BASOR*, 256 (1984).

22 Mohamed Abd el-Maksoud, "Project Sauvage Des Sites antiques Du Nor-Sinaï," *DE* 24 (1992) 7 – 12.

23 Maryvonne Chartier-Raymond, Claude Traunecker, and Fançoise Brien-Poitevin, "Reconnaissance archéologique à la pointe orientale du Delta Campagne 1992," *CRIPEL* 15 (1993) 62.

24 Ibid., 45 – 51; Bruno Marcolongo, "Évolution du paléo-environnement dans la partie orientale du Delta du Nile depuis la transgression flandrienne (8,000 B.P.) par rapport aux modèles de peuplement anciens," *CRIPEL* 14 (1992) 23 – 31.

25 I have discussed this problem with Dr. Weissbrod. As a result of my inquiry, he, along with Dr. Sneh, reexamined the aerial photographs of the Geological Survey of Israel. They are quite insistent that the line shown on their map published in *American Scientist* accurately reflects the visible remains from the air.

26 Sneh et al., *American Scientist* 63 (1975) 544.

27 The Epigraphic Survey, *The Battle Reliefs of King Sety I* (Chicago: Oriental Institute, 1986) pl. 6.

28 "The Ancient Military Road Between Egypt and Palestine," *JEA* 6 (1920) 99 – 116. The canal is actually shown running between Tjaru on the left and a building on the right where the Egyptian troops await the king's arrival. The relationship between these two structures is a problem dealt with in a forthcoming article of mine entitled "Ancient Tjaru: Tell Abu Sefeh or Hebua?"

29 *Urk.* IV, 647.12.

30 *Die Ostgrenze Ägyptens* (Leipzig: J. C. Hinrichs, 1911). Küthmann's dissertation apparently was not published.

31 K. A. Kitchen, *RITA*, vol. 1, 13 – 14.

32 Gardiner, *JEA* 6 (1920) 99, 104.

33 *The Battle Reliefs of King Sety I*, 16.

34 Sneh et al., *American Scientist* 63 (1975) 546.

35 The translation is my own, based on the critical edition in A. M. Blackman, *Middle Egyptian Stories*, Bibliotheca Aegyptiaca, vol. 2 (Brussels: Édition de la Fondation Égyptologique Reine Élizabeth, 1932) 35 – 36.

36 *AEO*, vol. 2, 202 – 203.

37 See chap. 3, n. 23.

38 *Egypt and the East Mediterranean World 2200–1900 B.C.: Studies in Egyptian Foreign Relations in the First Intermediate Period* (Beirut: American University Press, 1971) 34 – 35. This text was discussed at length in chap. 3, §I.

39 For a full treatment of this text and discussion of translation problems, see chap. 3.

40 "A Date for the Recently Discovered Eastern Canal of Egypt," *BASOR* 226 (1977) 37.

41 Blackman, *Middle Eastern Stories*, 11.

42 Shea, *BASOR* 226 (1977) 31 – 38.

43 Ward, *Egypt and the East Mediterranean*, 34.

44 Ibid., 36 – 38.

45 H. D. P. Lee, trans., *Aristotle Meteorologica* (Cambridge, Mass.: Harvard University Press, 1952) 117.

46 Horace L. Jones, trans., *The Geography of Strabo* (New York: G. P. Putnam's Sons, 1932) 77.

47 H. Rackham, trans., Pliny the Elder, *Natural History* (Cambridge, Mass.: Harvard University Press, 1942) 461.

48 Herodotus speaks of the legendary Sesostris frequently. Alan Lloyd, the most recent commentator on Herodotus, claims three types of usages of the name Sesostris occur in Herodotus: "Historical reminiscence of the XIIth Dyn. (1991 – 1786)"; "Historical reminiscence of post-XIIth Dyn. kings" (i.e., accomplishments of later kings ascribed to the great legendary figure); and "The Pharaonic Ideal." Thus, he concludes, "As applied to the Sesotris legend this has a crucial consequence. Many of his acts could be historical reminiscences of the XIIth Dyn. but they could also be nothing more than the presentation of Sesostris as an embodiment of the Pharaonic ideal." *Commentary 99–182* 16 – 17). Lloyd's categories might equally apply to later writers' use of Sesostris, thus allowing for the possibility that a real memory of one of the Sesostrises (or Senuserts) of Dynasty 12 is preserved.

49 "Le Canal du Nil a la Mer Rouge avant les Ptolémées," *CdÉ* 13 (1938) 268.

50 T. O. Lambdin, "Pi-hahiroth," *IDB*, vol. 3, 810 – 811; Cazelles, "Les localizations de l'Exode et la Critique Littéraire," *RB* 62 (1955) 353 and Donald Redford in *Egypt, Israel, Sinai: Archaeological and Historical Relationships in the Biblical Period*, ed. Anson Rainey (Tel Aviv: Tel Aviv University Press, 1987) 142 – 143. Subsequently, Redford has allowed for a Semitic root for this name in "Pi-Hahiroth," *ABD*, vol. 5, 371.

51 Lambdin, "Pi-hahiroth," 810 – 811.

52 Cazelles, *RB* 62 (1955) 330; W. F. Albright, "Exploring in Sinai with the University of California African Expedition," *BASOR* 109 (1948) 16.

53 *LEM*, 23.4.

54 In *Egypt, Sinai Israel* 153 n.10.

55 *Late-Egyptian Miscellanies*, Bibliotheca Aegyptiaca I (Brussels: Éditions de la Fondation Égyptologique Reine Élizabeth, 1932) 80.

56 *ABD* 5, 371.

57 *Wb*, vol. 3, 150 describes this deity as "neben Bastet." (Bastet the cat goddess is the patron of Bubastis.)

58 *BASOR* 109 (1948) 16.

59 Cazelles, *RB* 62 (1955) 351.

60 Sneh et al., *American Scientist* 63 (1975) 547.

61 *ABD* 5, 371.

62 *CAD*, vol. 6, 175.

63 Ibid., 114.

64 Ibid., 176.

65 *Hrt* means "to plow" in Ugaritic (J. Aisleitner, *Wörterbuch der Ugaritischen Sprache* [Berlin: Akademie-Verlag, 1974, 108) and "to scrape, to chisel" in Phoenician and Punic (R. S. Tomback, *A Comparative Semitic Lexicon of the Phoenician and Punic Languages* [Missoula, Mont.: SBL Diss. Series, 1978] 113). *Hrt* occurs only once in Hebrew (Exod. 32:16) and means "engrave" (KB, 338). Words derived from the same root in Arabic are rendered "to bore or drill a hole" (H. Wehr, *Arabic-English Dictionary* [Ithaca: Spoken Languages, 1976] 231).

66 KB, 753.

67 *Targums of Onkelos and Jonathan ben Uzziel on the Pentateuch*, trans. J. W. Ethridge, (New York: Ktav, 1968) 485. Numbers 33:8 transliterates the Hebrew in a shortened form, Ha-hiroth.

68 Sneh et al., *American Scientist* 63 (1975) 543.

69 The segment from Lake Timsah to El-Ballah Lake was discovered by de Belle-

fonds (*Mémoires sur les principaux travaux*, pl. 3) and identified as a trace of the Neco–Darius canal from the sixth century. Sneh and Weissbrod argue that this section is likely a part of the earlier Eastern Canal because of its size and alignment with the section north of El–Ballah Lake (*American Scientist* 63 [1975] 544–545).

70 For a popular report, see William F. Allman, "Finding Lost Worlds," U.S. News and World Report, 13 Sept. 1993, 69–72.

71 I recognize that Pharaoh's words could be interpreted as simply referring to the desert itself. However, the same desert that would prove difficult for the Israelites to pass through would have been equally troublesome for Pharaoh's chariots since Egyptian chariots had very thin wheels and would have had a most difficult time driving through the sand and rocky terrain of the Sinai.

8

THE GEOGRAPHY AND
TOPONYMY OF THE EXODUS

> Moses wrote down their starting places,
> stage by stage, by command of the Lord; and
> these are their stages according to their start-
> ing places. They set out from Rameses in the
> first month, on the fifteenth day of the first
> month"
>
> Num. 33:2–3a

I. The Exodus Itinerary

The geography of the exodus of the Israelites from Egypt has long been a subject for academic inquiry, so much so that most Bible dictionaries have an entry "the Exodus" or "The Route of the Exodus " that treats the geography and toponymy in the Pentateuch.[1] Similarly, Bible atlases try to chart the route by offering different reconstructions based on reading the toponymy in the light of the archaeological record.[2] A quick look over the standard dictionaries and atlases reveals a variety of interpretations of the data.

The reasons for the differences are often attributed to the various sources and traditions behind the Pentateuch. This is not the case, I will argue, and a coherent picture does emerge if biblical materials are rightly understood alongside the geography of the northeastern Delta and northwestern Sinai. By taking this position, the reader should not conclude that every toponym will be securely placed on a map, but a schematic route can be traced. This is an important realization because it demonstrates that the travels described in the Pentateuch did not occur in a hazy nonexistent Never Never Land.

A major problem for investigating the geography of the exodus is the general lack of knowledge of the archaeological history of the northeastern Delta. Over a century ago, Max Müller complained, "I need not explain how difficult, from want of monuments and the nature of the country, is the geography of the whole

Delta of Egypt, and especially the western part, about which the most celebrated of Egyptologists are very little in harmony."³ The picture has not improved significantly since the end of the last century. Indeed, though there has been important archaeological work going on in the Delta and Sinai region in recent decades, Egyptologists would agree that knowledge of the archaeological history and toponymy of the "land of Goshen" and Isthmus of Suez remains in an elementary stage. Many sites have been badly denuded because of agricultural activity, while a higher water table has made access to early levels difficult, if not impossible. On these problems, Donald Redford comments: "Many Delta sites had been picked over before archaeological excavations became the scientific endeavor it is today, while others have either permanently concealed their Middle Kingdom strata below a high water table."⁴

The biblical sources that trace the march from Egypt to freedom in Sinai are Exodus 12:37, 13:17–20, 14:2, and the itinerary in Numbers 33. The latter is a lengthy list that traces the movements of the Hebrews from their departure from Raamses/Rameses (i.e., Pi-Ramesses) to the arrival in Canaan at the end of the "wilderness period." The relationship between the toponyms in the Exodus passages and the list in Numbers 33 has been the subject of considerable discussion. Exodus 12:37 is usually assigned to the Jahwist (J) by source critics,⁵ while 13:20 and 14:2ff. are thought to derive from the Priestly (P) source,⁶ and Exodus 13:17 to 19 is attributed to the Elohist (E).⁷ The toponym list in Numbers 33 is thought to be a late compilation, the product of P, that may have drawn upon earlier material.⁸

Recent form-critical studies of Numbers 33 have concluded that this unit is an itinerary.⁹ Alternatively, a study by Benjamin Scolnic argues that this passage belongs to a separate genre: the list.¹⁰ He argues that "Biblical lists are interpolations which fit loosely into their present contexts," perhaps deriving from "ancient documents," but place their present context at a "relatively late date."¹¹ While he acknowledges this is a "presupposition," he offers no compelling evidence to support such an assumption. A further weakness to his approach is that when he investigates "Egyptian topographical lists," Scolnic does not consider important studies of these lists, like that by Donald Redford which demonstrates that some New Kingdom topographical lists functioned as itineraries.¹² I agree with Redford's observations and believe that they help confirm that Numbers 33 is an itinerary. However, it cannot be regarded as simply a compilation of the toponyms from other biblical sources, for it contains nearly twenty entries not attested elsewhere in the Pentateuch.

Source critics consider lists written in a laconic manner to be the trademark of the Priestly School.¹³ By default, then, Numbers 33 has been attributed to P. But it should be noted that itineraries from the ancient Near East, whether Egyptian, Assyrian, or Roman, exhibit the same rather terse, formulaic style.¹⁴ Thus, it appears that the literary character of the itinerary genre accounts for the particular style of Numbers 33 and not the hand of "the Priestly School."

In an investigation of the toponym list of Thutmose III at Karnak, Donald Redford has determined this list is a "group of itineraries for Western Asia as far north as the Euphrates."¹⁵ Such an itinerary would guide Egyptian couriers, as well as economic and military expeditions, in their travels through the Levant. Redford further observes that itineraries were not just a list of cities, but included such geographical features as mountains, valleys, streams, and springs that would assist the traveler in finding his way to a desired location.[16] Charles Krahmalkov has recently described the Egyptian toponym lists as "Egyptian maps of the Late Bronze Age Palestine."[17] It is worth noting that the Pentateuchal records include geographical features of the sort Redford has identified in the Thutmose III itinerary. For instance, Exodus 14:2 and 3 mention "the sea" (*hayyām*) and "the wilderness" (*hammidbār*), while Numbers 33:9 mentions the same features as found in the Exodus references and later in the journey mentions that "at Elim there were twelve springs and seventy palm trees." Subsequently, various mountains are named (i.e., Mount Shepher, Mount Hor: Num. 33:23–24, 37). Bearing in mind the types of geographical features Redford has identified in the New Kingdom Egyptian itinerary, it is clear that toponym lists in the Pentateuch share many of these same features.

Additionally, Krahmalkov has identified parallel sequences between some of the Transjordanian toponyms in Egyptian itineraries and those in Numbers. These factors lead him to conclude that the Hebrew itineraries are at home in the Late Bronze Age. Krahmalkov, furthermore, argues that the correspondence between the two sources shows that the biblical itineraries are reliable and historical, claiming "the account sounds credible enough, even authoritative, as if based on real and reliable sources. It certainly creates in the mind of even the most critical reader the impression of historical fact. After all, the historian is absolute and specific: He describes the Transjordanian route the invaders took in quite remarkable detail. . . . On the face of it, this passage (Numbers 33:45b–50) is an impressive and credible piece of ancient historical writing."[18]

Since the Hebrews did not intend to repeat the journey or return to Egypt, it does not appear that the purpose of the lists in the Pentateuch was exactly the same as Egyptian itineraries, even if one stands behind the Numbers material. The itinerary of Numbers 33 is introduced by stating that Moses recorded the trek by stages or encampments from the departure in Egypt to the arrival in Canaan. But the text offers no reason for this documentation. Graham Davies argues that the purpose of this itinerary was "to bind into a single unit the whole complex of narratives from the Exodus to the Conquest."[19] Gordon Wenham notes that this itinerary omits names found elsewhere in Numbers while adding others,[20] demonstrating that the itinerary is somewhat schematic. If the beginning (Raamses) and the concluding points are eliminated, Wenham suggests, forty names are recorded, which might correspond to the forty years in the wilderness (Num. 14:34). This may be a nice literary device or an interesting coincidence and nothing more. Wenham also observed that the list of forty-two toponyms can be divided into six groups of seven, that "similar events recur at the same point in the cycle," and that the names might be arranged in numerically significant patterns which correspond to special occurrences.[21] There is merit to these considerations, and if they are correct it might be conceivable that the itinerary served as a mnemonic for later writing of the narrative material in Exodus and Numbers. This practice is not dissimilar to the Egyptian scribal practice of recording an expedition in the "day book of the king's house," which contained rather terse entries on a daily basis, but later was used to create more detailed narratives, hymns, and annals, like those of Thutmose III.[22]

Having discussed the toponymic materials related to the departure from Egypt, we can now turn to the geographical questions. There is little doubt that either the city of Pi-Ramesses or its environs, the Qantir-Avaris (Tell el-Dabʿa), was the starting point of the exodus (cf. Exod. 12:37, Num. 33:3; for detailed discussion, see above, chap. 5).

II. Raamses to Succoth

Both Exodus 12:37 and the Numbers itinerary (33:5-6) agree that the first stop was Succoth, Hebrew *sukkōt* (סֻכֹּת). The term "Succoth" has long been regarded as a Hebrew writing for Egyptian *ṯkw*.[23] The site is widely believed to be located within the Wadi Tumilat, at Tell el-Maskhuta (west of modern Ismailiya), based upon the location of the tell relative to its placement in textual sources and because the Arabic Ma*skhut*a preserves the ancient name (figs. 2, 21).[24] From the Nineteenth Dynasty texts, *ṯkw* is normally written with throw-stick and foreign-land determinatives (𓏴 𓈉) and not usually with the city sign (𓊖).[25] This detail indicates that *ṯkw* was more than just a city or single site. Rather it shows it was an area within the Eighth Lower Egyptian nome,[26] the Wadi Tumilat,[27] and that it was on Egypt's frontier.[28]

At the same time, there is textual evidence to suggest that the term *ṯkw* could also be limited to a more specific settlement. A letter from a superior in Papyrus Anastasi 5 contains the order to another officer to bring a group of Medjai (Nubian mercenaries) to the senior officer "at Tjeku."[29] Since Tjeku is generally understood to be a region, this order would make little sense unless the soldiers also understood the term to mean a more specific location.[30] Perhaps this more specific location for Tjeku is *p3 sg3r n ṯkw*: "the enclosure of Tjeku," also from Papyrus Anastasi 5.[31] The term *sg3r* is identified with the Semitic root *sᵉgôr* (סְגוֹר), which has the same meaning as in Egyptian, "enclosure."[32] The wall hieroglyph "𓉻" accompanies *sg3r*, suggesting that a fortified feature is meant. In fact, John Wilson rendered this line "the enclosure wall of Tjeku,"[33] implying a defensive settlement or fort within the area *ṯkw*.

The region of Tjeku was clearly "a military zone near the eastern border of Egypt in Ramesside times," to use Edward Bleiberg's recent description.[34] The first line of evidence is textual references to military installations. Papyrus Anastasi 6 records a number of military installations by name, including "the fortress of Merneptah-hetep-hir-maat which is [in] Tjeku" (*p3 ḥtm n mr n ptḥ ḥr m33t nty ṯkw*).[35] Unless this fortress is one and the same as *p3 sg3r n ṯkw*—"the enclosure of Tjeku" of Papyrus Anastasi 5—which seems unlikely, then it should be considered a different military facility within the region of Tjeku. Bleiberg sees a total of four or five different "military outposts" in Tjeku, based upon the information provided in Papyrus Anastasi 5 and 6.[36] In view of the excavations at Tell el-Retabeh and Tell el-Maskhuta from the turn of the century and recent ones from the 1970's and 1980's, it is clear that the former site played a prominent role during the New Kingdom in the Wadi Tumilat,[37] while the latter superseded it at the end of the seventh century through the Persian period.[38] Other military installations from the New Kingdom mentioned in Papyrus Anastasi 6 were likely situated east of Maskhuta, at the eastern end of the Wadi Tumilat.

A text that has not widely been considered for the military significance of Tjeku is the fragmentary Deir el-Medineh ostracon 1076, a translation of which that apparently remains unavailable in published form. The following translation is offered through the kindness of Kenneth Kitchen.[39]

> 1) [Writer PN to addresse PN]: in life, prosperity and health, in the favour of all the gods of Tjeku! [. . . .] (2) [. . . .] to/for you, here, forever, you being in favour daily. Another matter [. . . .] (3) [PN came] at the time of evening, saying:
> "Thus one speaks in the Great House (*pr ᶜ3*), life, prosperity, health, [. . . .]
> (4) the great [meadow (?)] of Pi-Ramesse Great-of-Victories, [. . . .]; (5) and one sent to the horse-drovers ("keepers") who are in the [. . x . .], (6) there, at the three Waters of Pharaoh, life prosperity, health, who drive the droves ("herds") [of horses(?) . . . .] (7) [a]mong them, who shall fetch the grooms [. . . .] (8) the droves of horses [. . . .] (9) saying "The charioteers
> [. . . .] (10) [. . . .]

Here Tjeku is described as a place where horses and their grooms were stationed, and the city determinative is written with Tjeku, suggesting that a particular location, not a general region, was intended.[40] Kitchen suggests that the "three Waters of Pharaoh" may be one and the same as the "pools (*brkt*) of Pithom of Merneptah which is [in] Tjeku" of Papyrus Anastasi 6 (54–61).[41] When this ostracon is considered along with the existing body of textual evidence, it appears that Tjeku was a region and a specific locale within the area. Finally, the appearance of horses in the military setting of this frontier fort is precisely what would be expected. It is from such a fortress that we might expect the Egyptian chariotry, which would be stationed to defend Egypt, to have been dispatched in pursuit of the Israelites (Exod. 14:6–8).[42]

Further support for Tjeku being a militarized zone is found in military titles associated with officers assigned to defend that area. The earliest reference to Tjeku is found in the Eighteenth Dynasty. This text from Sinai is dated to the seventh year of Thutmose IV (ca. 1393 B.C.).[43] It names one Amenemhet who was "troop commander (*hry pdt*) of Tjeku."[44] Likewise, a communiqué in Papyrus Anastasi 5 is sent by a troop commander (*hry pdt*) in Tjeku to a fellow troop commander elsewhere. The appearance of this title at Tjeku illustrates that a very high ranking officer oversaw the military affairs in this strategic area.[45] Interestingly, the important fort of Tjaru (*htm n t3rw*) was also under the direction of a *hry pdt* in the New Kingdom.[46]

In a letter in Papyrus Anastasi 5 there is mention of a military officer (*idnw*) named May who is stationed at Tjeku.[47] Additionally, there are two letters that refer to Medjai in the Tjeku region in Papyrus Anastasi 5.[48] Medjai were Nubian paramilitaries who served as a police force, largely in the desert areas throughout the New Kingdom.[49] This combination of forts and the names and ranks of

officers who served at these posts demonstrate the military nature of this important region toward the east end of the Wadi Tumilat and Lake Timsah area.

Papyrus Anastasi 5 contains the oft-cited letter reporting on the movements of
two runaway servants through Tjeku that nicely correspond to the route taken by
the Hebrews in Exodus 13.39 and Numbers 33:5, namely, from Raamses to Succoth. The troop commander Ka-Kem-Wer who is investigating their disappear-
ance traces their movements beginning from Pi-Ramesses, going to "the *sg3r* of
Tjeku," south (*rsy*) to "the fortress" (*p3 ḥtm*) before reaching "the wall north of
the Fort (*mktr*) of Seti-Merneptah."[50] While the identity of "the fortress" (*p3 ḥtm*)
is uncertain, Bleiberg's proposed association with "the Fortress (*p3 ḥtm*) of
Merneptah-hetep-hir-maat which is [in] Tjeku" of Papyrus Anastasi 6 is a sensi-
ble correlation.[51] What is not clear is whether the "north wall" is a part of this fort
or yet another defensive structure near by. Ricardo Caminos rendered *t3 inbt mḥty
n mktr* as "the north fortification of the fortress,"[52] while John Wilson translated it
"the walled place north of the Migdol."[53] These interpretations suggest that a separate structure was in view, though its distance north of the "Migdol of Seti-
Merneptah" is not given, although it is situated in the desert (*ḥ3st*).

Gardiner's idea that "the Fort (*mktr*) of Seti-Merneptah" is located at Tell el-
Herr in north Sinai, between Qantara and Pelusium (figs. 2, 22), and is equated
with Migdol of the Exodus narratives has been rejected by Caminos and Bleiberg
on the grounds that Ka-kem-wer's movement from Pi-Ramesses to Tjeku and
beyond was going in a southerly or southeasterly direction.[54] There is no evidence that "captain of the host" or the runaways he was tracking turned north.
Furthermore, the distance from Tell el-Maskhuta (assuming that "the Enclosure of
Tjeku" is close to that site if not the tell itself) to Tell el-Herr is approximately
seventy kilometers in a straight line. Given the southern movement as described
in Papyrus Anastasi 5 and the considerable distance to Tell el-Herr, I concur that
it is not a likely candidate for this fortress. The military outposts mentioned in this
papyrus all appear to be within the region of Tjeku, perhaps between Tell el-
Maskhuta and east to the Lake Timsah area, although Redford and Goedicke have
suggested that "the Fortress (*p3 ḥtm*) of Merneptah-hetep-hir-maat which is [in]
Tjeku" was located at Tell el-Retabeh, fourteen kilometers west of Maskhuta.[55]

Thus, the toponym *tkw* is a well documented military zone in inscriptions of
the Ramesside period, as well as in the one occurrence cited above for the Eighteenth Dynasty, which illustrates that the Tjeku region was also a military zone at
that time. This suggests that just as the Israelites would have wanted to avoid the
fortress Tjaru by not taking the coastal highway route, they would have to carefully maneuver their way through the Tjeku and Succoth region, particularly the
eastern end of the Wadi Tumilat, to circumvent the several military posts and forts
in that area. Thus, the reference to Succoth in the Israelite departure from Egypt
need only mean that the region of Tjeku was traversed. They surely would not
have camped beside one of the fortresses in Tjeku. By traversing the eastern end
of the Wadi Tumilat, the Israelites were taking one of the main routes out of
Egypt,[56] especially if the destination was central or south Sinai.

III. Succoth to the Sea

Numbers 33:6 reports that the stop after Succoth was Etham, "which is on the edge of the wilderness," in agreement with Exodus 13:20. The meaning of the word 'ēṭām is obscure, which makes determining the location problematic. It has been associated with the Egyptian term ḥtm (fort), an attractive solution, but one that poses a serious linguistic problem that a number of scholars have recognized.[57] A shift from Egyptian ḥ to Hebrew aleph is improbable since the Egyptian ḥ normally corresponds to Hebrew ḥ.[58] If Etham is a writing for Egyptian ḥtm, one would have to admit an error in transmission or pronunciation, a point conceded by Cazelles.[59] Despite the linguistic problems posed by this correlation, not a few biblical scholars have associated Hebrew Etham with Egyptian ḥtm.[60] In view of the significant number of military installations at the east end of the Wadi Tumilat, this association is a tempting solution. But, as with Succoth, surely the fleeing Hebrews would not purposefully camp by an Egyptian fort.

Alternatively, Manfred Görg has suggested that Etham is shortened writing for the Egyptian p(r) itm, that is, Pithom (Exodus 1:11), but with the initial element Pi omitted as in the case of (Pi)Raamses in the Pentateuch.[61] He follows P. Weimer in believing that a late redactor is responsible for the toponymy in the Pentateuch.[62] It will be recalled that Redford too thought that the absence of pi in the name Raamses (Exod. 1:11, 12:37; Num. 33:3, 5) was indicative of the lateness of the tradition.[63] However, the only Egyptian pi-type toponym in the Hebrew Bible from an undeniable late source, Ezekiel 30:17 of the sixth century B.C., is Pi-beseth, which indeed preserves this element. Thus, the absence of pi cannot be used as evidence of lateness.

Another problem with Görg's proposal is that it fails to explain why the redactor would get the spelling Pithom right in Exodus 1:11, but omit the initial element in Exodus 13:20 and Numbers 33:6–8. While the LXX of Numbers 33:7 reads Βουθὰν, a corrupt writing that might support Görg's proposal, the LXX's reading of Pithom in Exodus 1:11 is Πειθώ. If the LXX translators thought Etham in the Hebrew text was Pithom, then one would expect the same writing as in Exodus 1:11, where there is no doubt about the reading. Thus, while Görg's suggestion is intriguing, textual support is lacking.

Given the specificity of Etham's location "on the edge of the wilderness," it appears that Etham, whatever the feature was, was situated at the eastern end of the Wadi Tumilat, east of Tell el-Maskhuta, perhaps in the Lake Timsah region.[64] Unfortunately, with the knowledge presently available, the location and nature of this encampment, as well as the meaning of Etham, will have to remain uncertain. From Etham, the Israelites moved on to "the sea" and a cluster of three toponyms.

IV. Pi-ha-hiroth, Migdol, and Baal-zephon

The biblical record agrees that the Hebrews camped next "in front of Pi-ha-hiroth, between Migdol and the sea, in front of Baal-zephon" (Exod. 14:2).[65] Similarly, Numbers 33:7 states, "And they set out from Etham, and they turned back to Pi-ha-hiroth, which is east (*ᶜal pᵉnê*) of Baal-zephon; and they encamped before Migdol." One of the interpretive problems posed by these descriptions is the uncertainty of the distance between these various toponyms. Then, too, differences in locating these names have resulted in scholars positing either a northern or a more southern, central route for the departure from Egypt.

The Northern-Route Theory

Otto Eissfeldt's influential work on the Israelite exodus has convinced many over the years that Baal-zephon is the shrine of Zeus Casius located on Ras Qasrun on the Mediterranean coast, with Lake Sirbonis being "the sea."[66] In support of Lake Sirbonis, Strabo and Diodorus report of problems various travelers had with changing water levels and becoming mired in the swampy soil, which perhaps would explain what happened to the Egyptian armies in Exodus 14.[67]

While there are certain merits to Eissfeldt's northern-route thesis, it is also fraught with problems. First of all, Exodus 13:17 explicitly states "God did not lead them by the way of the land of the Philistines, although that was near," which seems to preclude a northern route.[68] "The way of the land of the Philistines" (*derek ʿereṣ pᵉliŝtîm*) has been associated with the coastal highway or the military road (known to the Egyptians as "the Ways of Horus") which would have passed by Tjaru (Egypt's northeastern frontier town with Sinai) and on to Palestine.[69] Based on the reliefs and inscriptions of Seti I (1294–1279 B.C.) from the northern wall of the hypostyle hall at Karnak temple (figs. 10, 23), and the itinerary in Papyrus Anastasi I, Gardiner traced a series of military outposts between Egypt and Canaan. Beginning with the Fortress Tjaru (*ḥtm n ṯ3rw*) and ending with Gaza, twenty-three sites are recorded.[70] Gardiner was firmly convinced by Carl Küthmann's 1911 dissertation, which identified Tjaru with Tell Abu Sefêh (also called Tell Ahmar), located about three kilometers east of present-day Qantara (figs. 2, 22)[71] In fact, Gardiner believed "the question is finally settled."[72] Gardiner's stature as an Egyptologist influenced generations of scholars who accepted his locating Tjaru at Tell Abu Sefêh[73] even though archaeological evidence was limited and questionable.[74]

Despite the impressive size of Tell Abu Sefêh and the conviction of many that it covered ancient Tjaru, it has for decades awaited the scrutiny of archaeologists. Eliezer Oren conducted small-scale excavations and reports that he discovered no material dating to the New Kingdom from his site survey or his brief excavations.[75] Finally in the spring of 1994, full-scale excavations began under the direction of Mohamed Abd el-Maksoud. The finds from the first season are impressive. A massive Roman-period fort with a nearby harbor, complete with stone quays, has been exposed. By one of the quays, crocodile remains were found. Tell Abu Sefêh apparently was situated by one of the northeastern extensions of the El Ballah Lakes (figs. 2, 17, 22). But no remains dating to the New Kingdom have been uncovered,[76] indicating that the Ramesside blocks discovered on the surface of the site nearly a century ago were probably brought to the site at a later date.[77]

Because of the incredible amount of military activity during the Eighteenth and Nineteenth Dynasties that involved Tjaru, one would expect to find at least some New Kingdom sherds around the tell. This glaring absence suggests that Tell Abu Sefêh cannot be Tjaru. The importance of Tjaru as the launching point for New Kingdom military activities cannot be overstated, and I believe it holds the key for understanding why the Israelites did not take the northern route out of Egypt as Exodus 13:17 reports. Over a century ago, Max Müller recognized the importance of Tjaru in ancient Egypt and realized that it must have played a role in the movements of the Israelites; he declared that "no town of the eastern Delta frontier has a greater importance than Tharu [i.e. Tjaru], which was not only its largest town, but also the principal point for the defense of the entrance to Egypt, therefore also for the military and mercantile roads to the East."[78] He also felt that the route of the exodus could not be fixed with any certainty until Tjaru was positively located.[79]

Gardiner's work, based on textual evidence, and the survey by Oren along the military road across north Sinai demonstrate that this highly fortified region would not have been a logical choice for the fleeing Israelites, even if Canaan was their initial destination. Quite naturally, the Israelites did not want to come too near Egyptian troops, and the reason given for not taking the route was that the Israelites might see fighting and turn back (Exod. 13:17b). Roland de Vaux has pointed out that the Israelites would have avoided Tjaru or Sile because of the Egyptian military presence.[80] Bietak agrees, stating "one comes to the decision either to pass the frontier at Sile (Zaru) or to evade it and pass through the el-Ballah lakes in order to reach wells east of that lake."[81] Bietak's point is that departing Egypt via the coastal highway was difficult because of the lakes and the fortress at Tjaru, especially for the Israelites who would not have wanted to encounter Egyptian forces.[82]

In a recent article assessing the results of Oren's archaeological work in north Sinai, as well as that of geologist D. Niv, Graham Davies, who has done extensive work on the wilderness itinerary,[83] agrees that the northern route for the exodus must now be abandoned for the following reasons:

1. there is no archaeological evidence for Baal-zephon at Ras el Kasrum during the second millennium;
2. there is no evidence that the coastal strip that resulted in the formation of Lake Bardawil/Sirbonis (i.e., "the (reed) sea") existed in the second millennium; and
3. because of the major military presence along the coastal highway.[84]

Let us consider more closely the recent archaeological work in northern Sinai that supports and elucidates Davies's third point and militates against Eissfeldt's northern-route theory.

In the years following the 1967 Arab-Israeli war, Oren surveyed and excavated a number of sites along the so-called "Ways of Horus" across northern Sinai.[85] He discovered hundreds of sites between Qantara and Rapha, including many small campsites, whereas Tell Kedua (Oren's T-21) contained a large fort. Closer to Canaan, a fortress that was built in the Amarna period (end of fourteenth century) and continued in use through the time of Seti I and Ramesses II, has been uncovered at Deir el-Balah by Trude Dothan.[86] This new archaeological information confirms what has been known from textual sources; namely, that the coastal highway was a militarized zone established to protect Egyptian economic and military interests and to provide stopping-off points for Egyptian expeditions.

Perhaps the most important site in the region escaped Oren's survey of north Sinai. Tell Hebua served as a military camp during the Israeli occupation of Sinai from 1967 to 1979 and thus was apparently inaccessible to Oren. Hebua was known to an earlier generation of Egyptologists, but no excavations were ever conducted. Believing that Tell Abu Sefêh was Tjaru, Gardiner tentatively proposed that Hebua was "the Dwelling of the Lion," the third toponym but the second stop on the Seti I sequence of military posts.[87] Now that it is evident that Tell Abu Sefêh is not Tjaru, Hebua can hardly be "the Dwelling of the Lion."

In the mid-1980s, Abd El-Maksoud began excavating the site of Tell Hebua.[88] Hebua actually is comprised of four separate sites, making it a major metropolitan area, not just a military outpost or a solitary fort.[89] The area known as Hebua I has been the focus of the greatest attention and has yielded the remains of a massive fort, surrounded by a mud-brick wall, complete with protruding turrets. The outer wall measures about four hundred by eight hundred meters (fig. 24).[90] The state of preservation of the wall is very poor, with the superstructure completely denuded. The visible outline of the wall is just below the present-day surface of the sand and stands at about the street level of the New Kingdom. Large silos, officers' barracks, and stables are indicative of the military nature of this installation. In an area thought to date to the late Hyksos Period, a horse burial was discovered in 1994. The latter phase of the fort has good late New Kingdom pottery, and the site may have been used in the first millennium. Inscriptional evidence bearing the name of Seti I shows that the site was active during the New Kingdom.[91] That Seti I's name should be found here is not surprising given the witness of the Karnak reliefs portraying his movements through the network of forts on the coastal route to Canaan.[92] On the early end, materials dating back to the Second Intermediate Period have been discovered, including a stela with the name of King Nehesy,[93] the Fourteenth Dynasty king who Manfred Bietak believes was the founder of Avaris.[94]

Abd el-Maksoud is now convinced that this site is the New Kingdom frontier town of Tjaru.[95] There is much to be said in favor of this suggestion. First of all, it had a major, functioning military installation during the New Kingdom, the period in which Tjaru is often mentioned as the launching point for military campaigns into the Levant. Second, no other site thought to be Tjaru in northwest Sinai has produced any evidence of New Kingdom occupation. Third, Hebua is strategically situated upon a strip of land elevated one or two meters above the surrounding low-lying area. Upon this elevated strip ran the coastal highway leading to Canaan (figs. 2, 25).[96] This landform was surrounded on either side by a low-lying paleolagoon, which geomorphologist Bruno Marcolongo affirms was active during the entire period that the Pelusiac branch of the Nile flowed through that area (fig. 22).[97] The degeneration of the Pelusiac in this area began around A.D. 25 and it quickly thereafter dried up.[98] Certainly by the eighth century it was defunct, to judge from the failure of Arab geographers to refer to it when describing the early Islamic city of Pelusium.[99]

Finally, if Hebua is Tjaru, then it was surrounded by water. Situated on a high strip of land, Hebua I was an island with sections of the el-Ballah lake system around it (figs. 2, 22, 26). Today, however, the site and surrounding area is a desert with recent eolian dunes.[100] As the Pelusiac branch of the Nile deteriorated, the easternmost corner of the once fertile Delta gave way to the encroaching sands from central Sinai.

Texts from the New Kingdom confirm this geological evidence. A letter, most likely dispatched from Pi-Ramesses, containing a directive of Ramesses II regarding the shipment of three stelae, refers to passing by Tjaru and unloading the boats (n3 ꜥḥꜥw) at "the Dwelling of Ramesses Mery-Amun,"[101] likely the fuller name of "the Dwelling of Sese."[102] Another document lists the food supplies of Pharaoh and includes inw wgꜣs n ṯꜣrw, "gutted bolti-fish of Tjaru."[103] The inw-fish are identified with the genus Tilapia nilotica, which "are known to inhabit inshore waters, especially sheltered bays,"[104] and to prefer shallow water,[105] such as the marshy lakes of the northeastern Delta area in Pharaonic times.

A further witness to the proximity of a body of water and Tjaru is the Seti I relief at Karnak. It shows the monarch returning from the southern Canaan with POWs (fig. 10). Dividing the scene between the royal parade on the left and the fortress Tjaru with cheering Egyptian officials on the right is a body of water labeled t3 dnit, "the canal" or "the dividing waters."[106] One problem with interpreting this scene is in determining the distance between the fort and t3 dnit. While it appears they are very close, there actually could be some distance between the two. According to Marcolongo's reconstruction, the Pelusiac dips southwest from Pelusium and passes through a break in the elevated strip of land upon which Hebua and the road to the coastal highway are situated (see fig. 22). If this reconstruction is right,[107] then the Nile itself might be the feature depicted in the Karnak relief.[108] But the Karnak relief labels the waterway adjacent to Tjaru as t3 dnit, which is what one would expect for a canal, rather than for the Nile (for a more detailed discussion of this scene and the Eastern Frontier Canal, see chap. 7).

However, Sneh and Weissbrod's reconstruction of the Pelusiac's course shows it flowing in a straight line east to Pelusium (Tell Farama), about eight and a half kilometers north of Hebua (fig. 17).[109] Their reconstruction of the Eastern Frontier Canal runs about six kilometers south of Hebua (a site they did not know about in the early 1970s). It must be noted that Sneh and Weissbrod believed Tell Abu Sefêh was Tjaru (as almost everyone did), and hence they placed the section of the canal that was not visible either on the ground or in aerial photographs to correspond with the canal passing by Tjaru in the Seti I relief.

In 1994 I observed that the low-lying area around Hebua I was covered with a myriad of shells, and on the surface dark sediment could be seen mingled with the sandy plain.[110] In order to obtain data to clarify the nature of the water that was in this area, I returned to Hebua in April 1995 for further investigation. Eighteen probes were made with an auger of the low-lying area between Hebua I and Hebua II.[111] Beginning past the northeast end of Hebua I around its midpoint (30°56'19" N, 32°22'17" E), probes were sunk to a maximum depth of 2.75 meters every fifty meters, ending about a kilometer from the starting point (30°56'03" N,

32°22'33" E). The soil samples are still being scientifically studied. At this point, some preliminary observations can be made. In most areas, only ten to twenty centimeters of sand covered the area, followed by sandy brown soils for the next ten to fifteen centimeters before turning to a darker clay as far down as our auger was able to reach. The depth of the rich clay soil that frequently had shells in it suggests this area was long covered by water. The width of the area probed suggests that a branch of the Nile or a lake was what covered it. This information further suggests that the ancient city that occupied Hebua had a natural defense: water. Even if the Nile itself did not pass close by Hebua, it appears that a boat could have traveled most of the way up the Bubastite-Pelusiac branch from Pi-Ramesses before completing the trip on the lake or lagoon that was fed by the Nile.

Based on the archaeological, historical, and environmental data now available, the identification of Hebua with ancient Tjaru seems likely.[112] If this correlation is correct, then a number of nagging historical problems for understanding Egypt's frontier with western Asia are clarified and new light is shed on the Exodus narratives. Tjaru (or "The Ways of Horus") was the border town between Egypt and Asia and was the place from which the martial monarchs (e.g., Thutmose III, Seti I, and Ramesses II) of the New Kingdom launched their campaigns. Consequently, this massive military facility would have had troops stationed continuously throughout the New Kingdom. Therefore, it is most unlikely the Israelites would have taken this way out of Egypt. Should the escaping Israelites have chosen to go the northern route and try to skirt Tjaru, they would have run the danger of getting stuck in the marshy lagoon surrounding the elevated road towards the coastal highway. If they took the narrow elevated strip of land between the lagoons, they would have run into the huge fort at Hebua I. Interestingly, during the Israeli occupation of Sinai during the 1960s and 1970s, this same elevated strip of land had military camps stationed upon it, while the low-lying area surrounding the strip was mined.[113] Because of the strategic nature of this area, it was and is an ideal place to defend the main access route between the Nile Delta and the northern coast of Sinai and on to the Levant.

With this archaeological and topographical information about Hebua in mind, the meaning of Exodus 13:17 is now clear. The way to the coastal highway had an insurmountable barrier, the fortress Tjaru, surrounded by marshy lagoons (figs. 22, 25). A final barrier would likely have been the Eastern Frontier Canal which ran from Lake Timsah, north to El Ballah Lake, and from its north side up to the Mediterranean coast (see chap. 7).

"The Way of the Wilderness"

Another consideration against the northern route is that the Israelite destination was not Canaan but Mount Sinai (cf. Exod. 3:12), which is most likely situated in central or southern Sinai.[114] Thus, a route through the eastern end of the Wadi Tumilat (the Succoth or Tjeku region) is preferable to Eissfeldt's northern route. After denying that the Israelites took the coastal route (Exod. 13:17), the following verse (13:18) affirms that they went "by the way of the wilderness" (*derek hammidbār*), understood to be the road that connected the Wadi Tumilat with central Sinai. Exodus 15:22 calls the wilderness of 13:18, "Shur." According to biblical sources, the Wilderness of Shur is located on the other side of *yām sûp*. (Exod. 15:22), "east of Egypt" (1 Sam. 15:7), and "Shur and on toward Egypt" (1 Sam. 27:8).[115] The references from 1 Samuel are helpful because they refer to events taking place in the Negev and moving toward Egypt, squarely placing Shur or the Wilderness of Shur south of the coastal highway and north of central Sinai. In other words, Shur would be situated in Sinai, east of El Ballah Lake in the north and the Bitter Lakes to the south.[116]

The word Shur (*šûr*) means "wall,"[117] and its use in the Hebrew Bible has been associated with the line of forts that defended Egypt's frontier, thought to be the same as the "Walls of the Ruler" of "Sinuhe" and "Neferti" (Cf. chap. 3, §I).[118] With the discovery of the Eastern Frontier Canal, Weissbrod and Sneh propose that Shur refers to the canal and its embankments, which could be included in the Walls of the Ruler.[119] Others, however, maintain that Shur alludes to the beginning of the mountainous region east of Suez known as Jebel es-Sur or er-Rahah.[120] Thus while a number of plausible identifications for Shur in northeastern and north central Sinai have been suggested, a consensus has not developed around any one of these.

After leaving Etham, the Israelites "turned back" and arrived in the vicinity of Pi-hahiroth, Baal-zephon, Migdol, and *yam sûp* (Num. 33:7; Exod. 14:2). Ambiguities in the text make following the route difficult to reconstruct. First, as mentioned, Etham's location is problematic, as is the direction taken upon leaving that encampment. Second, the word rendered "turn back," *šûb*, does not mean turn left or right, or north or south. This second problem has resulted in different interpretations. For example, Simons believes that after leaving the Wadi Tumilat a northern direction was taken that was subsequently reversed (*šûb*), taking them southward.[121] On the other hand, Umberto Cassuto understood *šûb* to mean "turn around and not continue to travel in a south-easterly direction, which would bring them into the desert, but let them make a detour in a south-westerly direction and return to the edge of the inhabited country."[122] Unfortunately, the text is just not explicit. If the three toponyms could be identified with any certainty, then this question could be answered.

We turn now to the three toponyms, Pi-ha-hiroth, Migdol, and Baal-zephon, before trying to identify "the sea" (which will be dealt with in the following chapter). Exodus 14:2 reads: "Tell the people to encamp in front of Pi-ha-hiroth, between Migdol and the sea, in front of Baal-zephon, you shall encamp over against it, by the sea." While the toponyms of Raamses, Pithom, and Succoth are clearly associated with Egyptian cities or regions, I suggest that the three named in Exodus 14:2 and Numbers 33:7-8 are actually Semitic. This suggestion, if correct, explains the difficulty in locating these sites because they would not necessarily have been on known Egyptian itineraries. I have already treated Pi-hahiroth at length (chap. 7, §III), arguing that this toponym was the Hebrew description for the point where the Eastern Frontier Canal entered or exited from "the Sea of Reeds," one of the lakes in the central or southern section of the Isthmus of Suez (fig. 2). Let us now look equally closely at the remaining two toponyms.

Migdol   Exodus 14:2 places Pi-hahiroth between "the sea" and a site called Migdol (*bên migdōl ûbên hayyām*). Migdol is indisputably a Semitic word for "tower or watchtower,"[123] and it appears in Egyptian as *mktr*, a widely used loanword meaning "fort," "fortification," and "stronghold" during the New Kingdom.[124]

The fort "the Migdol of Men-maat-re (Seti I)," introduced above, is mentioned on the Seti war reliefs at Karnak as an early stop on the "military" or coastal road to Palestine.[125] Gardiner located this fort at Tell el-Herr,[126] (figs. 2, 17) and many have followed this identification.[127] Naturally, this location made good sense for a northern exodus-route theory. Tell el-Herr is currently being excavated by Dominique Valbelle of Lille University. A Roman-period fired-brick fort tops the tell, making it difficult to get at lower levels.[128] To date, no remains of Pharaonic Egypt have come to light. In view of this recent archaeological development and the clear biblical indicators that the Israelites avoided the coastal highway and moved in a southeasterly direction from Raamses to Succoth, Tell el-Herr seems an unlikely candidate for Migdol. Furthermore, it seems doubtful that this site could be the location of the fortress bearing the name of Seti I because it stands about three kilometers south of the coastal highway of the New Kingdom.

Another important site discovered during Oren's survey of north Sinai is Tell Kedua (T-21). It was briefly excavated by Oren's team. He believes this fort, which measures two hundred by two hundred meters and dates to the Saite-Persian period (ca. 650–500 B.C.), is the Migdol of Jeremiah and Ezekiel,[129] but he is quick to distinguish this site from Migdol of Exodus 14:2. He states: "T. 21 has nothing to do with the Exodus episode or with the Egyptian New Kingdom period."[130] A University of Toronto team headed by Donald Redford has continued investigating Tell Kedua. As of the 1993 season, nothing earlier than the Saite period had been discovered, which provisionally suggests that this fort did not exist in the New Kingdom.[131] Another factor that discourages identifying Tell Kedua with "the Migdol of Men-maat-re," is that the distance from Hebua I (assuming it is the "the fortress of Tjaru") is just ten kilometers, which seems to be too a short distance for a military force to stop after departing Tjaru.[132]

Given that the Israelites were in the area of Succoth (Exod. 13:37; Num. 33:5), it is logical to look for Migdol in or near this area. Evidence for such a fort in the area at the end of the Wadi Tumilat and Lake Timsah region is found in Papyrus Anastasi 5, 20. This Migdol is associated with the name of Pharaoh Merneptah (reigned 1212–1205 B.C.) in the late Nineteenth Dynasty.[133] If the toponym of Exodus 14:2 preserves a memory of the actual name, including the Semitic term Migdol, then this fort would be a good candidate. Unfortunately, at present, no site has been identified with this fort. The fact that the royal name "Merneptah" is incorporated in the fort's name in Papyrus Anastasi 5 does not mean that this installation was built by that monarch. Rather, the names of reigning monarchs were often attached to various defensive structures. For instance, the Fortress of Tjaru is called "the Fortress (*ḥtm*) of Ramesses, beloved of Amun, which is in Tjaru" in a text from the time of Ramesses II.[134] The fort name "the Dwelling of the Lion" under Seti is called "the Dwelling of Ramesses Mery-Amun,"[135] which is likely the fuller name of "the Dwelling of Sese"[136] built by his son.

Another possibility is that the Hebrew term "Migdol" might be a generic term for a fort rather than part of its name. As Papyri Anastasi 5 and 6 illustrate, there were a number of forts in the Wadi Tumilat and Tjeku area, and only one contains the element *mktr* (Migdol) in surviving written sources. With this consideration in mind, the toponym in Exodus 14:2 could refer to this military installation, probably closer to Lake Timsah than the main fortress at Tell el-Retabeh.

Baal-zephon   The identification of Baal-zephon (*ṣapôn*) remains problematic. The expression literally means "lord of the north" and is a deity in the Ugaritic pantheon associated with Mount Casius just north of Ugarit.[137] The origin of the name is clearly Canaanite. As noted, Eissfeldt identified Baal-zephon with the Mount Casius, modern Ras Qasrun, of Herodotus (*Histories* 2:6, 158; 3:5), but Baal-zephon need not be associated exclusively with mountains, since cult centers where he was worshipped were located in Memphis and Tell Defeneh.[138] Baal-zephon is included in a list of gods in the "house of Ptah" in Memphis in the late Ramesside era in Papyrus Sallier 4.[139] A cylinder seal depicting Baal-zephon as "protector of sailors" has come to light at Tell el-Dabᶜa from the Hyksos Period.[140] The deity is portrayed with each foot standing upon a mountain. It is plain, then, that Baal-zephon was at home in the Delta of Egypt throughout the second millennium B.C., and not just on the Mediterranean coast as Eissfeldt believed.

Noël Aimé-Giron, strongly influenced by a Phoenician papyrus that presented Baal-zephon as the principal deity of Tahpanhes, suggested that the toponym of the exodus narratives was the east Delta city Tell Defeneh (fig. 2).[141] Aimé-Giron was also persuaded by Eissfeldt's northern route, and hence was interpreting the archaeological data in that light. A problem with associating Baal-zephon with the city of Tahpanhes is that the biblical writers knew the name of this city (cf. Jer. 2:16; 43:7–9; 44:1; 46:14) and would likely have called it by its Egyptian name. Located eight kilometers west of Qantara, Tell Defeneh has been barely excavated. Whatever its earlier history was, it expanded and developed into a position of importance during the Twenty-sixth Dynasty in the late seventh and sixth centuries.[142] So while equating Tahpanhes/Tell Defeneh with Baal-zephon has some merit, complications exist.

There is nothing in the biblical records to suggest that a mountain was associated with Baal-zephon. But since Baal-zephon is near "the sea" in Exodus 14:2 and 9 and Numbers 33:7 and 8, and because this deity is associated with the sea and mariners,[143] a shrine devoted to this god may be behind the toponym. Interestingly, some of the Aramaic Targums understood Baal-zephon to be an idol.[144] Therefore, a shrine of Baal-zephon might have been located in the southern part of the Isthmus of Suez, near Lake Timsah, the Bitter Lakes or even the Gulf of Suez. The juxtaposition of Baal-zephon and "the sea" in Exodus 14:2 lends support to this suggestion.

A small fortified temple discovered earlier this century by Jean Clédat at Jebel Abu Hassa, west of the southern end of the Bitter Lakes (fig. 2), has been connected with Baal-zephon.[145] This structure, measuring only about sixteen square meters, has yielded reliefs that were usurped by Ramesses II; consequently, the original scene could go back to the Eighteenth Dynasty.[146] The principal deities associated with the temple, Hathor and Seth, are found on the relief.[147] Only the lower portion of the Seth animal (🐕) is preserved. Since the Seth animal is also used as a determinative with Baal,[148] the writing of Baal is certainly possible, especially since Baal occurs on one of the Ramesses II stelae found at the site.[149] The location of this Eighteenth or Nineteenth Dynasty fortified temple in the vicinity of the Bitter Lakes and the connection with Baal or Seth suggests that this feature might stand behind the toponym Baal-zephon in the exodus narratives. Alternatively, Simons suggested that this structure could be Migdol.[150]

Conclusions

To sum up then, the Bible portrays the Israelites leaving from Raamses, the area of Avaris/Pi-Ramesses, moving in a southeastern direction towards the Tjeku region in the eastern end of the Wadi Tumilat. At the end of this Wadi is Lake Timsah, and about twenty kilometers to its south is the northernmost of the Bitter Lakes. It is my hypothesis that somewhere around the Lake Timsah and the Bitter Lakes region is where the toponyms Etham, Pi-hahiroth, Migdol, and Baal-zephon are to be found, along with "the Sea of Reeds," the subject of the next chapter.

Notes

1 E.g., *IDB*, vol. 2, 197–199; *NBD*, 359–360; *ISBE*, vol. 2, 238–241; *ABD*, vol. 2, 703–704.

2 E.g., *OBA* 58–59; *ABL*, 10; *HAB*, 56–57; *MBA*, 40; *NBA*, 31–32; and *NIVAB*, 86–90.

3 "A Contribution to the Exodus Geography," *PSBA* 10 (1888) 467.

4 *Egypt, Canaan, and Israel in Ancient Times* (Princeton: Princeton University Press, 1992) 102–103.

5 Martin Noth, *Exodus* (Philadelphia: Westminster Press, 1962) 98–99; J. P. Hyatt, *Exodus* (Grand Rapids, Mich.: Eerdmans, 1980) 139; and Ronald E. Clements, *Exodus* (Cambridge: Cambridge University Press, 1972) 76. In contrast, S. R. Driver assigned the first part of the verse to P and only the second part to J (*The Book of Exodus* [Cambridge: Cambridge University Press, 1911] 100).

6 Noth, *Exodus*, 109–110; Brevard Childs, *Exodus* (Philadelphia: Westminster Press, 1974) 220; Hyatt, *Exodus*, 147; and Driver, *Book of Exodus*, 114.

7 Noth, *Exodus*, 106–107; Childs, *Exodus*, 220; Hyatt, *Exodus*, 147; Clements, *Exodus*, 81; and Driver, *Book of Exodus*, 111.

8 Noth, *Numbers* (Philadelphia: Westminster Press, 1968) 242; John Sturdy, *Numbers* (Cambridge: Cambridge University Press, 1976) 227–228; Philip Budd, *Numbers* (Waco: Word, 1984) 352.

9 George Coats, "The Wilderness Itinerary," *CBQ* 34 (1972) 135–152; Graham Davies, "The Wilderness Itineraries: A Comparative Study," *TB* 25 (1974) 46–81; J.T . Walsh, "From Egypt to Moab: A Source Critical Analysis of the Wilderness Itinerary," *CBQ* 39 (1977) 20–33; Graham Davies, *The Way of the Wilderness* (Cambridge: Cambridge University Press, 1979), and "The Wilderness Itineraries and Recent Archaeological Research," *VTS*, vol. 41, ed. J. A. Emerton (Leiden: Brill, 1990) 161–175.

10   *Theme and Context in Biblical Lists* (Atlanta: Scholars Press, 1995) chap. 2.

11   Ibid., 67.

12   Donald Redford, "A Bronze Age Itinerary in Transjordan (Nos. 89 – 101 of Thutmose III's List of Asiatic Toponyms)," *JSSEA* 9 (1982) 55 – 74.

13   Above, n.7. Scolnic also accepts P as responsible for the form and content of Numbers 33 (*Biblical Lists*, 113 – 116).

14   Davies, *TB* 25 (1974) 52 – 78; Donald Redford, *JSSEA* 9 (1982) 55 – 74.

15   Ibid., 59 – 60.

16   Ibid.

17   "Exodus Itinerary Confirmed by Egyptian Evidence," *BAR* 20 no. 5 (1994) 54 – 62.

18   Ibid., 56.

19   Davies, *TB* 25 (1974) 47.

20   *Numbers* (Downers Grove, Ill.: IV Press, 1981) 216 – 217.

21   Ibid., 217 – 218.

22   For a recent study on this subject, see James Hoffmeier, "The Structure of Joshua 1 – 11 and the Annals of Thutmose III," in *Faith, Tradition, and History: Old Testament Historiography in Its Near Eastern Context*, ed. A. R. Millard, J. K. Hoffmeier, and D. W. Baker (Winona Lake, Ind.: Eisenbrauns; 1994), esp. 169 – 172, which contains references to earlier studies.

23   W. F. Albright, *The Vocalization of the Egyptian Syllabic Orthography* (New Haven: ASOR, 1934) §20B; Wolfgang Helck, "*Ṯkw* und die Ramses-Stadt," *VT* 15 (1965) 35; William Ward, "The Biconsonantal Root *SP* and the Common Origin of Egyptian *ČWF* and Hebrew *SÛP*:'Marsh (-Plant),'" *VT* 24 (1974), although dealing with the Hebrew *sûp*, does explain the correspondence between Hebrew ס and Egyptian *ṯ*; Edward Bleiberg, "The Location of Pithom and Succoth," in *Egyptological Miscellanies*, ed. J. K. Hoffmeier and E. S. Meltzer, *Ancient World* 6 (1983) 21.

24   Donald Redford, "Exodus I 11," *VT* 13 (1963) 404 – 406; John S. Holladay, Jr., *Tell el-Maskhuta: Preliminary Report on the Wadi Tumilat Project 1978–1979, Cities of the Delta III*, *ARCE* Reports, vol. 6 (Malibu: Undena Publications, 1982); Davies, *Way of the Wilderness*, 79; and Redford, "An Egyptological Perspective on the Exodus Narrative," in *Egypt, Israel, Sinai: Archaeological and Historical Relationships in the Biblical Period*, ed. Anson Rainey (Tel Aviv: Tel Aviv University Press, 1987) 140. For a review of pertinent archaeological data from these sites, see chap. 3, §II.

25   *LEM*, 66.11; 67.1; 76.14, 15. The foreign-land determinative occurs alone in two occurrences of Tjeku on a Ramesside-period inscription found at Tell el-Retabeh. Flinders Petrie, *Hyksos and Israelite Cities* (London: British School of Archaeology in Egypt, 1906) pl. 31.

26   Pierre Montet, *Gèographie de l'Égypte Ancienne*, vol. 1 (Paris: Imprimerie Nationale, 1957) 213 – 214.

27   John Baines and Jaromír Málek, *Atlas of Ancient Egypt* (New York: Facts on File, 1980) 15. This point was recently noted by Bleiberg (*Ancient World* 6 [1983] 24).

28   Like the foreign-land sign, the throw-stick sign is associated with foreigners and foreign lands (A. H. Gardiner, *Egyptian Grammar*, 3d ed. [London: Oxford University Press, 1969] 513). I suggest that its use here is because of the frontier location of Tjeku. Interestingly, Nineteenth Dynasty writings of Tjaru also used the same sign combination (cf. *LEM*, 21.7; 24,7; 31:10; 52.1), because both Tjaru and Tjeku were frontier districts with forts, right on the edge of Sinai.

29   *LEM*, 66.8.

30   Bleiberg has observed that the city sign (◉) was not written with *ṯkw* until the

Twenty-second Dynasty, when he suggests *ṯkw* was understood to be a city. However, the evidence presented here suggests that this understanding could go back to the nineteenth dynasty.

31 *LEM*, 67.1.

32 KB, 649 and *Wb*, vol. 4, 324.

33 *ANET*, 259.

34 *Ancient World* 6 (1983) 24.

35 *LEM*, 76.13-14.

36 *Ancient World* 6 (1983) 24.

37 Hans Goedicke "Ramesses II and the Wadi Tumilat," *VA* 3 (1987) 13-24 and Hans Goedicke, "Papyrus Anastasi VI 51-61," *SAK* 14 (1987) 83-98.

38 Holladay, *Tell el-Maskhuta*, 19-24.

39 Discussed in an unpublished paper, "Raamses, Succoth and Pithom," a copy of which Professor Kitchen was kind enough to give me. The paper was originally presented at a conference "Who Was the Pharaoh of the Exodus" in April 1987 in Memphis, Tennessee.

40 Ibid., n.23.

41 Ibid.

42 Ibid.

43 Raphael Giveon, "A Long-Lost Inscription of Thutmose IV," *Tel Aviv* 5 (1978) 170-174.

44 The same determinatives (𓏤 𓎝) are found in this Eighteenth Dynasty occurrence of Tjeku.

45 The officer's title is *ḥry pḏt*, literally "Chief of Bowmen" (*LEM*, 66.11). Alan Schulman has shown that the *ḥry pḏt*, which he renders "commander of a host," was "one of the highest ranking officers, subordinate only to the 'general'" (*Military Rank, Title and Organization in the Egyptian New Kingdom*, Münchner Ägyptologische Studien, vol. 6 [Berlin: Verlag Bruno Hessling, 1964] 53). I prefer the more contemporary sounding translation, "commander of troops" or "troop commander" (*DLE*, vol. 2, 131).

46 Under Thutmose IV, Nebi was the *ḥry-pḏt* at Tjaru at the same time as his contemporary Amenemhet who is discussed below was the *ḥry-pḏt* at Tjeku. See Betsy Bryan, *The Reign of Thutmose IV* (Baltimore: The Johns Hopkins University Press, 1991) 288.

47 *LEM*, 70.12. An *idnw* is a lesser officer, a couple of rungs below the *ḥry-pḏt*. Schulman, *Military Rank, Title and Organization*, 34.

48 *LEM*, 66.5, 70.12.

49 *AEO*, vol. 1, 73-89. Schulman concurs with Gardiner's understanding of the function of the Medjai (*Military Rank, Title and Organization*, 24).

50 *LEM*, 66.16-67.5; translations available in *ANET*, 259 and Caminos, *Late-Egyptian Miscellanies* (London: Oxford University Press, 1954) 255.

51 *Ancient World* 6 (1983) 25.

52 *Late Egyptian Miscellanies*, 255.

53 *ANET*, 259.

54 *Ancient World* 6 (1983) 24 and *Late Egyptian Miscellanies*, 257.

55 Redford, in *Egypt, Israel, Sinai:*, 140; Goedicke, "Papyrus Anastasi VI 51-61," 91-93. Tell el-Retabeh is well within the Tjeku region, as a Ramesside inscription from Retabeh mentions Atum of Tjeku. Petrie, *Hyksos and Israelite Cities*, pl. 31, and figure 14.

56 Hermann Kees, *Ancient Egypt: A Cultural Topography* (Chicago: University of Chicago Press, 1961) 116-117; Holladay, *Tell el-Maskhuta*, 1-2; Baines and Málek, *Atlas of Ancient Egypt*, 166-167; Carol Redmount, *On an Egyptian/Asiatic Frontier: An Archaeological History of the Wadi Tumilat* (University of Chicago: UMI Dissertations, 1989) 1-2.

194   Israel in Egypt

57 This suggestion can be traced back to H. Brugsch, *History of Egypt*, vol. 2 (1879) 359; Henri Cazelles, "Les Localisations de l'Exode et la Critique Litteréraire," *RB* 62 (1955) 358; Umberto Cassuto, *A Commentary on the Book of Exodus* (Jerusalem: Magnes, 1967) 157.

58 J. Simons, *The Geographical and Topographical Texts of the Old Testament* (Leiden: Brill, 1959) §426. Davies, *Way of the Wilderness,* 79–80. For examples of Semitic *ḥ* becoming Egyptian *ḫ*, cf. *ḥbr* > *ḫbr* (*Wb*, vol. 3, 254), *ḥms* > *ḫmṯ* (Ibid., 285), *ḥlqḥ* > *ḫrkt* (Ibid., 330), *ḥt* > *ḫtȝ* (Ibid., 349). The Hebrew word *ḥtm* ("seal," KB, 344) appears in Egyptian as *ḫtm*, which also means "seal" and may be homophonous with the root for *ḫtm* meaning fort (*Wb* vol. 3, 353). Alternatively, the meaning "seal" could become attached to border forts as the place where international travelers would, as it were, have their entry visas stamped. For the Egyptian *ḫtm* meaning "fort" and "seal," both forms utilize the seal determinative (⊗; ibid., 352) while the writing *ḫtm* meaning "fort" includes the house sign ⊏⊐.

59 Cazelles, *RB* 62 (1955) 359.

60 E.g., Hyatt, *Exodus*, 149; Durham, *Exodus* (Waco: Word, 1983) 186; J. L. Mihelic, "Etham," *IDB*, vol. 2, 153; Norman Snaith, *Leviticus and Numbers* (London: Nelson, 1967) 335.

61 "Etham und Pitom," *BN* 51 (1990) 9–10.

62 *Die Meerwundererzählung. Eine redaktionaskritische Anallyse von Ex 13,17–14,31, ÄAT*, vol. 9, 264–265.

63 See discussion in chap. 5.

64 The *HAB* (57) locates Etham on the southeastern side of Lake Timsah, then has the Israelites turn back west and then pass through the Bitter Lakes, while Mihelic locates it on the northern side of the same lake (*IBD* 2 [1962] 153).

65 See Jean Louis Ska, *Le Passage De La Mer: Etude de la construction, du style et de la symbolique d'Ex 14,1–31* (Rome: Biblical Institute Press, 1986) for a stylistic study of Exodus 14 that is concerned with rhetorical issues, not questions of history and geography.

66 Otto Eissfeldt, *Baal Zaphon, Zeus Kasios und der Durchzug der Israeliten durchs Meer* (Halle: Niemeyer 1932). Examples of those following Eissfeldt include Siegfried Hermann, *Israel in Egypt* (London: SCM Press, 1973) 60–62; Noth, *Exodus*, 109-110 (Noth identified Exod. 14:2 as P's route); Redford, in *Egypt, Israel, Sinai*, 143 refers to Eissfeldt's identification as having been "persuasively" made.

67 For a discussion of these classical writers, see Herrmann, *Israel in Egypt*, 60–62.

68 This point was compelling to Simons. He further contended that Ras Qasrun was an unattractive identification for Baal-zephon since the discovery of the Ugaritic texts places Baal-zephon in Syria (*Geographical and Topographical Texts*, 249, n.217).

69 Alan H. Gardiner, "The Ancient Military Road Between Egypt and Palestine, " *JEA* 6 (1920) 99–116.

70 Ibid., 113. For a more recent translation, see Edward Wente, *Letters from Ancient Egypt*, SBL Writings from the Ancient World Series (Atlanta: Scholars Press, 1990) 109.

71 Ibid., 99. He held firmly to this identification in later writings, too, cf. *AEO*, vol. 2, 202–204. Küthmann, *Die Ostgrenze Ägyptens* (Leipzig: J. C. Hinrichs 1911).

72 *JEA* 6 (1920) 99.

73 Some authorities who have followed this identification include Caminos, *Late-Egyptian Miscellanies*, 73; Kees, *Ancient Egypt*, 190; William C. Hayes in *CAH*, vol. 2, pt. 1, 445 (while not specifically mentioning Tell Abu Sefêh, he locates it "near modern el-Qantara" which is suggestive of this site, whereas Hebua is about eight kilometers northeast of Qantara); Raymond Faulkner, "Egypt: From the Inception of the Nineteenth Dynasty to the Death of Ramesses III," ibid., pt. 2, 19; similarly, see Nahum Sarna, *Exploring Exodus* (New York: Schocken, 1987) 105; Baines and Málek, *Atlas of Ancient Egypt*,

167; George Kelm, *Escape to Conflict: A Biblical and Archaeological Approach to the Hebrew Exodus and Settlement in Canaan* (Fort Worth: IAR Publications, 1991) 11.

74 Part of an obelisk of Seti and a plinth of Ramesses II were discovered on the surface. For references, see Kitchen, *RITA*, vol. 1, 13 – 14.

75 "Migdol: A New Fortress on the Edge of the Eastern Nile Delta," *BASOR* 256 (1984) 35.

76 I visited this site in March 1994 and reported a month later at the *ARCE* annual meeting in Toronto that I thought some sort of water feature passed along the southeastern side of the tell based on my observations. It is precisely in the area that the harbor was uncovered. I was able to view these important discoveries in April 1995. No publication has yet appeared. I appreciate being briefed on site by Mr. Abdul Rahman el-Ayedi, the chief inspector for the Department of Antiquities.

77 See chap. 7, §II for information about these objects.

78 *PSBA* 10 (1888) 467.

79 Ibid., 477.

80 *Early History of Israel* (Philadelphia: Westminster Press, 1978) 376.

81 "Comments on the 'Exodus,'" in Rainey, ed., *Egypt, Israel, Sinai*, 167.

82 Bietak's ideas on the geography of the Exodus were detailed in an earlier study in *Tell El-Dabᶜa*, vol. 2 (Vienna: Verlag Der Österreichschen Akademie der Wissenschaften, 1975) 217 – 220, fig. 45.

83 See above, n.9.

84 *VTS* 41 (1990) 161 – 175.

85 *BASOR* 256 (1984) 7 – 44.

86 For a review of fifteen seasons of work at this site, cf. Trude Dothan, "Deir El-Balah," in *NEAEHL*, vol. 1, 343 – 347.

87 Gardiner, 113. *T3 dnit* is the second, which we believe was a canal, hence not a fortified encampment like the others.

88 "Une nouvelle forteresse sur la route d'Horus Tell Heboua 1986 (Sinaï Nord)," *CRIPEL* 9 (1987) 13 – 16.

89 Dominique Valbelle et al., "Reconnaissance archéologique à la pointe du Delta Rapport préliminaire sure les saisons 1990 et 1991," *CRIPEL* 14 (1992) 1 – 17, fig. 2.

90 Maksoud, *CRIPEL* 9 (1987) plan 1 and pl. 1a. The dimensions of the outer wall are projections based on a number of soundings along the northern wall that runs east to west. The southern wall has not been positively identified yet. This information was given to me by Mohamed Abd el-Maksoud when I visited the site in March 1994. I greatly appreciate the time he and his associate, Mr. Rifaat Gindy, spent with me during my stay. In my later visit, no further work on the outer wall had been undertaken.

91 Valbelle, *CRIPEL* 14 (1992) fig. 4.

92 Gardiner, *JEA* 6 (1920) 99 – 116 is now complemented by the full publication of this scene by the Epigraphic Survey, *The Battle Reliefs of King Sey I* (Chicago: The Oriental Institute, 1986) 16 – 22, pl. 6 – 7.

93 Mohamed Abd el-Maksoud, "Un Monument du Roi ᶜaa-sh-rᶜ nhsy à Tell-Habuoa (Sinaï Nord)," *ASAE* 69 (1988) 3 – 5.

94 "Zum Königreich des ᶜ3-zh-Rᶜ Nehesi," *SAK* 11 (1984) 59-75.

95 He communicated this to me during my March 1994 visit. The excavations at Hebua are ongoing.

96 Over forty years ago, Umberto Cassuto doubted the identification of Tell Abu Sefêh with Tjaru because it was not on or close to the maritime highway. *A Commentary on the Book of Exodus* (Jerusalem: Magnes Press, 1967; orig. 1951) 157.

97 "Évolution dur paléo-environnement dans la partie orientale du Delta du Nil

depuis las transgression flandrienne (8000 B.P.) par rapport aux modeles de pleulement ancients," *CRIPEL* 3 (1992) 24.

98 Amihai Sneh and Tuvia Weissbrod, "Nile Delta: The Defunct Pelusiac Branch Identified," *Science* 180 (1973) 59–61.

99 Bietak, *Tell el-Dabᶜa II*, 47–177.

100 Amihai Sneh, Tuvia Weissbrod, and Itamar Perath, "Evidence for an Ancient Egyptian Frontier Canal," *American Scientist* 63 (1975) 542.

101 *LEM*, 70.7–8.

102 Caminos, *Late-Egyptian Miscellanies*, 269. "The Dwelling of Sese" is the first stop on the itinerary after Tjaru in Anastasi 1 and the Seti I relief where it is called "The Dwelling of the Lion." (Gardiner, *JEA* 6 [1920]113).

103 *LEM*, 52.2; Bolti is the Arabic name for the fish, see *CDME*, 23 and Caminos, *Late-Egyptian Miscellanies*, 200.

104 Douglas Brewer and Renée Friedman, *Fish and Fishing in Ancient Egypt* (Cairo: American University Press, 1989) 77.

105 Ibid.

106 *Battle Reliefs of King Sety I*, pl. 2, 6. The translation "dividing waters" was offered by Gardiner (*JEA* 6 [1920] 104, but he understood the feature to be a canal (106).

107 In Sneh and Weissbrod's study (*Science* 180 [1973] 60, fig. 2) the Pelusiac runs due west to Pelusium and does not run northeast through the Qantara region. Cf. Sneh, Weissbrod, and Peruth's reconstruction of the Pelusiac and the Eastern Frontier Canal in *American Scientist* 63 (1975) 543, fig. 1.

108 The problem of whether *t3 dnit* is a canal or the Pelusiac is fully treated below.

109 *Science* 180 (1973) 59–61. In 1994, I asked Dr. Weissbrod his assessment of Marcolongo's reconstruction compared with his own. He reexamined the aerial photographs from which his map was made and reaffirmed the correctness of his 1973 map. I have also been in touch with Dr. Marcolongo, who is convinced of his reconstruction, which is based on Russian SPOT satellite images. Given the significant movement of this Nile branch over the centuries, it could be that both reconstructions accurately reflect different periods of the Pelusiac's history in the area. Sneh and Weissbrod may have found traces from the latest period while Marcolongo's evidence might date to the second millennium. I appreciate the time both of these geologists took to communicate with me on this matter.

110 I collected shells for analysis on both of my visits.

111 The team included Ronald Bull, an engineer from Wheaton, Ill., and junior inspectors Ahmed and El-Araby. The work was conducted on April 26–27, 1995.

112 Two recent studies that have discussed the location of Tjaru must be mentioned. Alessandra Nibbi ("The Problems of Sile and *t3rw*," *DE* 14 [1989] 69–78) rightly questions the long held association between Tjaru of Egyptian texts and Sile of the Roman period. In view of the recent archaeological work at Hebua and Tell Abu Sefêh, I wonder if the latter site with its massive Roman-period fort is not Sile. Sile in the Roman period would have served as an important stop en route from Egypt to Palestine. Despite Nibbi's awareness of the excavations at Hebua, she locates Tjaru in the south central Delta, southwest of Bubastis and north of Heliopolis (see her fig. 1). She also treats *t3 dnit* of the Seti relief as a place at the base of the Delta. Her reconstruction is misguided. Nibbi is interested in placing Canaan in the northeast Delta (which is patently absurd and without foundation) and therefore has to squeeze known northeast Delta toponyms further south. I think a look at Ramesses II's Battle of Kadesh inscriptions make Nibbi's thesis untenable. It is clear that the king and his forces started the march from the capital, Pi-Ramesses (without a doubt Qantir), before passing Tjaru and continuing on to Djahy, a broad term for Syria and Palestine (see KRI vol. 2, 2ff.; *ANET*, 255). If Tjaru is where

Nibbi suggests, the line of March from Pi-Ramesses to Tjaru to Djahy would be most convoluted.

The second work is that of Claude Vanderslayen ("Tjarou," *GM* 136 [1993] 85–87) who, like Nibbi, questions equating Sile with Tjaru. The point of his article is to equate the toponym Nay-Ramesses–Beloved of Amun with Tjaru based on a Ramesside-period scarab that in his mind connects the two. The connection he suggests escapes me and I am inclined to agree with Caminos (*Late-Egyptian Miscellanies*, 156) that this Delta location is "uncertain." Alternatively, Gardiner identifies this name as a temple in middle Egypt, near modern Ashmunein, ancient Hermopolis (*AEO*, vol. 2, 83).

113   Although the minefields are said to have been cleared, warning signs are still in place. Barbed wire still surrounds parts of the tell, and evidence of bunkers can be seen on the site.

114   For around 1500 years, tradition has identified Jebel Musa as Mt. Sinai or Horeb of the Pentateuch. This peak is situated in south central Sinai. Although archaeological evidence is lacking, there are other good reasons for placing Mt. Horeb somewhere in southern Sinai that will not be pursued here. A recent study on ecological factors in the Sinai supports a southern locale, cf. Aviram Perevolsky and Israel Finkelstein, "The Southern Sinai Exodus Route in Ecological Perspective," *BAR* 11 no. 4 (1985) 26–41; Itzhaq Beit-Arieh, "The Route Through Sinai—Why the Israelites Fleeing Egypt Went South," *BAR* 15 no. 3 (1988) 28–37. Emmanuel Anati's idea that Mt. Horeb or Sinai is Har Karkom in northeastern Sinai (*Har Karkom: Montagna Sacra nel Deserto dell'Esodo* [Milan: Jaca Book, 1984]) and *The Mountain of God: Har Karkom* (New York: Rizzoli, 1986) has not been taken seriously by biblical scholars and archaeologists; cf. Graham Davies, "Sinai, Mount" *ABD*, vol. 6 (1992) 48.

115   The translation of 1 Samuel 27:8 is from Kyle McCarter, Jr., *I Samuel* (New York: Doubleday, 1980) 411.

116   It is located in this area by most of standard Bible atlases, e.g., *NBA*, 86; *MBA*, 50; *OBA*, 58–59; and *ABL*, 10.

117   KB, 958; Müller suggested the Semitic *šûr* was that behind the word Tjaru. *PSBA* 10 (1888) 476. This suggestion has not been accepted by scholars working in Egyptian and Semitic etymologies.

118   *ABD*, vol. 5, 1230, Sarna, *Exploring Exodus*, 105; Sneh and Weissbrod, *American Scientist* 63 (1975) 547; Clements, *Exodus*, 94; and Cassuto, *Exodus*, 183.

119   *American Scientist* 63 (1975) 547.

120   *IDB*, vol. 4, 342, *ISBE*, vol. 4, 498.

121   Simons, *Geographical and Topographical Texts*, §§418, 422. A number of Bible atlases follow this northward movement before the turn south to Sinai, e.g., *ABL*, 10; *OBA*, 58–59.

122   *The Book of Exodus*, 159.

123   KB, 492–493.

124   *Wb*, vol. 2, 164; *DLE*, vol. 1, 249.

125   Gardiner *JEA* 6 (1920) 109, 113.

126   Ibid., 113.

127   E.g., Cazelles, *RB* 62 (1955) 344; Davies, *Way of the Wilderness*, 82.

128   Brigette Gratien and D. Soulié, "Le céramique de Tell el-Herr, campagnes 1986 et 1987. Etude préliminaire," *CRIPEL* 10 (1988) 23–55; Etienne Louis and Dominique Valbelle, "Les trois dernières fortresses de Tell el-Herr," *CRIPEL* 10 (1988) 23–55; Brigette Gratien and Etienne Louis, "Tell el-Herr: Premières observations sur l'aggromération antique," *CRIPEL* 12 (1990) 71–83.

129   Oren, *BASOR* 256 (1984) 10, 30–35.

130 Ibid., 31.

131 As reported by team member Dr. F. Terry Miosi at the annual meeting of *ARCE* held in Toronto, Ontario, on April 30, 1994 (see *ARCE* Annual Meeting Abstracts, 49). Personal communications with Donald Redford are hereby acknowledged and appreciated, see his brief report, "The Tale of Two Tells: Kedwa and Mendes, Part One - Kedwa," *ARCE Newsletter, North Texas Chapter* 3 no. 2 (1995) 7–8.

132 Based on Thutmose III's expedition, the distance from Tjaru to Gaza, about 150 miles or 240 kilometers, was covered in ten days. Hence, an average distance covered per day would have been fifteen miles or twenty-four kilometers; see Yohanan Aharoni, *The Land of the Bible: A Historical Geography* (Philadelphia: Westminster Press, 1967) 141 and my recent discussion on the distances traveled by Thutmose III, "Reconsidering Egypt's Part in the Termination of the Middle Bronze Age in Palestine," *Levant* 21 (1989) 184–185.

133 *LEM*, 67.4–5; translation in Caminos, *Late-Egyptian Miscellanies*, 254–258; *ANET*, 259.

134 *LEM*, 70.7.

135 Ibid., 70.7–8.

136 Caminos, *Late-Egyptian Miscellanies*," 269. "The Dwelling of Sese" is the first stop on the itinerary after Tjaru in Papyrus Anastasi 1 and the Seti I relief is known by its earlier name "The Dwelling of the Lion." Gardiner, *JEA* 6 [1920] 113.

137 William F. Albright, *Yahweh and the Gods of Canaan* (Winona Lake, Ind.: Eisenbrauns, 1968) 125; *IDB*, vol. 1, 332–333.

138 Noël Aimé-Giron, "Baʿal Ṣaphon et les Dieux de Tahpanhes dans un nouveau papyrus Phénicien," *ASAE* 40 (1941) 433–460.

139 *LEM*, 89.6–7.

140 Bietak, "Canaanites in the Eastern Delta," in Rainey, ed., *Egypt, Israel, Sinai*, 43; Edith Porada, "The Cylinder Seal from Tell el-Dabʿa," *AJA* 88 (1984) 485–488.

141 *ASAE* 40 (1941) 457–460. Albright was one among many who embraced this association. See "Baal-zephon," in *Festschrift Alfred Bertholet zum 80. Geburtstag*, ed. W. Baumgartner et al. (Tübingen: J. C. B. Mohr 1950).

142 W. M. F. Petrie, *Tanis, Part II: Nebesheh and Defenneh* (Tahpanhes) (London: Egypt Exploration Society, 1888) 97; A. L. Fontaine, "Daphnae," *Bulletin de la Société d'Etudes Historiques et géographiques de l'Isthme de Suez* 1 (1948) 41–57.

143 Albright, *Yahweh and the Gods of Canaan*, 125.

144 *Targums of Onkelos and Jonathan ben Uzziel of the Pentateuch*, tran. J. W. Ethridge (New York: KTAV, 1968), 485.

145 "Notes sur l'Isthme de Suez," *BIFAO* 16 (1919) 208–212; also discussed by Cazelles, *RB* 62 343-350.

146 Clédat, *BIFAO* 16 (1919) 209.

147 Ibid., 210.

148 *Wb*, vol. 1, 447. Seth and Baal are closely associated, as can be seen in the 400 Year Stela where Seth is honored but portrayed iconographically as the Canaanite Baal. Cf. Pierre Montet, "La Stèle de l'An 400 Retrouvée," *Kêmi* 4 (1933) 200–207.

149 Clédat, *BIFAO* 16 (1919) 206–208. For the text, see KRI, vol. 2, 406.

150 *Geographical and Topographical Texts*, §423.

9

THE PROBLEM OF
THE RE(E)D SEA

But God led the people round by the way of
the wilderness toward the Red Sea

Exod. 13:18

Then Moses stretched out his hand over the
sea; and the Lord drove the sea back by a
strong east wind all night, and made the sea
dry land, and the waters were divided. And
the people of Israel went into the midst of
the sea on dry ground

Exod. 14:21–22a

The exodus event reached its climax with the passage of the Hebrews through the
sea on Egypt's border. There Pharaoh's forces that had pursued the escaping Israelites met their doom, according to the biblical records (Exod. 14:26–31;
15:1–6). By this the Israelite's liberation from Egypt and the oppressive hand of
Pharaoh was achieved and they celebrated this triumph with song on the sea's
shore in the Sinai (Exod. 15:1–21). So important was this event that it was recalled in later historical retrospectives (Deut. 11:4; Josh. 2:2, 4:23, 24:6; Judg.
11:16) and remembered in Israel's hymnody (Ps. 78:13, 53; 106: 7, 9, 22; 136:13,
15).

But where is this "sea"? Did the biblical writers have a specific location in
mind? If so, can it be located now? In a review of English translations of the Old
Testament, one finds the body of water called "the sea," "the Red Sea," and "Sea
of Reeds," revealing the uncertainty found in the Hebrew and Greek versions.
The nature of the sea and its location are problems that can only be resolved with
a careful examination of the biblical text and its various manuscript traditions.

I. Source- and Text-Critical Issues

The identification of the sea of the exodus from Egypt has long been the subject
of academic inquiry as well as the subject of recent studies. In the Hebrew man-

uscript tradition, some passages identify the water simply as "the sea" (e.g., Exod. 14:2, 9, 16, 21, 23, etc.; 15:1, 4; Num. 33:8). Elsewhere it is called *yam sûp* in Hebrew (Exod. 13:18; 15:4, 22). The parallel use of the two expressions in the "Song of Moses" (Exod. 15:4), widely believed to have been the oldest portion of the exodus tradition, demonstrates that the two were understood to be one and the same body of water. *Yam sup*, in recent decades has been widely accepted as meaning "reed sea" and referring to one of the lakes between the Mediterranean and the Gulf of Suez—that is, the Red Sea.[1]

The reason for this translation is that Hebrew *sûp* means reeds, rushes or some type of rushes, or water plant (cf. Exod. 2:3, 5; Isa. 19:6).[2] Undoubtedly, the scholarly consensus that was developing in recent decades for interpreting *yam sûp* as "Sea of Reeds" led the translators of the Jerusalem Bible to render *yam sûp* as "Sea of Reeds" in Exodus and elsewhere in the OT. However, in many cases the LXX, the Greek translation of the Hebrew Scriptures translates *yam sûp* as *eruthrá thálassē* (ἐρυθρᾶ Θαλάσσῃ), which means "red sea."[3] The Latin Vulgate followed the Greek interpretation, rendering the sea as *mari Rubro,* "Red Sea." The Greek and Latin translation traditions have resulted in English translators, by and large, following their lead. The lone exception is the Jerusalem Bible (1968 English edition). In classical sources *eruthrá thálassē* applied to the Red Sea, the Persian Gulf, and the Indian Ocean.[4] Therefore, the association with the Red Sea, the northern segment of which is currently called the Gulf of Suez, is also thought to be a possible location for the crossing.

With the rise of source criticism in the last century, some scholars have contended that the confusion in the different versions merely reflects the multiplicity of oral and written traditions and their conflation in the Pentateuch.[5] Nevertheless, the understanding of "Reed Sea" as the correct translation of Hebrew *yam sûp* was not seriously challenged until Bernard Batto's 1983 study.[6] Because of the serious nature of the questions he has raised, careful consideration of his work is in order.

Batto argues that P in the fifth century B.C. was attempting to historicize and localize the rather ambiguous toponym "the sea" from earlier sources.[7] He observes: "The geographical framework of the received texts of Exod. 13:17–15:22 stems from the latest (P) redaction of the narrative."[8] Then he concludes, "it is clear that P consciously intended to historicize and localize the sea miracle at the Red Sea."[9] Gösta Ahlström has subsequently argued along similar lines.[10]

If indeed *yam sûp* is the Red Sea and P's attempt to localize the event, how is it that Exodus 13:18, assigned usually to E by many source critics,[11] mentions *yam sûp* while 14:2 to 31, thought to be P's account,[12] does not use this name? If P was responsible for localizing the event and giving us the name *yam sûp*, then surely one would expect to find this name in Exodus 14. This absence demonstrates that Batto's hypothesis that Exodus 14 is P's historicized version of Exodus 15 is untenable.

For Batto, the body of water represented by *yam sûp* is unquestionably the Red Sea (i.e., the Gulf of Suez). He contends that the Numbers 33 itinerary makes it impossible for "the sea" and *yam sûp* to be one and the same body of water. Numbers 33:8 reports that the Israelites passed through the sea near Migdol, Pi-ha-hiroth, and Baal-zephon, and then, two stops later, after several days of travel, they reached *yam sûp* (Num. 33:10). The problem posed by the Numbers itinerary has long been recognized. Jerome wrestled with this over fifteen hundred years ago. We shall return to his solution to the problem below.

As in Exodus 15:4, Joshua 24:6 employs *yam* and *yam sûp* in parallelism, and the judge Jepthah mentions *yam sûp* (Judg. 11:16); these both occur in the so-called Deuteronomic History, which predates P.[13] The late Robert Boling, along with some other scholars, considered Joshua 24:1 to 25 to be "pre-Deuteronomic."[14] If one were to follow Batto's contention that P has inserted *yam sûp* into the earlier sources he edited, why did the shorter name *yam* survive at all in the Pentateuch? Clearly source-critical analysis has not aided our understanding of the events or route of the exodus; rather, it has contributed to confusion. The lack of a consensus and the confusion over the sources in the exodus narratives was noted in 1964 by L. S. Hay: "The literary critics, despite the air of assurance with which they individually proceed, have been unable to convince one another of the precise, or even approximate limits of the major constituent strata of the narrative."[15] Hay's observation is equally true thirty years later.

II. The Song of the Sea

In the "Song of the Sea" (Exod. 15:4) *yam* and *yam sûp* occur in parallelism, and the Song is overwhelmingly thought to be one of the earliest pieces of Hebrew poetry, dating to the thirteenth century B.C., thanks to the work of Frank M. Cross and David N. Freedman, who found favorable comparisons between the Song and Ugaritic poetry.[16] Prior to their works there have been some who had argued for a late pre-exilic and post-exilic datings.[17] Faced with the convincing conclusions of Cross and Freedman, Batto accepts the early date of the Song but believes that at the latest stage of the tradition, P's influence came to bear on the hymn.[18] But this raises the question of why Priestly redactors would insert *yam sûp* in Exodus 15 but not in chapter 14, which is supposed to be P's version of the exodus.

Against the views of Cross and Freedman, Ahlström has argued that the Song is from much later in Israel's history, calling it "fictional historiography."[19] Some of the problems he raises for Freedman and Cross's late thirteenth to early twelfth-century date have long been recognized. For instance, he finds the terms "Philistine" (14) and "Yahweh's sanctuary" (17) indicators of a much later date. The problem is that the Philistines did not arrive in the Levant until early in the twelfth century as a part of the Sea Peoples migration or invasion. Freedman and Cross acknowledge that if a thirteenth-century date for the poem is correct, then the appearance of the term "Philistines" would be "an anachronism," and "its use here fixes the twelfth century as the *terminus a quo* for the poem in its present form."[20] For a different reason, John Durham does not think the appearance of "Philistines" in the poem is a criterion for dating. Rather, he believes that 15:14 to 16 was not a part of the original poem but subsequently added.[21]

This solution is not only extremely subjective, but creates problems for the strophic structure of the song. Freedman and Muilenburg agree that the poem is structured in a threefold stanza and refrain pattern, plus a fourth that is structured in a slightly different manner and is shorter;[22]

I.	Stanza	15:1b–5	Refrain 15:6
II.	Stanza	15:7–10	Refrain 15:11
III.	Stanza	15:12–16a	Refrain 15:16b
IV.	Concluding Stanza	15:17–18[23]	

With this structure in view, if Durham's suggested later addition of 15:13 to 15 is accepted, then the third stanza would have to be condensed to verses 12 and 16 only. Given the literary unity of this hymn and the clear strophic structure, Durham's solution creates more problems that it resolves.

The reference to Philistia here can, however, be interpreted in other, more plausible, ways:

1. It reflects the time of writing the poem from its earlier oral form.
2. It points to later editorial glossing or updating after the arrival of the Philistines.[24]

In support of this second proposal, the twelve spies' intelligence report of the "promised land" states that "the Canaanites dwell by the sea [i.e., the Mediterranean]," not the Philistines (Num. 13:29). On the other hand, Exodus 13:17 uses "Philistine" to describe the coastal area of southern Canaan when detailing the route not taken by the Hebrews when leaving Egypt. Numbers 13:29 demonstrates that the Israelites understood that prior to the arrival of the Philistines in the early twelfth century B.C., the area had been occupied by Canaanites.[25] This realization makes it dangerous to assume that the mention of Philistia or Philistines in the Pentateuch must point to a date after the arrival of this Indo-European people in the Levant for the origin of the entire unit.

As for the reference to Yahweh's sanctuary, Ahlström thinks it points to a time after the establishment of Jerusalem as Israel's worship center during or after the reign of David. It should be noted, however, that the text neither mentions Jerusalem nor Zion, which would be expected if in fact this cult center was in mind. Verse 17 does speak of "mountain" (har) "your abode" (mākôn lešibtekā) and "sanctuary" (miqdāš). Martin Noth maintained that these terms could refer to the entire land of Canaan as Yahweh's sanctuary,[26] while J. P. Hyatt proposed it referred particularly to the central hill country.[27] This latter suggestion has merit since this mountainous area housed Israel's early cult centers (i.e., Shechem and Shiloh) long before Jerusalem. The centrality of the mountain of the deity could also be at the root of the imagery in Exodus 15:17.[28] The absence of specific reference to Jerusalem or Zion suggests that Exodus 15:17 did not have Solomon's temple in mind. Because of this important silence, it seems that this pericope and the song as a whole predates the Davidic-Solomonic era, as Freedman, Cross, Muilenburg, and others have maintained.

Additionally, Ahlström attempts to use linguistic evidence to discredit Cross and Freedman's thirteenth or twelfth-century date for the "Song of the Sea." He is convinced that the term *sûp* in Exodus itself is really the Aramaic term *sôp*, which came into Hebrew in the second half of the first millennium.[29] To support this claim, Ahlström appeals to Roland de Vaux.[30] But de Vaux only refers to the "theory" that "*sôph* is an Aramaic word which was introduced into Hebrew at the late date," and he amply discusses and weighs the relationship with Egyptian *twf(y)*, concluding that the "uncertainties" surrounding the etymology and geographical location of "the sea" prevent the historian from drawing firm conclusions.[31] Clearly, de Vaux's cautious position should not be used to sustain Ahlström's position that *sôp* was Aramaic and evidence of lateness.

Interestingly, Ahlström's insistence that *sôp* in Exodus is indicative of its lateness represents a departure from his earlier work on the use of the same word in the book of Joel.[32] There he argued against automatically assigning a late date to the term because in the Hebrew of Daniel, *qēṣ* occurs instead of *sôp* in the Aramaic sections of Daniel. Consequently, Ahlström observes, "It is doubtful whether, as has been maintained, סוף must always be understood as an Aramaism for קץ."[33] One wonders why the occurrences of *sûp* in Exodus are not viewed by Ahlström in the same manner. If the text of Exodus is describing the mythological "Sea of the End,"[34] why was the expected term for end, *qēṣ*, not used?

In an even more recent monograph, Martin Brennen, like Ahlström, has argued for a date after the rebuilding of Jerusalem's walls in 444 B.C.[35] First of all, he trivializes the Ugaritic parallels, claiming that this influence could have been later and cannot be used to support an early date of Exodus 15.[36] His reason for late-dating the Song is based largely on comparison with biblical Psalms and passages in Isaiah that are thought to be late. However, basing the date of the "Song of Moses" on the assumption of a post-exilic date of, for example, Psalm 78 is methodologically questionable. Against this assumption, Walter Brueggemann correctly observes "it is not always clear (as with Psalm 78) that the parallel text is late. On the other hand and more importantly, it does not follow that because a text is parallel, it shares the date of the other text. Thus the conclusion is based on what I think is a series of non sequiturs."[37] The criticism of Ahlström above also applies here. Why would a fifth-century writer not mention Jerusalem or Zion, especially since the passages Brenner compares to Exodus 15 (Psalm 78 and Deutero-Isaiah) speak of the sanctuary in Zion?

Despite Ahlström's and Brenner's efforts to push Exodus 15 very late in Israel's history and to rob it of any historical value, Cross and Freedman's work stands because it links this poetic unit to thirteenth-century Ugaritic poetic material. In weighing the different attempts to date this poem, Brevard Childs supported Cross and Freedman stating that "of the various arguments brought forth the philological arguments carry the most weight. The cumulative evidence forms an impressive case for an early dating of the poem, particularly the tense system and the orthography."[38] The early dating of this hymn means that the reference to "the sea of reeds" cannot be dismissed as a late phenomenon but stands very close in time to the events celebrated therein.

III. The Etymology of *Sûp* and Bernard Batto's Thesis

Further investigation of Batto's study on *yam sûp* is now in order. While recognizing that the Hebrew *sûp* in Exodus 2:3 and Isaiah 19:6 means reeds or rushes, he declares that "the principal stay to this theory is the contention that *yam sûp* should be translated as 'Sea of Papyrus' or 'Sea of Reeds' because etymologically *sûp* is a loan-word from Egyptian *ṯwf(y)* papyrus (reeds)."[39] This statement is misleading at best and quite the opposite of what is found in the exegetical history of the expression *yam sûp*.

It was just over a century ago that the association between the Egyptian and Hebrew words was made.[40] But the translation "Sea of Reeds" is not solely the result of Egyptological influence on twentieth-century biblical scholarship. Aramaic Targums, such as those of Onkelos and Jonathan Ben Uzziel, which date from the end of the first to beginning of the second century A.D., render *yam sûp* as "sea of suph" in Exodus 15:4 and Numbers 33:10, and not Red Sea.[41] When Rashi wrote his commentary on Exodus at the end of the eleventh century, he consulted the Targums and concluded that *yam sûp* signified "a marshy tract in which reeds grow."[42] Martin Luther rendered it as *Schilfmeer* in his translation of the Bible. Also in the sixteenth century, John Calvin understood *yam sûp* similarly, writing, "it is called סוף, *suph*, either from the reeds or rushes with which it abounds, or from its whirlwinds; since this word is used in Scripture in both senses."[43] In the second half of the last century, C. F. Keil explained the reason for the name *sûp* was "on account of the quantity of sea-weed which floats upon the water and lies upon the shore."[44] None of these sources were aware of an etymological relationship between Egyptian *ṯwf(y)* and Hebrew *sûp*.

Another ancient source that Batto completely ignored is the Coptic (Bohairic or B) translation of the Old Testament. While the Sahidic version follows the LXX and reads "Red Sea," the Bohairic reads *pyom n ša(i)ri* (ϣⲓⲟⲙ ⲛ̄ϣⲁⲣⲓ).[45] It has been suggested that this means "sea of reeds or rushes," deriving from Old Egyptian *š i3r(w)*.[46] Indeed Egyptian *š* means lake[47] and *i3rw* means "reeds" or "rushes."[48] *Š i3r(w)*, "lake of reeds," is well known from the Pyramid Texts (PT, §§519, 1421), along with *šḫt i3r(w)* "field of reeds" (PT, §§275, 525–530, 981–989, 1132–1137, 1408–1415)[49] as the place where the deceased king was purified in the celestial sea.[50] The use of *š i3r(w)* is not restricted to the Old Kingdom, but continues in the Coffin Texts of the period 2200 to 1700 B.C. (CT, 1:94; 2:128, 369, 386; 3:55; 5:158; 7:265).[51] The "Lake of Reeds" is also found in the Book of the Dead from the New Kingdom (sixteenth century) through the Greco-Roman period (BD, 1, 15, 17, 136, 156, 168, 174).[52]

Other etymologies have been suggested for Coptic *pyom n ša(i)ri* (ϣⲓⲟⲙ ⲛ̄ϣⲁⲣⲓ). Jaroslav Černý suggested that *ša(i)ri* derives from Egyptian *h3rw*, "Syrian."[53] But this meaning makes little sense in the Exodus passages as "Syrian Sea," as in the "Tale of Wen-Amun," refers to the Mediterranean.[54] *Ḥʿr* is the root proffered by Wolfhart Westendorf, which would mean "the sea of the storm."[55] This possibility is intriguing in the light of the report in Exodus 14:21 which states that a strong east wind caused the parting of the waters. Despite these suggested alternative etymologies of the Coptic (B), in view of the fact that Hebrew *sûp* clearly means reeds or rushes in Exodus 2:3 and 5 and Isaiah 19:6, it appears that Coptic (B) translators understood this meaning and opted for a good Egyptian equivalent. They certainly did not follow the LXX. If this is the meaning of Coptic *pyom n ša(i)ri*, then translating Hebrew *yam sûp* as "sea of reeds" has ancient versional evidence, and the Greek tradition must be regarded as a secondary, erroneous interpretation of the Hebrew.

These sources, spanning from the beginning of the Christian era through medieval times and down to the last century, all associate *sûp* with some sort of swamp plant, and none of these translators and commentators knew the meaning of Egyptian *ṭwf(y)*, except possibly the Coptic (B) translators. If anything, the association with the Egyptian word supports the well-established exegetical tradition.

This brief history of translating the Hebrew *sûp* illustrates that the problem lies with the LXX's understanding of this term. Clearly, the LXX did not translate the Hebrew word *sûp*.[56] Concerning this point G. R. H. Wright has observed: "In short the Septuagint translators could have used *eruthra* because they knew (or thought they knew) that the Jews passed across these waters (whatever *yam suf* might stand for) or because they knew (or thought they knew) that *yam suf* in Hebrew designated the Red Sea (whatever waters the Jews passed through).[57] Put simply, the LXX translators may have thought that the body of water in question was the northern limits of the Red Sea. When the LXX translation was made, likely during the reign of Ptolemy II Philadelphus, the scribes engaged in considerable speculation and commentary on the Hebrew.[58] Melvin Peters has recently commented on this tendency: "To the degree every translation is a commentary, the LXX, as the first translation of the Hebrew Bible, provides insight into the art of translation of a sacred text and the subtle (and at times blatant) way in which it was reinterpreted in the process."[59]

Another factor that may have influenced the LXX's translation of *yam sûp* is that Ptolemy II was engaged in canal-building efforts through the Isthmus of Suez to the Red Sea.[60] Consequently, the scribes may have projected their knowledge of this area onto the biblical text.

It is true that *yam sûp* refers not only to the sea crossed by the Israelites during the exodus from Egypt, but also to the Gulf of Aqaba. The LXX of 1 Kings 9:26 renders *yam sûp* as "the extremity (εσχατης) of the sea in the land of Edom." In 1938, J. A. Montgomery thought the LXX of 1 King 9:26 might hold the clue to understanding the meaning of *sûp*.[61] He suggested that Greek *eschátēs* (ἐσχάτης), meaning "the end," was a translation of Hebrew *sôp*, which means "end." This idea was carried over into the Latin name *Mari Ultimum* for the Indian Ocean. Since the Red Sea is an extension of the Indian Ocean, the connection between the two was obvious to Montgomery. However, a full reading of the LXX of 1 Kings 9:12 reveals that Solomon's fleet was located at Eloth "on the shore of the extremity of the sea in the land of Edom" (i.e., the northern extremity of the sea, not the sea of the extremity).[62] Strangely enough, the Greek word ἐρυθρ ἀ, "red" is not used. Why in this case does the LXX depart from the usual translation of *sûp*?

Montgomery, followed by Norman Snaith,[63] Maurice Copisarow,[64] and more recently Batto,[65] suggested that the translators of the LXX were rendering the meaning of *sôp* meaning "end" and not *sûp* "reeds." But why they did it in this case while ignoring other references to the Gulf of Aqaba (e.g., Judg. 11:16) is not explained. Interestingly enough, had they translated Hebrew Edom into Greek, it would have been *eruthrá* (ἐρυθρᾶ), for red is what Edom means.[66] There still is no convincing explanation for the origin for the name "Red Sea" although a number of proposals have been made.[67] But since through much of Israel's history the area around the Gulf of Aqaba was controlled by the Edomites, it might locally have been called "the Edomite Sea" (as in the LXX of 1 Kings 9:12). Given the historic animosity between Israel and Edom,[68] the Israelites may have had a difficult time calling the Gulf of Aqaba by the name of their hated neighbors. To remedy the problem, perhaps the Hebrews extended the name of the body of water on the other side of the Sinai peninsula to the Gulf of Aqaba.[69] Even if we allow for the possibility that the land of Edom stands behind the name "Red Sea," when this term began to be used and by whom is not clear.

Taking Montgomery's theory a step further, Snaith suggested that the Greek *eruthrá thálassē* (ἐρυθρᾶ θαλάσση) was a vague term for distant, remote locations.[70] He then posited the presence of Canaanite mythic language in the "Song of the Sea."[71] These points greatly contributed to the more recent works of Batto and Ahlström.[72] While the Greeks understood that the Red Sea was connected to the Indian Ocean, the "ultimate sea," there is nothing in the Greek *eruthrá* (ἐρυθρᾶ), which clearly means "red," that suggests it had anything to do with "the end."[73]

There are other reasons for not relying upon the LXX to elucidate the name and location of Israel's exodus sea as Montgomery, Snaith, Batto, and Ahlström have done. First, the LXX does not actually translate the Hebrew term *sûp*; rather, it offers a historicized interpretation. Second, its translation of the Hebrew *yam sûp* is not consistent. *Yam sûp* is used in Hebrew for the sea through which the Israelites passed (Exod 13:18, 15:4; Josh. 24:6), the Gulf of Suez (Num. 33:10, 11) and the Gulf of Aqaba (Exod. 23:31; Deut. 1:40, 2:1; 1 Kings 9:26). But the LXX does not translate all occurrences of *yam sûp* by *eruthrá thálassē*. One such variant is found Judges 11:16. Jephthah's retrospective on the exodus and wilderness period to the conquest of the Transjordan is very brief and it is unclear if he is referring to the sea of passage or the Gulf of Aqaba.[74] Apparently owing to this ambiguity, the LXX simply transliterated the name of the sea as *thálassēs siph* (θαλάσσης σιφ)—that is, *yam sûp*.

The LXX's inconsistent handling of *yam sûp* in 1 Kings 9:26 and Judges 11:16 ought to caution against relying upon it to settle the meaning of the term *sûp* or the intended location of the sea in the Exodus 14 through 15. In fact, it has been argued that the LXX was historicizing when locating the event at the Red Sea (i.e., the Gulf of Suez).[75] Therefore, the search for the sea of the exodus should rest primarily on the Hebrew manuscript tradition and not on the LXX.

Having said this, we still have not resolved the problem raised by Numbers 33:8 through 10, which refers to the sea of passage as "the sea" and a location several days south as *yam sûp*.

IV. *Yām sûp*: The Bitter Lakes and the Gulf of Suez?

Saint Jerome (late fourth century A.D.), as mentioned above, recognized the geographical problem posed by Numbers 33:8-10. It is well known that he worked closely with Jewish rabbis and studied earlier Jewish writings, for he believed that in order to truly interpret the Hebrew Scriptures, one should work with the Hebrew text.[76] Jerome postulated that *sûp*, while meaning "red," might also mean "reed."[77] In short, Jerome thought that *yam sûp* could apply both to the Red Sea and the Reed Sea through which the Israelites passed. While this is an attractive solution, is there any historical or geological evidence to support Jerome's hypothesis?

Indeed, there are reasons to believe that the Gulf of Suez had been connected to the Bitter Lakes north of Suez. The French canal engineer Linant de Bellefonds, who did extensive survey work in the Isthmus of Suez, believed that the Bitter Lakes and the Gulf of Suez were actually connected in the first millennium.[78] De Bellefonds's geographical interpretation was accepted by Flinders Petrie, who actually went further, not only connecting the Red Sea and the Bitter Lakes but supposing the lake ran continuously from the east end of the Wadi Tumilat to the Gulf of Suez.[79] The engineer Aly Bey Shafei did not go as far as Petrie, but agreed with de Bellefonds.[80]

Three factors that may have contributed to and subsequently changed the connection between the two are the amount of flooding from the Nile, which affects lake levels; the level of the Red Sea; and the elevation of the ground around the Bitter Lakes.

The biblical geographer, J. Simons, also thought the Bitter Lakes and Red Sea were at least seasonally connected.[81] During the Nile's inundation (late August through early November) the Wadi Tumilat served as a path for overflow from Nile floodwaters. This is because this wadi is a defunct branch of the Nile that dried up in prehistoric times.[82] One noted example was the flood of A.D. 1800, which overwhelmed the Wadi, impacting the Isthmus of Suez. Carol Redmount describes the results based on earlier writers' observations: "flood waters streamed into the Wadi, bursting all dikes, inundating the valley along its entire length, and overflowing Lake Timsah. The waters even spread out into the Isthmus of Suez, finally stopping just north of the Bitter Lakes and [north to] approximately twenty kilometers south of Lake Manzeleh, at Ras el-Moyeh."[83] Such flooding was common prior to the building of the first Aswan Dam earlier this century.

Moreover, there is evidence that the Bitter Lakes may have extended further south in ancient times. The area north of the Gulf of Suez known in Arabic as *Shallûf* yielded crocodile teeth and hippopotamus bones during the excavation of the Suez Canal.[84] Interestingly, Karl Baedeker reports that these remains were discovered not far from the Darius canal stela.[85] The stela itself was situated on higher land.[86] Additionally, shells discovered on the floor of the Bitter Lakes correspond with ones found in the Gulf of Suez,[87] though their date was never established, making it difficult to know if the connection was in historic or prehistoric times.[88]

Furthermore, there is evidence to show that the level of the Red Sea was higher three to four thousand years ago than at present. Based on his work at Tell el-Kheleifeh on the Gulf of Aqaba, Nelson Glueck identified it with Ezion Geber, Solomon's port.[89] However, Gary Pratico's reassessment of Glueck's work at this site has shown that the structures attributed to Solomon's economic ventures, in fact, date to the eighth through sixth centuries.[90] If this fortified structure was located on the shore in this period which would make sense, it indicates that the Red Sea has retreated from its ancient shoreline by five hundred meters.[91]

When Darius completed the Red Sea canal, four stelae were erected at various points along the canal route. The southernmost was located around six kilometers north of Suez,[92] possibly marking the area where the canal debouched into the Gulf of Suez around 500 B.C. Edward Robinson, who studied the area north the Gulf of Suez in 1838 before work on the Suez Canal altered the ecology of the area and the freshwater canal made irrigation and farming possible, discovered evidence that suggested this area had been covered by water. He reported that a bay from the Gulf ran "further north (than at present and) it spread itself out into a broader and deeper bay."[93] Thus, the water level of the Red Sea from the beginning to the middle of the first millennium B.C. was higher than at the present time, making the connection between the Gulf and the Bitter Lakes closer than today.[94]

The level of the Red Sea in the second millennium seems to have been even higher, to judge from ocean levels and melting of glaciers during this period. Ocean levels reached a height over a meter above present levels around 2000 B.C. and gradually lowered to their present level at an estimated rate of ten millimeters per year between A.D. 0 and 1000.[95]

In more recent history, there is also evidence for a linking of the Gulf of Suez and the Bitter Lakes, at least periodically. When the tide comes in, the land between the Gulf and the southernmost of the Bitter Lakes becomes saturated, with water oozing to the surface, making the area impassable.[96] Napoleon, when campaigning in this area, experienced this sudden appearance of water that had not been there when he had passed by earlier. Others have been forced to use boats to traverse this area during high tide.[97] A testimony of the flooding that can occur in the land north of the Gulf of Suez from the Red Sea was made by S. C. Bartlett, a nineteenth-century explorer. He reported:

> I have already mentioned, that after a high wind and storm I saw water standing on low grounds, five and six miles north of Suez, along the line of the [Suez] canal, and was informed on the spot that it had recently been six feet deep; and was told by M. de Lessups that in extraordinary storms, once in fifteen and twenty years, it is driven far north. It is, therefore, not improbable that in earlier times the region between Chaloof and the present head of the Red Sea may have been a marsh region, and that the lagoons north of Suez may have extended beyond their present limits.[98]

Whether or not this northward-surging push of water from the Red Sea is the phenomenon behind the deliverance of the Hebrews from the Egyptian army is impossible to say.[99]

The elevation of the land surrounding the Bitter Lakes would have been a factor in the configuration of lakes and marshes in the area. It has already been demonstrated that the water levels in the Red Sea and the lakes in the Isthmus of Suez were higher than in the past two millennia. However, tectonic activity in the Isthmus would also alter the terrain around the lakes and the lakes themselves. Tuvia Weissbrod of the Geological Survey of Israel believes that some sort of upheaval in the Ismailiya area occurred sometime between the second and the first millenniums, hampering Neco's canal-excavating efforts. Currently, there are tectonic fractures in the area between Lake Timsah and the Gulf of Suez that according to Manshe Har-el contributed to the forming of the Bitter Lakes.[100] The tectonic activity in this area will be the subject of future investigation by Weissbrod.[101]

Geological, oceanographic, and archaeological evidence suggests that the Gulf of Suez stretched further north than it does today and that the southern Bitter Lake extended further south to the point where the two could have actually been connected during the second millennium. This linking may have stood behind the Hebrew naming the lake *yam sûp* as well as the Red Sea to which it was connected.

A logical question presents itself if this scenario is correct. Could a saltwater marsh, lake, or sea support reeds or rushes as reflected in the name *yam sûp*? Over the years a number of scholars have rejected translating *yam sûp* as "Reed Sea" because they believed that the sea could not have been the Gulf of Aqaba (1 Kings 9:26; Num. 21:4), the Gulf of Suez (Num. 33:10), and at the same time, an inland sweet-water lake in the Isthmus of Suez in which reeds and rushes grow. Batto says, "*yam sûp* clearly has nothing to do with papyrus because papyrus does not grow in these waters."[102] First, it should be noted that the Egyptian term *twf(y)* is not restricted to the meaning "papyrus," but can apply to other marsh plants,[103] a point Batto fails to recognize. Second, salt-tolerating reeds and rushes, called halophytes, do thrive in salt marsh areas. The lakes in the Isthmus of Suez have long had the reputation for being highly salinated even before the Suez Canal brought seawater into them. In the 1929 edition of his classical traveler's guide to Egypt, Baedecker commented on Lake Timsah: "The lake, which is now about 5 ½ sq. miles in area and of a beautiful pale-blue colour, was, before the construction of the canal, a mere pond of brackish water, full of reeds."[104] The reeds in Lake Timsah were reported by travelers in the last century to reach six or seven meters in height.[105] After being connected with the Suez Canal, Lake Timsah was enlarged by the influx of seawater. And yet even today in these lakes, which have water from the Mediterranean and the Red Sea, a variety of reeds and rushes grow (fig. 27), and even along the Suez Canal one can see reeds growing (fig. 28).[106]

In view of these observations, it is possible that the body of water called *yam* and *yam sûp* in the exodus narratives, Numbers 33:8 through 10, and elsewhere in the Old Testament could refer to the line of lakes (especially the Bitter Lakes) on Egypt's border with Sinai as well as the northern limits of the Red Sea. If either scenario is correct, the problem Batto saw in Numbers 33:8 through 10 is removed, and Jerome's solution is validated by geological and botanic evidence.

Alternatively, if the (Reed) sea mentioned in Exodus 13:18; 14:2, 21 through 29, and Numbers 33:8 is one of the more northern lakes such as El-Ballah or

Timsah, then the reference to the *yam sûp* in Numbers 33:10 that was reached after the crossing could be the Bitter Lakes and not the Gulf of Suez as Batto supposed (fig. 2). Interestingly, in the Egyptian story of Sinuhe, it reports that he camped in the Timsah and Bitter Lakes region (*km wr*), and shortly thereafter was overcome by thirst,[107] not unlike the Israelites in Exodus 15:22 to 26 who after passing through *yam sûp* could not find drinkable water in the Bitter Lakes area. Both stories bear witness to the salinity of the water.

V. The Lakes of the Isthmus of Suez

The biblical and Egyptological data do not allow for firm conclusions on the location of *yam sûp*. Nevertheless, plausible scenarios can be constructed by examining the geographical, biblical, archaeological, and Egyptian textual evidence. Consequently, a brief examination of the prominent lakes in the Isthmus of Suez, in the light of the toponymic evidence of the previous chapter, is in order. This survey moves from north to south.

Lakes Manzeleh and Bardawil

Situated adjacent to the Mediterranean coast are Lakes Manzeleh and Bardawil (fig. 2). *Sḫt ḏc* is likely the Egyptian name for the marshy region called Manzeleh today that lies west of the city of Port Said.[108] When it was thought that Tanis (San el-Hagar) was Pi-Ramesses, Manzeleh was a logical choice for *yam sûp* and accepted by a number of Bible atlases.[109] Psalm 78:12 and 13 locates the events of the exodus "in the fields of Zoan (Tanis)," which reflects the time when Tanis was the dominant city of the northeastern Delta (ca. 1180 B.C. onwards), after Pi-Ramesses was abandoned.[110] The dating of this Psalm is difficult, with a proposed range from the time of David to the post-exilic period.[111] Whatever the precise date of Psalm 78, locating the area of the events of Exodus 1 to 13 in the area of Tanis is a secondary interpretation by later biblical writers.[112] Gardiner and Caminos thought that the marshy area known as *p3 ṯwfy* in Papyrus Anastasi 3 (2.11–12) is Lake Manzeleh and that this lake was in the mind of the biblical writer.[113] However, the Ballah Lakes have also been equated with *p3 ṯwfy* (see next section). Now that the Tanis/Pi-Ramesses equation has been abandoned,[114] Lake Manzeleh should no longer be considered a candidate for *yam sûp*.

Lake Bardawil or Sirbonis is located around twenty-five kilometers east of Pelusium and is separated from the Mediterranean by a narrow strip of land. For Eissfeldt and his followers who adhered to the northern-route theory, this lake was *yam sûp*. However, as has been demonstrated above (chap. 8, §IV), the biblical, geological, and archaeological evidence does not support this location. It is my contention that this body of water should no longer be considered an option for the "Sea of Reeds" of the exodus event.

Lake El-Ballah

The ancient configuration of this lake is difficult to determine since it was largely drained when the Suez Canal was cut through the center of it in the last century, and there has been significant agricultural and urban development in the area west of the canal (figs. 2, 17).[115] East of the Suez Canal, eolian dunes have covered the area, making the ancient lake bed virtually impossible to trace from the surface, although some of the area once covered by the lake is still made up of small marshy patches in which various reeds abound, particularly between Qantara West and Ismailiya (fig. 29). These marshes give us a hint at what the area was like in Pharaonic times.

Based upon the parallel use of *p3 š ḥr* and *p3 ṯwfy* in Papyrus Anastasi 3 (2.11–12), Manfred Bietak believes that these two lakes were close to each other.[116] He suggests that the former is the long narrow lake which is north of and parallel to the narrow strip of land on which the so-called "Ways of Horus" (i.e., the coastal highway) was situated and that the later is the Ballah Lakes, south of the same land form.

This lake remains a viable candidate for *yam sûp* particularly if the Hebrews went north when they "turned back" after camping at Succoth (Exod. 14:2; see above chap. 8, §IV). Furthermore, if I am right in associating Pi-ha-hiroth with the Eastern Frontier Canal's point of entry into "the sea" (ibid.), then the juncture between the ancient canal traces and this lake would be necessary. In fact, traces of the ancient canal do intersect Lake El-Ballah on the southwest side (32°15' E, 30°44' N; figs. 2, 17). This union could mark the area mentioned in Exodus 14:2 and Numbers 33:7 and 8. The location of Tell Defeneh, thought by some to be Baal-zephon, about seventeen kilometers to the northwest, seems to be too far removed from this area of the lake to have been Baal-zephon.[117] Alternatively, the canal would also have exited from some point on the north side of the lake, but this spot has not yet been identified. From the north side of the lake, Tahpanhes would be three to five kilometers closer than to the southern section of the lake.

While this latter scenario is a tempting one, it seems less likely since this would place the Israelites four to five kilometers from Fort Tjaru, the major military zone on Egypt's frontier with Sinai that the Hebrews clearly wanted to avoid (Exod. 13:17). On the other hand, the advantage to the northern side of El-Ballah is that proposed locations for the four place-names of Exodus 14:2 and Numbers 3:7 and 8 can be identified within this region: Pi-ha-hiroth (the canal's exit point from the lake), Migdol (Fortress Tjaru), Baal-zephon (Tahpanhes) and the sea (Lake El-Ballah). However, careful consideration of the wording of Exodus 14:2 suggests that Baal-zephon and Pi-ha-hiroth were beside each other in view of the placement of the preposition *lipnê*, ("before" or "in front of") preceding both toponyms.

Thus, while the el-Ballah lake system remains a possibility for the Sea of Reeds, and one favored by a number of scholars,[118] problems exist which prevent us from drawing firm conclusions.

Lake Timsah

"Crocodile" Lake, the Arabic and Egyptian meaning of Timsah,[119] is situated at the east end of the Wadi Tumilat (figs. 2, 17, 27). The city of Ismailiya, founded in connection with the digging of the Suez Canal during the last century, occupies the northern shore of the lake.

Lake Timsah has been associated with the Egyptian toponym *km wr*, "the great black," which probably included the Bitter Lakes to the south.[120] The determinative $\approx$, or $\rightleftarrows$, or a combination of the two indicates that a body of water was understood by *km wr*. Since after departing Raamses/Pi-Ramesses the Israelites traversed Succoth, the eastern Wadi Tumilat region, Lake Timsah is an obvious choice for *yam sûp*. Because they had been moving in a southeasterly direction from Pi-Ramesses to Tjeku, when they "turned back" a more northeasterly direction could have placed the Hebrews on the north side of Lake Timsah. The traces of the ancient canal discovered in the last century by de Bellefonds connect the north side of Lake Timsah and the southern part of Lake El-Ballah (figs. 17, 20), placing Pi-ha-hiroth in the vicinity of Ismailiya (fig. 2). The numerous forts in the Tjeku and Succoth region have already been discussed, one of which in the Nineteenth Dynasty is called "the Migdol (*mktr*) of Men-maat-re." The textual evidence situates this fort somewhere at the eastern end of the Wadi Tumilat. The possible association of the toponyms Pi-ha-hiroth and Migdol with Lake Timsah, which could certainly have been labeled *yam sûp* by the Israelites, suggests that this lake must remain a candidate for the events described in Exodus 14 and 15.

The Bitter Lakes

The southernmost chain of lakes in the Isthmus of Suez is the Bitter Lakes (fig. 2). Along with Lake Timsah, the Bitter Lakes were probably included under the Egyptian name *km wr*.[121] If the Bitter Lakes had at least periodic connections with the Gulf of Suez, it could explain how *yam sûp* could be both the sea of passage and the Red Sea (the Gulfs of Suez and Aqaba). The exodus toponyms can be linked to this area, too. Baal-zephon could be associated with the New Kingdom fortified temple discovered by Clédat (chap. 8, §IV). Alternatively, it has been suggested that this structure could be Migdol,[122] in which case, Baal-zephon would remain unidentified.

Israel Geological Survey members who studied the Eastern Frontier Canal hypothesize that Neco was actually attempting to reopen a canal from the second millennium that had silted up. Consequently, the canal would have to go south from the Timsah–Wadi Tumilat area to the greater (or northern) Bitter Lake.[123] If this hypothesis is correct, then Pi-ha-hiroth would be the entry point of the canal into the northern Bitter Lake. The Bitter Lakes is a spot favored by many historical geographers who consider *yam sûp* to be one of the lakes in the Isthmus of Suez.[124] The narrow area where the lesser and greater Bitter Lakes join has been proposed as a more specific point because the water can be so shallow at times as to allow the area to be forded.[125]

VI. Mythological Considerations of the Sea Crossing

Working on the mistaken assumption that the sea was called *sôp*, "Sea of the End," Snaith believed that creation-myth language associated with defeating a sea monster was used in the "Song of the Sea" (Exod. 15:1-21).[126] Batto expanded on Snaith, opining that "Such mythological motifs account rather patently for the presence of *yam* (Sea dragon) in the poem" and that "earth" in 15:7 really stood for "the Underworld."[127] For Batto, and Ahlström, the mythological nature of this poem renders the events described therein as "historicized."[128] The mythic language contributes to Ahlström's radical conclusion that the exodus material is "fictional historiography" and "is definitely not one of empirical history."[129]

Several critical observations are in order. First, the poetic or hymnic description of the sea passage of Exodus 15 does not disagree with the main points of the narrative version in Exodus 14:21 to 31 despite the apparent presence of mythological terms. Second, when Hebrew writers elsewhere used mythic allusions or language, it applied to specific historical realities. For instance, both Isaiah 30:7 and Ezekiel 29:3 liken the Saite Pharaoh and his might to Rahab and Tannim.[130]

The setting of Isaiah's oracle is thought to be Sennacherib's invasion of Judah in 701 B.C. and the Twenty-fifth Dynasty's attempt to intervene by sending Tirhaka (Taharka) to engage the Assyrians,[131] or in response to Hoshea of Samaria's appeal to Egypt prior to the northern kingdom's demise in 722 B.C.[132] In either case, Isaiah attaches the mythological Rahab, whom Yahweh had defeated at creation, to a weak Pharaoh of the Third Intermediate Period who could not withstand the power of Assyria. Ezekiel uses the "great Tannim" (as in Gen. 1:21) in much the same way as Isaiah did with Rahab. The historical context of this oracle is 586 B.C., the time of Jerusalem's destruction at the hand of Chaldeans.[133] Once again, an appeal to Pharaoh's help was made (Ezek. 17:15), and Apries (Hophra) offered a feeble response (Jer. 37:5, 44:30; Ezek. 30:20-25).[134]

These two examples demonstrate that the Hebrew writers could use mythic language and images to depict specific historic situations. Evidently, the use of this type of language in the Hebrew scribal tradition in no way detracted from the historicity of the events being discussed. Interestingly, Ahlström in his monumental, posthumously published *History of Ancient Palestine* mentions the fall of the Jerusalem and Apries's role in trying to assist Judah, stating, "the Egyptian army was of no help."[135] This is precisely the point of Ezekiel's application of Canaanite mythological symbols to Pharaoh Hophra and Egypt's military frailty at the end of the six-century B.C. Clearly in this case Ahlström did not reject the historic value of a text because it utilized mythic terminology regarding Pharaoh. I maintain the same is true of Exodus 15. There may be mythological images used in the "Song of the Sea," but that should not automatically render its contents unhistorical. Rather, mythic language was a tool in ancient Israel's historiographical repertoire.

Another line of mythological investigation of the exodus sea event has concerned Egyptian, as compared with Canaanite or Mesopotamian, sources. It is suggested that the "Sea of Reeds" (*š i3rw*) or "Field of Reeds" (*sḫt i3rw*), which are closely related in Egyptian funerary texts,[136] stand behind the Hebrew *yam sûp*.[137] Towers points to the Coptic (B) version where *yam sûp* is normally translated as *pyom n ša(i)ri* (ⲯⲓⲟⲙ ⲛ ϣⲁ ⲣ ⲓ), "Sea of Reeds."[138] In Exodus 15:22 and 23:31, the variant translation *pyom n ḥзḥ* (ⲯ ⲓ ⲟ ⲙ ⲛ ϩ ⲁ ϩ) occurs in Coptic (B), which Towers believed to be the writing for Egyptian *š n ḥз* or *ḥзḥз*.[139] In the Pyramid Texts, these two lakes are found in parallelism, which suggests to Towers that it was an obvious synonym for *pyom n ša(i)ri*. The deceased, in Egyptian funerary literature, would pass through the lake or marsh and be purified (*wᶜb*) in its waters before ascending to new life in the realm of Re or Osiris.[140] Towers and others associate the regeneration of the Egyptian dead with the Israelites' passage through the "Sea of Reeds" where they were born as a nation.[141]

My response to the theorized Canaanite and Mesopotamian mythological influence on the passage through the sea accounts apply as well to an Egyptian theological perspective. A mythological connection is an intriguing possibility, especially in light of the Coptic (B) variants, but that could represent a Coptic or Egyptian scribal interpolation. The Hebrews may well have attached such symbolic national-birth motifs to the exodus story, and in the process employed various Near Eastern mythological images and terminology, which it did with reference to historical reality, not concocted events.

VII. Conclusion

If the term *sûp* is related to Egyptian *ṭwf(y)*—and I think this is virtually certain in light of Ward's rigorous linguistic investigation of the word[142]—then *yam sûp* may have been the Hebrew for the proper name *p3 ṭwfy*, a marshy region of the eastern Delta.[143] Alternatively, *yam sûp* in the exodus narratives may simply be a descriptive term that could have applied to any marshy lakes in the Isthmus of Suez.

The crossing of the sea signaled the end of the sojourn in Egypt and it certainly was the end of the Egyptian army that pursued the fleeing Hebrews (Exod. 14:23–29, 15:4–5). After this event at *yam sûp*, perhaps the verb *sôp*, meaning "destroy" and "come to an end," originated (cf. Amos 3:15; Jer. 8:13; Isa. 66:17; Psa. 73:19).[144] Another possible development of this root is the word *sûpah*, meaning "storm-wind."[145] Often such winds have destructive capabilities (cf. Amos 1:14; Hos. 8:7; Jer. 4:13; Isa. 5:28, 17:13). Recall in this connection the strong east wind that drove back the waters and made the Israelite escape possible (Exod. 14:21). The meanings "end" and "storm wind" would have constituted nice puns on the event that took place at the *yam sûp*.

After crossing *yam sûp* and ending the sojourn in Egypt, the Numbers itinerary traces the trek of the Hebrews through Sinai, concluding in Moab. At another place called *sûp* Moses renewed the covenant with Israel (Deut. 1:1). The name of this site might serve to signal the "end" of the wandering period, thus producing a symmetrical pattern in the narrative for the beginning of the exodus (passing through *yam sûp*) to the conclusion of the wandering period (arriving at *sûp* in Moab).

One final literary observation should be made. The eighth plague in the cycle comprised of swarms of locusts that devoured vegetation in Egypt (Exod. 10:3–20). The plague ended with the Lord sending a strong west wind to drive the locusts into *yām sûp* (Exod. 10:19).[146] Elsewhere in the OT, locusts are symbolic of ravaging armies (cf. Joel 1:4, 2:25). The drowning of locusts may have foreshadowed the termination of the Egyptian army in *yam sûp*.

In the foregoing section I have sought to show that the exodus traditions present a coherent picture of the route taken by the Israelites to freedom in Sinai. The problems of comprehension often lie with our inadequate knowledge of the geography and toponymy rather than confusion among the various literary traditions. The sea through which the Israelites passed most likely was one of the lakes in the Isthmus of Suez; most likely the Ballah Lakes, Lake Timsah, or Bitter Lakes region (figs. 2, 17), and it could interchangeably be called "the sea" or *yam sûp*, the latter being a more descriptive name.

In the final analysis, our inability to locate the sea with certainty does not diminish the historicity of the event or its importance for Israel's religious and national history. The scope of this book does not permit me to delve into the phenomenon of the miracle at the sea, but I am sympathetic with Bright, who observed, "If Israel saw in this the hand of God, the historian certainly has no evidence to contradict it!"[147]

Notes

1 John Bright, *A History of Israel* (Philadelphia: Westminster Press, 1981) 121; Siegfried Herrmann, *Israel in Egypt*, Studies in Biblical Theology, 2d series, vol. 27 (London: SCM, 1973) 56–64; Roland de Vaux, *The Early History of Israel* (Philadelphia: Westminster Press, 1978) 377.

2 KB, 652.

3 Henry Liddell and Robert Scott, *Greek-English Lexicon* (Oxford: Clarendon Press, 1968) 693.

4 Ibid.

5 See de Vaux, *Early History of Israel*, 376, where a chart records the analyses of Noth, Eissfeldt, and Fohrer regarding the toponyms of Exodus 12–14 and Numbers 33.

6 "The Reed Sea: *Requiscat in Pace*," *JBL* 102 (1983) 27–35.

7 Ibid., 29–30.

8 Ibid., 28.

9 Ibid., 30.

10 *Who Were the Israelites?* (Winona Lake, Ind.: Eisenbrauns, 1986) 49.

11 Martin Noth, *Exodus: A Commentary* (Philadelphia: Westminster Press, 1962) 106–107; J. Philip Hyatt, *Exodus* (London/Grand Rapids, Mich.: Marshall, Morgan, and Scott/Eerdmans, 1971) 147; Brevard Childs, *The Book of Exodus* (Philadelphia: Westminster Press, 1974) 220. De Vaux's solution to this dilemma was to consider 13:18 "an addition" (*Early History of Israel*, 378). The practice of assigning a later intrusion into the text to salvage one's literary assumptions about the text is hardly a satisfactory methodology.

12 Noth, *Exodus*, 109–111; Hyatt, *Exodus*, 148; Childs, *Exodus*, 220.

13 John Gray, *Joshua, Judges, Ruth* (London: Nelson, 1967); Trent Butler, *Joshua* (Waco: Word, 1983) xxvii–xxix.

14 Robert Boling and G. Ernest Wright, *Joshua* (Garden City, N.Y.: Doubleday, 1982)

533. For others holding to an earlier origin, Kenneth Kitchen, *The Bible in Its World* (Exeter, England: Pater Noster, 1977) 81-85 and Richard Hess, *Joshua: An Introduction and Commentary* (Downers Grove, Ill.: IV Press, 1996) 49-51, 299-300 both consider the covenant structure in chap. 24 to point to a date around 1200 B.C.

15 "What Really Happened at the Sea of Reeds?" *JBL* 83 (1964) 399.

16 Cf. F. M. Cross and D. N. Freedman, "The Song of Miriam," *JNES* 14 (1955) 237 - 250; James Muilenburg, "A Liturgy on the Triumphs of Yahweh," *Studia Biblical et Semitica* (Wageningen: Veenman, 1966) 233 - 252; F. M. Cross, "The Song of the Sea and Canaanite Myth," *JTC* 5 (1968) 1 - 25; F. M. Cross and D. N. Freedman, *Studies in Ancient Yahwistic Poetry* (Missoula, Mont.: Scholars Press, 1975) 45 - 65; D. N. Freedman, "Strophe and Meter in Exodus 15," in *A Light Unto My Path*, ed. H. N. Bream et al. (Philadelphia: Temple University Press 1975) 163 - 204; D. N. Freedman, "Divine Names and Titles in Early Hebrew Poetry," in *Magnelia Dei: The Mighty Acts of God*, ed. F. M. Cross et al. (New York: Doubleday, 1976) 55 - 107 and "Early Israelite Poetry and Historical Reconstruction," *Symposia Celebrating the Seventy-Fifth Anniversary of the American Schools of Oriental Research (1900–1975)*, ed. F. M. Cross (Cambridge, Mass.: ASOR, 1979) 85 - 96.

17 These earlier studies were unaware of the Ugaritic parallels; cf. R. Tournay, who dates the Song just prior to the exile ("Recherches sur la Chronologie des Psaumes," *Revue Biblique* 65 [1958] 321 - 357), while Paul Haupt lowered the date to the post-exilic period ("Moses' Song of Triumph," *AJSL* 20 [1904] 149 - 172).

18 *JBL* 102 (1983) 30 n.13.

19 *Who Were the Israelites?* 46 - 55.

20 *Studies in Ancient Yahwistic Poetry*, 62 n.42.

21 *Exodus* (Waco: Word, 1987) 208.

22 Freedman, *Light Unto My Path*, 163 - 204 and "The Song of the Sea," in *Pottery, Poetry and Prophecy: Studies in Early Hebrew Poetry*, ed. D. N. Freedman (Winona Lake, Ind.: Eisenbrauns, 1980) 179 - 186; and Muilenburg, in *Studia Biblical et Semitica,* 238 - 245. For a more linguistic analysis of the poetry of Exodus 15, see Michael O'Connor, *Hebrew Verse Structure* (Winona Lake, Ind.: Eisenbrauns, 1980) 471 - 475.

23 According to Muilenburg, this last strophe is different because "it is designed to bring the worshipping congregation to the present" (249). Freedman (*Pottery, Poetry, and Prophecy*, 183) argues that the closing stanza parallels the opening "Exordium" (1b - 2). Robert Alter (*The Art of Biblical Poetry* [New York: Basic Books, 1985] 50 - 54) has recently reaffirmed the threefold strophic structure of the "Song of the Sea," but it is unclear how he handles 17 - 18. Earlier than Muilenburg and Freedman, Umberto Cassuto had argued for a three-strophe structure, while holding that 17 - 18 constituted the epilogue (*Commentary on Exodus* [Jerusalem: Magnes, 1967; orig. Hebrew ed., 1951] 173 - 177).

24 The practice of later editorial glossing or updating geographical terms is attested to elsewhere in the Pentateuch: e.g., Gen. 14:2, 3, 7, 8, 17; Num. 32:38 (?), 33:36; Deut. 2:10 - 12, 20 - 23, and the practice is also found outside of the Torah: e.g., Josh. 15:8, 9, 10, 25, 49, 54, 60; Judg. 1: 10, 23.

25 Gezer, a city on the edge of the coastal plain, remained in Canaanite control until the time of Solomon (1 Kings 9:16), when it was conquered by the Egyptian pharaoh who handed it over to Solomon. Subsequently, Philistine cultural remains began to appear. Cf. W. G. Dever et al. *Gezer I* (Jerusalem: Hebrew Union College, 1970) 58 - 61.

26 Noth, *Exodus*, 125.

27 Hyatt (*Exodus*, 168) assigns this meaning only to the phrase "your own mountain," whereas the other expressions in the verse do refer to Solomon's temple.

28 Durham, *Exodus*, 209.

29 *Who Were the Israelites?*, 51.

30 *Early History of Israel*, 377.

31 Ibid., 377–378.

32 *Joel and the Temple Cult of Jerusalem*, *VTS*, vol. 21 (Leiden: Brill, 1971) 2.

33 Ibid.

34 We shall return to the possible mythological dimension of "the sea" in §5 of this chapter.

35 *The Song of the Sea: Ex 15:1–21* (New York/Berlin: de Gruyter, 1991) 174–177.

36 Ibid., 9–11.

37 Review of Martin L. Brenner, *The Song of the Sea*, in *JBL* 112 (1993) 127.

38 *Exodus*, 245–246. Childs does allow for the possibility that archaizing might be at work here, but concludes that the hymn contains "genuine archaic elements" (246).

39 *JBL* 102 (1983) 27. On the etymology, see the authoritative article by William Ward, "The Semitic Biconsonantal Root *SP* and the Common Origin of Egyptian *ČWF* and Hebrew *SÚP*: "Marsh (Plant)," *VT* 24 (1974) 340–342.

40 One of the early Egyptologists to see a connection between the Hebrew and Egyptian terms was Max Müller, "A Contribution to the Exodus Geography," *PSBA* 10 (1888) 474–475. In 1911 S. R. Driver mentioned the correlation: "it seems to correspond to the late Eg. *thuf.*" *The Book of Exodus* (Cambridge: Cambridge University Press, 1911) 111. See also Gardiner, *AEO*, vol. 2, 202.

41 *The Targums of Onkelos and Jonathan Ben Uzziel of the Pentatuech*, trans. J. W. Ethridge (New York: Ktav, 1968) 331, 379, 461. Onkelos comes from sometime around the end of the first to the third centuries A.D. but apparently relied on earlier Targumic works.

42 *Rashi's Commentary*, trans. M. Rosenbaum, A. M. Silberman, and L. Joseph (London: Shapiro, Vallentine, 1929–1930) 67.

43 *Commentary on the Old Testament in Ten Volumes*, vol. 1: *The Pentateuch* (Grand Rapids, Mich.: Eerdmans, 1983; rep. of orig. 1869–1870) 497.

44 Ibid.

45 Melvin K. Peters, *A Critical Edition of the Coptic (Bohairic) Pentateuch*, vol. 2: *Exodus*, Septuagint and Cognate Studies, vol. 22 (Atlanta: Scholars Press, 1986) 37.

46 John R. Tower, "The Red Sea," *JNES* 18 (1959) 150–153; Maurice Copisarow, "The Ancient Egyptian, Greek and Hebrew Concept of the Red Sea," *VT* 12 (1962) 4–5.

47 Ibid., *Wb*, vol. 4, 397.

48 Ibid., vol. 1, 32.

49 For the Pyramid Texts, see Kurt Sethe, *Die Altaegyptischen Pyramidentexte* (Leipzig: J. C. Hinrichs, 1908). For a translation, see R. O. Faulkner, *The Ancient Egyptian Pyramid Texts* (Oxford: Clarendon Press, 1969).

50 James K. Hoffmeier, "The Possible Origins of the Text of Purification in the Egyptian Funerary Cult," *SAK* 9 (1981) 167–177.

51 See Adriaan de Buck, *The Egyptian Coffin Texts* (Chicago: University of Chicago Press, 1935–1961).

52 A variant expression "lakes of the field of Rushes" is found in BD, 179. This expression appears to be a conflation of *sht i3r(w)*, "field of reeds/rushes" and *š i3r(w)*, "lake of reeds." The former expression is widely found in the Pyramid and Coffin Texts, as well as the Book of the Dead, and may be one and the same place. What is clear is that both bodies of water in the Pyramid Texts played a central role in the purification of the deceased king in his preparation for ascending to heaven (cf. Hoffmeier, *SAK* 9 [1981] 174–176. Sources for the BD include T. G. Allen, *The Book of the Dead of Going Forth By Day* (Chicago: University of Chicago Press, 1974) and R. O. Faulkner, *The Book of the Dead* (London: The British Museum, 1985).

53 *Coptic Etymological Dictionary* (Cambridge: Cambridge University Press, 1976) 251.

54 A. H. Gardiner, *Late-Egyptian Stories*, Bibliotheca Aegyptiaca, vol. 1 (Brussels: Éditions de la fondation égyptologique Reine Élizabeth, 1932) 66.5.

55 *Koptisches Handwörterbuch* (Heidelberg: Universitätsverlag, 1965) 324. I would like to thank Professor Kitchen for bringing these other etymologies to my attention.

56 Graham I. Davies, *The Way of the Wilderness* (Cambridge: Cambridge University Press, 1979) 70.

57 "The Passage of the Sea," *GM* 33 (1979) 57.

58 John Wevers, "Septuagint," *IDB*, vol. 4, 273; Melvin Peters, "Septuagint," *ABD*, vol. 4, 1093–1104.

59 Ibid., 1102.

60 Alan K. Bowman, *Egypt After the Pharaohs* (Berkeley and Los Angeles: University of California Press, 1986) 20. For a recent discussion, see Carol Redmount, "The Wadi Tumilat and the 'Canal of the Pharaohs,'" *JNES* 54 (1995) 127–135.

61 "Hebraica," *JAOS* 58 (1938) 131–132.

62 1 Kings 9:12 of the MT is found in 3 Kings in the LXX.

63 "יַם־סוּף: The Sea of Reeds: The Red Sea," *VT* 15 (1965) 395–398.

64 *VT* 12 (1962) 1–13.

65 Batto, *JBL* 102 (1983) 31–32.

66 Cf. Gen. 25:30; KB, 12.

67 For a good review of some of the standard explanations, see Wright, *GM* 33 (1979) 55–57.

68 The national antagonism is traced back to Num. 20:14–21 when the Israelites tried to pass through Edom after departing Kadesh Barnea. This event is recalled in later history (Judg. 11:17–18). There was also periodic warfare between the nations that exacerbated the hostility (E.g., 1 Sam. 14:47; 2 Sam. 8:13–14; 1 Kings 11:15–16; 2 Chron. 20:1). Other Hebrew literature expresses disdain for Edom (e.g., Ps. 137:7–9; Obad.; Jer. 49:7–22).

69 This practice is analogous to Arab nations no longer using the name "Persian Gulf" but the "Arabian Gulf," or Greeks calling "Turkish" coffee "Greek" coffee.

70 *VT* 15 (1965) 395–398.

71 Ibid., 397–398.

72 *JBL* 102 n. 1 (1983) 30–35 and *Who Were the Israelites?*, 45–55.

73 Liddell and Scott, *Greek-English Lexicon*, 693.

74 Recently, John Huddlestun has acknowledged this ambiguity, but opts for the Gulf of Aqaba ("Red Sea," *ABD*, vol. 5, 633).

75 Wright, *GM* 33 (1979), 63.

76 Herman Hailperin, *Rashi and the Christian Scholars* (Pittsburgh: University of Pittsburgh Press, 1963) 5–7.

77 Davies, *Way of the Wilderness*, 70.

78 *Mémoires sur les principaux travaux d'utilité publique exécutés en Egypte depuis la plus haute antiqué juscqu'à nos jours*, 2 vols. (Paris: Arthus Bertrand, 1872–1873).

79 *Egypt and Israel* (New York: E. S. Gorham, 1912) 39, fig. 7.

80 "Historical Notes on the Pelusiac Branch, the Red Sea Canal and the Route of the Exodus," *Bulletin de la Société royale de Géographie d'Egypte* 21 (1946) 244.

81 *The Geographical and Topographical Texts of the Old Testament* (Leiden: Brill, 1959) §423.

82 Karl Butzer, *Early Hydraulic Civilization in Egypt* (Chicago: University of Chicago Press, 1976) 24; E. M. el Shazly, "The Ostracinic Branch, A Proposed Old Branch of the River Nile," *DE* 7 (1987) 69–78. In a personal communication from Tuvia Weissbrod, he

expresses this doubt that this branch of the Nile flowed, as el-Shazly prosed, to the area east of Lake Bardawil or Ostracine, based on the presence of Nilotic deposits in that area. Weissbrod, who did some investigation in this area, believes they could have come from the Pelusiac and Tanitic branches and were deposited east along the Sinai coast because of the prevailing Mediterranean currents which run west to east along Egypt's coast.

83 Carol Redmount, *On an Egyptian/Asiatic Frontier: An Archaeological History of the Wadi Tumilat* (Ann Arbor: University Microfilms International, 1989) 39.

84 Karl Baedeker, *Egypt and the Sudan* (Leipzig: Baedeker, 1908) 182.

85 Ibid.

86 Redmount, *JNES* 54 no. 2 (1995) 127–128.

87 S. C. Bartlett, *From Egypt to Palestine Through the Wilderness and the South Country* (New York: Harper, 1879) 157–159.

88 Manashe Har-el, *The Sinai Journeys: The Route of the Exodus* (San Diego: Ridgefield, 1983) 143.

89 *The Other Side of the Jordan* (Cambridge, Mass.: *ASOR*, 1970) 106–137.

90 "A Reappraisal of the Site Archaeologist Nelson Glueck Identified as King Solomon's Red Sea Port," *BAR* 12 no. 5 (1986) 24–35.

91 Glueck, *Other Side of the Jordan*, 107.

92 Redmount, "Canal of the Pharaohs," 128; Simons, *Geographical and Topographical Texts*, §423.

93 *Biblical Researches in Palestine and the Adjacent Regions*, 2 vols. (Boston: Crocker and Brewster, 1860) 61. I gratefully acknowledge receiving this reference from Dr. Rodger Dalman.

94 The present distance between the Bitter Lakes and the Gulf of Suez is about eighteen kilometers.

95 H. H. Lamb, *Climate: Present, Past and Future*, vol. 2 (London: Methuen, 1977) 347 and Ronald Pearson, *Climate and Evolution* (New York: Academic Press, 1978) 204.

96 Cassuto, *Commentary on Exodus*, 167. Dr. Weissbrod told me he has seen a watery section of the Isthmus of Suez transformed in a matter of hours by a dust storm into hard land—in other words, the phenomenon opposite to that encountered by Napoleon and others.

97 Ibid.

98 *From Egypt to Palestine*, 163–164.

99 For a recent discussion of the possible circumstances of the Israelite crossing of the sea, cf. Doron Nof and Nathan Paldor, "Are There Oceanographic Explanations for the Israelites' Crossing the Red Sea?" *Bulletin of the American Meteorological Society* 73 no. 3 (1992) 305–314. For a recent treatment of the Israelite sea crossing compared with other historical analogies, cf. Stanislav Segert, "Crossing the Waters: Moses and Hamilcar," *JNES* 53 (1994) 195–203.

100 *The Sinai Journeys: The Route of the Exodus* (San Deigo: Ridgefield, 1983) 312.

101 Dr. Weissbrod has kindly passed this information on to me. He anticipates that space-shuttle radar images will assist in determining tectonic activity in this region.

102 *JBL* 102 n. 1 (1983) 28.

103 Ward, *VT* 24 (1974) 340–342.

104 *Baedeker's Egypt 1929* (London: Allen and Unwin, 1929) 198.

105 Redmount, *On an Egyptian/Asiatic Frontier*, 36–37.

106 In the United States, halophytes grow along the coast of Virginia, South Carolina, and Georgia in swamps connected to the Atlantic Ocean, and the concentration of salt in these swamps is actually higher than the seawater. I owe this information on halophytes to

my former colleague Dr. Dorothy Chappell who was then professor of biology and chair of the biology department at Wheaton College, and now dean of Gordon College.

107 A. M Blackman, *Middle Egyptian Stories*, Bibliotheca Aegyptiaca, vol. 2 (Brussels: 1932) 12–13 (B 21–22).

108 Bietak, *Tell el-Dabᶜa*, vol. 2, pl. 10.

109 *OBA*, 58–59; *NBA*, 31.

110 The city was used as his Delta residence by Smendes, the founder of the Tanite, Twenty-first Dynasty, who reigned 1089–1063 B.C. K. A. Kitchen, *The Third Intermediate Period*, 2d ed. (Warminster: Aris and Phillips, 1986) 466 and Redford, "Zoan," *ABD*, vol. 6, 1106.

111 For a recent, helpful review of the various positions on dating, see Marvin Tate, *Psalms 51–100* (Waco: Word, 1990) 284–286. Ahlström (*Who Where the Israelites?*, 48 n.6) argues for a post-exilic date for Psalm 78 because the verb *bqᶜ* ("split") in 78:13 is also used in Neh. 9:11, a fifth-century work. This is a spurious argument because *bqᶜ* is also attested in Ugaritic texts from the twelfth century and earlier (KB, 143), which indicates that it could have existed in Hebrew at an earlier date, too. When a word is attested over a long period of history, it cannot be a criterion for dating a text early or late.

112 So Bietak correctly argues in "Comments on the Exodus," in *Egypt, Israel, Sinai: Archaeological and Historical Relationships in the Biblical Period*, ed. Anson F. Rainey (Tel Aviv: Tel Aviv University Press, 1987) 165–166.

113 *AEO*, vol. 2, 201; Ricardo Caminos, *Late-Egyptian Miscellanies* (London: Oxford, 1954) 79.

114 See discussion of this problem in chap. 5. Gardiner abandoned his identification of Pelusium (Tell Farama) with Pi-Ramesses, accepting Qantir as its location (*AEO* vol. 2, 171–174), but he continued to correlate Manzeleh with *p3 ṯwfy* (ibid., 201).

115 See Bietak's map, *Tell el-Dabᶜa* (Vienna: Verlag Österreichschen Akademic der Wissenschaft, 1975) vol. 2, pl. 10.

116 *LEM*, 22.13–14; Bietak, "Comments on the Exodus," 167.

117 See chap. 8, §IV.

118 Bietak, in *Egypt, Israel, Sinai*, 167; *ABL*, 10.

119 Hans Wehr, *Arabic-English Dictionary* (Ithaca: Spoken Language Service, 1976) 98; *Wb*, vol. 2, 136. The Egyptian word, going back to the Old Kingdom, is *msh*. The *t* in Timsah reflects the definite article *t3* in late Egyptian.

120 Pierre Montet, *Géographie de l'Égypte Ancienne*, vol. 1 (Paris: Imprimerie Nationale, 1957) 216; *Wb*, vol. 5, 126.

121 Ibid.

122 Henri Cazelles, "Les Localisations de l'Exode et la Critique Littéraire," *Revue Biblique* 62 (1955) 346–350; Simons, *Geographical and Topographical Texts*, §423, 425.

123 Amihai Sneh, Tuvia Weissbrod, and Itamar Perath, "Evidence for an Ancient Egyptian Frontier Canal," *American Scientist* 63 (1975) 546.

124 Simons, *Geographical and Topographical Texts*, §423; Manashe Har-el, "The Exodus Route in Light of Historical-Geographic Research," in *Geography in Israel*, eds. D. Amiran and Y. Ben-Arieh (Jerusalem: Tzur-ot Press, 1976) 373–396, and *Sinai Journeys*; *NIVAB*, 86–88; *HAB*, 56–57; George Kelm, *Escape to Conflict: A Biblical and Archaeological Approach to the Hebrew Exodus and Settlement in Canaan* (Fort Worth: IAR Publications, 1991) 79–80.

125 Simons, *Geographical and Topographical Texts*, §§ 423, 425; Har-el, *Sinai Journeys*, 351–353.

126 *VT* 15 (1965) 396–398. Other scholars see mythological images and language in the song, e.g., Frank E. Eakin, Jr., "The Reed Sea and Baalism," *JBL* 86 (1967) 378–384; Brevard Childs, "A Traditio-Historical Study of the Reed Sea Tradition," *VT* 20 (1970)

412–414; Frank Moore Cross, *Canaanite Myth and Hebrew Epic* (Cambridge, Mass: Harvard University Press, 1973) 112–144; Robert Luyster, "Myth and History in the Book of Exodus," *Religion* 8 no. 1 (1978) 155–171; Walter Wifall, "The Sea of Reeds as Sheol," *ZAW* 92 (1980) 325–332. An unpublished dissertation by Rodger W. Dalman ("Born as a Witness: The Polemics of Israel's Red Sea Crossing" [1992]) recognizes the mythic elements in Israel's sea crossing but suggests that the exodus texts are intended to be a Yahwistic polemic against Canaanite and Egyptian mythology.

127 *JBL* 102 (1983) 31, 33.

128 Ibid., 30 and Ahlström, *Who Where the Israelites?*, 49.

129 Ibid., 55.

130 Based on his book *Slaying the Dragon: Mythmaking in the Biblical Tradition* (Louisville: Westminster/John Knox Press, 1992), it is clear that Batto realized that the biblical writers could use mythic images and language to describe real historical situations. See his treatment of Ezekiel 29. In chapter 6, "Egypt and Gog as Mythic Symbols in Ezekiel," (cf. 163–166). In his *JBL* article, however, Batto dismissed the historicity of the sea crossing because of the presence of mythic language. He thus displays an inconsistent method of interpreting mythic material in the OT.

131 Childs, *Isaiah and the Assyrian Crises* (London: SCM, 1967) 32–35; Otto Kaiser, *Isaiah 13–39* (Philadelphia: Westminster Press, 1973) 283–284; Klaus Koch, *The Prophets I: The Assyrian Period* (Philadelphia: Fortress, 1978) 128–129; A. S. Herbert, *Isaiah 1–39* (Cambridge: Cambridge University Press, 1973) 180.

132 John Hayes and Stuart Irvine, *Isaiah: The Eighth-century Prophet* (Nashville: Abingdon, 1987) 336–338; and Hoffmeier, "Egypt as an Arm of Flesh: A Prophetic Response," in *Israel's Apostasy and Restoration: Essays in Honor of Roland K. Harrison*, ed. A. Gileadi (Grand Rapids, Mich.: Baker, 1988) 88–89.

133 Ezekiel 29:3 precisely dates the oracle to "the tenth year the tenth month." Concerning the accuracy of Ezekiel's dates, see K. S. Freedy and D. B. Redford, "The Dates in Ezekiel in Relation to Biblical, Babylonian and Egyptian Sources," *JAOS* 90 (1970) 462–485.

134 Anthony Spalinger believes that only a "small relief army" was dispatched to Judah. "The Concept of the Monarchy during the Saite Epoch—An Essay of Synthesis," *Orientalia* 47 (1978) 24.

135 (Minneapolis: Fortress, 1993) 796.

136 I have suggested that the one could be a part of the other, but their precise relationship is unclear. *SAK* 9 [1981] 174–175.

137 Towers, *JNES* 18 (1959) 150–153; Wright, *GM* 33 (1979) 55–68.

138 Towers, *JNES* 18 (1959) 152.

139 Ibid., 152–153.

140 Cf. Whitney Davis, "The Ascension-Myth in the Pyramid Texts," *JNES* 36 (1977) 161–179; Hoffmeier, *SAK* 9 (1981) 167–177.

141 *JNES* 18 (1959) 153. Tower's conclusion were endorsed by Wright, *GM* 33 [1979] 60–63.

142 *VT* 24 (1974) 340–342.

143 Gardiner, *AEO*, vol. 2, 201–202; Montet, *Géographie*, vol. 1, 200–201. Bietak equates *p3 twfy* with Lake El-Ballah (in *Egypt, Israel, Sinai*, 167). Caminos identified *p3 twfy* with Lake Manzeleh (*Late-Egyptian Miscellanies*, 79).

144 KB, 652. An analogy from recent American political history comes to mind. When Judge Robert Bork was denied confirmation for the Supreme Court in the 1980s, a verb "to bork" was heard around Washington to describe the process of discrediting an individual so as to deny them a political or judicial appointment.

145 Ibid.

146 Exodus 10:1–20 is thought to be a blend of J and P by Noth (*Exodus*, 82), but J. L. Mihelic and G. E. Wright (*IDB*, vol. 3, 823) argued that it is a compilation of J and E. While Noth thought the pericope containing *yām sûp*, is P, Mihelic and Wright assigned it to J.

147 *History of Israel*, 122.

10

CONCLUDING REMARKS

I began this book by posing a number of key questions that I have sought to answer in the nine preceding chapters. Let us review them to see what picture emerges regarding Israel's national origins in Egypt as the Bible records. The major question was, Is the picture portrayed in Genesis 39 through Exodus 15 compatible with what is known from Egyptian history? I think we have answered that in the affirmative, but let us consider the more specific questions. Did Semitic-speaking peoples from western Asia come to Egypt for relief during times of drought and famine as the Patriarchal stories of Genesis suggest? It was shown that in nearly all periods there were Asiatics (ʿ3mw or pdtyw according to Egyptian documents) living in Egypt, especially in the First and Second Intermediate Periods. As the Middle Kingdom was breaking up or early in the Second Intermediate Period appears to have been the most likely time when the family of Jacob emigrated to Egypt and Joseph served as a court official. After a century (or slightly more) of domination of Egypt by the Hyksos, the Theban liberators and rulers of the Eighteenth Dynasty, it seems that repressive measures were taken against the remaining Semitic-speaking peoples in Egypt. They were forced to work in state labor projects, as were tens of thousands of POWs taken during the Asian campaigns of the warring kings of the Eighteenth Dynasty. There is no reason to exclude the Israelites from this type of bondage.

Another question posed was, Could a Semite like Joseph have advanced to such a high post in the Egyptian court. The evidence is clear. If during the New Kingdom a Semitic official such as Aper-el could occupy the office of the Vizier of Lower Egypt and other non-Egyptians were appointed to ranking positions in the government, then surely the same could have occurred to a Hebrew named Joseph anytime from the Thirteenth Dynasty through the Hyksos Period. In a similar vein, Eighteenth Dynasty sources showed that during this period many foreign princes were reared and schooled in the Egyptian court in the "Royal Nursery" and bore the title "Child of the Nursery," ḥrd n k3p. It is my belief that Moses was a product of this institution. It was also shown that the name "Moses" is at home in the New Kingdom. His birth story, so commonly associated with the Sargon legend from Mesopotamia, attests to the presence of terms with Egyptian etymologies, suggesting that this unit had an unquestionable Egyptian connection.

Similarly, the first six plagues in the series of the nine neatly fit the setting of the Nile's annual inundation season, and the seventh through ninth plagues are not out of place in the Nile Valley. These nine created havoc for Egypt, especially the institution of the kingship. Pharaoh, the incarnation of Horus and the one responsible for maintaining cosmic order and the fertility of the land, proved impotent against Yahweh and his agents Moses and Aaron. This catastrophe proved to be a frontal assault on "Pharaoh and the gods of Egypt," with the emphasis, I proposed, being on the king.

Finally, important geographical questions were answered that demonstrate that a coherent and singular route is described in Exodus and Numbers 33 for the departure from Egypt to Sinai, despite not being able to plot it on a map with absolute certainty. New light from recent excavations in north Sinai has shown why the Israelites did not exit Egypt via the northern or coastal road. The massive new fortress, Tjaru, discovered at Hebua in the 1980s, plus a clearer picture of the lake and marsh system north of the Wadi Tumilat, along with the recently discovered frontier canal indicate that a route through the Succoth/Tjeku region was followed even though there were forts there as well. The Anastasi Papyri from the Nineteenth Dynasty provide information about a number of forts in the Wadi Tumilat and Lake Timsah region. However, the more southerly route apparently posed fewer dangers than departing by the coastal highway.

The canal discovered by Weissbrod's team of geologists in north Sinai and the way it connected the lakes along the Isthmus of Suez may explain the entrapment the Israelites felt when trying to reach Sinai. The juxtaposition of Pi-ha-hiroth (the Semitic writing for "the mouth of the canal") and the Sea of Reeds (yām sûp) in Exodus 14:2 and Number 33:7 and 8 suggest that the body of water in question is one of the lakes along the Isthmus, although a more precise identification is impossible with the current state of knowledge of the area.

How should the Genesis and Exodus narratives be treated once the supporting evidence presented above is taken into account? To reject it out of hand would be pure obscurantism. A second approach is to accept that there is some or even a considerable amount of Egyptian realia in the biblical narratives, but these influences were borrowed by the Hebrew writers because of the overwhelming influence of figures like Ramesses II and his massive building projects. Baruch Halpern, for example, believes that the Genesis and Exodus narratives contain "historical reflections" of Israel's stay in Egypt but that this "folklore" was influenced by real, Egyptian historical events, such as the 400 Year Stela of Horemheb inspiring the four hundred-year sojourn of Israel.[1] Likewise, the shadow of Ramesses the great and his colossal construction activities and the use of foreign labor and prisoners of war left its mark on the Israelite historians who connected their own history to Nineteenth Dynasty Egypt. So Halpern claims "on a historiographic plane, what this means is that the image of Ramses II determined the reconstruction of the Exodus story. The Pharaoh of the Oppression was the Pharaoh of Construction, of monument-building, of public works, *par excellence*. The biblical tradition reflects familiarity with the practice, especially under Ramses, of using Semitic population of the eastern Delta for forced labor."[2] If I correctly understand Halpern, he is saying that the later Israelite historian (from the time of David and Solomon?) believed that his ancestors spent some time in Egypt, but the precise details were lost or garbled in the folklorist traditions that had survived. Consequently, information was obtained from Egypt during the Twenty-first Dynasty through contact between the two courts and impacted the writer in his reconstruction of Israel's origin in Egypt.

This approach is intriguing because it recognizes the Egyptian influence on the Pentateuchal narratives, rather than ignoring it or minimizing it as many recent studies on the origins of Israel debate have done. However, this argument has a serious flaw: it implies that the Israelites know more about Egypt's history than their own. It is inconceivable that early Israelites were incapable of preserving their early history, in either oral or written form, from the second half of the second millennium onward. Only by special pleading can the minimalist argue that during the Late Bronze Age the Israelites were the only nation who could not record historical events. Certainly they cannot be considered "illiterate" because they were a pastoralist tribe, be they indigenous to Levant or having come from desert regions beyond Canaan, as a story during the judgeship of Gideon illustrates. Admittedly, this story dates to early in the Iron I period, but one episode reports of the capture of an Ishmaelite/Midianite foe who was able to write out the names of officials and leaders of the Transjordanian area (Judg. 9:14). If there was at least a degree of literacy among these tribes, who have often been closely associated with the early Israelites, then it is just as likely that among early Israel there were select individuals who could write. And if I am correct in believing that there was an historical Moses who was a product of the royal nursery, then he would have been trained in the Egyptian scribal tradition. During the New Kingdom, some Egyptian scribes connected to the court had to be bilingual to deal with communiqués that came to Pharaoh from the far reaches of the empire, like the Amarna Letters, written in cuneiform. Because of the close connection between figures like Joseph and Moses and the Egyptian court, it seems that there is reason to believe the biblical tradition that ascribes to Moses the ability to record events, compile itineraries, and other scribal activities. This is not to say that he is the sole author of the Pentateuch, but he cannot be ruled out as having had the role in its formation that the Bible reports (cf. Exod. 17:14; Num. 33:2; Deut. 31:9, 22, 24).

The body of evidence reviewed in this book provides indirect evidence which shows that the main points of the Israel in Egypt and exodus narratives are indeed plausible. After arguing that the Egyptianisms of the exodus are datable to the Persian period, Donald Redford determines that the "exodus is a post-Exilic composition which, in the absence of genuine historical detail, was obliged to draw on contemporary toponymy: but to draw such a conclusion is not, needless to say, tantamount to branding the Biblical tradition a wholly late fabrication."[3] Despite his overall skepticism about the accuracy of particular events in the biblical story, Redford is forced to concede:

1) There was an early and strong reminiscence of a voluntary descent into Egypt by pastoralists, in which one Jacob played a leading part, and was later to achieve a reputation as an ancestral figure,

2) Those who made the descent had not only prospered and multiplied, but had also for a time become exceedingly influential in Egypt.

3) Subsequently, strong antipathy had arisen between the autochthonous inhabitants and the Asiatic newcomers.

4) This had resulted in the enforced retirement of the intrusive element to the Levantine littoral which they had emerged.[4]

I cannot disagree with any one of these points, except that Redford thinks these events derived from the Hyksos experience in Egypt—their migration, period of dominance, followed by their forced exodus.[5] For him a particular group of Shasu (Bedouin) who lived in Sinai and the Negev are the forebears of Israel. This tribe embraced the story of the Hyksos as their own. The problem with this interpretation, like that of Halpern, is that the Israelites recall little or nothing of their own origin but know about the Hyksos from a thousand years before. The essentials of the Hyksos story are recalled, Redford speculates, and then they were combined with Persian-period data from Egypt to create the biblical narratives. I find this model to explain how the story of Genesis 39 to Exodus 14 was formed requires a greater leap of faith than to believe the narratives are historical in nature and were preserved by Hebrew scribes, beginning toward the end of the Late Bronze Age.

There is ample supporting evidence from Egypt, some of which has been presented here, to come to this conclusion, not to mention hundreds of references and allusions to the Israel in Egypt and exodus events in the remainder of the Hebrew Bible.[6] Because of the weight of these two lines of evidence, it seems premature to dismiss the biblical traditions of Israel's birth as a nation in Egypt, an event still commemorated annually by Jews when Passover is observed.

Notes

1 "The Exodus and the Israelites Historians," *Eretz Israel* 24 (1993) 92–93.
2 Ibid.
3 "An Egyptological Perspective on the Exodus Narratives," in *Egypt, Israel, Sinai; Archaeological and Historical Relationships in the Biblical Period*, ed. A. F. Rainey (Tel Aviv: Tel Aviv University Press, 1987) 150.
4 Ibid.
5 Ibid., 150–151.
6 See Kitchen's recent survey of some of this material in *ABD*, vol. 2, 701.

SUBJECT INDEX

TERM INDEX

EGYPTIAN

HEBREW